Treating Young Veterans

*Promoting Resilience Through Practice
and Advocacy*

D0879395

Diann Cameron Kelly, PhD, is an Associate Professor at Adelphi University, School of Social Work, Garden City, New York. Dr. Kelly is an editorial board member for *Youth & Society*, a former Fahs-Beck Fellow (2007–2008), and consults with various organizations to inform and evaluate service delivery within sustainable communities.

Sydney Howe-Barksdale, PhD, JD, is the Director of the Public Interest Resource Center and a Professor of Legal Methods at Widener University School of Law in Wilmington, Delaware. Dr. Howe-Barksdale is a Legal Anthropologist and examines the impact of legal systems on individual rights and local cultures. Dr. Howe-Barksdale is admitted to practice in the State of Maryland, and is a member of the ABA, NBA, and Philadelphia Bar Association.

David Gitelson, DSW, LCSW, is Director, Social Work Department, VA Hudson Valley Health Care System, Montrose, NY, Fellow of the New York Academy of Medicine, and Senior Adjunct Professor, Adelphi University, School of Social Work. He also teaches Social Welfare Policy at New York University Graduate School of Social Work, and Mercy College, BSW Program, Dobbs Ferry, New York.

Treating Young Veterans
Promoting Resilience Through Practice and Advocacy

Diann Cameron Kelly, PhD
Sydney Howe-Barksdale, PhD, JD
David Gitelson, DSW, LCSW
Editors

SPRINGER PUBLISHING COMPANY
NEW YORK

Copyright © 2011 Springer Publishing Company, LLC

Springer Publishing Company, LLC
11 West 42nd Street
New York, NY 10036
www.springerpub.com

Acquisitions Editor: Jennifer Perillo
Senior Editor: Rose Mary Piscitelli
Composition: Nick Barber/Techset

ISBN: 978-0-8261-0709-1
E-book ISBN: 978-0-8261-0710-7

11 12 13/ 5 4 3 2 1

The author and the publisher of this Work have made every effort to use sources believed
to be reliable to provide information that is accurate and compatible with the standards
generally accepted at the time of publication. The author and publisher shall not be liable for
any special, consequential, or exemplary damages resulting, in whole or in part, from the
readers' use of, or reliance on, the information contained in this book. The publisher has no
responsibility for the persistence or accuracy of URLs for external or third-party Internet
Web sites referred to in this publication and does not guarantee that any content on such
Web sites is, or will remain, accurate or appropriate.

CIP data is available from the Library of Congress

Printed in the United States of America by Hamilton Printing

We dedicate this body of work to all who have
silently cried, ached, lost, and felt lost ...
on the field of battle during war and peace ...
and to your loved ones who have yet to
breathe deeply and exhale.
We, the Editors and Contributors, salute you.

A Special Mention to

In Memoria

Commander Charles Keith Springle[1]
U.S. Navy, Army 55th Medical Company
Combat Stress Center, Camp Liberty
Baghdad, Iraq. Felled by assailant's
gunfire on 5/11/2009.

Lieutenant Colonel Juanita Warman, NP
U.S. Army Reserve, Maryland Army
National Guard
Yellow Ribbon Faculty Member. Felled
by assailant's gunfire at Fort Hood on
11/5/2009 while assisting fellow soldiers
to safety.

John M. Kelly
U.S. Air Force

In Honor

Harry S. Cameron, Sr.
Master Sergeant, U.S. Army, 82nd Infantry
(1945–1963)

Christopher S. Cameron
E-5, U.S. Navy (2007–present)

JoAnn Kelly
Captain, U.S. Army
(Reserves & Operation Desert Storm)

Mark & Mimi Branker
U.S. Air Force

Peter B. Vaughan
Captain, U.S. Army
Active Duty—1966–1968
Reserves—1964–1970

Scott F. Butler
E-4, U.S. Army (1978–1981)

Thomas Reed
2nd Lieutenant, USMC. U.S. Navy ROTC
Midshipman; Air Medal received, 1965
Dominican Republic Crisis

---

[1]University of North Carolina School of Social Work has set up the Charles Keith Springle, PhD Memorial Scholarship Fund that will support military-dependent students in the Masters of Social Work. Contributions may be made to the UNC School of Social Work (payee) c/o UNC School of Social Work Development Office. Please contact Mary Beth Hernandez, (919) 962-6469, marybeth@email.unc.edu.

As well as dedications to:

My grandfather, Samuel Mallow (WWI), my great uncle, Mitchell "Mike" Feder (U.S. Army, WWII), my uncles, Nathan Carroll Mallow (U.S. Coast Guard, WWII) and Thomas Mallow (Army Air Corp, WWII), and my stepson, Frank DeMonte (U.S. Navy). This chapter is also dedicated to Francis Walsh, an orphan, who in 1941 enlisted in the Navy, leaving behind his fiancée and a chance to build a family for the country he cherished. He perished on the *USS Juneau*, sunk in the Pacific in 1942.

—*Alissa Mallow*

All of my uncles, and cousins, the Mitchell and Williams men who served with honor, humor, and strength in Korea, Germany, the Middle East, on ships, abroad, stateside, and places unspoken. To my uncle Cecil Mitchell, Jr, a Navy man whose brilliant mind and sensitive heart helped to heal the broken at Walter Reed Hospital. To Dr. James D. Wilson, Sr, Special Forces, for a lifetime of commitment and honor and in recognition of his sacrifices, to keep us safe, especially after Vietnam. I am honored to recognize the resiliency our veterans, our country's true unsung heroes for so many generations.

—*Brenda Williams-Gray*

Chia Hsing Chen, who is presently serving a second tour in Iraq and whose homecoming experiences inspired this work.

—*Donna Caplin and Katharine Kranz Lewis*

This is dedicated with love, honor, and profound respect to all of the men and women in the Howe, Barksdale, Pease, Vaughan, DeBourg, McCurdy, Dignan, Clarke, and Stell families who have served in every conflict since we came to this country.

—*Sydney Howe-Barksdale*

On behalf of my family, I personally dedicate this to my dad (U.S. Army), my nephew (OEF), my niece-in-law (OEF), late uncles (WWII, Korea), my grandfather (WWI), and most importantly my great-great grandfather, Burl Isham (Union Army, Civil War), who began our family's commitment to national service—military and nonmilitary. My brother, our cousins and I, we thank all of you from the bottom of our hearts.

—*Diann Cameron Kelly*

CONTENTS

CONTRIBUTORS

Jonathan Alex, LCSW   Assistant Professor, Department of Social Work, Lehman College/CUNY, Bronx, NY.

Deirdre Barry   Alumna of Berkshire Community College and Westfield State College, and member of a military family.

Patrick S. Calhoun, PhD   Associate Director, VA Mid-Atlantic MIRECC; Research Associate, VA Center for Health Services Research in Primary Care; and Assistant Professor, Department of Psychiatry and Behavioral Sciences, Duke University, Durham, NC.

Donna Caplin, RN, MSN   Completed this study as a graduate student at the University of Hartford, West Hartford, CT; currently Adjunct Faculty, University of Connecticut, School of Nursing.

Joan DeSimone, PhD   Instructor, Johns Hopkins University, Division of Public Safety Leadership, Baltimore, MD.

Leah Dillard   Alumna of Berkshire Community College and Elms College, and member of a military family.

Lieutenant Colonel Michael Gafney   Maryland Army National Guard Director of Reintegration Programs, and Officer-in-Charge (OIC), Maryland National Guard Deployment Cycle Support Program; presently assigned to the 29th Combat Aviation Brigade.

Jennifer M. Gierisch, PhD, MPH   AHRQ Fellow in Health Services Research, Durham VAMC, Center for Health Services Research in Primary Care and Department of Medicine, Duke University Medical Center, Durham, NC.

Godfrey Gregg, PhD, LCSW   Clinical Assistant Professor, Adelphi University, School of Social Work, Garden City, NY.

Christina Harnett, PhD, MBA   Assistant Professor, Johns Hopkins University, Division of Public Safety Leadership; Faculty, Maryland National Guard, Yellow Ribbon Program; Member, All Services Resiliency Task Force, Department of Defense, Defense Centers of Excellence, Yellow Ribbon Reintegration Program; Major, Maryland Defense Force, 10th Medical Regiment.

Justin Holbrook, JD   Associate Professor of Law and Director of the Veterans Law Clinic at Widener University Law School, Widener University, Delaware campus. Served as an active duty judge advocate in the U.S. Air Force from 2004 to 2010; deployed twice in support of OEF and OIF, and served as Chief of Military Justice and Chief of International Law in Japan.

Wesley Kasprow, PhD, MPH   Associate Research Scientist at Yale Medical School Department of Psychiatry, New Haven, CT, and Associate Director of the Department of Veterans Affairs Northeast Program Evaluation Center (NEPEC), West Haven, CT.

Wayne Klug, PhD   (Boston College), Professor of Psychology, Berkshire Community College; recipient of the Society for the Psychological Study of Social Issues' 2010 Award for Outstanding Teaching and Mentoring for Community College Faculty.

Katharine Kranz Lewis, PhD, MSN, MPH, RN   Assistant Professor, Department of Nursing, University of Hartford, West Hartford, CT; Executive Director, Connecticut Public Health Policy Institute.

Harold Kudler, MD   Associate Director, VA Mid-Atlantic MIRECC and Associate Clinical Professor, Department of Psychiatry and Behavioral Sciences, Duke University, Durham, NC.

Alissa Mallow, DSW, LCSW   Vice President for Quality Improvement Systems, Basics/Promesa, Bronx, NY. Formally, Assistant Professor, Department of Social Work, Lehman College/Bronx, NY. Associate Editor, End Page for the *Journal of Social Work Practice in the Addictions*.

Jamila S. Miah, LCSW, CGP   Doctoral student at NYU Silver School of Social Work, and Clinical Social Worker at the Psychosocial Rehabilitation and Recovery Center, VA Hudson Valley HealthCare System, Montrose, NY.

Anne O'Dwyer, PhD   (Boston College), Dean of Academic Affairs, Bard College at Simon's Rock; Past President, New England Psychological Association.

Haili Polo-Neil   Alumna of Berkshire Community College and New England Institute of Art; graduate student at Rochester Institute of Technology; and member of a military family.

Elizabeth Quinn, PhD   Associate Professor of Psychology at Marist College, Poughkeepsie, NY; author of *The Community Mental Health System: A Navigational Guide for Providers* and *Community Psychology: A Common Sense Approach to Mental Health*. Currently a clinical psychologist working with chemically dependent individuals, many of whom are military veterans.

Thomas Quinn, LCSW   Team Leader for the Danbury Vet Center, a Department of Veterans Affairs counseling center for combat veterans; maintains a private practice providing mental health services to Vietnam veterans; also an Adjunct Lecturer at Adelphi University, School of Social Work, Hudson Valley Program.

Elizabeth Rahilly, LMSW   Social Worker, VA Hudson Valley Health Care System, Montrose, NY.

Thomas Reed, JD   Taishoff Professor of Law at Widener University School of Law, Wilmington, DE.

Robert Rosenheck, MD   Professor of Psychiatry and Epidemiology and Public Health at Yale Medical School, Department of Psychiatry, and Senior Investigator at the New England Mental Illness, Education and Research Center (MIRECC 151D).

Kristy Straits-Tröster, PhD   Assistant Director, VA Mid-Atlantic Mental Illness Research, Education and Clinical Center (MIRECC); Assistant Professor, Department of Psychiatry and Behavioral Sciences, Duke University, Durham, NC.

Jennifer L. Strauss, PhD   Health Scientist, Center for Health Services Research in Primary Care, Durham VA Medical Center; Research Associate, VA Mid-Atlantic MIRECC and Assistant Professor, Psychiatry & Behavioral Sciences, Duke University Medical Center, Durham, NC.

Kristen Tuttle, LCSW   Clinical Social Worker, VA Hudson Valley Health Care System, Montrose, NY.

William Valente, BA, MFA   MSW student at Hudson Valley Campus, Adelphi University School of Social Work, Garden City, NY.

Peter B. Vaughan, PhD   Dean of the Graduate School of Social Service, Fordham University, New York, NY. Previously, social work officer US Army, Medical Service Corps with the rank of captain who served as the American Division Social Worker, and OIC USARV Stockade in the Republic of Vietnam from July 1967 to June 1968.

Corrine Voils, PhD   Health Scientist, Center for Health Services Research in Primary Care; Associate Professor, Department of Medicine, Duke University Medical Center, Durham, NC.

Shari Ward, MSN, NP-Psychiatry   Director of the Substance Abuse Rehab Facility at Arms Acres, in Carmel, NY; maintains a private practice providing intensive mental health treatment to individuals, couples, and families throughout the Hudson Valley region of New York.

Megan Warriner   Alumna of Berkshire Community College and University of Massachusetts, and member of a military family.

Brenda Williams-Gray, DSW   Assistant Professor, Department of Social Work, Lehman College/CUNY, Bronx, NY.

FOREWORD

No one said "Welcome home" when we deplaned at Travis Air Force Base after spending a year in the Republic of Vietnam. The servicemen and servicewomen at U.S. Customs and Immigration, who processed returning military personnel back into the United States, were at best indifferent as they rummaged through and scattered our belongings. At worse they were rude. All of these agents wore Vietnam Campaign Ribbons, indicating that they had completed a tour of duty in there as had we. I suspect they were assigned to in-processing duty because they had themselves experienced it. My sense of their demeanor was that because they had completed a tour of duty in Vietnam, their treatment of returnees could be less than welcoming and was maybe even sanctioned by those in command of that unit. This was yet another example of "suck it up," which was what all too many men and women in uniform of that era were expected to do without protest when faced with adverse situations.

A number of Vietnam veterans have reported similar or worse experiences when they returned to Reception Centers. Those returning and who were remaining in the service would most likely find the routine of military duty and the familiarity of the military post or base an anchoring point to continuing their lives. In all probability, there would be other Vietnam veterans at those locations with whom they could share their experiences; and if not normalize them, they would at least be able to ventilate and have a sympathetic ear. For many of those veterans who were being separated from the military at their point of return, stateside life would be permanently altered.

Families and communities that were so familiar to them before their Vietnam deployment had become unfamiliar. Warm and open friends with whom they used to be comfortable could no longer be depended on to respond in a way that made them feel welcome to be back in the old fold. "You've changed" was a common response to the sadness, anger, isolation, lack of motivation, and search for meaning in life for returning veterans.

Of course they had changed, and little help was available to them as they tried to make sense of their commitment of time and effort to support what had been sold to them as service in defense of democracy and one's nation. In addition to suffering physical injury in the course of their service, many veterans sacrificed their physical and psychological well-being, economic stability, and family integrity. Systems of care were not in place to address the needs of these veterans and their families, and well-intentioned professionals who staffed facilities and agencies that offered them care were more often than not ill equipped to understand the depths of anguish and suffering of this group of veterans.

Those close to the veterans felt pain in their relationships with them, because of not knowing how to be supportive as their loved ones struggled to transition from the battlefield to the homeland. Added to these veterans' problems associated with intimacy, motivation, and future orientation was the response of a number of fellow Americans during that era who expressed openly not only how much they hated the war, but also how much they despised the warriors.

As problems continued to be manifested by many veterans of the Vietnam War, such as bizarre public behavior, homelessness, chronic substance abuse, and criminality that persisted long after many service people returned home and several years after the end of the war, researchers began to ask the difficult question of how this group of women and men could be helped. Researchers began to ask questions about the link between veterans' behaviors and certain types of war activities, behaviors and exposure to certain stressors. Also, researchers explored the links of toxic substances used in fighting the war that may have been associated with certain physical and mental conditions of those veterans. Given the broken bodies of many returning Vietnam veterans, by the early to mid-1980s there was a growing awareness that perhaps something was also broken in the minds, spirits, and social experiences of Vietnam veterans.

This brokenness was different from that of veterans of World War II and the Korean War, and family members, service providers, the uniformed services, and the veterans themselves began to recognize this difference. In response to some new information, the diagnosis of post-traumatic stress disorder was added to the *Diagnostic and Statistical Manual of Mental Disorders.* This was in large measure because the behaviors that were exhibited by Vietnam veterans did not neatly fit other psychiatric diagnostic categories that were being ascribed. Vet Centers came into existence, VA hospitals tried to devise new treatment modalities, and teams of researchers studied the physical, psychological, and spiritual effects of the war on Vietnam veterans. Troubled warriors of the Vietnam War, at last, no longer were being told to "suck it up."

Unlike the Vietnam War, in subsequent wars and U.S. military operations against hostile forces, there has been at least a recognition that war causes many continuing adverse effects for the individuals who are called on to fight them and for the families and communities to which they return. Deployments to the Iraq War and the war in Afghanistan have been different from other wars. Persons may be deployed multiple times, and along with regular military personnel we have seen the deployment of many Reserve Units and National Guard Units which, heretofore, focused on domestic issues. Women now constitute a sizeable portion of military personnel being deployed to those theaters. Additionally, there has been the deployment of husbands and wives, with children being left behind sometimes and with insufficient care arrangements having been made for them. Not only are the dynamics of deployment to military service overseas very different from previous wars, overseas military engagements and the readjustment needs and patterns for those returning are different as well.

For many of us who were mental health professionals during the Vietnam War, we relied on knowledge gained during our formal education. But we quickly recognized that much of what we knew was not easily applied to soldiers in combat situations where the beginning, middle, and end of a mental health intervention or encounter may last for only minutes. After serving as a social work officer in the Republic of Vietnam, first as a division social worker and then heading a mental hygiene operation in the United States Army Vietnam Stockade, I felt at the end of the tour of duty that I had mastered the knowledge and skills to provide well-targeted mental health services to members of the military and to veterans of that war. Other mental health professionals who served in Vietnam returned stateside and were able to provide effective treatment and interventions with veterans of that war because of their own experiences in the combat theater of operations. Learning-by-doing characterized our work in Vietnam. It was in the theater of combat operations where much of our learning about how to treat combatants came about as we were doing it.

Fortunately, there has been a new awareness on the part of governmental departments and agencies that serve the Veteran population. Public and private social service agencies, police and sheriff departments, and faith communities also seek to respond to the needs of returning veterans, and the families and communities to which they return. Many have vowed that never again will we endure the disrespect for our servicemen and servicewomen, which was accepted and even promoted when the Vietnam veterans returned and tried to begin their lives anew.

The editors of *Treating Young Veterans* and the authors of the individual chapters have taken the approach that by providing practitioners with essential information about the needs, desires, and possibilities for veterans of the wars of Iraq and Afghanistan, those veterans and their families will be able to achieve wholeness in their interpersonal relationships and in their communities. In addition, the larger society will be able to benefit from the training and knowledge, discipline, teamwork, and patriotism that characterized their military service as they are helped to reestablish themselves. This book represents a thoughtful, sensitive, and sensible approach to working with military personnel and veterans who have been deployed to wars in the Persian Gulf, Iraq, and Afghanistan.

It is remarkable that *Treating Young Veterans* considers the multiple diversities of servicemen and servicewomen and veterans and their families. It offers ways in which professionals in helping professions can intervene with and on behalf of returning veterans and their families at an individual and family level, and at community and organizational levels. The combined efforts of these professionals and veterans will bring about social change, which will promote the health and well-being of veterans of recent wars as they return to the multiple roles they performed prior to deployment.

Peter B. Vaughan, PhD
Dean, Graduate School of Social Service
Fordham University

ACKNOWLEDGMENTS

Every large endeavor stands on the broad shoulders of supporters, leaders, and advisers. The same is true for this two-year trek to produce *Treating Young Veterans*.

First, we thank each contributor to this body of work. From the beginning, each of you demonstrated a commitment to the men and women in our Armed Forces, and a strong desire to see their well-being improved. No matter the varied challenges that arose for all of us as we developed this body of work for the public, you remained steadfast in contributing to a text that is a service to one of our nation's treasures—our veterans. For your diligence, insight, empirical data, and your wonderful humor, we thank you!

In addition to our contributors, we could not have completed this body of work if it were not for the external reviewers. These reviewers did not just review manuscripts. At times, they gave critical insight into terminology, existing services, and practice implications. But most importantly, they took a great deal of time out of their schedules to make certain we achieved our goal of providing a literary service to veterans. These reviewers were

Katherine Bent, RN, PhD, CNS
   Chief, Healthcare Delivery & Methodologies
   NIH-Center for Scientific Review
   Division of AIDS, Behavioral & Population Sciences
   Bethesda, MD

Roni Berger, PhD, LCSW
   Professor, Adelphi University, School of Social Work, Garden City,
      NY

Elaine P. Congress, DSW
   Professor & Associate Dean, Fordham University Graduate School
      of Social Service
   New York, NY

Christopher R. Erbes, PhD, LP
   Assistant Professor and Program Manager
   Minneapolis Veterans Affairs Medical Center

Department of Psychiatry Medical School-PTS Team
Minneapolis, MN

Kathryn Herr, PhD
   Professor, Montclair State University
   College of Education & Human Services
       Montclair, NJ

Monica M. Matthieu, PhD, LCSW
   Associate Professor, Washington University in St Louis
   George Warren Brown School of Social Work,
   St Louis, MO

Penelope J. Moore, DSW, ACSW
   Associate Professor, Iona College School of Social Work
       New Rochelle, NY

Christopher Parker, PhD
   Assistant Professor,
   University of Washington
   Department of Political Science
   Seattle, WA

We owe them a debt of gratitude. In addition to these reviewers, we also thank the cadre of military officers/retired military officers and veterans who reviewed portions of this work to ensure accuracy and relevancy. In particular, we are deeply grateful for the guidance, direction, and support of Col. Will Barnes, Col. Dick Schnell (Ret.), and Lieutenant Colonel Michael Gafney.

We are indebted to Peter B. Vaughan, Dean, Fordham University, Graduate School of Social Service, and a veteran, for contributing his voice to this body of work in the Foreword. But also, we thank him for his mentorship and direction in the early and final days of this project. Before this project commenced, Councilwoman Suzanna Sullivan Keith, Rye, New York, inspired conversations and connections with everyone she knew to help complete a body of work for United States veterans. She brought two of the editors together, and connected two of the reviewers/contributors to the project. *Treating Young Veterans* owes a debt of gratitude to this wonderful businesswoman and public servant who remains a humble benefactor. Thank you Suzanne.

Edited compilations too often forget the tireless, diligent work of editorial assistants and coordinators. Our editorial coordinator is William "Bill" Valente, an MSW student at Adelphi University, School of Social Work. He also serves as the graduate research assistant for

Diann Kelly. Prior to attending Adelphi University and working on this project, Bill worked as a daily news reporter with outlets such as the *Poughkeepsie Journal*. He was also an English teacher in Spain, and Community Program Manager for the Mediation Center of Dutchess County. Our work could not have been completed without him, and thus we humbly thank him for all of his work. In addition to Bill, we want to acknowledge two other former graduate students who worked on the project during its early days—Scott Butler (also a veteran) and Jeanette Corrow. We thank them for their efforts as well.

David Gitelson expressed specific thanks to the veterans with whom he directly works, who teach him every day about courage and resilience. In addition, "I'd like to thank my colleagues, who teach me ... about commitment, and my family, who teach me everything that's important."

The authors Kristy Straits-Tröster, Jennifer Gierisch, Patrick Calhoun, Jennifer Strauss, Corrine Voils, and Harold Kudler would also like to thank the veterans and their families who volunteered their time for their project. In addition, they acknowledge Patricia Vanderwolf and Stephen Dienstfrey of *abt SRBI* for their partnership in this effort and their dedication to veterans' health and well-being. "We [also] credit our late friend and colleague, Dr. Mimi Butterfield for her early vision, encouragement and contribution to this project."

At the time of these analyses, Dr. Gierisch was funded by a fellowship from the Agency for Healthcare Research and Quality (grant 2-T32-HS000079). Dr. Strauss was funded by a Department of Veterans Affairs Research Career Development Award (RCD-06-020).

Christy Harnett and Lieutenant Colonel Michael Gafney express sincere gratitude to members of the National Guard and the Army Reserve, who contributed to the development of their chapter. "Thank you for your assistance and for your services to our country." Further, Alissa Mallow acknowledged the contributions of veterans and noted, "I am humbled by the strength, resiliency, and valor of not only the men in my family but for all the service men and women who have served, are serving, and will serve in the armed forces. Thank you for protecting and defending the freedoms, liberties, and rights I cherish as an American."

Donna Caplin and Katharine Kranz Lewis note that their study would not have been possible without the veteran volunteers who generously agreed to participate in this important study. They give "[s]pecial thanks to the Hartford Hospital School of Nursing Alumnae Association who supplied funding for the research study

'The homecoming experiences of Connecticut veterans of Iraq (OIF) and Afghanistan (OEF).'"

In the end, there are three key groups that are the most important as we offer our gratitude. First, we are especially thankful to Springer Publishing for acknowledging this work and choosing to bring it to fruition. More importantly, we thank Jennifer Perillo who remains a phenomenal editor. Thank you, Jennifer!

Further, we thank all veterans, active duty personnel, and veteran families for inspiring our body of work. What you endure, during peace time and during war, remains unfathomable. We hope our contribution to your community enhances services and outreach programs to positively impact quality of life for today's veterans . . . and those tomorrow.

Finally, we thank our families, our children, and our spouses for their enormous support throughout this journey. We could not have achieved this if it were not for you. Thank you for allowing us to be of service to others.

> *Perhaps on earth I never shall behold,*
> *With eye of sense, your outward form and semblance;*
> *Therefore to me ye never will grow old,*
> *But live forever young in my remembrance!*

—Dedication, *The Seaside and the Fireside*, 1850
Henry Wadsworth Longfellow

Introduction

TODAY'S YOUNG VETERANS: SERVING A RESILIENT COMMUNITY

Diann Cameron Kelly

> *... let us strive on to finish the work we are in; to bind up the nation's wounds; to care for him who shall have borne the battle, and for his widow, and his orphan—to do all which may achieve and cherish a just, and a lasting peace, among ourselves, and with all nations.*
>
> —PRESIDENT ABRAHAM LINCOLN, 2ND INAUGURAL ADDRESS, 1865

The strength of our veterans is not just embodied in their erect carriage, confident walk, or firm resolve which defines their presence. Their strength is in their resilience, which overcomes adversity in the face of insurmountable odds. This resilience is demonstrated by the veteran's quiet tenacity to face the diagnosis of posttraumatic stress disorder (PTSD) or traumatic brain injury (TBI); or the hopeful smile on the mask of a stoic face of grief and depression; or a caring, empathetic heart deeply camouflaged by the wounds of isolation and rage.

Treating Young Veterans captures the strengths, needs, and concerns of young servicemen and women making the transition from active combat duty to veteran status and a return to civilian life. This text reexamines the human costs and sacrifices attached to combat. Veterans' experiences with loss, extensive physical and emotional separations, along with lasting visible and nonvisible wounds appear normal in the combat arena. However, when servicemen and women transition home and attempt to reintegrate into civilian society, they find that the skills, coping mechanisms, beliefs, and social mores which allowed them to survive in combat make it harder to return to civilian life (Jarrett, 2008; Vogt, Samper, King, King, & Martin, 2008; Wheeler & Bragin, 2007). All of these put them at increased risk for the following: PTSD, TBI, chronic health issues, substance abuse, domestic violence, homelessness, unemployment, divorce, and overall social and emotional instability (Erbes et al., 2007; Frisman & Griffin-Fennell, 2009; Jarrett, 2008; Vogt et al., 2008).

Treating Young Veterans brings to life the practice, outreach, and advocacy opportunities that facilitate a healthy and socially engaged reintegration for traditional veterans (i.e., enlisted and career military personnel) and nontraditional veterans (i.e., reservists and national guardsmen and women) between 18 and 40 years. Further, it combines knowledge from across disciplines to promote thoughtful and purposeful interventions and future research aiding reintegration of young, socially developing veterans into civilian communities.

This work comprises nearly 15 chapters divided into three parts: (1) Assessment and Practice Approaches to Promote Resilience; (2) Outreach and Practice With Special Communities; and (3) Advocacy Practice to Promote Young Veterans' Well-Being. Each part is preceded by a summary written by members of the editorial team that details the material to the reader. After these parts, the editors offer an Epilogue summarizing significant steps needed in practice, outreach, and advocacy to improve the quality of living and well-being for veterans, their families, and their communities.

Treating Young Veterans is designed to enhance practice and research to inform services to veterans and their families, and ensure this community is not marginalized again after another war conflict. Currently, of the 23 million U.S. veterans, about 60% are under the age of 65 years (National Center for Veterans Analysis & Statistics, 2010). With approximately 21% of veterans between the ages of 18 and 24 years unemployed compared with 16% of nonveteran young adults in the same age group (Bureau of Labor Statistics, 2010) and many attempting to self-manage their mental health and physical health needs, vigorous outreach and contemporary practice strategies are needed for this community as there are only about 1000 VA Vet Centers (260) and VA community-based outpatient clinics (773) across the nation (National Center for Veterans Analysis & Statistics, 2010).

Our emphasis on trauma, cognitive dissonance, and pathways toward social and emotional triumph is informed by the diverse contributions of many scholars, practitioners, and veterans. This includes the work of Wesley Kasprow and Robert Rosenheck of Yale Medical School's Department of Psychiatry and the Northeast Program Evaluation Center focusing on veterans dealing with homelessness. In addition, we have scientists and practitioners from Duke University Medical Center and the VA Mid-Atlantic MIRECC who discuss the transition of veterans to civilian life and the effects of transition on families; and law professors Thomas Reed and Justin Holbrook of Widener University Law School who respectively provide information on the VA claims process as well as the nation's Veteran Courts across the United States that ensures issues related to veterans' mental health are not further misconstrued or ignored in a civilian context and costs the veteran his or her freedom postdeployment.

This text answers the call for creative early responses to and comprehensive interventions for our veterans prior to their return from combat and throughout their reintegration into civilian society. Knowing what we know now, veterans should return home with their expectancy of honor ... expectancy of duty, ... and expectancy of responsive services being met from the partnerships between their veteran care systems and the civilian community. They should also expect to return to a fully functional life comparable to that which they had before deploying.

Treating Young Veterans is a tribute to the honorable duty these men and women have shown in the face of turmoil and chaos, and is a humble response to their need for services ... but most of all, their sacrifice.

REFERENCES

Bureau of Labor Statistics. (2010). *The employment situation—February 2010.* U.S. Department of Labor, USDL-10-0256 (http://www.bls.gov/news.release/archives/empsit_03052010.pdf), as cited in *Washington Post* (2010). Unemployment rate for young veterans hits 21.1 percent, March 13, 2010. Retrieved October 12, 2010, from http://www.washingtonpost.com/wp-dyn/content/article/2010/03/12/AR2010031204123.html

Erbes, C. R., Polusny, M. A., Dieperink, M., Kattar, K., Leskela, J., & Curry, K. (2007, November). Care for returning service members: Providing mental health care for military service members returning from Iraq and Afghanistan. *Minnesota Psychologist,* 1–4.

Frisman, L. K., & Griffin-Fennell, F. (2009). Suicide and incarcerated veterans—Don't wait for the numbers. *Journal of American Academy Psychiatry Law,* 37(1), 92–94.

Jarrett, Maj. T. (2008, July–September). Warrior resilience training in operation Iraqi freedom: Combining rational emotive behavior therapy, resiliency and positive psychology. *The Army Medical Department Journal,* 32–38.

National Center for Veterans Analysis and Statistics. (2010). *VA benefits & health care utilization.* Veterans Administration, VETDATA, Retrieved October 12, 2010, from http://www1.va.gov/VETDATA/Pocket-Card/4X6_summer10_sharepoint.pdf

Vogt, D. S., Samper, R. E., King, D. W., King, L. A., & Martin, J. A. (2008). Deployment stressors and posttraumatic stress symptomology. Comparing active duty and National Guard/Reserve personnel from Gulf War I. *Journal of Traumatic Stress,* 21(1), 66–74.

Wheeler, D., & Bragin, M. (2007). Bringing it all back home: Social work and the challenge of returning veterans. *Health and Social Work,* 12(4), 297–300.

Treating Young Veterans

*Promoting Resilience Through Practice
and Advocacy*

Part I

ASSESSMENT AND PRACTICE APPROACHES TO PROMOTE RESILIENCE

David Gitelson and William Valente

P art I of *Treating Young Veterans* offers a distinct portrait of the assessment, issues and concerns regarding veterans and their families. It immerses the reader in assessment opportunities for working with veterans and recognizing and fostering hallmarks of resiliency in the face of reintegration and through the symptomatic challenges of post-traumatic stress disorder (PTSD).

The clash of war-time demands and home-life expectations overload the psyche of many returning veteran and is a theme throughout the book. Diann Cameron Kelly looks at those identifiers that present challenges to veterans returning from war. This information gives veterans and those who serve them a more profound recognition of their worldview in a moment of crisis while providing tools for helping professionals to improve well-being in the face of reintegration.

Veterans have their own internal tools to cope with life post-combat. Alissa Mallow, Brenda Williams-Gray, and Jonathan Alex, along with Diann Kelly consider five of these protective tools that may foster veterans' resilience. Utilizing these factors can be an excellent way for veterans and helping professionals to promote post-traumatic growth. Further, PTSD has its own course of development, and Thomas Quinn and Elizabeth Quinn identify the stages of development and how to use this knowledge in flexible, specific, and superior assessment and treatment. Wayne Klug, Anne O'Dwyer, along with alumna from Berkshire Community College offer a comprehensive presentation on cognitive dissonance and its relationship to combat. Finally, Diann Kelly returns with colleague Shari Ward to discuss how the combat trauma experienced by veterans, equally affects their children across the life span. She identifies these individuals, dealing with secondary traumatization, as "veterans-by-proxy".

The views and research expressed in Part I posit that veterans dealing with trauma, who are attempting to reintegrate into civilian life, face a unique and brutal set of challenges. Assessment of how these challenges manifest in each veteran, followed by appropriate, professional, and consistent responses, is society's responsibility—a responsibility that is often given to the helping professions.

THE CONTEXTUAL CHALLENGES FOR YOUNG VETERANS

Diann Cameron Kelly

The day soldiers stop bringing you their problems is the day you have stopped leading them. They have either lost confidence that you can help them or concluded that you do not care.

COLIN POWELL (1995)

C oming home from combat is not an easy task for veterans. Soldiers do not get on a plane, leave the war theater, and then disembark in a small town with a myriad of waving flags, grand bandstand music, and deafening cheers from family, friends, and neighbors. Actually, soldiers are informed they are finally leaving the combat environment a short time before departure (often after many weeks, if not months, of uncertainty of when their actual departure may be) (Department of Defense, 2009). They must, then, stay alive to ensure they can get to the safety of the *demobilization site*—their last step before coming home to the United States.

During their time in demobilization, soldiers go through a myriad of screenings to address any physical and mental health needs before they arrive home. One of the more essential documents is the *Post Deployment Health Assessment*. This document's stated purpose is to assess the health of soldiers after their deployment, and identify issues that can "assist military healthcare providers" and other health care providers in providing care to veterans (Department of Defense, 1999). The Health Assessment portion of the form is no more than six questions (Department of Defense, 1999, p. 2):

1. Would you say your health in general is ... (choices are five indicators ranging from "Excellent" to "Poor" of which only one indicator is chosen).

2. Do you have any unresolved medical or dental problems that developed during this deployment?
3. Are you currently on a profile or light duty?
4. During this deployment have you sought, or intend to seek, counseling or care for your mental health?
5. Do you have concerns about possible exposures or events during this deployment that you may feel may affect your health?
6. Do you have any questions or concerns about your health?

While critical to the Department of Defense as well as the Veterans Administration, as there is an electronic record of this information following the veteran, there is not one question on this health assessment that identifies the likelihood or existence of posttraumatic stress disorder (PTSD) symptoms, substance use during combat, or stability factors once state side, including employment prospects and housing. Stability factors address the quality of life and well-being domains of overall health for the veteran (Department of Defense, 2009; Fontana & Rosenheck, 2004; Hoge et al., 2004; Monson, Taft, & Fredman, 2009).

Further, during this transition period, returning soldiers attend a myriad of briefings, in essence, on how to live state side (Department of Defense, 2009; Koppes, 2010; Manderscheid, 2007). For some of the returning soldiers, many of the briefings ask about suicidal ideation, substance use and dependency, or lack of stability on the home front, and are likely to occur before tens of peers and commanding officers (C. Quinn, personal communications, September 12, 2010, October 13, 2010, October 15, 2010). The presence of confidentiality is minimal if not stifled during this context.

And then they return home.

According to Dr. Constance Quinn (2010), a Social Worker and Clinical Coordinator of Inpatient Psychiatry at the Hudson Valley Health Care System of the Veterans Administration, when soldiers return home "they often go underground."

> They try to regain normalcy. That's what going underground means. They rejoin families and friends, and they attempt to reclaim their civilian jobs or find new employment. Unfortunately, the Post Deployment Health screening is done in the demobilization [site], and people tell you what you want to hear just to move on from [combat]. We [at the VA] may not see them until a year later or maybe even more when life as a new civilian is just too difficult to manage.
>
> —*Quinn, 2010*

CONTEXTUAL CHALLENGES TO MANAGING REINTEGRATION

The presumption that most veterans, returning from combat zones, experience some form of debilitating outcome such as a severe mental illness or incarceration is not sound (Department of Defense, 2009; Fontana & Rosenheck, 2004; Hoge et al., 2008; Jarrett, 2008; Manderscheid, 2007). In fact, a large amount of veterans return to the United States and present as the *resilient warrior*, one who does well during transition and early reintegration, has a cohesive, supportive social network of family and friends, is able to secure employment, and also has or has access to private insurance beyond the benefits available through the Veterans Administration (Fontana & Rosenheck, 2004; Hoge, Auchterloine, & Milliken, 2006; Jarrett, 2008; Manderscheid, 2007).

In addition, many returning veterans also have the protective factors of living in municipalities or states that overtly support veterans with consumer opportunities (i.e., discounted products) solely for veterans and their families, and communities that are overly supportive of veterans (Quinn, 2010). However, there are many veterans who face significant contextual challenges that increase the likelihood for debilitating outcomes such as severe mental illness, substance abuse, and suicide, among others (Brenda & Belcher, 2006; Friedman, 2006; Hoge et al., 2008; Jones, Young, & Leppma, 2010; Kang & Hyams, 2005; Keuhn, 2009; Meichenbaum, 2009; Pompili et al., 2009). These challenges negatively affect veterans' transition to civilian status (Lapierre, Schwegler, & LaBauve, 2007; Seal, Bertenthal, Miner, Sen, & Marmar, 2007), becoming public health concerns.

Gehlert et al. (2008) developed a social epidemiological model to facilitate the study of factors that increase the likelihood for socio-behavioral and physical health disparities and rates primarily among individuals confronting significant chronic illnesses. Gehlert et al. (2008) suggested that when we know what environmental and social issues influence public health, and fuel the perpetuation of social and behavioral challenges and maladies, we are better able to address it through early, targeted, and comprehensive intervention.

> ... social factors [represent] upstream determinants [defined] as features of the social environment, such as socioeconomic status and discrimination that influence individual behavior, disease and health status. Viewing health disparities through a lens that incorporate

social/environmental conditions ... better allows us to design and implement interventions targeted at levels downstream from those conditions.

—*Gehlert et al., 2008*

When looking specifically at the determinants before, during, and after veterans' deployment, we find a myriad of conditions that may increase the likelihood for public health concerns within and among this community. Given the greater weight to upstream determinants, these conditions are (1) environmental, (2) social, (3) behavioral, and (4) biological (Gehlert et al., 2008) (see Figure 1.1).

Combat exposure is one of the more significant environmental conditions that place veterans at risk for debilitating outcomes postdeployment (Friedman, 2006; Hoge et al., 2004; Lapierre et al., 2007). Long-term and frequent exposure to combat, as well as direct involvement in the causing of casualties of enemy combatants and civilians, imparts a significant level of stress on the individual (Friedman, 2006; Hoge et al., 2004; Kang & Hyams, 2005; Meichenbaum, 2009). The veteran must cognitively detach himself or herself from that stressor in order to complete the military task.

In addition, the deployments in the current Global War on Terror (GWOT) are frequent and long (i.e., often 12–18 months) with minimal or infrequent home/base stays away from combat (Felker et al., 2008; Hoge et al., 2004; Lapierre et al., 2007). As such, the soldier attempts to succeed at tasks that remain consistently harmful to his or her own perception of self and interpretation of his or her own actions, amid a tenuous, uncertain environment where fatalities are a daily possibility.

Along with combat exposure, environmental conditions also include a diminished socioeconomic history that decreases social capital prior to deployment and can inform the likelihood of stability during reintegration (Department of Defense, 2009; Manderscheid, 2007). In addition, a history of domestic violence (Monson et al., 2009) along with minimal education and employment options also increase the likelihood of repeating this postdeployment history, especially when combined with combat exposure and other stressors (Manderscheid, 2007).

Social conditions follow environmental conditions, and speak to the factors that enhance or detract from one's quality of living (Fontana & Rosenheck, 2004; Jarrett, 2008). Key conditions are housing and employment losses as well as low educational attainment

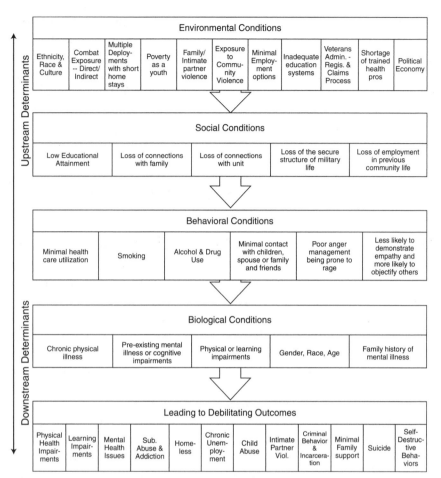

FIGURE 1.1 Downward causal model of contextual challenges to reintegration increasing gateway risk factors for returning veterans. *Source*: Adapted from Gehlert, S., Sohmer, D., Sacks, T., Mininger, C., McClintock, M., & Olopade, O. (2008). Targeting health disparities: A model linking upstream determinants to downstream interventions. *Health Affairs, 27*(2), 339–349.

and connections with a supportive social network (Manderscheid, 2007). The behavioral conditions, following the social conditions, involve minimal health care utilization (Hoge et al., 2006), smoking, alcohol, and other drug use (Brenda & Belcher, 2006; Meichenbaum, 2009; Pompili et al., 2009), along with poor anger management and being unable to connect with loved ones or demonstrating empathy to others (Monson et al., 2009).

When combined with the biological conditions, including pre-existing medical or mental health issues (Collins & Kennedy, 2008; Hoge et al., 2008), there is a higher likelihood that veterans will require early and more intensive interventions to secure and stabilize their reintegration into the civilian context. This social epidemiological model facilitates our understanding of the contextual challenges for veterans, and informs a more polytrauma perspective toward intervention.

A POLYTRAUMA PERSPECTIVE TO EARLY INTERVENTION

Combat exposure diminishes a returning soldier's ability to directly enhance his or her own quality of living when transitioning to civilian society (Koppes, 2010; Manderscheid, 2007). This is not to say that the veteran is unable to accomplish the task of reintegration. However, the task of reintegration is an intergroup and interdisciplinary task that includes the veteran, family, his or her reintegration partner(s) (i.e., Chaplain, veteran mentor, military "buddy," etc.), as well as inter-disciplinary professionals engaged with the veteran to secure his or her transition home and facilitate reintegration into the civilian arena (Jarrett, 2008; Koppes, 2010; Manderscheid, 2007).

Collins and Kennedy (2008) maintain that combat produces such visible and nonvisible injuries that the therapeutic care needs to be mul-tifaceted and polytrauma-focused. A polytrauma model, as emphasized by their "Polytrauma Rehabilitation Centers," asserts that attending to daily living, cognitive functioning, emotional attunement, and social connectedness ameliorates long-term issues and medical needs (Collins & Kennedy, 2008). The goal is to inform, support, and motivate veterans and their families through a paradigm of "action-oriented, strength-based, and solution-focused ..." service goals (Collins & Kennedy, 2008, p. 994).

Primarily used to address medical issues emerging from traumatic brain injury (TBI), the polytrauma perspective identifies a multitude of stressors that impact the overall well-being and propensity of well-being for the veteran. This includes (1) multiple outcomes of combat exposure, including the consistent uncertainty of death or extensive injury as well as contributing to the harm of another; (2) treatment that is specific to the veteran's complex issues; (3) presence or lack of family support; (4) social characteristics, including marital status, employment, or housing; and most importantly, (5) loss of access to "military environment and culture" (Collins & Kennedy, 2008, pp. 995–996). Collins and Kennedy (2008) assert that

> [t]he ultimate goal of [this model] is to optimize quality of life by maximizing independent functioning and community integration. Toward this end, treatment occurs in multiple setting, including the community.
>
> —*Collins & Kennedy, 2008, p. 994*

Thus, returning soldiers (highly resilient, moderately resilient, and minimally resilient) require a comprehensive, multifaceted approach to support their home-bound efforts as early as possible.

WHERE DO WE BEGIN?

Many researchers from within the military and in the veteran/civilian community assert or imply that transition from the combat arena must begin before the demobilization site (Collins & Kennedy, 2008; Felker, Hawkins, Dobie, Gutierrez, & McFall, 2008; Jarrett, 2008; Lapierre et al., 2007; Manderscheid, 2007; Pietrzak et al., 2010; Seal et al., 2007). Their rationale for this belief is that early intervention is the key to better socio-behavioral and physical health outcomes postdeployment. Knowing about addiction, suicidal ideation, along with minimal familial support and lack of housing or unemployment are essential contextual challenges to address in order to achieve strong postcombat health screenings. But more importantly, there is no gestalt or one-size-fits-all strategic plan to reintegrate veterans. Each veteran requires a personalized strategy based on the causal determinants specific to the veteran—their environmental, social, behavioral, and biological determinants (risk and protective factors) that may diminish or enhance the quality of life and well-being for the returning veteran.

With these issues facing today's young veteran, emerging from GWOT operations, there is a high likelihood that these young veterans can be marginalized, disappear, and embark on a pursuit to reclaim their lives through an existential vacuum. This existential vacuum embodies social alienation and a struggle to find purpose and meaning amid loneliness, despair, apathy, and cynicism that can lead to distress, depression, and aggression (Frankl, 1992; p. 111; Mascaro & Rosen, 2005).

In fact, no veteran should ostensibly disappear from the national landscape. When veterans disappear from the national landscape, it is indicative of the environmental context of our nation—an oppressive contextual challenge of apathy and low regard toward today's young veteran.

REFERENCES

Brenda, B., & Belcher, J. (2006). Alcohol and other drug problems among homeless veterans: A life course theory of forgiveness. *Alcoholism Treatment Quarterly, 24*(1/2), 147–170.

Collins, R. C., & Kennedy, M. C. (2008). Serving families who have served: Providing family therapy and support in interdisciplinary polytrauma rehabilitation. *Journal of Clinical Psychology: In Session, 64*(8), 993–1003.

Department of Defense. (1999). *Post Deployment Health Assessment,* DD Form 2796, 10 U.S.C. 136 Chapter 55. 10/41, 3013, 5013, 8013, and E.O. 9397.

Department of Defense. (2009). *Report of the Second Quadrennial Quality of Life Review.* Office of the Deputy Under Secretary of Defense (Military Community and Family Policy). Retrieved from http://cs.mhf.dod.mil/content/dav/mhf/QOL-library/PDF/MHF/QOL%20Resources/Reports/Quadrennial%20Quality%20of%20Life%20Review%202009.pdf

Felker, B., Hawkins, E., Dobie, D., Gutierrez, J., & McFall, M. (2008). Characteristics of deployed Operation Iraqi Freedom military personnel who seek mental health care. *Military Medicine, 173*(2), 155–158.

Fontana, A., & Rosenheck, R. (2004). Trauma, change in strength of religious faith, and mental health service use among veterans treated for PTSD. *The Journal of Nervous and Mental Disease, 192*(9), 579–584.

Frankl, V. E. (1992). *Man's search for meaning: An introduction to logotherapy.* Boston: Beacon Press.

Friedman, M. J. (2006). Posttraumatic stress disorder among military returnees from Afghanistan and Iraq. *American Journal of Psychiatry, 163*(4), 586–594.

Gehlert, S., Sohmer, D., Sacks, T., Mininger, C., McClintock, M., & Olopade, O. (2008). Targeting health disparities: A model linking upstream determinants to downstream interventions. *Health Affairs, 17*(2), 339–349.

Hoge, C. W., Auchterloine, J. L., & Milliken, C. S. (2006). Mental health problems, use of mental health services and attrition from military service after returning from deployment to Iraq or Afghanistan. *Journal of the American Medical Association, 295*, 1023–1032.

Hoge, C. W., Castro, C. A., Messer, S. C., McGurk, D., Cotting, D. I., & Koffman, R. L. (2004). Combat duty in Iraq and Afghanistan, mental health problems, and barriers to care. *New England Journal of Medicine, 351*(1), 13–22.

Hoge, C. W., McGurk, D., Thomas, J. L., Cox, A. L., Engel, C. C., & Castro, C. A. (2008). Mild traumatic brain injury in U.S. soldiers returning from Iraq. *New England Journal of Medicine, 358*, 453–463.

Jarrett, Maj. T. (2008, July–September). Warrior resilience training in operation Iraqi freedom: Combining rational emotive behavior therapy, resiliency and positive psychology. *The Army Medical Department Journal*, 32–38.

Jones, K. D., Young, T., & Leppma, M. (2010). Mild traumatic brain injury and post traumatic stress disorder in returning Iraq and Afghanistan war veterans: Implications for assessment and diagnosis. *Journal of Counseling & Development, 88*, 372–376.

Kang, H. K., & Hyams, K. C. (2005). Mental health care needs among recent war veterans. *New England Journal of Medicine, 352*(13), 1289.

Keuhn, B. M. (2009). Soldier suicide rates continue to rise: Military, scientists work to stem the tide. *Journal of the American Medical Association, 301*(11), 1111–1113.

Koppes, C. R. (2010). *The hidden casualties of war: Promoting healing and resiliency for U.S. service members and their families—A two day symposium* [PPT]. Retrieved from http://uwf.edu/cap/HCW/brief/KoppesBrief.pps

Lapierre, C. B., Schwegler, A. F., & LaBauve, B. J. (2007). Posttraumatic stress and depression symptoms in soldiers returning from combat operations in Iraq and Afghanistan. *Journal of Traumatic Stress, 20*(6), 933–943.

Manderscheid, R. W. (2007). Helping veterans return: Community, family, and job. *Archives of Psychiatric Nursing, 21*(2), 122–124.

Mascaro, N., & Rosen, D. H. (2005). Existential meaning's role in the enhancement of hope and prevention of depressive symptoms. *Journal of Personality, 73*(4), 985–1014.

Meichenbaum, D. (2009). Trauma and substance abuse guidelines for treating returning veterans. *Counselor: The Magazine for Addiction Professional, 10*(4), 10–15.

Monson, C. M., Taft, C. T., & Fredman, S. J. (2009). Military-related PTSD and intimate relationships: From description to theory-driven research and intervention development. *Clinical Psychology Review, 29*, 707–714.

Pietrzak, R. H., Goldstein, M. B., Malley, J. C., Rivers, A. J., Johnson, D. C., & Southwick, S. S. (2010). Risk and protective factors associated with suicidal ideation in veterans of Operations Enduring Freedom and Iraqi Freedom. *Journal of Affective Disorders, 123*, 102–107.

Pompili, M., Innamorati, M., Lester, D., Akiskal, H. S., Rihmer, Z., Del Casale, A. et al. (2009). Substance abuse, temperament and suicide risk: Evidence from a case control study. *Journal of Addictive Diseases, 28*, 13–20.

Powell, C. L. (1995). *My American journey*. New York: Random House/ Ballantine Books.

Seal, K. H., Bertenthal, D., Miner, C., Sen, S., & Marmar, C. (2007). Bringing the war back home: Mental health disorders among 103,788 U.S. veterans returning from Iraq and Afghanistan seen at Department of Veterans Affairs facilities. *Archives of Internal Medicine, 167*(5), 476–482.

2

LIVING BEYOND THE INTERSECTION OF WAR THEATER AND HOME: PROTECTIVE FACTORS FOR HEALTHY REINTEGRATION

Alissa Mallow, Brenda Williams-Gray,
Diann Cameron Kelly, and Jonathan Alex

Never in the field of human conflict was so much owed by so many to so few.

WINSTON CHURCHILL, August 20, 1940

C olloquially "war is hell." But for servicemen and servicewomen in contemporary wars, emerging from the battle arena is even more complicated than ever before (Brenda & Belcher, 2006; Fontana & Rosenheck, 2004). Today's servicemen and servicewomen, especially those serving in Iraq and Afghanistan, must live with and survive in the war theater while addressing and managing the stressors of the home environment in real time (Friedman, 2006; Kang & Hyams, 2005; Meichenbaum, 2009; Vogt, Samper, King, King, & Martin, 2008). There remains little separation between the two environments as servicemen and servicewomen attempt to address the school or health issues of their children and manage household finances, while keeping up with the well-being of their parents or spouses all while staying on mission in the combat arena.

War theater is more than a geographical area. It contains various symbols, rules, orthodox structures, protocols, and the cultural contexts of power and uniformity (Friedman, 2006; Jarrett, 2008; Kuzmics, 2009). Veterans emerging from war theater have risked bodily injury, fought enemies that may be void of conventional uniforms, or traveled along roads with improved explosive devices (IEDs), while confronting stressors and news from home via the Internet (i.e., social networking media; computer-based voice and video calling; etc.) and mobile phone access. Surprisingly, direct and frequent contact with family and friends in the civilian contexts during combat may improve servicemen's and servicewomen's morale, provide family support, and allow veterans to feel involved in the resolution of family problems at home, while in the midst of war theater (Bell, Schumm, Knott, & Ender, 1999; Wong & Gerras, 2006).

Further, the intersection of home life and war theater connects servicemen and servicewomen to the realities of their lives at home and may support stability in the war arena (Fontana & Rosenheck, 2004; Friedman, 2006; Jarrett, 2008) until their permanent return home. For many veterans, distance and disconnectedness from familial or cultural ties during combat diminish resilience levels and make reintegration into civilian contexts even more difficult (Beck & Schlichte, 2007; Kang & Hyams, 2005; Manske, 2006; Wheeler & Bragin, 2007). This is more likely due to extensive immersion in combat zones through frequent and extended deployments as well as the values and institutionalized processes characteristic of military order within the chaos of war (Beck & Schlichte, 2007; Friedman, 2006; National Center for PTSD, 2006; Vogt et al., 2008).

Before achieving veteran status, Iraq and Afghanistan service personnel, in particular, have extended lengths of service, two years on average, in the war theater with short breaks between repeated deployments (Department of Defense, 2007) that increase exposures to traumatic stressors (Lomsky-Feder, Gazit & Ben-Ari, 2008). However, the degree of posttraumatic stress for veterans can be mitigated by specific protective factors before, during, and after deployment to influence the transition and reintegration for young veterans (Friedman, 2006; Wheeler & Bragin, 2007). These protective factors are self-esteem and other self-isms; cognitive processing; use of self and social competence; and personality and personal values (Jarrett, 2008; Williams-Gray, 1998).

IDENTIFYING VETERANS' PROTECTIVE FACTORS

The aftermath of war zone combat can produce behavioral, physical, and emotional reactions that are normative responses to horrific circumstances within combat arenas (Friedman, 2006; Lomsky-Feder et al., 2008; Vogt et al., 2008). The coping styles, prior traumatic histories, the strength of connections to their former units and missions, and pre-combat trainings/preparations impact levels of stress and recovery among veteran personnel (Herman, 1992; Huckans et al., 2010; Wheeler & Bragin, 2007). However, the veterans' level of resilience and particularly their protective factors can diminish the effect of *gateway risk factors* (i.e., suicidal ideation, substance abuse and addiction, likelihood of violence and limited impulse control, etc.) on self-destructive behaviors, social disconnectedness and mental impairment, homelessness, and even incarceration (Brenda & Belcher, 2006; Department of Defense, 2007; Fraser, Richman, & Galinsky, 1999; Jones, Young, & Leppma, 2010; Kang & Hyams, 2005; Meichenbaum, 2009; National Center, 2006).

Resilience is not just a trait. Resilience is how we interact with our environment and the resources we call upon, apply, and contribute to the environment in stressful situations (Begun, 1993; Bernard, 1994; Fraser et al., 1999; Greene & Livingston, 2002; Luthar & Ziglar, 1991; Pompili et al., 2009). Masten, Best, and Garmezy (1990) define resiliency as "the process of, or capacity for, or outcome of successful adaptation despite challenging or threatening circumstances" (Masten et al., 1990, p. 426). Research demonstrates that moderately high to highly resilient veterans emerging from war theater are able to demonstrate positive outcomes despite high-risk circumstances, consistent competency even under stress, and the ability to recover from trauma (Fontana & Rosenheck, 2004; Friedman, 2006; Jarrett, 2008).

While there are many external processes and factors that serve to protect the veteran and promote well-being after combat (i.e., connections to home; connections to unit or other veterans; gaining employment and educational opportunities), veterans are also able to demonstrate successful adaptation through a series of internal processes that emerge from that positive intersection of war and home theater to promote resiliency and healthy reintegration (Fontana & Rosenheck, 2004; Jarrett, 2008; Jones et al., 2010). As illustrated in Figure 2.1, these internal protective factors are:

1. "Self-isms" (self-esteem, efficacy, internal locus of control, sense of purpose).
2. Cognitive processing or internal feedback systems (the process of thinking through one's own lens, insight, achievement, mental stamina, problem-solving, intellectual skills, hope, sense of direction, realistic expectations of self and environment, recognizing what is not within one's control).
3. Use of one's self in the world (social cognitive skills and relatedness, adaptive distancing, pro-activity, sense of competence, ability to make friends, recruit others for support, secure attachment).

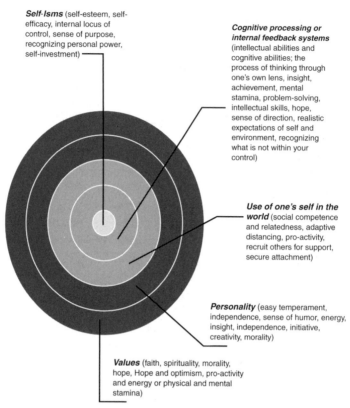

Self-Isms (self-esteem, self-efficacy, internal locus of control, sense of purpose, recognizing personal power, self-investment)

Cognitive processing or internal feedback systems (intellectual abilities and cognitive abilities; the process of thinking through one's own lens, insight, achievement, mental stamina, problem-solving, intellectual skills, hope, sense of direction, realistic expectations of self and environment, recognizing what is not within your control)

Use of one's self in the world (social competence and relatedness, adaptive distancing, pro-activity, recruit others for support, secure attachment)

Personality (easy temperament, independence, sense of humor, energy, insight, independence, initiative, creativity, morality)

Values (faith, spirituality, morality, hope, Hope and optimism, pro-activity and energy or physical and mental stamina)

FIGURE 2.1 Internal protective factors promoting resilience and healthy reintegration.

4. Personality (easy temperament, independence, sense of humor, energy).
5. Values (faith, spirituality, morality, hope). (DeNeve & Cooper, 1998; Fontana & Rosenheck, 2004; Grassman, 2010; Kelly, 2008; Park, 2004; Williams-Gray, 1998.)

Self-isms refer to self-esteem, positive self-concept, locus of control and self-efficacy, and a realistic understanding of one's environment (including strengths and limitations) and are key protective factors for the veteran (DeNeve & Cooper, 1998; Jarrett, 2008) and critical to post-traumatic growth (PTG). In particular, internal locus of control is the ability to be self-directed, take power and responsibility for one's decisions and life (Valentine & Feinauer, 1993). Self-efficacy is "confidence that one's internal and external worlds are predictable, controllable and hopeful" (Kaplan, Turner, Norman, & Stillson, 1996, p. 159). These selfisms enable individuals to perceive and take in (internalize) their gifts and resources amid feelings and experiences of uncertainty, impatience, and sorrow (Jarrett, 2008; Park, 2004; Valentine & Feinauer, 1993). Further, selfisms enable the process of self-forgiveness and moving beyond the inability to undo the past (Fontana & Rosenheck, 2004; Jarrett, 2008; Park, 2004).

Cognitive processing refers to being more than how we think but also how we behave, the motivations behind our behavior, and how we rationalize our actions and our beliefs (Fontana & Rosenheck, 2004; Huckans et al., 2010; Jones et al., 2010; Park, 2004). Our cognitive processes allow us to problem solve, acquire, and strengthen our skills and remove challenges and opporunities (Friedman, 2006; Huckans et al., 2010; National Center for Post Traumatic Stress Disorder, 2004). However, for many veterans with traumatic brain injuries and posttraumatic stress disorder, even those with mild cases (Jones et al., 2010) can exhibit diminished resiliency when these issues are undiagnosed or undetected. Traumatic brain injuries and mild traumatic brain injuries are physical injuries to the brain (e.g., concussions) that disturb or disrupt cognitive functioning (Huckans et al., 2010; Jones et al., 2010). With about 20% of Operation Iraqi Freedom/Operation Enduring Freedom (OIF/OEF) veterans returning to civilian society with mild traumatic brain injuries alone, this is a significant issue (Hoge, Goldberg, & Castro, 2009; Jones et al., 2010). Early detection through imaging devices and immediate occupational and speech/language assessments and treatments followed by immediate and intensive cognitive behavioral treatment (Hoge et al., 2009; Jarrett, 2008; Jones et al., 2010) can address the interpersonal relations and desired occupational performances of reintegrating veterans who are themselves attempting to intersect the field with home.

Use of self refers to the use of one's self in the world and is a significant characteristic of resilience (Beardslee, 1989; Fraser et al., 1999; Greene & Livingston, 2002). Further, use of one's self aids PTG to engage in and with varied elements in society (Jarrett, 2008; Kozaric-Kovacic, 2001). Use of one's self encompasses social competence and relatedness, adaptive distancing, pro-activity, recruitment of others to receive support and strength, and secure attachment (Blum, 1998; DeNeve & Cooper, 1998; Williams-Gray, 1998), especially civilian society. Use of self also includes use of cultural literacy and skills such as prosocial rituals to enhance well-being, along with civic literacy and skills such as vocal activism and volunteerism (DeNeve & Cooper, 1998; Kelly, 2008; Park, 2004) to promote a steady and stable reintegration. For veterans, this use of self is critical because it strengthens the veterans' engagement in society as well as their self-evaluation of their quality of life in a civilian context.

Personality refers to our ability to relate to others (DeNeve & Cooper, 1998). It encompasses our temperament, sense of humor, energy, insight, independence, initiative, and creativity as well as our level of and interpretation of morality (DeNeve & Cooper, 1998). Temperament, in particular, facilitates human relatedness and our capacity to connect to others, to love and be loved, and to care for and be cared about, as well as to trust others and the world around us (DeNeve & Cooper, 1998; Kelly, 2008). The veterans' temperament, positive energy, initiative, and creative processing are influenced by and influence their social networks. The presence of these support systems enables veterans to further cope with postcombat stressors and overcome physical, emotional, and social dysfunction (Friedman, 2006; Jarrett, 2008).

Personal values refer to the ability to relinquish pain, embrace forgiveness, and use spiritual tools and resources to invoke peace to the person's social and emotional contexts (Brenda & Belcher, 2006; DeNeve & Cooper, 1998; Fontana & Rosenheck, 2004; Jarrett, 2008). PTG and resilience are enhanced by the overarching themes of faith, spirituality, hope, and morality (Blum, 1998; Calhoun & Tedeshi, 2006; DeNeve & Cooper, 1998; Fontana & Rosenheck, 2004; Hawley & DeHaan, 1996; Jarrett, 2008; Park, 2004). Faith, or spirituality, is noted consistently in the literature of factors fostering resiliency, especially among military personnel and veterans. Fontana and Rosenheck (2004) assert that veterans treated for posttraumatic stress disorder (PTSD) struggle to find meaning and purpose in their lives. The weakening of religious faith can be tied to excessive combat exposure and possibly increased guilt from a myriad of actions in the combat arena that appear dissonant with actions and values gained from the home arena (Fontana & Rosenheck, 2004; Jarrett, 2008). Faith has a strengthening affect on the psyche, on social relations, and most importantly on one's perception of self (Brenda & Belcher, 2006; Fontana & Rosenheck, 2004) in that faith (religious faith, spiritual faith, moral beliefs, and internalizations) supports the newly minted veteran's quest for answers to life's meaning and purpose *post-war theater*.

Brenda and Belcher (2006), in their study with homeless veterans with co-occurring substance abuse and depression, validate optimistic outcomes for those with low social capital when faith or spiritual constructs were present in the belief system of the individual. Their findings support the relationship of forgiveness and spiritual well-being as a means of enhancing PTG and resilience after war theater.

> Loving and secure attachments and spiritual well-being ... encourage a healthy sense of self-efficacy and ego identity, and buffer one against adverse feelings such as depression and stress and destructive thoughts and behaviors.
>
> —*Brenda and Belcher, 2006, p. 152*

These protective factors are critical for enhancing resilience levels and aiding post-PTG. PTG focuses on one's capacity for renewed functioning and positive change after enduring trauma and adversity (Calhoun & Tedeshi, 2006). For young veterans, this includes relatedness to others, personal and spiritual strength, appreciation for life, and openness to choices and opportunities (Calhoun & Tedeshi, 2006) to mediate healthy reintegration.

CONCLUSION

The protective factors are essential to comprehensive assessments of veterans returning from war theater. Although these protective factors are internal representations and tell only half the narrative of veterans, these factors do allow for a comprehensive review of the individual's ego functioning and their perception of their capacity to successfully reintegrate into their home environment (Brenda & Belcher, 2006; Fontana & Rosenheck, 2004; Friedman, 2006; Jarrett, 2008; Wheeler & Bragin, 2007).

Young veterans navigating the intersection of war theater and the home environment can be at-risk for the destabilizing effects of PTSD. The capacity to harness PTG by internalizing protective factors associated with resiliency is an indication of hopefulness and optimism. This intersection is a fluid relationship between two environments (Lomsky-Feder et al., 2008) that have a significant impact on the mind, heart, strength, and will of the young veteran.

As Hoge et al. (2009) noted, the care and well-being of veterans should be of the highest priority. Promoting resiliency enhances the veterans' abilities and skills to exhibit self-advocacy and self-determination upon their reintegration into civilian society and home theater after combat. By promoting resiliency through a comprehensive assessment, practitioners aid young veterans in effectively planning for life beyond war theater.

REFERENCES

Beardslee, W. (1989). The role of self understanding in resilient individuals: The development of a perspective. *American Journal of Orthopsychiatry, 59,* 266–277.

Beck, T. K., & Schlichte, K. (2007). Nature and civilization in the habitus of the warrior (Serbia and Angala). *Micropolitics of Armed Groups, 1,* 1–16.

Begun, A. (1993). Human behavior and the social environment: The vulnerability, risk and resilience model. *Journal of Social Work Education, 29*(1), 26–34.

Bell, D. B., Schumm, W. R., Knott, B., & Ender, M. G. (1999). The desert fax: A research note on calling home from Somalia. *Armed Forces and Society, 25*(3), 509–521.

Bernard, C. (1994). Resiliency: A shift in our perception? *The American Journal of Family Therapy, 22*(2), 135–143.

Blum, D. (1998). Finding strength: How to overcome anything. *Psychology Today,* May, 1998, 66–73.

Brenda, B., & Belcher, J. (2006). Alcohol and other drug problems among homeless veterans: A life course theory of forgiveness. *Alcoholism Treatment Quarterly, 24*(1/2), 147–170.

Calhoun, L. G., & Tedeshi, R. G. (2006). *Handbook of posttraumatic growth: Research and practice.* Mahwah, NJ: Lawrence Erlbaum Associates.

DeNeve, K. M., & Cooper, H. (1998). The happy personality: A meta-analysis of 137 personality traits and subjective well-being. *Psychological Bulletin, 124*(2), 197–229.

Department of Defense. (2007). *An achievable vision: Report of the Department of Defense Task Force on Mental Health.* Falls Church, VA: Defense Health Board.

Fontana, A., & Rosenheck, R. (2004). Trauma, change in strength of religious faith, and mental health service use among veterans treated for PTSD. *The Journal of Nervous and Mental Disease, 192*(9), 579–584.

Fraser, M. W., Richman, J. M., & Galinsky, M. J. (1999). Risk, protection and resilience: Toward a conceptual framework for social work practice. *Social Work Research, 23,* 129–208.

Friedman, M. J. (2006). Posttraumatic stress disorder among military returnees from Afghanistan and Iraq. *American Journal of Psychiatry, 163*(4), 586–594.

Grassman, D. L. (2010). Peace at last: Stories of hope and healing for veterans and their families. *Chaplaincy Today, 26*(1), 44.

Greene, R., & Livingston, N. C. (2002). A social construct. In R. R. Greene (Ed.), *Resiliency: An integrated approach to practice, policy and research* (pp. 63–94). Washington, DC: NASW Press.

Hawley, D., & DeHaan, L. (1996). Towards a definition of family resilience integrating life-span and family perspectives. *Family Process, 35,* 283–295.

Herman, J. (1992). *Trauma and recovery.* New York, NY: Basic Books.

Hoge, C. W., Goldberg, H. M., & Castro, C. A. (2009). Care of war veterans with mild traumatic brain injury—Flawed perspectives. *New England Journal of Medicine, 360*(16), 1588–1591.

Huckans, M., Pavawalla, S., Demadura, T., Kolessar, M., Seelye, A., Roost, N. et al. (2010). A pilot study examining effects of group based Cognitive Strategic Training treatment on self-reported cognitive problems, psychiatric symptoms, functioning and compensatory strategy use in OIF/OEF combat veterans with persistent mild cognitive disorder and history of traumatic brain injury. *Journal of Rehabilitation Research & Development, 47*(1), 43–60.

Jarrett, Maj. T. (2008, July–September). Warrior resilience training in operation Iraqi freedom: Combining rational emotive behavior therapy, resiliency and positive psychology. *The Army Medical Department Journal,* 32–38.

Jones, K. D., Young, T., & Leppma, M. (2010). Mild traumatic brain injury and post traumatic stress disorder in returning Iraq and Afghanistan war veterans: Implications for assessment and diagnosis. *Journal of Counseling & Development, 88,* 372–376.

Kang, H. K., & Hyams, K. C. (2005). Mental health care needs among recent war veterans. *New England Journal of Medicine, 352*(13), 1289.

Kaplan, C., Turner, S., Norman, E., & Stillson, K. (1996) Promoting resilience strategies: A modified consultation model. *Social Work in Education, 18*(3), 158–166.

Kelly, D. (2008). In preparation for adulthood: Exploring civic participation and social trust among young minorities. *Youth & Society, 40*(4), 526–540.

Kozaric-Kovacic, D. (2001). Assessment of post traumatic stress disorder and comorbidity. *Military Medicine, 166*(8), 677–680.

Kuzmics, H. (2009). Concept for validating the theoretical potential of historical sources. The case of analyzing long-term changes in the Habsburg military habitus. *Historical Social Research, 34*(1), 270–304.

Lomsky-Feder, E., Gazit, N., & Ben-Ari, E. (2008). Reserve soldiers as transmigrants. *Armed Forces and Society, 34*(4), 593–614.

Luthar, S. S., & Ziglar, E. (1991). Vulnerability and competence. *American Journal of Orthopsychiatry, 61*(1), 6–22.

Manske, J. (2006). Social work in the Department of Veterans Affairs: Lessons learned. *Health and Social Work, 31*(3), 233–238.

Masten, A. S., Best, K. M., & Garmezy, N. (1990). Resilience and development: Contributions from the study of children who overcame adversity. *Development and Psychology, 2*(4), 425–443.

Meichenbaum, D. (2009). Trauma and substance abuse guidelines for treating returning veterans. *Counselor: The Magazine for Addiction Professional, 10*(4), 10–15.

National Center for Post Traumatic Stress Disorder. (2004). *Iraq War clinician guide* (2nd ed., pp. 1–20). Department of Veteran Affairs.

National Center for Post Traumatic Stress Disorder. (2006). *Returning from the war zone: A guide for families of military members* (pp. 1–11). Department of Veteran Affairs.

Park, N. (2004). The role of subjective well-being in positive youth development. *ANNALS, AAPSS, 591,* 25–39.

Pompili, M., Innamorati, M., Lester, D., Akiskal, H. S., Rihmer, Z., Del Casale, A. et al. (2009). Substance abuse, temperament and suicide risk: Evidence from a case control study. *Journal of Addictive Diseases, 28,* 13–20.

Valentine, L., & Feinauer, L. (1993). Resilience factors associated with female survivors of childhood sexual abuse. *The American Journal of Family Therapy, 21*(3), 216–223.

Vogt, D. S., Samper, R. E., King, D. W., King, L. A., & Martin, J. A. (2008). Deployment stressors and posttraumatic stress symptomology. Comparing active duty and National Guard/Reserve personnel from Gulf War I. *Journal of Traumatic Stress, 21*(1), 66–74.

Wheeler, D., & Bragin, M. (2007). Bringing it all back home: Social work and the challenge of returning veterans. *Health and Social Work, 12*(4), 297–300.

Williams-Gray, B. (1998). *Individual protective factors and resiliency: A literature review.* Unpublished manuscript, The Graduate Center/CUNY, New York.

Wong, L., & Gerras, S. (2006). *CU@the FOB: How the forward operating bases is changing the life of combat soldiers* (United States Army War College). Retrieved from www.strategicstudiesinstitutearmy.mil/monograph

3

TRAUMA AND THE DEVELOPMENTAL COURSE OF PTSD POSTDEPLOYMENT

Thomas Quinn and Elizabeth Quinn

When a man seats before his eyes the bronze face of his helmet and steps off from the line of departure, he divides himself . . . in two parts. One part he leaves behind. That part which takes delight in his children, which lifts his voice in the chorus, which clasps his wife to him in the sweet darkness of their bed. That half of him, the best part, a man sets aside and leaves behind. He banishes from his heart all feelings of tenderness and mercy, all compassion and kindness, all thought or concept of the enemy as a man, a human being like himself. He marches into battle bearing only the second portion of himself, the baser measure, that half which knows slaughter and butchery and turns the blind eye to quarter. He could not fight at all if he could not do this.

PRESSFIELD, 1998, p. 115

For all of time, societies have relied upon their warriors. No civilization can advance without the warrior class, and yet the cost to the warrior and his society is high. The requirements for being a good soldier include emotional detachment, a kill-or-be-killed mentality, the rejection of one's civility, and a departure from one's humanity. At best, reintegration into society postdeployment, the reclaiming of a part of the self the veteran left behind to go into battle (Pressfield, 1998), is complicated. Often, the complexity of reintegration is exacerbated by posttraumatic stress disorder (PTSD).

PTSD is a psychological disturbance that is developmental in nature; the longer you have it, the more internalized it becomes (Friedman, 2006; Grinage, 2003; Miah, 2010; University of Western Ontario, 2007; Yehuda, 2002). Over time, PTSD symptomatology becomes ego syntonic in that it defines the individual (Benderly, 2008; Lapierre, Schwegler & LaBauve, 2007; Schnurr et al., 2000; Teten et al., 2010; Yehuda, 2002). The longer the veteran is forced to endure the trauma symptoms, the greater the risk for loss of self. Maladaptive coping skills become internalized and the veteran relies on a smaller, more constricted repertoire of coping strategies (Allen, 2005; Grinage, 2003; Teten et al., 2010; University of Western Ontario, 2008). Some coping strategies typical of individuals with PTSD are: hyper-vigilance; anger; substance abuse; and avoidance.

For PTSD to develop, the individual must experience, witness, or have been confronted with an event or events that involve actual or threatened death or serious injury, or a threat to the physical integrity of one's self or to others (Benderly, 2008; Iversen et al., 2008; Yehuda, 2002). His or her response involves intense fear, helplessness, or horror (*DSM-IV-TR*, 2000; Teten et al., 2010). Efforts to reduce the individual's perception of helplessness in the face of such threats to life may reduce the potential for PTSD symptoms to develop.

Veterans experiencing PTSD often recall combat experience from a frame of memory that leads them to speculate that if they had only done more, acted in a more forceful or heroic manner, history may have been changed; fallen comrades might have been saved; and the reality of one's own present subjective distress, therefore, would be mitigated (Geisinger Health System, 2008; University of Western Ontario, 2008; Yehuda, 2002).

Veterans may also experience shame and guilt for either the acts they were part of in combat or for surviving while many of their friends were killed (Friedman, 2006; Lapierre et al., 2007; Shay, 1994; Teten et al., 2010). One Vietnam veteran who went into combat as a 19-year-old private was promoted to squad leader. On what was to be his last night as an active soldier, he unknowingly led a group of soldiers into an ambush. Even though he was so seriously wounded and discharged due to the gravity of his injuries, he carried the guilt of knowing that some other young men in his squad were killed. Thirty years later, he was invited by other Vietnam veterans to accompany them to the Vietnam Veterans Memorial in Washington, DC, for Memorial Day. He refused. He eventually found the words in the group to express his belief that the names of the young men who were killed in his squad that terrible night of combat, and etched into The Wall for all to see, were an indictment of him and proof he had been unable to save them. As he lived his life and experienced a succession of normal developmental milestones—college, marriage, the birth of children, he was always reminded that others, men he was responsible for, would never have those experiences. For decades, his feelings of shame became consuming because they were left unchallenged.

The extent to which PTSD develops and progresses is impacted by age of onset, the individual's level of resilience, his or her baseline psychological functioning, the severity of the trauma, and whether he or she has experienced a single trauma or multiple exposures (Benderly,

2008; Friedman, 2006; Lapierre et al., 2007; Teten et al., 2010). Studies indicate that untreated PTSD becomes a "developmental psychopathology" with social and emotional difficulties remaining across the lifespan (Schnurr et al., 2000; Teten et al., 2010).

Scientific research illustrates how traumatic exposure can damage and alter neural functioning, leading trauma victims to experience problems with short-term memory, attention, concentration, and mood (Fontana, Rosenheck, & Desai, 2010; Lapierre et al., 2007). The hallmark of PTSD among veterans is troubled sleep, usually with horrifying dreams which recall combat experiences (Fontana et al., 2010; Geisinger Health System, 2008; Lapierre et al., 2007; Teten et al., 2010). Research shows childhood trauma increases the potential for victimization and PTSD in adults (Grinage, 2003) and being married may protect one from developing PTSD (University of Western Ontario, 2007).

PTSD also has a genetic component. Pingxing et al. (2009) found the 5-HTTLPR genotype interacted with adult traumatic events and childhood trauma to increase the risk for PTSD, especially for those with multiple traumas. The genotype may impact serotonin in the brain, affecting an individual's anxiety levels and altering the arousal response to fear. Risk factors (Table 3.1) tend to be exponential rather than additive. Multiple exposures over time are likely to overwhelm any and all protective factors, which are no match for repeated trauma (Iversen et al., 2008).

Acute and more immediate reactions to combat trauma may be ameliorated through prompt debriefing-type interventions designed to help the veteran analyze and, as much as possible, normalize the experience. However, we have learned from the Vietnam era, veterans who have adapted to symptoms from as long as 30 or 40 years ago will need treatment targeting coping skills to help them minimize and manage their reactions to trauma that may never entirely disappear (Allen, 2005; Geisinger Health System, 2008).

TABLE 3.1 Risk factor to chronic PTSD

	Risk Factors	Protective Factors
Internal	Vulnerability (preexisting psychological condition)	Resilience (predeployment psychological health)
	Age of onset	
External	Severity of trauma	
	Multiple exposures over time	

Further exacerbating the treatment of PTSD is the prevalence of co-morbid disorders. Grinage (2003) found 80% of individuals with PTSD have at last one other co-occurring disorder and are at higher risk for major depression, panic disorder, generalized anxiety disorder, and substance abuse (Yehuda, 2002).

The developmental nature of PTSD indicates a therapeutic need to evaluate symptomatology from a developmental stage perspective. The developmental stages are often fluid, and when PTSD is treated early in its development, optimal outcomes are more likely. However, when veterans with PTSD are left untreated for a long period of time, treatment may also have to focus on education and teaching the veteran how to cope with his or her illness.

THE DEVELOPMENTAL COURSE OF PTSD

According to the literature, PTSD has several stages: (1) reaction to trauma; (2) symptom formation; (3) symptom internalization; and (4) symptom reinforcement (Benderly, 2008; Geisinger Health System, 2008; Iversen et al., 2008; Lapierre et al., 2007; Miah, 2010; Schnurr et al., 2000; Teten et al., 2010; University of Western Ontario, 2007; van der Kolk, 2006; Yehuda, 2002). The following describes each stage as it relates to veterans, postdeployment.

Reaction to Trauma

A reaction of distress to trauma should be expected and considered "normal," and trauma for the combat veteran is likely to be repeated exposure rather than a single event. The duties of a soldier in war theater may present multiple trauma-producing events unlikely to occur in civilian life: handling the dead and wounded, witnessing others being killed and wounded in a variety of ways (possibly including noncombatants), suffering one's own physical wounds, living in fear of death, and, perhaps most importantly, taking human lives (Friedman, 2006; Lapierre et al., 2007; Teed & Scileppi, 2007; Teten et al., 2010).

Trauma triggers fear that activates the fight or flight response, a biological response to physical threat, which stimulates the release of catecholamine. This neuromodulator arouses the heart and muscles to prepare for battle while "turning off" the prefrontal cortex of the brain which is responsible for logical thought, decision-making, and the values and goals of the individual (American Academy of

Neurology, 2007; Benderly, 2008; University of Western Ontario, 2007; van der Kolk, 2006). From an evolutionary standpoint, this response enables the individual to flip on "autopilot" and focus solely on survival. For the soldier, in particular, this response is perfected through his or her military training and a developing soldier identity (Fontana et al., 2010; Lapierre et al., 2007; National Center for PTSD, 2006; Schnurr et al., 2000). Ideally, posttrauma, one regains a homeostatic balance, but repeated trauma may result in a continual state of fear that negatively impacts the individual's ability to regain any sense of safety, thereby perpetuating a constant state of arousal and affective dysregulation (Benderly, 2008; Lapierre et al., 2007; Teten, 2010; Yehuda, 2002).

Reaction to repeated exposure to trauma may meet the diagnostic criteria for acute stress disorder, including a subjective sense of numbing, detachment, or absence of emotional responsiveness, a reduction in awareness of his or her surroundings, derealization, depersonalization, or dissociative amnesia (the inability to recall an important aspect of the trauma) (*DSM-IV-TR*, 2000; Grinage, 2003; Yehuda, 2002). Veterans often experience guilt, shame, anger, or depression as they attempt to understand the trauma and their perceived role in it. The emotional response at this stage of reaction to trauma is likely to tax individuals' coping skills as they have become overwhelmed in attempting to regain homeostatic balance. Previous defensive strategies are inadequate for coping with the trauma so the veteran psychologically retreats to more primitive strategies (denial, regression, avoidance) that will ultimately become symptoms of behavioral and/or mood disorders, where social, interpersonal, and occupational difficulties begin to emerge (Benderly, 2008; Fontana et al., 2010; Friedman, 2006; Geisinger Health System, 2008; Teten et al., 2010). In addition, Geisinger Health System (2008) warns that without early intervention, soldiers will develop serious health problems in the future.

Symptom Formation

This stage is characterized by experiencing the symptoms of PTSD including hyperarousal, reexperiencing the affective states of trauma, and avoidance, which escalates into behaviors targeting escape from the negative trauma responses (Benderly, 2008; Lapierre et al., 2007; University of Western Ontario, 2008). The veteran begins to construct a new reality based on irrational cognition; she/he creates a hostile environment by generalizing the combat experience to his or her entire life (Benderly, 2008; Lapierre et al., 2007; Teten et al., 2010). For example, in combat, crowds were dangerous (a rational belief relative to experience), yet postdeployment, crowds continue to feel dangerous to the veteran and she/he experiences anxiety and agitation being among and around crowds of people. Such generalization is complicated by the veteran feeling isolated by, and "different" because of, his or her symptoms (Friedman, 2006; Geisinger Health System, 2008).

When soldiers come home, they may be given a hero's welcome locally, which may create some dissonance because they are unsure of how they are perceived. Some soldiers describe their military combat experience as being so "out of real world" they do not know if others view them as objects of curiosity (Benderly, 2008; Geisinger Health System, 2008; Teten et al., 2010). They begin to immediately project "you cannot possibly understand what I've experienced," and their own conflict about such experiences is predictive of their need to isolate from others. Veterans report this is exacerbated by a negative self-concept that carries the cognitive distortions informing them the same people celebrating their service would recoil from them if they knew what these soldiers might have done in the chaos of combat (Benderly, 2008; Lapierre et al., 2007; Teten et al., 2010). However, at this stage, the symptoms are ego dystonic in that they are experienced as pathological or unusual for the individual given the proximity in time to experiences considered normal during deployment.

Symptom Internalization

Symptom internalization is characterized by the previously ego dystonic features of PTSD (e.g., negative self-concept, irrational cognition, excessive worry or unrealistic fear, etc.) becoming ego syntonic (Lapierre et al., 2007; Teten, 2010; Yehuda, 2002). Paradoxically, as the veteran attempts to cope with the symptoms, they become internalized. The symptoms begin to define the veteran as a person: a soldier with PTSD becomes defined as disabled, or as a "crazy person" (Benderly, 2008; Lapierre et al., 2007). As the veteran becomes defined by his or her symptoms, a parallel process occurs: his or her family and society stop believing this can change. The interpersonal and emotional retreat from the veteran by his or her family can reinforce the veteran's belief about, and feelings of, isolation, alienation, and unworthiness (Friedman, 2006; Lapierre et al., 2007; National Center for PTSD, 2006). While probably unintentional and a self-protective reaction for the family member(s), the veteran in turn internalizes this retreat as his or her new reality (Lapierre et al., 2007; National Center for PTSD, 2006; University of Western Ontario, 2008).

Primary care physicians are often the first to identify somatic symptoms of PTSD, but according to Yehuda (2002), they may be mistaken for those of depression or other anxiety disorders, especially when physicians do not ask patients about the occurrence of traumatic events. University of Western Ontario (2007) reported Iraq combat veterans with migraines were twice as likely to have co-occurring symptoms of PTSD, depression, or anxiety than those who did not have migraines.

Symptom Reinforcement

The now chronic PTSD is characterized by a reinforced pathology feedback loop. The autonomic nervous system adapts to trauma symptoms which become integrated into the personality. Shay (1994) cautions the *DSM-IV* criteria fail to capture the full extent of the damage to the character that results from the devastating trauma and results in a complete loss of self as exhibited by:

- A hostile or mistrustful attitude toward the world.
- Social withdrawal.
- Feelings of emptiness or hopelessness.
- A chronic feeling of being on the edge, as if constantly threatened.
- Estrangement (World Health Organization, 1992)

These symptoms are sufficiently pervasive to cause veterans to become alienated from the world around them.

CONCLUSION

Conceptualizing PTSD along a developmental continuum allows the clinician to direct treatment toward the stage specific to the symptoms presented by the veteran. There are various approaches that address the development of PTSD over time. However, clinicians should be flexible and recognize the fluid nature of treatment, as well as the continual need for suicide assessment and prevention regardless of the stage of PTSD.

For practitioners working with homecoming veterans of the current conflicts, assessment of here-and-now behaviors and emotional states is critical. Further, debriefing and revisiting the events immediately following trauma help the individual to recognize not only the nature of behaviors while experiencing a stressful event, but also to realize the positive acts of courage or selflessness that may have occurred so quickly as to be almost forgotten (Benderly, 2008; Lapierre et al., 2007). Because veterans may strongly identify with strength and courage, traumatization can be perceived as weakness or failure, thereby fracturing the self-image. Debriefing of a possible trauma-producing event as soon as possible may help the veteran to have a much more realistic memory of what happened. The goal for the PTSD sufferer is to alter the memory of the event so it is not the defining characteristic of the personality.

Finally, Cognitive Behavioral Therapy helps the veteran explore the extent to which trauma has distorted cognition and such changes have impacted various domains of functioning, that is, occupationally, socially, and so on. Attempts to reconcile who he or she was before the trauma with who he or she has become are helpful for personality reintegration for the veteran.

Regardless of whether or not veterans were involved in combat, or their emotional well-being is impaired, treatment approaches must address subjective well-being and quality of life (University of Western Ontario, 2008). Clinicians are cautioned against simply measuring symptom reduction without objectively assessing improved quality of life, well-being, and community reintegration.

Treatment for PTSD needs to be sufficiently flexible to target idiosyncratic symptoms born from each individual's experience but structured enough to follow established and tested treatment protocols through the developmental course of PTSD.

REFERENCES

Allen, J. G. (2005). *Coping with trauma: Hope through understanding* (2nd ed.). Washington, DC, VA: American Psychiatric Publishing Inc.

American Academy of Neurology. (2007, May 4). For Iraq veterans, migraines may be sign of other problems. *ScienceDaily*. Retrieved November 1, 2009, from http://www.sciencedaily.com/releases/2007/05/070503075228.htm

American Psychiatric Association. (2000). *Diagnostic and statistical manual of mental disorders (DSM-IV-TR)* (4th ed.). Washington, DC: American Psychiatric Association.

Benderly, L. B. (2008). Paving the road home: Returning veterans and behavioral health. *SAMHSA News*, September/October, 16(5), http://www.samhsa.gov/samhsaNewsletter/Volume_16_Number_5/ReturningVeterans.aspx

Fontana, A., Rosenheck, R., & Desai, R. (2010). Female veterans of Iraq and Afghanistan seeking care from VA specialized PTSD programs: Comparison with male veterans and female war zone veterans of previous eras. *Journal of Women's Health, 19*(4), 751–757.

Friedman, M. J. (2006). Posttraumatic stress disorder among military returnees from Afghanistan and Iraq. *American Journal of Psychiatry, 163*(4), 586–594.

Geisinger Health System. (2008, February 15). Post-traumatic stress disorder is a medical warning sign for long-term health problems, study suggests. *ScienceDaily.* Retrieved September 13, 2008, from http://www.sciencedaily.com/releases/2008/02/080213090510.htm

Grinage, B. (2003). Diagnosis and management of post-traumatic stress disorder. *American Family Physician, 68*(12), 2401.

Iversen, A., Fear, N., Ehlers, A., Hacker Hughes, J., Hull, L., Earnshaw, M. et al. (2008). Risk factors for post-traumatic stress disorder among UK Armed forces personnel. *Psychological Medicine, 38,* 511–522.

Lapierre, C. B., Schwegler, A. F., & LaBauve, B. J. (2007). Posttraumatic stress and depressive symptoms in soldiers returning from combat operations in Iraq and Afghanistan. *Journal of Traumatic Stress, 20*(6), 933–943.

Miah, J. S. (2010). Impact of the military culture on female service members. *NASW-New York State Chapter, 34*(6).

National Center for Post Traumatic Stress Disorder. (2006). Returning from the war zone: A guide for families of military members. *Department of Veteran Affairs,* 1–11.

Pingxing, X., Kranzler, H., Poling, J., Stein, M., Anton, R., Brady, K. et al. (2009). Interactive effect of stressful life events and the serotonin transporter 5-HTTLPR genotype on posttraumatic stress disorder diagnosis in 2 independent populations. *Archives of General Psychiatry, 66*(11), 1201.

Pressfield, S. (1998). *Gates of fire: An epic novel of the battle of Thermopylae.* New York, NY: Bantam.

Schnurr, P., Ford, J., Friedman, M., Green, B., Dain, B., & Sengupta, A. (2000). Predictors and outcomes of posttraumatic stress disorder in World War II veterans exposed to mustard gas. *Journal of Consulting and Clinical Psychology, 68*(2), 258–268.

Shay, J. (1994). *Achilles in Vietnam: Combat trauma and the undoing of character.* New York, NY: Simon & Schuster.

Teed, E., & Scileppi, J. (2007). *The community mental health system: A navigational guide for providers.* New York, NY: Allyn and Bacon.

Teten, A. L., Miller, L. A., Stanford, M. S., Retersen, N. J., Bailey, S. D., Collins, R. L. et al. (2010). Characterizing aggression and its association to anger and hostility among male veterans with post-traumatic stress disorder. *Military Medicine, 175*(6), 405.

University of Western Ontario. (2008, October 3). Whether combat or peacekeeping, PTSD impacts veterans' well-being. *ScienceDaily.* Retrieved November 7, 2009, from http://www.sciencedaily.com/releases/2008/10/081001145118.htm

University of Western Ontario. (2007, December 15). Predicting post-traumatic stress disorders in deployed veterans. *ScienceDaily.* Retrieved November 7, 2009, from http://www.sciencedaily.com/releases/2007/12/071213120937.htm

van der Kolk, B. (2006). Clinical implications of neuroscience research in PTSD. *Annals of the New York Academy of Sciences, 40,* 1–17.

World Health Organization. (1992). *The ICD-10 classification of mental and behavioral disorders: Clinical descriptions and diagnostic guidelines.* Geneva, Switzerland: Author.

Yehuda, R. (2002). Post-traumatic stress disorder. *The New England Journal of Medicine, 346*(2), 108–115.

4

THE BURDEN OF COMBAT: COGNITIVE DISSONANCE IN IRAQ WAR VETERANS

Wayne Klug, Anne O'Dwyer, Deirdre Barry, Leah Dillard, Haili Polo-Neil, and Megan Warriner

Will American soldiers who saw combat in Iraq seek to reduce dissonance by disparaging their victims? Defined as the discomfort one feels when simultaneously holding two psychologically incompatible beliefs, such as "I am humane" and "I have killed," cognitive dissonance is likely experienced by young veterans who have witnessed or perpetrated battlefield casualties; this conflict, if unresolved, may haunt them and create difficulties in reintegrating to civilian life. Sixty-eight Iraq war veterans responded to a three-page questionnaire soliciting demographic, ratings, and narrative data about their war experiences. When asked to rate Iraqis and Americans on various traits, the combat sub-group that had only witnessed killings (W) gave lower ratings to Iraqis than did either the sub-group directly involved in killings (DI), or the non-combat group (NA). Unexpectedly, both combat sub-groups did, however, give lower ratings to Americans, whom some described as "weak" or "cowards." The DIs were overrepresented among those objecting to fellow citizens who "protest the soldiers." Further demonstrating dissonance, DIs were more inclined to see the war as beneficial to both countries. These findings suggest the moral challenges confronting soldiers and offer clues for understanding the conflicting cognitions experienced by combat veterans. The findings' clinical and policy implications are discussed.

It is to no purpose, it is even against one's better interest, to turn away from the consideration of the affair because the horror of its elements excites repugnance.

—*Carl von Clausewitz, On War, 1832*

In a recent special issue of *The New Yorker* devoted to "Soldiers' Stories," Captain Lisa Blackman, an Army psychologist stationed in Qatar, describes her work with combat veterans of the Iraq war:

At home I ask people if they have ever experienced or witnessed a traumatic event or abuse. But out here I ask, "Have you ever been in combat?" Apparently, this is a question with the power to unglue, because all four of these troops burst into tears at the mention of the word "combat."

And when I say burst, I mean splatter—tears running, snot flowing, and I literally had to mop my floor after one two-hour session. In other words, I mean sobbing for minutes on end, unable to speak, flat-out grief by an otherwise healthy, strong, manly guy who watches football on the weekends and never puts the toilet seat down.

Each time, I sit there with not a clue what to say ... offering tissues ... saying I'm sorry ... trying to normalize ... trying to say, "It was not your fault that so-and-so died" and "If you could have done differently, you would have" and "You had a right to be scared." And, even worse, "You had to shoot back," and "Yes, you killed someone, and you still deserve to go back to your family and live your life."

Next time you are hanging out with a friend, think about what you would do if he turned to you and said, "My boss made me kill someone, and I know I'm going to Hell for it, so why bother?" What would you say to "normalize" that? ...

I can't stop thinking about the fact that these folks have lost something that they will never get back—innocence (and a life free of guilt). My heart hurts for them.

—Blackman, 2006, pp. 127–128

A social psychologist wishing to engage in a "consideration of the affair" confronts provocative questions: How does a soldier justify his taking of life in the face of the powerful sanctions against this act that likely informed his upbringing? Does his subsequent struggle with guilt, grief, and cognitive dissonance suggest a moral indictment of war? May such an indictment help him to heal? And can the accumulated knowledge of our field effectively assist in exploring these questions?

This knowledge likely began with the groundbreaking work of Leon Festinger (1957), who introduced cognitive dissonance as key to self-concept and adaptive ego defenses. Defined as the discomfort one feels when simultaneously holding two psychologically incompatible beliefs, cognitive dissonance characteristically involves a preexisting view of one's self, and a subsequent behavior or belief that challenges that view (Aronson, 2008, p. 192; Festinger & Carlsmith, 1950). The study of its dynamics—how individuals attempt to resolve dissonance—is dominated by 50 years of experimental data on subjects' aggression toward victims, most of it gathered in civilian laboratory settings (Bandura, 1999; Cooper, 2007; Glass, 1964; Harmon-Jones & Mills, 1999; Klass, 1978). This is research largely reflecting the concerns of social psychology, a discipline interested in the effects on individual behavior of other individuals, groups, and institutions.

These studies have reached a consensus useful to the present inquiry. "Knowledge of immoral actions that contradict one's values," the theory holds, "creates uncomfortable dis-equilibrium that persons will seek to right" (Klass, 1978, p. 766). Some researchers see acts of aggression as "producing inequity between actor and victim," with the actor motivated to restore equity (Berscheid et al., 1968; Walster, Berscheid, & Walster, 1970, p. 185). This "righting" or "restoration" may take a *psychological* form, either through denial of responsibility (Brock & Buss, 1964, p. 410) or through derogation, as seen in perpetrators' subsequent dislike for their victims (Glass, 1964, p. 548; Lerner, 1970, p. 266). Or it may take an *actual* form, either through compensation of victims or through self-punishment (Berscheid & Walster, 1967; Walster et al., 1970, p. 185). But the underlying motivation is seen as inescapable, since "one of the most uniform findings in the transgression literature is that negative feelings about one's action do result from breaking moral rules" (Klass, 1978, p. 758).

How might soldiers deal with transgressions committed on the battlefield? At one end of the spectrum, and mirroring experimental findings, practitioners have identified psychological maneuvers predictably employed by antagonists in an effort to deflect personal accountability. They observe that in conflict "everyone rationalizes, justifies, fabricates, diverts attention, changes the subject, becomes defensive, counterattacks, minimizes, and grandstands," and suggest that such maneuvers are especially likely when the accountability being deflected concerns behavior in warfare (Cloke, 2001; Holbrook, 2007, p. 547).

At the other end of the spectrum, and also echoing experimental findings, Veterans Administration clinicians have identified feelings of guilt among veterans who have killed, "result[ing] in suicidal behavior or in actions carried out in the hope of receiving punishment" (Bradshaw, Ohlde, & Horne, 1993, p. 473). Of special interest here, veterans who were "directly involved" in killing "had more severe symptoms than those who 'only saw' those events" (MacNair, 2001, p. 274).

Deriving from both laboratory and clinical studies is the belief that perpetrators may resolve their dissonance in a healthier and more rational direction by acknowledging their error, seeking forgiveness, and offering restitution—that is, restoring equity to the victim or the victim's group, rather than punishing oneself (Aronson, 2008, pp. 250–251; Paquette, 2008, p. 145; Walster et al., 1970, p. 185). This option requires considerable ego strength, and support either from those in similar circumstances or from helping professionals.

As this spectrum suggests, veterans react to combat in a variety of ways, healthy and unhealthy. By examining the dynamic of cognitive dissonance among those who have perpetrated or witnessed killings, we may better address the suffering to which, in a substantial number, dissonance appears to give rise—from substance abuse and domestic violence, to posttraumatic stress disorder (PTSD) and combat-related suicidality—and reduce the likelihood that veterans will isolate themselves from necessary support as they struggle to make sense of their experience and resume civilian lives.

The authors were struck by the absence of any systematic empirical research into cognitive dissonance among combat veterans. At a time when our nation's identity was bound up in the simultaneous waging of two protracted wars, this deficiency captured the authors' interest and spawned the present study. They borrowed their hypothesis from laboratory research on cognitive dissonance, which demonstrates that those who harm another individual are likely to disparage that individual (Glass, 1964, p. 548; Lerner, 1970, p. 266); the social comparison literature adds that this effect will extend to other members of the victim's group as well (Bandura, 1999, p. 200; Staub, 1989). The study therefore predicted that Iraq war veterans who had perpetrated or witnessed killings would hold more negative views of Iraqis than veterans who had not.

METHOD

Several veterans' organizations and service agencies were involved in recruiting participants. These included a VA hospital, a Red Cross Military Family Support Group, and a private agency offering counseling to veterans in two New England locations. To these agencies, the authors mailed approximately 295 packets containing cover letters, questionnaires, and stamped envelopes, addressed to a post office box set up for the study. The agencies then recruited Iraq war veterans from among their members and clients. The authors mailed or e-mailed an additional 25 questionnaires to veterans or active-duty soldiers known to them, who were asked to forward it to others they knew. As of January 2007, 68 questionnaires had been returned—64 mailed back from participants in Maine, Massachusetts, Vermont, Rhode Island, Connecticut, Delaware, and Alabama, and 4 returned via e-mail—yielding a response rate of 21%. (Four questionnaires with incomplete ratings were excluded from the quantitative analysis.)

Participants

The majority of the sample were male (91%) and young—two-thirds of them under the age of 30. The overwhelming majority (85%) had joined the military before turning 21, and fully half had joined at or before the age of 18. But as shown in Table 4.1, their ages also varied considerably, with a range from 20 to 56. Some three-fourths reported having attended college for a period of time, but only about half of those had obtained a degree. Approximately two-thirds came from families with an income at or below $50,000.

One-third of the sample were at the rank of Private or Corporal/ Specialist; about half held the rank of Sergeant or Master Sergeant;

TABLE 4.1 Characteristics of the sample (N = 68)

Measure	#[a]	%	Mean	Standard Deviation	Minimum	Maximum
Respondent age	64	100	29.7 years	8.4	20	56
Gender						
Male	59	91				
Female	6	9				
Age joined military						
Joined before age 21 years	55	85	19.3 years	2.7	17	27
Family income[b]						
<$50K	42	66	2.3	1.1	1	5
Education level[c]						
At least some college	47	72	3.3	1.2	1	6
Rank of personnel						
Private or corporal/ specialist	22	34				
Sergeant/master sergeant	34	53				
Chief warrant officer	1	1.5				
Lieutenant	3	5				
Captain	3	5				
Major	1	1.5				

[a]Four respondents completed only the qualitative sections of the survey.
[b]Family income (in 1000s): 1 (under $25); 2 ($25–$50); 3 ($50–$75); 4 ($75–$100); 5 ($101+).
[c]Education Level: 1 (no high school); 2 (high school degree); 3 (some college); 4 (AA degree); 5 (BA degree); 6 (graduate school).

and the remainder had earned higher ranks, namely Chief Warrant Officer, Lieutenant, Captain, or Major. While the questionnaire did not request such information, the authors' personal knowledge of the population served by the recruiting agencies suggests that participants were members of the U.S. Army or, less frequently, the National Guard; and that at the time of the survey, the majority had completed a single deployment to Iraq and had returned to the United States.

The Questionnaire

The questionnaire was designed to gather data in four thematic areas: (1) casualty exposure groups; (2) veterans' attitudes toward Iraqi citizens; (3) social experiences while in Iraq; and (4) attitudes toward the Iraq war. In addition to these four areas, the survey also presented open-ended questions. The thematic areas and questions are detailed below.

Exposure Groups

To test the study's main hypothesis, respondents were asked: "To what extent were you involved in an Iraqi casualty?" Response options were *"not at all," "witnessed,"* or *"directly involved."*

Veterans' Attitudes Toward Iraqi Citizens

Veterans' attitudes—positive or negative—toward the people of Iraq comprised the study's main outcome variables. Respondents were asked to "Please indicate to what extent you feel each of the listed traits describes the individuals in the [following] groups": (a) Iraqi soldiers; and (b) Iraqi civilians.[1] Festinger (1957) held that if one disparages another individual or group, one will view oneself or one's group more positively. Thus, respondents were also asked to rate (c) American civilians and (d) American soldiers. The six traits rated were: "dedicated," "intelligent," "ambitious," "moral," "humane," and "loyal," and ratings were made using a 5-point scale ranging from 1 (very little) to 5 (very much); consistently high ratings indicated a more positive evaluation of the target group.

Respondents' attitudes toward each group were evaluatively consistent, since reliabilities (Chronbach's alpha) of respondents' ratings

---

[1]Respondents were also asked to indicate how they felt about "insurgents" (members of the armed resistance to the American occupation). However, this item was not labeled as "Iraqi," and the lower reliability of these trait ratings (alpha = 0.61) suggests respondents may not have known to which group this term referred. Evaluative responses to this item were not included in these analyses.

across the six traits, within each of the four groups, were strong—ranging from 0.69 to 0.85—suggesting a consistent bias toward either the negative or the positive. Thus, based on the principle of evaluative consistency (Heider, 1958), the six trait ratings were combined into a single overall measure of the respondents' attitude toward each target group, wherein a high score indicated a more positive attitude, and a low score indicated a more negative attitude.

Social Experiences While in Iraq

Respondents were asked how often they had socialized with Iraqi civilians while on duty and during free time. Ratings were on a 5-point scale ranging from 1 (never) to 5 (constantly). In an open-ended format, they were also asked to indicate in what ways they socialized with Iraqis.

Attitudes Toward the Iraq War

Several items on the questionnaire asked respondents to indicate their own perception of the war in Iraq. These included: "Disregarding financial aspects, how beneficial *to the U.S.* do you think it is for us to be in Iraq?" and "Disregarding financial aspects, how beneficial *to Iraq* do you think it is for us to be in Iraq?" The response scale ranged from 1 (extremely unbeneficial) to 5 (extremely beneficial).

Open-Ended Questions

Respondents were asked to answer several open-ended questions: (a) "What were some of the ways, if any, in which you socialized with Iraqi civilians?" as described above; (b) "What do you believe is America's primary reason for being in Iraq?"; (c) "Some soldiers say that, after being in Iraq, their ideas about the war have changed. If this describes you, please explain how your ideas have changed."; and (d) "What are your feelings about the anti-war protests in America?"

RESULTS

Involvement With Iraqi Casualties

Respondents were asked if they had witnessed, or been directly involved in, an Iraqi casualty. Their responses resulted in assignment to one of three "exposure groups." Sixteen reported no involvement at all in a casualty (the "NA" group); 27 had witnessed a casualty, but had not been directly involved in it (the "W" group); and 22 had been directly involved in a casualty (the "DI" group).

Test of the Cognitive Dissonance-Reduction Hypothesis

The cognitive dissonance hypothesis holds that those directly involved in harming another individual will likely disparage that individual, with the effect extending to other members of the victim's group as well (Bandura, 1999, p. 200; Staub, 1989). The study therefore predicted that Iraq war veterans who had seen combat would hold more negative views of Iraqis. As shown in Figure 4.1, mean ratings were only partially consistent with the hypothesis. Respondents did evaluate Americans— both soldiers and civilians—more positively than they did Iraqis—both soldiers and civilians. Comparing respondents' ratings of Americans, mean = 3.76, SD = 0.42, with their ratings of Iraqis, mean = 2.86, SD = 0.68, the difference was significant, $F(1,61) = 95.57$, $p < 0.001$, and was consistent across the three exposure groups.

But the pattern of mean ratings of *Iraqi civilians* ran counter to expectation. As shown in Figure 4.1, it was the *W*—and not the *DI*— group that produced the lowest mean rating of Iraqis. Planned comparisons across the three groups revealed significant differences. The rating by those in the *W* group (mean = 2.71, SD = 0.63) was significantly lower than that in the *DI* group (mean = 3.08, SD = 0.51, $t(45) = 2.16$,

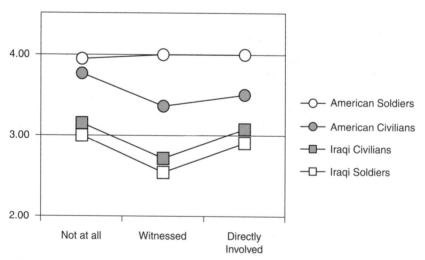

FIGURE 4.1 Differences in Iraq war veterans' perceptions of Iraqis and Americans by level of exposure to Iraqi casualties.

$p < 0.04$), and marginally lower than that in the *NA* group (mean = 3.13, SD = 0.89, $t(38) = 1.77$, $p < 0.09$). The latter two groups did not differ in these ratings, $t(35) < 1.0$. Finally, although failing to attain significance, the three groups' ratings of *Iraqi soldiers* followed a similar pattern: ratings by those in the *W* group (mean = 2.54, SD = 0.97) were lower than both those in the *NA* group (mean = 2.99, SD = 0.84, $t(38) = 1.54$, $p < 0.13$) and those in the *DI* group (mean = 2.91, SD = 0.31, $t(45) = 1.63$, $p < 0.11$), and the latter two group means did not differ, $t(35) < 1.0$.

Across the three groups, the pattern reflecting respondents' views of *American civilians* was similar to those above. As also shown in Figure 4.1, those who had *witnessed* Iraqi casualties rated American civilians more negatively than did either the *NA*s or the *DI*s.

Here, too, planned comparisons revealed the differences to be significant. Respondents who *witnessed* Iraqi casualties gave the lowest mean rating to American civilians, mean = 3.36, SD = 0.57—significantly lower than those in the *NA* group, mean = 3.76, SD = 0.52, $t(39) = 2.28$, $p < 0.03$. Although not significantly so, $t(45) < 1.0$, the *W* group's mean rating was also lower than that of the *DI* group, mean = 3.50, SD = 0.55. Further, the *NA* and *DI* groups did not differ significantly in their ratings, $t(36) = 1.47$, $p < 0.15$, although the *DI*s' mean rating was lower. Finally, in contrast to the general pattern found in the prior analyses, the exposure groups did not differ in their ratings of *American soldiers* (*DI*s mean = 3.99, SD = 0.49; *W*s mean = 4.00, SD = 0.55; *NA*s mean = 3.94, SD = 0.58) (all *t*-values <1.0), whom all three groups rated highly.

Demographic Differences Between Exposure Groups

Could differences in the groups' ratings be explained by predeployment characteristics (e.g., age or political views)? Researchers explored this question and, as shown in Table 4.2, found no significant demographic differences between groups in education level, military rank, political orientation, or family income prior to deployment. They did, however, find a marginally significant difference in the age at which respondents had joined the military. But even this finding reflected a disparity between the *DI*s, who had enlisted at a younger age, mean = 18.4, and the *NA*s, who had enlisted some two years later, mean = 20.2, $t(36) = 2.07$, $p < 0.05$. The enlistment age of the *W*s— whose ratings inspire particular interest—fell between those of the other two groups, mean = 19.5, and did not differ significantly from

TABLE 4.2 Demographic group difference by exposure group

	Not at All Involved	Witnessed	Directly Involved	Significance
Sample size (n)	16	27	22	
Respondent age	Mean = 31.75 (SD = 7.56)	Mean = 29.74 (SD = 8.00)	Mean = 28.19 (SD = 9.58)	$F < 1$
Age joined military	Mean = 20.19 (SD = 3.23)	Mean = 19.48 (SD = 2.61)	Mean = 18.41 (SD = 2.09)	$F = 2.27$, $p < 0.11$
Gender	Male n = 16	Male n = 22 Female n = 5	Male n = 21 Female n = 1	
Education level[a]	Mean = 3.25 (SD = 1.12)	Mean = 3.19 (SD = 1.30)	Mean = 3.32 (SD = 1.21)	$F < 1$
Average family income[b]	Mean = 2.03 (SD = 0.90)	Mean = 2.36 (SD = 1.29)	Mean = 2.32 (SD = 1.00)	$F < 1$
Rank[c]	Mean = 1.69 (SD = 0.45)	Mean= 1.60 (SD =0.49)	Mean = 1.81 (SD = 0.73)	$F < 1$
Politics[d]	Mean = 3.06 (SD = 0.77)	Mean = 2.93 (SD = 0.55)	Mean = 3.23 (SD = 0.53)	$F = 1.51$, ns

[a]Education level: 1 (no high school); 2 (high school degree); 3 (some college); 4 (AA degree); 5 (BA degree); 6 (graduate school).
[b]Family income (in 1000s): 1 (under $25); 2 ($25–$50); 3 ($50–$75); 4 ($75–$100); 5 ($101+).
[c]Rank: 1 (private); 2 (corporal/specialist); 3 (sergeant); 4 (sergeant first class); 5 (master sergeant); 6 (chief warrant officer); 7 (second lieutenant); 8 (first lieutenant); 9 (captain); 10 (major).
[d]Politics: 1 (extremely liberal); 2 (liberal); 3 (moderate); 4 (conservative); 5 (extremely conservative).

either one. Demographic characteristics, therefore, do not appear to explain why those who witnessed Iraqi casualties would rate both Iraqis and American civilians more negatively.

Differences Between Exposure Groups in Social Experiences

Researchers wondered if soldiers' involvement with Iraqis in nonmilitary contexts would mediate the effect of combat. Would socializing with Iraqis differ across the three exposure groups, and might any such differences affect each group's view of Iraqis? As shown in Figure 4.2, American soldiers report socializing with Iraqis more often while on duty, mean = 3.20, SD = 1.23, on a 5-point scale, than during free time, mean = 2.20, SD = 1.09, $t(64) = 7.82$, $p < 0.001$. The DI group socialized significantly more often than did the others—both on duty (DIs mean = 3.95, SD = 1.09; Ws mean = 3.00, SD = 1.18; NAs mean = 2.50, SD = 1.16) and on free time (DIs mean = 2.86,

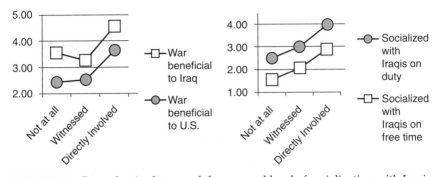

FIGURE 4.2 General attitude toward the war and level of socialization with Iraqis by exposure group.

SD = 1.13; Ws mean = 2.04, SD = 0.98; NAs mean = 1.56, SD = 0.73), $F(2,62) = 8.87$, $p < 0.001$ and $F(2,62) = 8.81$, $p < 0.001$, respectively—raising the possibility that a greater familiarity with Iraqis might dampen an American soldier's inclination to disparage them.

Differences Between Exposure Groups in Attitude Toward the War

The cognitive dissonance hypothesis predicts that those involved in casualties would tend to view the war more positively. As further shown in Figure 4.2, the DIs viewed the war as more beneficial both to the United States (DIs mean = 3.64, SD = 1.05; Ws mean = 2.52, SD = 1.22; NAs mean = 2.44, SD = 1.09, $F(2,62) = 7.48$, $p < 0.001$), and to Iraq (DIs mean = 4.55, SD = 0.51; Ws mean = 3.26, SD = 1.26; NAs mean = 3.56, SD = 1.32), $F(2,62) = 8.95$, $p < 0.001$).

Responses to Open-Ended Questions

Participants' written responses to four open-ended questions were transcribed into a separate Excel spreadsheet, accompanied only by their subject numbers, ensuring that coding was conducted blind to the veterans' exposure group status. All responses were coded separately by the two lead authors, whose interrater reliability rate was 0.86.

Questioned about their views as to **reasons the United States went into Iraq**, respondents' answers fell into two general categories: (1) those consistent with the U.S. government's stated reasons (to rid the country of Saddam Hussein, to find WMDs, and/or to find terrorists); and (2) those critical of the war (for access to Iraqi oil, for power or influence in the region, and/or for political gain in the United States). About half (55%) of the sample mentioned reasons consistent with the government's, and 36% mentioned those more critical (five mentioned both); the remaining 9% indicated they did not know the reasons or left the question blank. As the dissonance-reduction hypothesis would predict, it appeared that many *DI*s (78%) endorsed the U.S. government's rationale and fewer endorsed the more critical view—which, in turn, was more strongly endorsed by the *W*s and *NA*s (58% and 45%, respectively), although these differences did not reach statistical significance, $\chi^2(1,2) = 4.26$, $p < 0.12$.

Responses to a question on **frequency of socialization with Iraqis** revealed that about half (49%) of the respondents had socialized primarily in the context of their military responsibilities there—while on escort, transport, or watch duty, on patrol in the communities, or working with Iraqis who had been contracted by the U.S. military. This pattern—of socializing while on duty—was consistent across the three exposure groups, $\chi^2(1,2) < 1.0$. Less frequently, respondents mentioned one or more of several different off-duty interactions: teaching classes, tending to the wounded, playing soccer, or being invited to festivals or family gatherings. Fewer than 10% of the sample ($n = 6$) mentioned developing relationships with specific individuals or families. Rates of off-duty socializing, again, were consistent across the three exposure groups.

The question on how respondents' **ideas about the war had changed since serving in Iraq** elicited the most varied responses. Giving rise to this variability was the fact that almost one half (42%) chose not to answer the question, and almost one quarter (23%) indicated that their ideas had not changed. Of the remaining 35%, who did describe a change, similar percentages said they had become more critical ($n = 10$), or more supportive ($n = 12$), of the U.S. government and military since serving.

This question, nonetheless, elicited the greatest difference across the three exposure groups. Of those who indicated that they had become more critical of the government, all but one had *witnessed* an Iraqi casualty (see Table 4.3). In contrast, among those who reported that they had become more supportive of U.S. policies, the distribution was more evenly divided, $\chi^2(1,2) = 7.57$, $p < 0.03$.

Finally, responses to the question on the veterans' **feelings about antiwar protests** were coded on a 5-point scale of 1 (very negative) to 5 (very positive). The mean rating of their responses was 2.6 on the 5-point scale—slightly more negative than neutral. Respondents differed marginally in these feelings by exposure group, with *DI*s

TABLE 4.3 Representative comments critical of the war or of President Bush

I believe Americans *should* protest the war. No war anywhere, any time is a good thing for humanity.

I thought while there, that we were not supposed to be there, and to this day, I feel the same way.

The war is directed toward the greed and gains of the Bush administration. There are no reasons for American soldiers to die when the Iraqi Army only turns tail and runs when there is danger.

A lot of them are getting rich from this war.

It's all lies and propaganda.

My ideas have been the same since day one. We don't need to be over there.

The war is now taking us down the same road as the old Soviet regime. Strategically, financially, and emotionally, it can't be sustained to a victory. It will end like Vietnam, or like Afghanistan for the Soviet Union.

The lesson for anyone who chooses a long-term commitment to the military is that, eventually one might be forced to participate in a war that they do not approve of, under a Commander-in-Chief whom they detest.

No comment other than that I can't stand President Bush. He has not served his country and I do not respect him as Commander in Chief. I do not fight for him!

I believe that the antiwar protests were instrumental in turning public opinion against our immoral war in Iraq.

Note. No respondent directly involved in killing [DI] made such comments.

more negative than the other two groups, but not significantly so, $F(2,55) = 2.09$, $p < 0.14$ (*DI*s mean = 2.05, SD = 1.0; *NA*s mean = 2.79, SD = 1.10, *W*s mean = 2.62, SD = 1.28). Interestingly, almost all respondents ($n = 63$) mentioned the right to protest, but a third ($n = 21$) felt that the protesters were ignorant about the war. Some ($n = 8$) said protesters should focus on the politics, not the troops (see Table 4.4).

DISCUSSION

Summary of Results

The purpose of this study was to describe dynamics of those veterans who were directly involved (*DI*) in Iraqi casualties, those who witnessed (*W*) casualties, and those who had no exposure (*NA*) to casualties—and to test a hypothesis, based on previous cognitive dissonance research, that those directly involved in harming another person will be more

TABLE 4.4 Representative comments critical of American antiwar protests, from those directly involved in killing [DI]

Everyone has a right to protest. Just do not protest the soldiers.

Society wanted to go to war after September 11, 2001. When we went to war, people realized that people will die. That's what war is. Americans wanted [it], now we have it and have to deal with the consequences of that decision.

No one hears about the good things.

[Protest] isn't exactly what I want to see on my return, but it is a civil liberty.

It all depends on how they protest. I think that the protests at a funeral for a soldier killed in combat are deplorable. When a citizen spits on a soldier, that act is inexcusable.... The rowdy and rude protesters forget that the people that ensure they have the right to protest, are their targets. They have lived their whole lives under a blanket of safety. They don't have to worry about government police coming into their homes in the middle of the night and arresting them for speaking out against the president.

They're disrespectful.

Fuck all of them! The military is fucked up also by the way they treat their own. The military is supposed to look out for their own and doesn't, and 60% of civilians are against the war. Also, the Mothers of America shit make the military soft. Let the military be tough on your sons and daughters—or America as a whole will be weak. Americans in general are weak.

likely to disparage that person. Sixty-eight American veterans indicated which of the three levels of involvement described their experience while serving in Iraq. Inconsistent with the hypothesis, those who had witnessed casualties rated Iraqis more negatively than those who had perpetrated them. Interestingly, the W group also rated American civilians more negatively than did those not at all involved.

Limitations

The main limitations of the current study are a potential sampling bias, deriving from the "convenience" technique by which the sample was obtained, as well as its modest size, which prevented further exploration of subgroup differences.

The sample included only 68 participants, all of them voluntary, raising a question as to its representativeness of Iraq war veterans. Sixty-eight respondents do not comprise a large group from which to make sturdy inferences about a population numbering in the tens of thousands, and any conclusions drawn here are necessarily preliminary—and fodder for future studies. Some of the sample's strengths, however, include its representativeness of a range of military ranks and a considerable variation in age, from 20 to 56. Likewise, more than half the sample had attended college, with one quarter having completed a bachelors degree or higher; and almost two-thirds described themselves as holding moderate—neither liberal nor conservative—political views.

One group characteristic of potential concern is that female participants were few, with almost all (5 out of 6) belonging to the group that gave the most negative ratings to Iraqis (W). Gender, however, fails to explain differences across the three groups, as the same pattern of mean ratings is found with the six female veterans removed from the analysis, and the difference in ratings between W and DI groups remains significant ($p < 0.03$). Nonetheless, that such a large percentage of female participants witnessed casualties prevents gender comparisons between groups; it also raises a question about roles and responsibilities assigned to female soldiers in Iraq.

As is generally the case with new findings, the study may raise more questions than it answers. While the questionnaire solicited information on military rank, it failed to do so on branch or type of service. Gathering from both qualitative data and their personal knowledge of the agencies that recruited participants; however, the authors think it likely that most of those involved were members of the Army and National Guard. Qualitative data on respondents' *type* of service are few. Nonetheless, this missing information would seem to be of questionable relevance to the hypothesis, since whatever their duties or branch of service, soldiers either perpetrate, witness, or are uninvolved in casualties.

Despite the limitations described here, the study is the first to examine cognitive dissonance in soldiers, adding empirical data to a considerable body of theoretical, clinical, and personal narrative literature that attest to the experience of dissonance by those who participate in war.

General Implications

Although the present study failed to demonstrate that DIs would give lower ratings to Iraqis, it demonstrated by other measures that they experienced cognitive dissonance. In devising the study's hypothesis, the authors assumed that dissonance among soldiers on the battlefield would be expressed in the same manner, and toward the same targets, as it is among participants in the laboratory. Results showed this to be a flawed assumption. However, the *DIs'* disparagement of Americans, the *Ws'* disparagement of Americans and Iraqis, and both groups' disparagement of antiwar critics in particular—especially in the absence of such disparagement by the *NAs*—provides unanticipated evidence of cognitive dissonance. Thus, it was the choice of targets, not the prediction of dissonance, that was mistaken. The findings should be replicated in new research, using a revised methodology.

The evidence in the present study is further supported by differences in the way exposure groups rate the war's benefit. Those who were not involved in killings see the war as unbeneficial to the United States and barely beneficial to Iraq, while those who *were* involved see the war as beneficial to the United States and "extremely" beneficial to Iraq. These results are consistent with findings from classic studies which demonstrate that we value outcomes requiring great effort, discomfort, or sacrifice (Aronson & Mills, 1959, p. 177; Gerard & Mathewson, 1966, p. 278)—even if its application is especially ironic here: Those who have killed citizens of Iraq see the war as extremely beneficial to that country (Laufer, 2006, p. 29).

Two quite different effects, respectively—one demonstrated by Glass (1964) and the other by Aronson and Mills (1959)—informed the present hypothesis, and subsequently offered support for it. The manner in which dissonance was reduced certainly differed between each of those earlier studies, whose participants were exposed to dissonance-arousing circumstances in two distinct domains. Albeit not experimental in design, the current study examined a third domain, and appears to have discovered another form in which individuals may attempt to reduce dissonance. Notwithstanding obvious differences between the "independent variables" of shocking a fellow participant (Glass), expending great effort (Aronson & Mills), and being exposed to battlefield casualties (the current study), all three forms demonstrate participants' subsequent need for self-justification—the hallmark of dissonance (Aronson, 2008, p. 215).

Can all wars be expected to create dissonance? The moral and religious upbringing of most soldiers predicts such an outcome, suggests a U.S. Army major:

> Most soldiers are unknowingly conscientious objectors. They try to avoid taking a human life. This is ... a reflection of a strong moral upbringing. Getting most soldiers to pull the trigger on another human being requires great effort.
>
> *—Pierson, 1999, p. 60*

Similarly, an American officer in World War II has observed:

> It is a crucial moment in a soldier's life when he is ordered to perform a deed that he finds completely at variance with his own notions of right and good. ... He is conscious of the pacifistic injunctions of his faith and has not been able, in all likelihood, to make the easy distinctions between destroying life in peace and in war that governments insist upon.
>
> —*Gray, 1959, pp. 184, 120*

A personal account illustrates the point:

> He was entangled in the harness so I shot him with a .45 and I felt remorse and shame. ... I sobbed, in a voice still grainy with fear: "I'm sorry." Then I threw up all over myself ... [and] urinated in my skivvies. ... It was a betrayal of what I'd been taught since a child. ... I knew I had become a thing of tears and twitchings and dirtied pants. I remember wondering dumbly: *Is this what they mean by "conspicuous gallantry"?*.
>
> —*Manchester, as quoted in Grossman, 1995, p. 116*

For those who have killed in Iraq, the same clash of values is likely responsible for the dissonance they too experience, even if, in this study, the official enemy seems not to be the focus of their efforts to reduce it. What might explain the *DIs'* unexpected failure to disparage their victims?

As the group reporting significantly more socializing with Iraqis, on duty and off, the *DIs* may have come to know, and perhaps befriend, the local people more consistently than have other soldiers. This relative intimacy and knowledge of the culture would encourage identification with Iraqis and discourage these soldiers from subsequently denigrating victims whom they perceive as less alien than do others.

A related hint may lie in discussions by a U.S. Army colonel and other military observers of the "fellow-feeling" that gave rise to fraternization between enemy forces throughout the last century:

> During Christmas of 1914 British and German soldiers in many sectors met peacefully, exchanged presents, took photographs and even played soccer. Holmes (1985) notes that "in some areas the truce went on until well into the New Year, despite the High Command's insistence that it should be war as usual."
>
> —*Grossman, 1995, p. 160*

Identification with putative enemies persists into more recent times, as when "some of the Marines came to see the young Vietnamese they had killed as allies in a bigger war of individual existence ... with whom they were united against the impersonal 'thems' of the world" (Holmes, as quoted in Grossman, 1995, p. 38). The World War II officer adds an observation on the separateness of military culture:

> The understanding of his opponent's motives, a precondition of sympathy, is usually easier for a trained military man than is the comprehension of the motives of his own political superiors or the civilian mentality of his people.... He may discover in himself, if he is reflective, more genuine respect for the enemy he is annihilating than for a great number of those he is risking his life to protect. This commonly recognized fact should surprise nobody, for the military profession, like few others, is a way of life that forms its subjects in relative isolation from modern sentiments ...
>
> —Gray, 1959, pp. 145–146

The notion that an underlying mutual respect between combatants might play a role here, too, gains credibility if we consider the relative inapplicability to this study of research that lacks the mundane realism of the battlefield. Experimental results obtained in private from subjects believing they had merely administered shocks to individuals whom they later disparaged (Glass, 1964, p. 548) may not be replicated by those who feel responsible for actual deaths in the traumatically violent and public domain of war. The sheer enormity of what they have done may not permit it. For resolving this degree of dissonance, civilian critics and their "mentality" may seem the more attractive targets.

Once killing has become part of these soldiers' experience, a kind of innocence is lost—one they see as continuing to beguile their families and friends. One researcher observes that "perpetrators do not escape with impunity ... [they] do not simply kill and then go on as if they had killed vermin. ... [They demonstrate a] 'psychic numbing' and sense of unreality" (MacNair, 2001, pp. 281, 277). From that point forward, so it appears to them, "we have nothing to do with a world not at war. When we return home we view the society around us from the end of a very long tunnel. There they still believe" (Hedges, 2002, p. 40).

Feeling the deaths they caused were necessary, these veterans likely resent the implicit disapproval of other Americans—to whom they give lower ratings, and whom several soldiers describe as "uninformed," "weak," and "cowards." To say, as several do, that "only those who served could possibly understand," is not only to acknowledge their "relative isolation from modern sentiments," but also to discount their fellow citizens' moral standing and thereby deflect their judgment.

Indeed, this is a cause the *DIs* espouse quite openly. Questioned about the antiwar movement, they lead with responses such as "Don't protest the soldiers" and "Don't take it out on the troops." Comprising only a fourth (26%) of the sample's combat group (*DIs* and *Ws* combined), *DIs* nonetheless represent almost half (46%) of those within that group who make such comments, with the *Ws* comprising the balance.

Surprisingly, it is these witnesses (*Ws*) who display the predicted dissonance effect by evaluating Iraqis more negatively than do either the *DIs* or the *NAs*. What characteristic of theirs might account for this? The group comparisons revealed no demographic explanation. Yet, lacking both the "psychic numbing" and the particular burden of guilt carried by the *DIs*, could these *Ws* be the soldiers who replicate experimental findings by "blaming the victims"—and coming to the defense of their friends? If so, then the same effect may account for their giving the lowest ratings to American civilians as well.

This is not to suggest that witnesses are without guilt. Some of them may believe they failed to prevent an unnecessary killing. Others may feel responsible for having failed to shoot, thereby obliging a fellow soldier to do so. And if that comrade is killed, the experience of the witness is profoundly disturbing: "For those who know that they have not fired while their friends died around them, the guilt is traumatic" (Grossman, 1995, p. 90). Or they may simply recognize that they are part of a violent enterprise in which people die. "At some level every psychologically healthy human being who has engaged in *or supported* killing activities believes that his action was 'wrong' and 'bad,' and he must spend years rationalizing and accepting his actions" [emphasis added] (Grossman, 1995, p. 279). As they proceed with this daunting task, those who have witnessed traumatic events assign the lowest ratings to both Iraqis and American civilians.

It may be more than accidental that the comparative prevalence of dissonance among perpetrators and witnesses finds an analogue in the comparative prevalence of posttraumatic stress symptoms in such groups studied elsewhere. The American Psychiatric Association (2000) identifies the witnessing of death or injury to others as a causal factor in PTSD. According to Freedberg (2007, p. 28), the Surgeon

General's Mental Health Advisory Team found only 13% of soldiers and 14% of Marines reporting that they were "directly responsible for the death of an enemy combatant, [yet] ... 28 percent of those who had the most combat experience reported 'acute stress' symptoms suggestive of some level of PTSD"—that is, two times as many sufferers as perpetrators. A similar lifetime rate (30.9%) had been found among Vietnam veterans (Kulka et al., 1990), and even a more modest rate of 18.7%, identified in a reanalysis 16 years later, exceeded the proportion of those "directly responsible" among the 15% of veterans who had served in a combat role during that war (Dohrenwend et al., 2006, p. 980).

The sensitivity of the entire combat group (*DI*s and *W*s), moreover, may be heightened by historical circumstances in which a controversial war is being fought by a volunteer army. If, during a previous conflict, a mandatory draft inspired suspicion of those who avoided service, then 30 years later it is the volunteers themselves who may be viewed warily—at least from the perspective of economically more comfortable strata, and notwithstanding the political rhetoric of gratitude.

Some Iraq veterans—echoed by participants in the present study—convey a sense that they and their colleagues are regarded as the "stepchildren" of polite American society, a sense enhanced by the insufficient rehabilitative support available to them upon returning (Korn, 2008; Tanielian & Jaycox, 2008)—and to a country whose population by then opposes the war (Angus Reid, 2006; Cohen & Balz, 2007). As evidenced in comments by several of the study's respondents (see Table 4.4), their sometimes-apocryphal remarks about being personally disrespected, protested, and spat upon—echoes of the Vietnam era—capture their sense of disenfranchisement. "The military is supposed to look out for their own and doesn't, and 60% of civilians are against the war," one respondent complains. Is it therefore surprising that Americans should become the resented focus of their efforts to reduce dissonance?

Responses to the study's open-ended questions suggest that a good portion of the combat group's disparagement of Americans is directed to critics of the war. It would be reasonable to ask: Whom else would they disparage? For the *DI*s at least, Iraqis may be off-limits for reasons already discussed, and the Bush administration may have escaped critical scrutiny by soldiers who, having killed, now prefer to believe that the war is beneficial to all concerned—as their ratings of the war indicate they do. Indeed, no *DI* in the sample uttered a word of reproach against President Bush or the war, despite the many such words uttered by colleagues who had not killed. For the sake of reducing dissonance, it would seem that the taking of life in war may also forestall development of more nuanced political analyses.

Does wartime killing also preempt toleration of criticism by anyone else? Although the current antiwar movement has sought to avoid vilifying individual soldiers, the *DIs* in particular appear to take quite personally any opposition to the policy of war, even citing iconic accounts from the Vietnam era, as noted above. Perhaps this posture is to be expected among those who now depend on that policy to justify their actions. Critics who fault the war are seen as faulting the soldiers who killed on its behalf. Cognitive dissonance may therefore require that the fault-finders should fare poorly in both ratings and comments by these veterans.

Quite distinct from the *DIs'* sentiments are those expressed by their antiwar counterparts. In this study, self-described liberals represent just 10% of the entire sample but 29% of the antiwar subsample, thus demonstrating a threefold increase in liberals among war opponents. But the overwhelming majority of antiwar sentiments (71%) nonetheless come from those describing themselves as moderate or conservative. This unexpected finding contradicts claims of war supporters that the antiwar movement is dominated by liberals who are out of touch with the American mainstream. At least in the present military sample, it is moderates and conservatives who dominate, suggesting that opposition to the Iraq war cuts across political ideologies.

But such sentiment, as noted above, was absent among the *DIs*. Though not significantly so, *DIs* also appear to have rated themselves as somewhat more conservative than their *W* and *NA* counterparts. Since it is unlikely that already-conservative soldiers are more inclined to kill, these interesting data raise the possibility that some individuals who behave violently may subsequently adopt a conservative, pro-war ideology as a means of justifying their aggression and resolving dissonance—a prospect consistent with the notion within dissonance theory that behaviors induce attitude change, and not vice versa (Aronson, 2008, pp. 340, 342; Buss & Brock, 1963, p. 349).

Clinical and Policy Implications

For most American civilians, war's horrific nature remains tastefully obscured. In considering some implications of this study, it may be useful to sample the experiences that give rise to veterans' cognitive dissonance, often to PTSD, and sometimes, apparently, to suicidality. Laufer (2006) provides frank accounts from several Iraq veterans:

> That's what made me mad in Iraq. You can take human lives at a fast rate and all you have to do is say, "Oh, I thought they threw a grenade. I thought I seen this, I thought I seen that." You could mow down twenty people each time and nobody's going to ask you, "Are you sure?" They're going to give you a high five and tell you that you was doing a good job (p. 2).

> To kill someone, that's one thing. But to actually witness on an almost weekly basis an Iraqi that gets victimized by a car bomb, to see the carnage, to see the blood and the guts laying on the side of the road, to see a little girl's pink sandal smoldering, with her foot still in it, smoldering in the gutter, these are the images that you're going to have to live with the rest of your life (pp. 130–131).

> We turned a real sharp right and all I seen was decapitated bodies. The heads laying over here and the bodies over here and U.S. troops in between them. I'm thinking, "Oh my God, what in hell happened here? What's caused this?" ... [Then] I see two soldiers kicking the heads around like a soccer ball. I just shut my mouth, walked back, got inside the tank, shut the door, and it was like, I can't be no part of this (p. 1).

Those who have made careers in the military, reported on wars, or studied military history often argue that such scenes, even the last of those quoted above, are neither unusual nor extreme in warfare: "The dead are abused in wartime ... If you kill your enemy his body becomes your trophy, your possession, and this has been a fundamental part of warfare since before the Philistines beheaded Saul" (Hedges, 2002, p. 30).

For several years before this study's respondents could legally drink in the United States, they could legally kill in Iraq. Youthful proxies with expectations of nobility, they soon found themselves perpetrating the countless killings envisioned by their elders, and struggling to square their values with their actions, rhetoric with reality. "The adolescent soldier against whom such propaganda is directed is desperately trying to rationalize what he is being forced to do" (Grossman, 1995, p. 161)—a scenario he was unlikely ever to have imagined (Al-Arian, 2008; Craven & Miller (producers), 2006).

The psychological predicament of a typical combatant is untenable. Inspired by the ancient credo of military honor, the credulous youth is catapulted into a landscape of chaos, where belligerents who seem indescribably foreign employ roadside bombs to mark his arrival. With every panicked firing of his weapon, the young soldier may be triggering, unforeseen, his own psychiatric casualty as an adult. Whether he or his comrade does the shooting, each transgression violates the values of his upbringing, provides a bitter rationale for transgressions yet to come, and shapes his scorn for those still residing "under a blanket of safety" in a world that has forsaken him, but who would nonetheless presume to judge.

Each generation of soldiers makes this discovery for itself, under unexpectedly harsh circumstances. "For the most part, these youths must take leave of their lives under conditions of exposure, away from home, without the possibility of the dignity and ceremony that help to moderate death's shocking character" (Gray, 1959, p. 100). Further, the exposure is likely to fundamentally alter their view of the world:

> The horror one feels in relation to such sights can be traumatic and perhaps permanent; it works in ways we do not understand, depriving us not of self-esteem but of something equally important to the ego's health: a sense of a habitable world and of trustworthy human connections.
>
> —*Marin, 1981, p. 79*

When cases of PTSD can be traced to such experiences, the "accumulation of trauma" is believed to account for a "greater severity of symptoms" (MacNair, 2001, p. 280)—helping to clarify the link between extensive combat exposure and the condition's elevated prevalence (Freedberg, 2007, p. 28). Key to this clarification is the recognition that soldiers have not merely stumbled upon a scene of devastation as if by natural disaster, but have themselves perpetrated—or witnessed others perpetrating—man-made horrors. A senior officer at West Point has observed:

> When the military lists wartime causes of mental illness, they talk about, "Oh, it's hot; oh, it's scary," looking at what happens to soldiers without any mention of the violent things soldiers actually do. ... People don't have nightmares about, "It's another Groundhog Day." They have nightmares about the killing they've done and seen.
>
> —*Weinstein, 2008, p. 22*

If they are to overcome their reluctance to kill, "combatants need what psychologists call 'over-learned, over-practiced training.' It gets down there in the deep brain—not the cortex—where it doesn't require any thought" (Freedberg, 2007, p. 30). But in most cases, "thought" eventually intrudes: Training "makes soldiers able to kill even if they are not willing to kill. Conditioning soldiers to reflexively engage targets prepares them to deal with the enemy, but it does not prepare them to deal with their own consciences" (Gettelman, 2007; Kilner, 2002, p. 28).

Reckoning with his actions after the passage of several decades, a veteran of an earlier war confessed, "I thought you go to Vietnam and kill a few people and forget about it. I thought guys who complained were full of it" (Winerip, 2009, p. ST2). In reality, "the inability to forget what they did in the name of war is the private hell many veterans live with for the rest of their lives. Externally they are heroes; internally they judge themselves to be monsters" (Paquette, 2008, p. 143). "This is killing me," said former U.S. Senator Bob Kerrey about his Vietnam experience. "I'm tired of people describing me as a hero and holding this inside" (Farney, 2001, p. A22).

Moreover, since the time of that earlier war, the lethality of weaponry has increased almost exponentially. By way of illustration, a military historian notes that at the start of the Persian Gulf war, "U.S. forces 'ground up' twenty-nine Iraqi *divisions* within a hundred *hours*" (Gabriel, 1991). Killing on such a massive scale predicts "accumulation of trauma" in both perpetrators and witnesses. "Some psychiatric casualties have always been associated with war," the American colonel observes, "but it is only in this century that our physical and logistical capability to sustain combat has completely outstripped our psychological capacity to endure it." Alluding to a classic World War II "combat exhaustion" study that found a need for soldiers to be evacuated after 30 days of sustained fighting (Swank & Marchand, 1946), he notes that "war is an environment that will psychologically debilitate 98 percent of all who participate in it for any length of time" (Grossman, 1995, pp. 45, 50).

The Language of Dissonance

Perhaps the primary mechanism for coping, several observers agree, lies in the way soldiers speak of their experiences: "Even the language of men at war is full of denial of the enormity of what they have done. Most soldiers do not 'kill', instead the enemy was wasted, greased, taken out" (Grossman, 1995, p. 92). Examples of "sanitizing language" abound:

> By camoflaging pernicious activities in innocent or sanitizing parlance, the activities lose much of their repugnancy. ... Bombing

missions are described as "servicing the target," in the likeness of a public utility. The attacks become "clean, surgical strikes," arousing imagery of curative activities. The civilians whom bombs kill are linguistically converted to "collateral damage."

—*Bandura, 1999, p. 195*

The hijacking of language is fundamental to war ... we all speak with the same cliches and euphemisms. [We] use words to mask reality.

—*Hedges, 2002, p. 34*

All professions have their special vocabularies, but the military's is perhaps distinctive in the mythic poeticism by which its mission is identified as heroic—a style one detects in phrases used by the present study's respondents: "I was called to duty" ... "my brothers and sisters at arms" ... "my nation called upon me to go to war, I answered the call." Even Colonel Grossman's debt to this rhetorical tradition can be heard in his occasional use of archaic language: "They answered their nation's call and heeded not the cost" (Grossman, 1995, p. xxxii).

This diction can be seen as serving the psychological function of reducing dissonance, not only for recruits—"I suspect that at some level of consciousness many of these soldiers recognize their image to be false and that their rationalization is a way of making things easier for themselves" (Gray, 1959, p. 151)—but also for the society at large:

The potency of myth is that it allows us to make sense of mayhem and violent death. It gives a justification to what is often nothing more than gross human cruelty ... It allows us to believe we have achieved our place in human society because of a long chain of heroic endeavors, rather than accept the sad reality that we stumble along a dimly lit corridor of disasters .... We are elevated above the multitude. We march toward nobility.

—*Hedges, 2002, pp. 23–24*

What the myth obscures is a kind of moral abdication:

"The adoption of the cause means adoption of the language of the cause. When we speak within the confines of this language we give up our linguistic capacity to question and make moral choices."

—*Hedges, 2002, p. 148*

Even some in the clinical professions may encourage this abdication by employing an eviscerated language that seeks to rob the soldier's conduct of its moral dimension:

> One notices again and again the ways in which various phrases and terms are used to empty the vets' experience of moral content ... one feels a kind of madness at work. Repugnance toward killing and the refusal to kill are routinely called "acute combat reaction," and the effects of slaughter and atrocity are called "stress."
>
> —Marin, 1981, p. 72

The linguistic sleight-of-hand appears chiefly to serve the needs of those clinicians who

> have few useful ways to approach moral pain or guilt [which] remains for us a form of neurosis or a pathological symptom, something to escape rather than something to learn from, a disease rather than—as it may well be for the vets—an appropriate if painful response to the past. ... [One] VA psychologist told me that he and his colleagues never dealt with problems of guilt. Nor did they raise the question of what the vets did in the war: "We treat the vets' difficulties as problems in adjustment."
>
> —Marin, 1981, p. 71

Such anecdotal reports find confirmation in empirical research conducted prior to the Iraq wars (although some recent intiatives, reviewed below, suggest that the VA now seeks to address the problem): "The 'great majority' of veterans turning to mental-health services were not asked about their combat experiences, let alone their personal kills" (Stellman & Stellman, as cited in Grossman, 1995, p. 293).

This strategy seems designed to reduce cognitive dissonance by marginalizing the moral aspect of the conflict, in the vain hope that "the individual is released as far as possible from regret for past deeds and from the hard duty to improve his character." But the cost to such clients may outweigh the benefits, if "because they rarely can feel remorse, they experience no purgation and cannot grow" (Gray, 1959, pp. 57, 174).

In this account, remorse appears central to the process of healing; "it is the ethical lesson life teaches those who attend to the consequences of their actions."

> But because our age is what it is and because most Americans flee from such knowledge, this wisdom is especially hard for the vets to bear. Though it ought to bring them deeper into the human community, it isolates them instead, sets them irrevocably apart,

locks them simultaneously into a seriousness and a silence that are as much a cause of pain as are their past actions.

—Marin, 1981, p. 74

PTSD and Suicidality

Does moral pain, and the dissonance it arouses, find tangible expression in the symptoms of posttraumatic stress? Would such symptoms likely arise in soldiers who experienced events that were *not* morally proscribed? If not, then we may reasonably assume that the extent of exposure to such events will predict the intensity of symptoms. Indeed, mirroring findings of the Surgeon General's Mental Health Advisory Team, a Rand Corporation study draws a similar conclusion: "The No. 1 major risk factor for PTSD ... is the amount of combat trauma soldiers experience" (Korn, 2008). These findings are further supported by the Department of Defense in its prospective Deployment Health Research, which found

> a threefold increase in new onset self-reported PTSD symptoms or diagnosis among deployed military personnel who reported combat exposures. The findings define the importance of PTSD in this population and emphasize that specific combat exposures, rather than deployment itself, significantly affect the onset of symptoms of PTSD after deployment
>
> *—Smith et al., 2008, p. 1*

At increasing rates, moreover, some active duty soldiers—and veterans—of the Iraq war appear to find unbearable the simultaneous presence of moral pain, posttraumatic stress, and isolation from the human community, a form of "co-morbidity" that is thought to induce suicidality. These accounts exemplify the experience:

> The first time was when she called from Iraq weeping and weeping and saying, "Oh, mom, I can never come home. I just killed a 12-year-old boy." I knew from that point on she was suicidal.
>
> *—Korn, 2008*

> His father ... came home to find his [23-year-old] son had hung himself with a hose in the cellar of their house. The dog tags of two Iraqi prisoners he said he was forced to shoot unarmed, lay on his bed.
>
> *—Goodman, 2004*

"While nobody is sure what leads a veteran to attempt suicide ... many believe [PTSD] serves as a precursor to suicide among those who do not get help" (Korn, 2008). A spokesperson for Vietnam Veterans of America has testified: "It is our obligation not to utter empty claims that combat has little or nothing to do with the suicides of troops who have experienced it," but rather to explore "a connection between the type of combat waged in Iraq and suicide" (Weidman, 2007).

Examination of one state's statistics supports the claim that veterans face a variety of elevated risks, and underscores the vulnerability of the youngest among them:

> Oregon troops serving in Iraq and Afghanistan are more likely to die of suicide than in combat. In 2005, 19 Oregon soldiers died in combat in Iraq and Afghanistan. That same year, 153 Oregon veterans of all ages, serving in various wars, committed suicide. ... The rate of suicide among Oregon men who are veterans is more than double that of Oregon men in general ... [and] the age group in the state health statistics showing the greatest differential between veteran and nonveteran suicides, by far, are those between ages 18 and 24.
>
> —*Korn, 2008*

Data also support claims by those who speak of a "suicide epidemic." The VA's suicide hotline, for example, opened in July of 2007; by August 2008, it had received more than 22,000 calls (Korn, 2008). As for those currently deployed, between 2003 and 2006, the rate of completed U.S. Army suicides was almost 40% higher than that seen previously, and continued to grow through early 2010, when the present manuscript was being prepared, and when the rate of veterans' suicides had reached 18 per day (Hefling, 2010; Maceda, 2009; Mental Health Advisory Team IV, 2007, p. 262; Miklaszewski, 2010; Nesson, 2010; Weidman, 2007; Williams, 2009).

What is known about the prevalence of underlying psychiatric disorders—and the quality of their treatment—among these veterans?

> The Rand study found that one in five veterans from the wars in Iraq and Afghanistan—more than 300,000 people—suffer from either post-traumatic stress or depression. But just more than half sought help and only one in four received acceptable care.
>
> —*Dohrenwend et al., 2006, p. 979; Korn, 2008; Tanielian and Jaycox, 2008*
>
> A report by the Army [October 2007] suggests that the quality of care ... is a factor in the rising incidence of suicide among *active-duty* service members. This report notes that *more than half of the 948 soldiers who attempted suicide in 2006 had been seen by mental health providers before their attempt.*
>
> —*Weidman, 2007*

The Rand study elaborates on the availability of rehabilitative care:

[The VA] faces challenges in providing access to returning service-members, who may face long wait times for appointments. ... Our survey found that only 53 percent of returning troops who met criteria for PTSD or major depression sought help from a provider for these conditions in the past year. The gap is even larger for those reporting a probable TBI [traumatic brain injury]: 57 percent had not been evaluated by a physician for a brain injury.

—Tanielian and Jaycox, 2008

Assessing the "acceptability" of the care that veterans do receive, the study.

identified gaps in the delivery of quality care. Of those who had PTSD or depression and also sought treatment, only slightly over half received a *minimally adequate treatment* (defined according to the duration and type of treatment received). The number who received *high-quality care* (treatment supported by scientific evidence) would be even smaller. ... The study also identified gaps in the care systems' ability to promote and monitor quality care.

—Tanielian and Jaycox, 2008

Not surprisingly, then, correspondence internal to the Department of Veterans Affairs acknowledges "that 12,000 veterans *under VA treatment* attempt suicide each year, and that more than 6,000 veterans succeed" (Korn, 2008). Most likely because it has no way of doing so, the VA does not track attempted or completed suicides among those who are *not* registered in its system—the vast majority of the nation's 25 million veterans.

This failure to connect with soldiers' experience can be seen as the military analogue of a larger civilian avoidance: "Killing comes with a price ... [but] in many ways it is simply too painful for society to address what it does when it sends its young men off to kill other young men in distant lands" (Grossman, 1995, p. 191, p. 95). Even the medicalization of their pain as "posttraumatic stress disorder" may provide an opportunity for society to reduce its own dissonance "by transforming warriors into victims, [which] lets us declare our recognition of war's horror and absolves us for sending them ... [in] a prolonged failure to contextualize and accept our own collective aggression" (Dobbs, 2009, p. 69).

In light of the accounts and critiques quoted above, "acceptable care" would require that clinical services understand their ethical responsibility to engage the soldiers' memories and feelings of guilt, and assist them in coming to terms, as far as possible, with the consequences of their actions.

Clinical Approaches to Healing

Cognitive-behavioral therapies would appear to address at least the first part of that process. In exploring clients' guilt and depression, these therapies identify an irrational component of "self-statements" that inspires avoidant behavior, in turn reinforcing the psychological symptoms (Meichenbaum, 1994, 1996, p. 8). With what success may variations involving cognitive challenges, behavioral homework, and prolonged exposure to memories of trauma, be applied to therapeutic work with veterans suffering from PTSD? Over the past decade, several clinical studies have produced mixed results, which, while promising, suggest a reduced effectiveness in veteran samples.

Prolonged exposure therapy (PE) employs *in vivo* exposure to the "trauma-related situations that the client avoids" and imaginal exposure consisting of "repeatedly recounting memories of the traumatic event." The therapist and client then process the resulting thoughts and feelings. Homework involves *in vivo* exercises and listening to a tape recording of the session (Foa et al., 2007; Riggs, Cahill, & Foa, 2006, p. 66).

Some 18 reviewed studies of civilian samples cite global improvement in clients with traumas involving rape, domestic violence, childhood sexual abuse, and automobile accidents. Only three studies involving combat veterans are reviewed (Riggs et al., 2006, pp. 78–79). Of these, one found significant improvement in PTSD reexperiencing symptoms and depression, but no effect on emotional numbing and social avoidance (Keane, Fairbank, Caddell, & Zimering, 1989, p. 245). A second, somewhat contradictory, study found improvement in subjective anxiety and sleep disturbance, but no effect on depression (Cooper & Clum, 1989, p. 381). And a third found significant improvement in positive, but not negative, symptoms (Glynn et al., 1999, p. 243).

Why should results that are strong among civilians be mixed among veterans? Both groups experienced traumas perpetrated against them, but only the veterans had also perpetrated traumas against others (or observed colleagues doing so), which may account for the discrepancy. A stronger sense of responsibility and guilt surrounding the latter may limit the effectiveness of therapeutic interventions not specifically focused on the moral dimension of perpetrated trauma.

Cognitive processing therapy (CPT), likewise, exposes clients to traumatic memories, but places greater emphasis on challenging associated beliefs. The course of treatment proceeds from identifying "problematic beliefs" in an initial "impact statement"; through clients' efforts to "recall and better contextualize traumatic events," while learning to question "their assumptions and self-statements"; and finally to challenging "overgeneralized beliefs in five areas as they relate to self and other" (Monson et al., 2006, p. 901).

Posttreatment, 24 of 60 participants no longer met PTSD criteria, and another 30 made more modest improvements that extended to co-occuring symptoms of depression and anxiety. Compared to PE, CPT also "produced statistically significant improvements in some aspects of trauma-related guilt (i.e., hindsight bias [and] lack of justification)." Here, too, the uniqueness of veteran samples is noted—"the overall effect size from the veteran studies was statistically lower than [those] found in other trauma groups"—though with a slightly altered finding:

> In civilian samples, all symptom clusters are generally found to improve, and, in veteran samples, the emotional numbness/avoidance symptoms tend to be less treatment responsive (e.g., Glynn et al., 1999). In this study, reexperiencing and emotional numbing symptoms significantly improved in the CPT versus the wait-list condition, but behavioral avoidance and hyperarousal symptoms did not . . . .

> —*Monson et al., 2006, pp. 899, 898, 904*

The researchers note that although guilt-related distress decreased among their clients, guilt-related cognitions persisted. "This suggests that the nature but not the presence of these cognitions may change"— implying that CPT may provide a "more rational" basis for exploring the moral implications of veterans' guilt. Indeed, they argue:

> We believe an important aspect of CPT that makes it well suited to the veteran population is the ability to address cognitions related to committing, witnessing, and experiencing acts of violence, which often co-occur in the context of combat traumatization.

> —*Monson et al., 2006, pp. 905, 904*

Both of the treatments discussed above have now "been rolled out on a national scale at VA, and are mandated to be available at all VA medical centers" (anonymous reviewer, personal communication, June 28, 2010).

Finally, *cognitive therapy for trauma-related guilt* (CT-TRG) proceeds through three phases: assessment, guilt incident debriefings, and "procedures for correcting thinking errors that lead to faulty conclusions associated with guilt." Underlying this approach is the notion that trauma survivors tend to distort four cognitive components of guilt:

> First, many survivors believe, in retrospect, ... that they "knew" what was going to happen before it was possible to know, or that they dismissed or overlooked clues that "signaled" what was going to occur *(foreseeability and preventability distortion)*. Second, [they] accept an inordinate share of responsibility for causing the trauma ... *(responsibility distortion)*. Third, [they] believe that their trauma-related actions were less justified ... *(justification distortion)*. Fourth, [they] believe they violated personal or moral convictions ... *(wrongdoing distortion)*.
>
> —*Kubany and Ralston, 2006, p. 261*

Two treatment-outcome studies of CT-TRG with groups of battered women found reductions in guilt, depression, and PTSD symptoms, though "definitive studies have yet to be conducted" (Kubany & Ralston, 2006, p. 269). Nor have studies been undertaken with groups of veterans, although one day-long session with a single Vietnam veteran suggested an outcome similar to that of the battered womens' groups.

The distinction between traumas experienced and traumas perpetrated may be relevant as well to a consideration of the four "cognitive distortions" cited above, which perhaps apply more clearly to battered women than to combat veterans. Entering a war zone and trained to kill, the latter group are more likely to have foreseen at least some of what would occur, to feel some responsibility for their actions, and—even if after the fact—to suspect that their behavior has violated their moral convictions.

Curiously, the authors take scant notice of this distinction and appear to question the legitimacy of soldiers' guilt:

> Included in this group are many combat veterans who engaged in deliberate brutality or used excessive force in the war zone (e.g., "atrocities") but who feel bad when they think about what happened. They may even be tormented by guilt. CT-TRG is definitely applicable for such individuals.
>
> —*Kubany and Ralston, 2006, p. 271*

The sense conveyed in this passage (highlighted by use of the word "but") that the psychological outcome is surprising and that treatment to "fix" it is warranted, suggests a belief that it may be more valuable to medically erase, than to learn from, the consequences of a person's behavior. This recalls the early critics' disdain for therapies that view all guilt as pathological and that aim to "release" the individual from "regret for past deeds" (Gray, 1959, p. 174; Marin, 1981, p. 71).

The authors offer examples of what they see as "resistance" by clients who sense that "mentally 'tricking' oneself into reducing guilt might be thought of as avoiding taking responsibility for what happened, thus a 'cop-out'" (Kubany & Ralston, 2006, p. 270). But while reducing guilt is undoubtedly therapeutic—especially if clients are then better able to learn from it—perceived attempts to eliminate it altogether, if such were possible, would offer a false resolution of cognitive dissonance and disparage the clients' humanity.

The authors summarize their experience with the Vietnam veteran who, prior to his day-long session of CT-TRG, experienced severe guilt over having mutilated a dead Vietnamese soldier:

> What bothers me so much is ... that I took out a knife and cut off a human ear and wore it on a bracelet around my wrist as a war souvenir. At the time I was proud of it.

Arguably, the therapeutic task here was to help the client to reassess the *extent* of his guilt by coming to appreciate the effects of a situation rife with chaos and fear:

> This veteran was helped to realize that many American troops in Vietnam were impaired in their capacity to experience compassion, empathetic distress, and guilt because they had become numbed by the trauma of war. ... a certain degree of social consensus that extreme or brutal behavior might be excusable or necessary ... certainly raised the probability that extreme or brutal behavior would occur.
>
> —*Kubany and Ralston, 2006, p. 271*

For cognitive approaches, then, the therapeutic task may be seen as one of degree. If those associated with warfare, from privates to Joint Chiefs, are easily able to shed guilt about their role in its predictable atrocities, then it is reasonable to ask what our society as a whole will have learned about the policy of war. If history forgotten is history repeated, then it may be socially as well as individually therapeutic for those in the military who designed and fought the wars—and those in civilian society who embraced them—to remember. But is this form of memory even possible without the guidance offered by rational and humane remorse?

What requires therapeutic intervention, as these cognitive practitioners plausibly assert, is the disabling quality of guilt based on extreme self-blame and other irrational thoughts—but not, arguably, guilt itself. Once its excessive quality has been shed, rational guilt may be instructive. The enabling experience of exploring it via therapy can empower veterans to critique the policies that predicted their individual acts of brutality and thus victimized them as well. "Guilt fuels my fire," is the way one Iraq war veteran, now an antiwar activist, describes his newfound sense of social responsibility (Foulkrod, 2006). It would be difficult to view this veteran's calling as an example of "resistance" to trauma-related guilt therapy, as its practitioners might be tempted to claim.

Those who seek a humanistic framework for delivering the full benefit of cognitive therapies may find it in Marin's injunction:

> Therapy must enter those areas in which the therapist and patient become comrades, where what has been discovered about one's own experience and its related pain raises questions not only about psychological wholeness but also about moral responsibility ... . No one will be much use to the vets without taking these questions seriously and understanding that at the heart of each life ... lie fundamental moral questions about choice, responsibility, and the doing of good, [to] be answered with action that comes from one's deepest commitments.
>
> —*Marin, 1981, p. 80*

Self-Help Approaches to Healing

Even when therapists are not involved, these commitments are now helping Iraq war veterans to heal, as they navigate three diverse approaches to transforming remorse. Perhaps the most widely adopted are those modeled on traditional 12-step programs which allow for "full, frank discussion among people who share the same basic problem and who, therefore, understand each other's problem as no outsider could" (Stichman & Schoenberg, 1972, p. 156). Especially for veterans craving this kind of support, "a group of peers [can be] far more powerful than a single therapist" (Bartle, 2007, p. 5). Once underway,

> it is possible to resolve feelings of guilt ... by using the ritual of confession, forgiveness, compensation, and self-forgiveness. The 12-step

Recovery Movement includes a step where the individual takes responsibility for the people he or she has harmed. It is a relief to acknowledge these actions and discover a way to resolve guilt.

—Paquette, 2008, p. 145

These components may require applications in both private and semipublic settings, as in the case of confession, which "can be done on an individual basis or in a . . . group setting through traditional talk-based therapies." As for the others,

> compensation can take the form of positive actions: reaching out to others in need [or] speaking to groups of people who will be affected by hearing their stories . . . Self-forgiveness occurs when the soldier finds a place within her- or himself to truly forgive . . . his behavior as human, if not humane. Grieving the loss of life is necessary in recovering ones' own humanity . . . [We] can help facilitate the process of forgiveness by providing compassion, patience, and a readiness to listen to the "unacceptable." When forgiven, veteran soldiers can begin the process of healing and growth.

—Paquette, 2008, p. 145

As suggested by these passages, such groups may function well on a "self-help" basis but need not exclude clinicians, who may be seen as having not only a clinical, but also a social, responsibility of their own. For the sake of both veterans and the larger society, the hope is that therapists will "accompany" these clients through "those regions of the self into which the vets have been led and for which we have few words and little wisdom."

> Our actions will play a significant part in defining not only the social and moral life of our own people, but the future of countless and distant others as well, whose names we will not know and whose faces we will not see until perhaps, a decade from now, other American children view them through the sights of guns. The responsibility of the therapist, then, neither begins nor ends with the individual client, and the client's responsibility neither begins nor ends with himself or herself. Both extend far outward, from the past into the future, to countless other lives.

—Marin, 1981, p. 80

Art Therapy as an Approach to Healing

A second strategy employs politicized innovations in art therapy that involve the creation of poetry or art in transforming war trauma—for example, a network of poetry workshops called Warrior Writers, or the Combat Paper Project, in which veterans make paper from their shredded fatigues. Here they write poems disavowing their battlefield experiences and affirming the humanity they share with those who lost their lives. One veteran gives an account of the spontaneous and therapeutic experience that led to the group's founding:

> "I got completely dressed in my desert uniform. I hadn't put that thing on my body since Iraq," he said. "I was thinking about it systematically at first. Where do I cut? Then I started feeling this overwhelming feeling of empowerment and emotional expression. I started ripping and pulling at my uniform until I was down to my skivvies," he said. "I refer to it as an act of liberation."
>
> —Rappaport, 2008, p. 1-A

For veterans involved in this project, the shredding and transformation of uniforms symbolizes both their rejection of past violence and affirmation of future healing.

> When you arrive in the war zone, that uniform stands for destruction and chaos and death and so to come back and take that symbol, that piece, to destroy it, to create something new out of it and make a positive thing from that uniform, it's got that feeling that you're moving on from that and stepping onto a new path.
>
> —Nesson, 2010

Through papermaking workshops, public performances, and exhibits of their works, participants are finding that

> the gap between veterans and civilians narrows and the door for dialogue opens. This opening is reflected in an unexpected change—the VA has begun to see the CPP as an effective new model for art therapy. A discussion to implement the project into their programs has begun, a positive step toward healing.
>
> —Nesson, 2010

In a similar manner, the Warrior Writers and other soldier-poets produce and publicly read poetry that explores the significance of what they have seen and done in Iraq (Turner, 2005). Reflecting the chiefly therapeutic purpose of the writing, however, many of these works

> are remarkable for their reluctance to comment broadly on politics or ideology ... . The soldier-poets writing about Iraq have not yet mounted that kind of political attack on the politicians responsible

for the war. Their moral sensibility tends to be local and personal, not yet global.

—Winn, 2008, p. B16

But the focus is predicted to shift, as if embodying a developmental process: "The best of these poets will ultimately train their moral lasers on the rest of us" (Winn, 2008, p. B17). Meanwhile, the transformative nature of these activities is clear to many of those involved: "Writing, performing, and papermaking have been my healing. My young life was taken, but I believe I've been given another" (Black, 2008, p. 9-A).

Both approaches discussed above—a more traditional self-help group model that operates removed from the public, and a more innovative art therapy approach that requires engagement with the public—share certain features. Their participants

> are learning that speaking publicly about their experiences and problems brings some release and comfort. They are finding power in numbers, and this reinforces their resolve "not to let themselves off the hook" for their misguided behavior that left so many innocent people dead. Instead they are finding some measure of redemption by helping others [to] face the same demons.
>
> *—Paquette, 2008, p. 144*

Despite their compelling testimony about the therapeutic value of such activities, veterans and their caregivers would benefit from an outcome evaluation of these approaches, which has yet to be undertaken.

"The Call to Activism" as an Approach to Healing

Still other veterans are taking a third, more expressly political, path to working through trauma, transferring blame to the architects of war and adopting a critical perspective that reveals their own victimization. This form of reconciliation typifies organizations like Iraq Veterans against the War, which embody the activist approach of community psychology.

Departing from the more traditional self-help model that chiefly serves to increase emotional support, the activist group

> strives to articulate the embeddedness of individual conflicts in a more explicitly political frame of reference. As such, engagement

helps to recast both consciousness and capacity in social and political—rather than simply personal and emotional—terms. Together, participants in the organization learn and create the strategies, resources, and basic grammar of elementary political literacy.

—Kieffer, 1984

The IVAW organization pursues a three-pronged intervention strategy: "visiting military bases and their surrounding communities to inform servicemen and servicewomen of their rights; protecting and supporting members of the military who resist the war; and telling potential recruits about the realities of serving in the military" (Curtis, 2008, p. 8-A). Perhaps unexpectedly, it also partners with the CPP and Warrior Writers. "Part of pushing back is music, is writing, is art as much as it is protests and political discussion" (Rappaport, 2008, p. 1-A).

Some might regard the idea of soldiers pursuing activities such as these to be counter-intuitive. Why would veterans who had volunteered for service—of all people—join an organization such as IVAW? It may be that activism is a pathway by which the member, driven by disillusionment, achieves a kind of reconciliation with his victims.

This is exemplified in the aftermath of a 2007 incident in Baghdad, made famous in April 2010 by an anonymous leak of video footage showing an attack on civilians by a helicopter gunship. The leak prompted two of the veterans involved to issue a public apology to the victims' families:

"What was shown in the Wikileaks video only begins to depict the suffering we have created," reads an open letter from McCord and Stieber to the Iraqis who were injured or lost loved ones in the attack. . . . "The soldier in the video said that your husband shouldn't have brought children to battle, but we are acknowledging our responsibility for bringing the battle to your neighborhood, and to your family. We did unto you what we would not want done to us. Our heavy hearts still hold hope that we can restore inside our country the acknowledgment of your humanity, that we were taught to deny."

—Lazare and Harvey, 2010

The letter embodies both their desire to "right" or "restore" equity to their victims, as described in the early literature on cognitive dissonance (Walster et al., 1970, p. 185), and also their seeking of forgiveness as a healthy means of resolving dissonance (Paquette, 2008, p. 145).

That activism may be a pathway to reconciliation is further exemplified by another veteran interviewed in the film *The Ground Truth*, who explains that

> he may never be able to forgive himself for what he did "over there." But the guilt reinforces his resolve to help stop the war and get medical attention for its survivors. The call to activism is common among those who have suffered a traumatic event. In the case of these soldiers, helping others appears to be helping them return to a normal, civilian life
>
> —*Dreyer, 2008, p. 218*

In a poignant twist, this veteran—now a playwright—adds: "I don't want to be healed. I want it to always hurt me. That guilt fuels my fire" (Foulkrod, 2006). "Such a soldier will discover his future mission in life to be as far removed as possible from the destructive work of war. He will be absorbed in the reconstructive, the simple, and the truly humane arts" (Freedberg, 2007, p. 29; Gray, 1959, p. 211).

Dissonance as the Core of Distress—And a Guide to Healing

Based on the present study's results, the authors believe it likely that most soldiers who witness or perpetrate casualties experience cognitive dissonance, deriving from their sense of having been party to a transgression. This dissonance need not be disabling but only sufficiently uncomfortable to produce the kind of ratings and comments reviewed above. In severely traumatic instances, however, it is reasonable to predict that dissonance may give rise to PTSD and even suicidality.

What strikes the authors as particularly compelling about the self-help, artistic, and "political" forms of therapy discussed here is the necessity inherent in each for veterans to explore guilt and acknowledge remorse, as the cognitive therapies may help them to do—but also, ultimately, to understand and critique the policies that led to their distress, thereby resolving dissonance by comprehending its context and encouraging future involvement in altruistic—and redemptive—activities.

In the same vein, it is reasonable to predict that veterans who experience guilt but continue to embrace those policies may remain in a state of dissonance. Whether through one of the cognitive therapies or the more "political" means reviewed in this chapter, those who rationally come to attribute some of their battlefield behaviors to the power of the situation, may anticipate further gains by confronting the policies that led to it. As Aronson puts it:

> Before we can write off [our] behavior as ... merely villainous, it would be wise to examine the situation that sets up the mechanism for this kind of behavior. We can then begin to understand the terrible price we are paying for allowing certain conditions to exist. Perhaps, eventually, we can do something to avoid these conditions. Dissonance theory helps to shed some light on this mechanism.
>
> *—Aronson, 2008, p. 231*

Without taking this activist step, the casualties of war may appear, especially to this group, to have been in vain. And from this perception it is likely a short step to the cynicism and social avoidance that often plague combat veterans.

Dissonance as an Indictment of War

To what larger questions may the findings of the present study lead? Sometimes initially attractive, always subsequently horrific, war spawns a profound disillusionment about humanity in many of its veterans, leading them into years of isolation, bitterness, and shame.

> The moral cynics, which modern wars generate in great numbers, testify to a lost hope in mankind. Where cynicism is not mere shallowness and show, it is the cry of men who have not been able to endure the tension between their inner ideal and outer reality.
>
> *—Gray, 1959, p. 209*

Does the fact of their dissonance suggest an indictment of war? Would combat soldiers experience this "tension," and the cluster of anguished emotions that surround it, without the recognition of having betrayed the values by which they learned to live? Do they recognize that what they have seen and done in a particular war—to soldiers and civilians alike—belongs to the taking of life on a vast scale, in all previous wars, in which they have now been made complicit? (Hedges & Al-Arian, 2007; Phillips, 2010; Slim, 2008; Wolfe & Darley, 2005) Though unaffected civilians may prefer not to visualize it, combat veterans have no choice:

> There are many of the living who have had burned into their brains forever the unnatural sight of cold dead men scattered over the hillsides and in the ditches along the high rows of hedge throughout the world. Dead men by mass production—in one country after another—month after month and year after year. Dead men in winter and dead men in summer. These are the things that you at home need not even try to understand.
>
> —*Pyle, as quoted in Hedges, 2002, pp. 166 and 167*

In the 20th century alone, military organizations and their recruits have perpetrated the unimaginable slaughters of World War I and World War II, invasions and genocides, the firebombing and atomic bombing of entire cities and incineration of their civilian populations. "In wars of the twentieth century not less than 62 million civilians have perished, nearly 20 million more than the 43 million military personnel killed." To this legacy of more than 100 million dead must be added the unknown number, likely in the hundreds of thousands, of American soldiers and veterans who have, not surprisingly, taken their own lives. "Modern industrial warfare may well be leading us, with each technological advance, a step closer to our own annihilation. We too are strapping explosives around our waists. Do we also have a suicide pact?" (Hedges, 2002, p. 13).

Any discussion of veterans' dissonance will likely point to war itself as the institution that demands the most profound moral compromises of its participants, thus provoking their psychological struggle in the first place. It is not scientifically or ethically viable to explore dissonance as though it were a natural phenomenon apart from human societies and the choices they make.

A well-understood tenet of community psychology holds that prevention is greatly superior to treatment (Albee, 1981, p. 10). What would it mean to apply this principle to conflict among nations? Perhaps this: "Our age is caught in a painful contradiction for which there is no resolution other than the renunciation of wars" (Gray, 1959, p. 182). For in this era, "war may be a cruel fact of human life, but it is not a necessity" (Dreyer, 2008, p. 218). The passage of a half-century has done little to fault the wisdom of this observation inspired by World War II:

> More productive certainly will be our efforts to eliminate the social, economic, and political injustices that are always the immediate occasion of hostilities. Even then, we shall be confronted with the spiritual emptiness and inner hunger that impel many men toward combat. Our society has not begun to wrestle with this problem of how to provide fulfillment to human life, to which war is so often an illusory path.

—*Gray, 1959, pp. 57–58*

REFERENCES

Al-Arian, L. (2008, April 7). Winter soldiers speak. *The Nation*. Retrieved July 29, 2010, from http://www.thenation.com/article/winter-soldiers-speak

Albee, G. (1981). Politics, power, prevention, and social change. In J. M. Joffe & G. W. Albee (Eds.), *Prevention through political action and social change* (pp. 5–25). Hanover, NH: University Press of New England.

American Psychiatric Association. (2000). *Diagnostic and statistical manual of mental disorders* (4th ed.)—*Text revision*. Washington, DC: Author.

Angus Reid Global Monitor. (2006, March 19). *Opposition to Iraq War at 62% in U.S.* Retrieved July 18, 2010, from http://www.angus-reid.com/polls/view/11939

Aronson, E. (2008). *The social animal.* New York: Worth Publishers.

Aronson, E., & Mills, J. (1959). The effect of severity of initiation on liking for a group. *Journal of Abnormal and Social Psychology, 59,* 177–181.

Bandura, A. (1999). Moral disengagement in the perpetration of inhumanities. *Personality and Social Psychology Review, 3*(3), 193–209.

Bartle, S. (2007, Fall). A recent case of PTSD from Iraq. *Mental Health Journal of the Berkshires, VIII*(3), 5.

Berscheid, E., & Walster, E. (1967). When does a harm-doer compensate a victim? *Journal of Personality and Social Psychology, 6,* 435–441.

Berscheid, E., Boyce, D., & Walster, E. (1968). Retaliation as a means of restoring equity. *Journal of Personality and Social Psychology, 10,* 370–376.

Black, L. (2008, July 18). Iraq veterans turn warrior writers. *Vineyard Gazette, 163*(11), 9-A.

Blackman, L. (2006, June 12). Soldiers' stories. *The New Yorker,* 127–128.

Bradshaw, S. L., Ohlde, C. D., & Horne, J. B. (1993). Combat and personality change. *Bulletin of the Menninger Clinic, 57*(4), 466–478.

Brock, T. C., & Buss, A. H. (1964). Effects of justification for aggression and communication with the victim on postaggression dissonance. *Journal of Abnormal and Social Psychology, 68*(4), 403–412.

Buss, A. H., & Brock, T. C. (1963). Repression and guilt in relation to aggression. *Journal of Abnormal and Social Psychology, 66*(4), 345–350.

Clausewitz, C. M. von (1832/1976). *On war.* Princeton: Princeton University Press.

Cloke, K. (2001). *Mediating dangerously: The frontiers of conflict resolution.* San Francisco: Jossey-Bass.

Cohen, J., & Balz, D. (2007, January 11). Poll: most Americans opposed to Bush's Iraq plan. *The Washington Post.* Retrieved July 18, 2010, from http://www.washingtonpost.com/wpdyn/content/article/2007/01/11/AR2007011100282.html

Cooper, J. (2007). *Cognitive dissonance: Fifty years of a classic theory.* London: Sage Publications.

Cooper, N. A., & Clum, G. A. (1989). Imaginal flooding as a supplementary treatment for PTSD in combat veterans: A controlled study. *Behavior Therapy, 20*(3), 381–391.

Craven, J., & Miller, R. (producers) (2006). *After the fog: Interviews with combat veterans* [film]. Available from Kingdom County Productions, 949 Somers Road, Barnet, VT 05821.

Curtis, H. (2008, August 29). Soldier, summer visitor stuns crowd at Iraq Veterans against the War event. *Vineyard Gazette, 163*(17), 8-A, 9-A.

Dobbs, D. (2009, April). The post-traumatic stress trap. *Scientific American, 300*(4), 64–69.

Dohrenwend, B. P., Turner, J. B., Turse, N. A., Adams, B. G., Koenen, K. C., & Marshall, R. (2006). The psychological risks of Vietnam for U.S. veterans: A revisit with new data and methods. *Science, 313,* 979–982. doi: 10.1126/science.1128944.

Dreyer, R. (2008, July). There could never be a "peace traumatic stress disorder." *Perspectives in Psychiatric Care, 44*(3), 216–218.

Farney, D. (2001, April 25). Kerrey discloses his wartime role in civilian killings. *The Wall Street Journal,* A22.

Festinger, L. (1957). *A theory of cognitive dissonance.* Stanford, CA: Stanford University Press.

Festinger, L., & Carlsmith, J. M. (1959). Cognitive consequences of forced compliance. *Journal of Abnormal and Social Psychology, 58,* 203–210.

Foa, E. B., Hembree, E. A., & Rothbaum, B. O. (2007). *Prolonged exposure therapy for PTSD: Emotional processing of traumatic experiences: Therapist guide.* New York: Oxford University Press.

Foulkrod, P. (producer and director) (2006). *The ground truth: After the killing ends* [film]. Available from The Ground Truth, 137 South Robertson Boulevard, Beverly Hills, CA 90211.

Freedberg, S. J., Jr (2007). Intimate killing. *National Journal, 39*(29), 26–32.

Gabriel, R. (1991, March 19). The human dimension of modern warfare. Contribution to a symposium on *The Gulf War and Its Aftermath.* Boston College, Boston, MA.

Gerard, H., & Mathewson, G. (1966). The effects of severity of initiation on liking for a group: A replication. *Journal of Experimental Social Psychology, 2*, 278–287.

Gettelman, E. (2007, January/February). Inside "The Sandbox". *Mother Jones, 32*(1), 75.

Glass, D. (1964). Changes in liking as a means of reducing cognitive discrepancies between self-esteem and aggression. *Journal of Personality, 32*, 531–549.

Glynn, S. M., Eth, S., Randolph, E. T., Foy, D. W., Urbaitis, M., & Crothers, J. (1999). A test of behavioral family therapy to augment exposure for combat-related posttraumatic stress disorder. *Journal of Consulting and Clinical Psychology, 67*, 243–251.

Goodman, A. (2004, August 11). *Parents mourn son's suicide after returning from Iraq duty.* Retrieved January 23, 2010, from http://www.democracynow. org/2004/8/11/parents_mourn_ sons_suicide_after_returning

Gray, J. G. (1959). *The warriors: Reflections on men in battle.* New York: Harper & Row.

Grossman, D. (1995). *On killing: The psychological cost of learning to kill in war and society.* New York: Back Bay Books.

Harmon-Jones, E., & Mills, J. (Eds.) (1999). *Cognitive dissonance: Progress on a pivotal theory in social psychology.* Washington, DC: American Psychological Association.

Hedges, C. (2002). *War is a force that gives us meaning.* New York: Public Affairs.

Hedges, C., & Al-Arian, L. (2007, July 30/August 6). The other war. *The Nation, 285*(4), 11–31.

Hefling, K. (2010, January 11). *Increase in suicide rate of vets.* Retrieved January 11, 2010, from http://news.yahoo.com/s/ap/20100111/ap_on_ bi_ge/us_veterans_suicide

Heider, F. (1958). *The psychology of interpersonal relations.* New York: Wiley.

Holbrook, J. (2007). Reflections on war and killing. *Legal Studies Forum, 31*(2), 547–548.

Holmes, R. (1985). *Acts of war: The behavior of men in battle.* New York: Free Press.

Keane, T. M., Fairbank, J. A., Caddell, J. M., & Zimering, R. T. (1989). Implosive (flooding) therapy reduces symptoms of PTSD in Vietnam combat veterans. *Behavior Therapy, 20*, 245–260.

Kieffer, C. (1984). Citizen empowerment: A developmental perspective. *Prevention in Human Services,* 0270–3114, *3*(2). Retrieved July 29, 2010, from http://www.informaworld.com/smpp/content~db=all~content= a904473187. Doi: 10.1300/J293v03n02_03.

Kilner, P. (2002). Military leaders' obligation to justify killing in war. *Military Review, 82*(2), 24–31.

Klass, E. T. (1978). Psychological effects of immoral actions: The experimental evidence. *Psychological Bulletin, 85*(4), 756–771.

Korn, P. (2008, August 21). "Suicide epidemic" hits veterans. *Portland Tribune.* Retrieved January 8, 2010, from http://www.portlandtribune.com/news/ story.php?story_id=121926671416052100.

Kubany, E. S., & Ralston, T. C. (2006). Cognitive therapy for trauma-related guilt and shame. In V. M. Follette, & J. I. Ruzek (Eds.), *Cognitive-behavioral therapies for trauma* (2nd ed., pp. 258–289). New York: Guilford Press.

Kulka, R., Schlenger, W., Fairbanks, J., Hough, R., Jordan, K., Marmar, C. et al. (1990). *Trauma and the Vietnam War generation: Report of findings from the National Vietnam Veterans Readjustment Study.* New York: Brunner Mazel.

Laufer, P. (2006). *Mission rejected: U.S. soldiers who say no to Iraq.* White River Junction, VT: Chelsea Green Publishing.

Lazare, S., & Harvey, R. (2010, August 16/23). WikiLeaks in Baghdad. *The Nation, 291*(7,8), 24–27.

Lerner, M. J. (1970). The desire for justice and reactions to victims. In J. Macaulay, & L. Berkowitz (Eds.), *Altruism and helping behavior* (pp. 205–229). New York: Academic Press.

Maceda, J. (2009, December 20). Active duty suicides are at record levels. *NBC Nightly News.* New York: NBC News.

MacNair, R. (2001). Psychological reverberations for the killers: Preliminary historical evidence for perpetration-induced traumatic stress. *Journal of Genocide Research, 3*(2), 273–282.

Manchester, W. (1980). *Goodbye, darkness: A memoir of the Pacific war.* Boston: Little, Brown.

Marin, P. (1981, November). Living in moral pain. *Psychology Today, 15*(11), 68–80.

Meichenbaum, D. (1994). *A clinical handbook/practical therapist manual for assessing and treating adults with post-traumatic stress disorder (PTSD).* Waterloo, ON: Institute Press.

Meichenbaum, D. (1996). *Mixed anxiety and depression: A cognitive-behavioral approach.* New York: Newbridge.

Mental Health Advisory Team IV. (2007, November). Soldiers' and Marines' mental health: Assessment of those serving in Iraq. *Congressional Digest, 86*(9), 262–263.

Miklaszewski, J. (2010, July 29). Wounds of war. *NBC Nightly News.* New York: NBC News.

Monson, C. M., Schnurr, P. P., Resick, P. A., Friedman, M. J., Young-Xu, Y., & Stevens, S. P. (2006). Cognitive processing therapy for veterans with military-related posttraumatic stress disorder. *Journal of Consulting and Clinical Psychology, 74*, 898–907. Doi: 10.1037/0022006X.74.5.898.

Nesson, S. (producer and director). (2010). *Iraq, paper, scissors* [film in production]. Retrieved from http://web.mac.com/snesson/iWeb/iraqpa perscissors/Home.html

Paquette, M. (2008, July). The aftermath of war: Spiritual distress. *Perspectives in Psychiatric Care, 44*(3), 143–145.

Phillips, J. E. S. (2010). *None of us were like this before: How American soldiers turned to torture.* London: Verso.

Pierson, D. S. (1999). Natural killers: Turning the tide of battle. *Military Review, 79*(2), 60–65.

Pyle, E. (1986). *Ernie's war: The best of Ernie Pyle's World War II dispatches.* New York: Simon & Schuster.

Rappaport, J. (2008, July 25). War in pieces: Combat paper project sees veterans use uniforms to heal. *Vineyard Gazette, 163*(12), 1-A, 6-A.

Riggs, D. S., Cahill, S. P., & Foa, E. B. (2006). Prolonged exposure treatment of posttraumatic stress disorder. In V. M. Follette & J. I. Ruzek (Eds.), *Cognitive-behavioral therapies for trauma* (2nd ed., pp. 65–95). New York: Guilford Press.

Slim, H. (2008). *Killing civilians: Method, madness, and morality in war.* New York: Columbia University Press.

Smith, T. C., Ryan, M. A. K., Wingard, D. L., Slymen, D. J., Sallis, J. F., & Kritz-Silverstein, D. (2008). New onset and persistent symptoms of posttraumatic stress disorder self reported after deployment and combat exposures: Prospective population based US military cohort study. *British Medical Journal, 336,* 366–371. doi: 10.1136/bmj.39430.638241.AE.

Staub, E. (1989). *The roots of evil: The origins of genocide and other group violence.* New York: Cambridge University Press.

Stellman, J. M., & Stellman, S. (1988). Post-traumatic stress disorders among American Legionnaires in relation to combat experience: Associated and contributing factors. *Environmental Research, 47*(2), 175–210.

Stichman, J. A., & Schoenberg, J. (1972). Heart wife counselors. *Omega, 3*(3), 155–161.

Swank, R. L., & Marchand, W. E. (1946). Combat neuroses: Development of combat exhaustion. *Archives of Neurology and Psychology, 55,* 236–247.

Tanielian, T., & Jaycox, L. (Eds.) (2008). *Invisible wounds of war: Psychological injuries, their consequences, and services to assist recovery.* Santa Monica, CA: Rand Corporation. Retrieved January 19, 2010, from http://www.rand.org/pubs/monographs/MG720/

Turner, B. (2005). *Here, bullet.* Farmington, Maine: Alice James Books.

Walster, E., Berscheid, E., & Walster, B. (1970). The exploited: Justice or justification? In J. Macaulay & L. Berkowitz (Eds.), *Altruism and helping behavior* (pp. 179–204). New York: Academic Press.

Weidman, R. (2007, December 12). *Statement of Vietnam Veterans of America before the U.S. House of Representatives Veterans' Affairs Committee: Suicide among America's military personnel and veterans.* Retrieved January 8, 2010, from http://www.vva.org/testimony/2007/121207.html

Weinstein, A. (2008, September/October). Kill and tell. *Mother Jones, 33*(5), 22–25.

Williams, B. (2009, November 13). Military stress: Army suicides are way up. *NBC Nightly News.* New York: NBC News.

Winerip, M. (2009, September 6). Vietnam's damage, four decades later. *The New York Times,* ST1–ST2.

Winn, J. A. (2008, April 11). A waste of shame. *The Chronicle Review,* B16–B17.

Wolfe, R. J., & Darley, J. (2005). Protracted asymmetrical conflict erodes standards for avoiding civilian casualties. *Peace and Conflict: Journal of Peace Psychology, 11*(1), 55–61.

ACKNOWLEDGMENTS

The authors are grateful to Michael Gerardi, Barbara Kuhlman, Kathy Lama, and Jesslyn Schnopp for their research assistance; to Susan Opotow and Ray Paloutzian for their encouragement; and to the many Iraq war veterans for their participation.

5

VETERANS-BY-PROXY: AMENDING LOSS OF SELF AMONG THE CHILDREN OF COMBAT VETERANS

Diann Cameron Kelly and Shari Ward

Our nation owes a great deal to what I call "the power behind the power"—the families of all those who are serving. While our men and women in uniform may be called to pay the highest price, their families ... make a considerable sacrifice as well.

—Secretary of Defense Robert M. Gates, DEPARTMENT OF DEFENSE, Military Spouses Day, Washington, DC, May 6, 2008

Children experience war through their parents, as trauma and absence overwhelm even the best parental intentions of active and veteran military personnel. More than two million children from the United States have suffered a parent's absence at some time during the Global War on Terror (GWOT) (Flake, Davis, Johnson, & Middleton, 2009; Lamberg, 2008). In fact, the research of Lamberg (2008), Flake et al. (2009), as well as the Department of Defense (2008) demonstrates that during 2007 the number of children under the age of 21 years with a parent serving in GWOT was about 700,000, and by 2008 that number rose to about 1.2 million. Combat impacts not only those engaged in it, but also tens of millions of loved ones, especially millions of children.

When you are a child of a combat veteran, you are your own *veteran ... by-proxy*, dealing with secondary trauma, ambiguous loss, and insecure attachment from the fractured parental responsiveness and involvement you receive or believe to receive. Certainly, it is difficult to fully comprehend the experiences of combat veterans. The war-time seasons of these veterans are littered with memories that frequently return the conscious and unconscious structures of their minds to the images, smells, and sounds of war. However, when you are a young child of a combat veteran or a fully matured adult who is a child of a veteran, what you may see, think, hear and imagine to be the context of war is formed through the lens of that veteran (Bissell, 2007), and his or her own trauma-induced perspectives (APA, 2007; Chartrand & Siegel, 2007; Dekel & Monson, 2010; Flake et al., 2009; Rosenheck & Nathan, 1985).

The concept of proxy suggests that one individual represents another or acts on behalf of another individual. Proxy is vicarious in nature, in which an individual who witnesses or hears about the acts or experiences of another individual begins to experience the same, that is, vicarious pleasure, punishment, or trauma (McCann & Perlmann, 1990; Rosenheck & Nathan, 1985). With vicarious trauma, in particular, the witness observes the trauma experienced by another and attempts to adjust to and cope with the perceived elements of the trauma (McCann & Perlman, 1990).

Vicarious trauma is more than secondary stress experienced as a parallel process to another's primary trauma. Across the life span, but especially for maturing children witnessing their parents' traumatic experiences (Daud, Skoglund, & Rydelius, 2005), a witness of another's trauma struggles with the loss of self and subsequently presents with symptoms comparable to posttraumatic stress disorder (PTSD) (Chartrand & Siegel, 2007; Lincoln, Swift, & Shorteno-Fraser, 2008; Mmari, Roche, Sudhinaraset, & Blum, 2009; Rosenheck & Nathan, 1985). Whether the parent is a victim of rape or torture, as identified in the research of Daud et al. (2005), or a combat veteran, as presented in the research of Dekel and Monson (2010) and Rosenheck and Nathan (1985), these transmissions of traumatic stress can threaten one's ability to self-regulate and can increase the likelihood for loss of self (i.e., low self-efficacy, limited self-regulation, and poor social relatedness). Aided by a review of the literature, narratives from veterans-by-proxy and a conceptual model, we will learn that secondary traumatization is a significant issue and, as such, a dynamic of proxy.

VETERAN-BY-PROXY STATUS

Parents who are present in a child's life transmit cultural information, values and beliefs across the life span. This transmission of values and information informs children's process of gaining meaning, purpose, direction, and security in their lives (Bridges, Connell, & Belsky, 1988; Corwyn & Bradley, 1999; Dollahite & Hawkins, 1998; Landau, 2007; Lincoln et al., 2008; Pruett, 1997). One common method for this transmission is frequent communication—overt and implicit, through daily activities such as having dinner conversation, running errands, helping children with their own accomplishments (i.e., school or work), or even knowing children's friends and their parents which is part of being engaged in the child's social universe (Bridges et al., 1988; Christiansen & Palkovitz, 2001; Corwyn & Bradley, 1999; Erbes et al., 2007; Landau, 2007).

In contrast, research shows war combatants often transmit traumatic stress to their children, or "veterans-by-proxy," along with expected or unexpected pain and ambiguity, instead of affirming values and beliefs (Chartrand & Siegel, 2007; Daud et al., 2005; Dekel & Goldblatt, 2008; Lincoln et al., 2008; Mmari et al., 2009; Motta, Joseph, Rose, Suozzi, & Leiderman, 1997; Rosenheck & Nathan, 1985).

This transmission is not static, but rather fluid across the life span. It affects school, work, intimate relationships within and outside the home environment, and most importantly the individual's relationship with themselves (Dekel & Monson, 2010; Huebner, Mancini, Wilcox, Grass, & Grass, 2007; Lincoln et al., 2008; Nelson & Wright, 1996). Veteran-by-proxy children have a tendency to act out physical aggression as a protective response against the insurmountable adversities associated with traumatic stress that is transmitted by the combat veteran parent (Chartrand & Siegel, 2007; Erbes et al., 2007; Mmari et al., 2009). Violence, in particular, toward self and others, is used by veterans-by-proxy to effectively deal with the perceived threat in their lives. This includes hypervigilance, suspicion of adult authority figures as well as their peers, and even acting impulsively or disconnecting from others as a need to protect one's self from the pain of the transmitted trauma (Chartrand & Siegel, 2007; Huebner et al., 2007; Mmari et al., 2009).

While not all of these children, or veterans-by-proxy, present with the behaviors of excessive fighting, intimidating others, cruelty or violence toward others or destruction of property, or even social alienation and withdrawal (Dekel & Monson, 2010; Lincoln et al., 2008; Mmari et al., 2009), the issue with secondary trauma and its related factors is that it can significantly affect the proxy's cognition, emotional regulation, and social involvement (Dekel & Monson, 2010; Huebner et al., 2007; Mmari et al., 2009). These dynamics and others result in secondary traumatic stress (STS), ambiguous loss, and insecure attachment (Figure 5.1) (Chartrand & Siegel, 2007; Dekel & Monson, 2010; Huebner et al., 2007; Perrier, Boucher, Etchegary, Sadava, & Molmar, 2010; Walker, 2008) as a result of their veteran-by-proxy status.

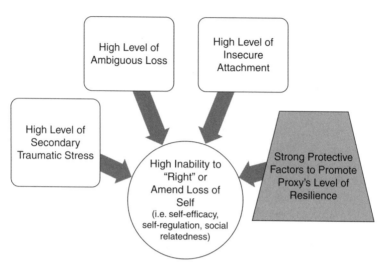

FIGURE 5.1 Conceptual framework amending loss of self post-secondary traumatic stress (STSD).

Secondary Traumatic Stress

Secondary traumatization or secondary traumatic stress (i.e. STS) relates to behaviors, conditions, and presentations exhibited in an individual who is in close proximity to the person immediately exposed to and recovering from the traumatic event (e.g., combat) (Dekel & Goldblatt, 2008; Dekel & Monson, 2010; McCann & Perlman, 1990). Secondary traumatic stress incorporates symptoms that are commonly associated with PTSD, except that the individual dealing with secondary traumatic stress experiences the traumatic event indirectly (Daud et al., 2005; Dekel & Monson, 2010; Rosenheck & Nathan, 1985).

For many maturing children with veteran-by-proxy status, secondary traumatic stress symptoms can include emotional numbness, anxiety, memory losses, cognitive distortions, poor concentration, academic underachievement, and educational disengagement (Chartrand & Siegel, 2007; Dekel & Monson, 2010; Huebner et al., 2007; Lincoln et al., 2008; Mmari et al., 2009; Motta et al., 1997; Rosenheck & Nathan, 1985). These symptoms presented by the veteran-by-proxy emerge from the transmission of distress and stress from the combat veteran parent (Collins & Kennedy, 2008; Dekel & Goldblatt, 2008; Erbes et al., 2007; Mmari et al., 2009; Motta et al., 1997; Rosenheck & Nathan, 1985).

The combat veterans' behaviors, emotionality and cognitive perceptions influence the social and emotional behaviors, emotionality, and cognition of their proxy (Dekel & Goldblatt, 2008; Mmari et al.,

2009; Rosenheck & Nathan, 1985). Specifically, Motta et al. (1997) and the work of Dekel and others (2008, 2010), citing the extensive works of Charles Figley (1995), propose that the negative impact of trauma is dispersed to the maturing child or veteran-by-proxy during close and continued contact with the combat veteran over a period of time (Dekel & Goldblatt, 2008; Mmari et al., 2009; Motta et al., 1997). This recurring proximity to the combat veterans' traumatic responses (i.e., PTSD) results in negative responses for the veteran-by-proxy similar to PTSD but seemingly less severe (Motta et al., 1997).

Reviewing research performed to investigate the intergenerational transmission of PTSD, Dekel and Goldblatt (2008) cited various studies. One about combat veterans from the Vietnam War showed that 40% of the children-of-combat-veterans/veterans-by-proxy used illegal drugs with another 35% reporting behavioral problems. In addition to the Beckham et al. (1997) study, Dekel and Goldblatt (2008) also cited the work of Parsons, Kehle, and Owen (1990) who looked at 191 children whose veteran parents were diagnosed with and without PTSD. In this study, researchers noted that those combat veterans with PTSD were more likely to see their children as having maladaptive behaviors—that is, social and emotional, and difficulties in keeping friendships with their peers. Finally, citing the research of Rosenheck and Fontana (1998a), when combat veterans exhibited more violence postdeployment, the children of these veterans demonstrated more behavioral issues than their peers whose combat veteran parents did not demonstrate such violent, abuse tendencies.

For the child of the combat veteran, or the veteran-by-proxy, the recurring proximity to the combat veterans' traumatic stress results in secondary traumatic stress for the proxy, as well as ambiguous loss and insecure attachment (Benjamin, 2006; Boss, 2007; Levy & Orlans, 1998; Perrier et al., 2010; Walker, 2008).

Secondary trauma in the proxy mirrors the posttraumatic stress exhibited by the combat veteran parent. It is not uncommon to see the maturing child, now a proxy, wrestle with the psychological battering from emotional distress, feelings of sadness and loneliness that seem unending, and even behavioral and psychological disturbances that for some children of combat veterans appear to increase in severity depending upon preexisting family conditions (i.e., family discord, low educational attainment, substance abuse, etc.) (Chartrand & Siegel, 2007; Dekel & Monson, 2010). It is as though the proxy walks a path along with the combat veteran that is unknown to both, but equally felt by each.

The Proxy's Narrative I

We walked around on eggshells a lot growing up with my dad (a combat veteran). I remember being taught from early on never to wake him from his nap. We were never told why, just told never to do it. I remember being 8 years old and watching my dad take a nap on the living room couch. He wasn't peaceful. In fact he looked angry in his sleep, with sweat pouring off his head and his shirt drenched. His fists were clenched and his mouth was moving as though he were talking. But I didn't hear anything. I wanted to shake him awake, maybe help him escape the nightmare, but I remembered what mama taught us ... 'don't wake him no matter what!' I was gripped with fear watching him and couldn't move for the life of me. At the same time, he screamed himself awake and yelled obscenities, I dropped back and fell to the floor. He asked me 'What did you do?' I was silent. He screamed 'Why did you pour water on me?!' I still couldn't speak. But I looked into my father's eyes and I didn't know him. He was a stranger as his eyes were dark and empty. I was punished with a spanking for doing something I didn't do and didn't have the voice to stand up for myself. To this day I cannot awaken anyone from a nap without clearly remembering that moment of fear. It was the first of many times I would see those dark and empty eyes look into my soul.

—*Adult Veteran-by-Proxy*

Ambiguous Loss

Ambiguous loss refers to loss experienced by an individual that is unclear and lacks certainty (Boss, 2007; Dekel & Monson, 2010; Huebner et al., 2007). It is an emotional context where little or no information is known about a loved one, which increases trauma for the proxy. This individual is left to wonder whether their loved one is alive or dead in many instances (Boss, 2007; Dekel & Monson, 2010; Huebner et al., 2007). Ambiguous loss also inhibits the proxy from grieving and reconciling loss through various coping strategies (i.e., crying, expressing anger, or engaging in self-soothing rituals) (Boss, 2007; Huebner et al., 2007). Further, it diminishes one's cognition and one's ability to understand the separation as a temporary loss and forces the individual to internalize the loss as life-altering, with the contradictions heightening emotional insecurity, anxiety, guilt, and even distress (Benjamin, 2006; Boss, 2007; Huebner et al., 2007; Levy & Orlans, 1998). These paradoxical obstacles for the proxy are the knowing the loved one is emotionally lost and yet physically found, emotionally absent and yet physically present, or even emotionally distant and yet physically nearby.

Ambiguous loss produces stress beyond the distress involved with secondary traumatic stress. Further, while data are not known on how ambiguous loss impacts or is associated with PTSD directly, the theory presumes that the affected individual withdraws further from the traumatized parent (i.e., combat veteran) influencing the feelings of ambiguous loss (Boss, 2007; Dekel & Monson, 2010). This is a self-protective strategy, albeit an unconscious coping mechanism, to guard against further emotional numbing and detachment that are associated with secondary traumatic stress (Boss, 2007).

The Proxy's Narrative II

Our dad was a great provider. I don't know how he did it, but we never knew we didn't have much. Actually, we always ate well (nice steaks, great desserts, I could go on), and he loved taking us out whether it was to the park, bike riding, or to the zoo. It was our time with our dad. But his emotions were so erratic and his temperament so unpredictable, we never knew "which dad" would show up on a given day. That's the part of him I can actually say I hated. I hated that he just couldn't be normal—whatever normal was. When he came home from work (blue collar union man), you knew he was in a good mood because he would speak and ask about your day. He would take an interest in you. The sad part was that it didn't last long … not even a full day's worth. It could be the next day, he'd come home and we would be swept up into his emotional turmoil. Not only could you not breathe, as his presence was all consuming, you knew not to breathe because he might actually notice you during his sulking moments over his alcohol-laced coffee … and then anything fueled his anger. Maybe we didn't wash the dishes, maybe there wasn't enough milk for his coffee, maybe someone left a jacket on the couch, maybe, just maybe, we were in his way in the small hallway as we tried to get out of his way! He would just lash out. Most of the time, it was just safer to stay in our rooms and run away through books, drawing, writing poems, etc. Either way, I know we felt like it was an emotional prison – inescapable and also painful because of our love for him and our hope that he would change.

—Adult Veteran-by-Proxy

As Nelson and Wright (1996) noted in their investigation, families of combat veterans with PTSD are often immersed in confusion, fear, and unmet needs. This correlates with the work of Huebner et al. (2007) and indicates that family members (i.e., the proxy) would more likely sacrifice their own needs in pursuit of gaining power over the confusion in order to increase certainty. Unfortunately, ambiguous loss is so pervasive that by sacrificing their own needs the proxy only serves to further isolate themselves, while experiencing internal familial discord and interpersonal difficulties (Boss, 2007; Dekel & Goldblatt, 2008; Huebner et al., 2007; Nelson & Wright, 1996).

> As a result of continuous ambiguity ... , [the proxy] may experience symptoms of depression, anxiety, guilt and distressing dreams. In addition, lack of clarity over the status of one family member immobilizes other family members ....
>
> —*Dekel and Monson, 2010, p. 305*

The concern is that the increased withdrawal employed as one coping strategy by the veteran's child distances the veteran-by-proxy from the combat-veteran parent, and perpetuates the issue of insecure attachment.

Insecure Attachment

An individual employs attachment behaviors to keep the attachment figure close with the hope that the desired figure is responsive and available to the maturing child (Ainsworth, 1973; Bowlby, 1982a; Fonagy, 1997; Kobak & Sceery, 1988; Lewis, Feiring, & Rosenthal, 2000; Perrier et al., 2010). The parents' responsiveness and attunement to the maturing child, in general, satisfy their need for physical and emotional security (Bowlby, 1982b; Crittenden, 2000; Kelly, 2008; Waters, Weinfield, & Hamilton, 2000). However, when parents are unresponsive, unavailable, and thwart a maturing child's ability to attach, the results are insecure attachments (Crittenden, 2000; Fonagy, 1997; Kobak & Sceery, 1988; Levy & Orlans, 1998; Waters et al., 2000).

Insecure attachments (whether avoidant, resistant, or disorganized), especially among veterans-by-proxy, are, in part, results of the parent's inability to respond to the proxy's needs, reassure in the face of anxiety and distress, or maintain contact even when the parent is close by or away from the proxy (Ainsworth, 1973; Crittenden, 2000; Fonagy, 1997; Huebner et al., 2007; Lewis, Feiring & Rosenthal, 2000; Walker, 2008). When parent's responsiveness to the veteran-by-proxy hinders attachment, and the proxy experiences their parent as distant or emotionally depriving, the proxy's cognitive strategies change and form perceptions that appear to favor the combat veteran's perceived rejection of the proxy (Crittenden, 2000; Fonagy, 1997; Levy & Orlans, 1998).

The veteran-by-proxy is, then, more likely to deem themselves as undesirable, based upon the combat veteran's perception of the child (Benjamin, 2006; Huebner et al., 2007; Walker, 2008). This dynamic stunts the maturing proxy's ability to cope, and instead increases the likelihood of poor attachment relationships, disengagement from social arenas, and possibly the presentation of violent behaviors (Fonagy, 1997; Levy & Orlans, 1998).

One can opine that the stressors and factors associated with the trauma of combat and postcombat experiences diminish a combat veteran's ability to attune and respond to their child (Benjamin, 2006; Crittenden, 2000; Fonagy, 1997; Huebner et al., 2007; Levy & Orlans, 1998; Perrier et al., 2010). Attunement refers to the parents' perception of the child's behavior and interpretation of the child's needs (Crittenden, 2000; Levy & Orlans, 1998). Responsiveness relates to the parents' ability to appropriately interpret and respond to their child's needs, as well as the parents' capacity to meet those needs in a timely and effective manner (Crittenden, 2000; Levy & Orlans, 1998).

When combat-veteran parents provide their proxy child with minimal emotional supports in the attachment relationship, the veteran-by-proxy experiences severe stress. The outcome for the veteran-by-proxy is poor coping skills while experiencing the combat veteran parent as a stranger rather than an engaged parent (Bridges et al., 1988; Fonagy, 1997; Kelly, 2008; Waters et al., 2000). Because the parent is experienced as stranger, the veteran-by-proxy is less likely to believe or feel they are protected and instead feels emotionally abandoned with the child experiencing rejection, isolation, hostility, deprivation and even destructive thinking (Fonagy, 1997; Kelly, 2008; Kobak & Sceery, 1988; Levy & Orlans, 1998; Waters et al., 2000).

This leads to narcissistic injury that impacts self-efficacy, self-regulation, and social relatedness (Bowlby, 1982a, b; Fonagy, 1997), and occurs because combat veteran parents experiencing several traumas may have a higher tendency to repeat their own experiences of suffering through traumatic experiences transmitted to the veteran-by-proxy (Chartrand & Siegel, 2007; Dekel & Monson, 2010; Lincoln et al., 2008; Motta et al., 1997; Rosenheck & Nathan, 1985). Based on the research of resilience, a resilient proxy is one who is able to overcome this dynamic and exhibit moderately high to high levels of self-efficacy, self-regulation, and social relatedness (Fraser, Richman, & Galinsky, 1999; Greene & Livingston, 2002; Kelly, 2006; Walker, 2008).

The Proxy's Narrative III

For the last ten years, every Father's Day, my dad asks "was I a good dad?" What the hell am I supposed to say, "No!" I don't think so. For years I have said "yes," while simultaneously remembering the butchery and the pain at his hands and his mouth. I said "I thank you for whom I've become, you made me who I am." I still don't know what I meant by that, but it sounded supportive. All I know is I spent my entire life supporting my dad, while living under the weight of his thumb. Excelling in school was important, but with him you could not fail. Perfection was expected. You had to exceed your peers, and your teachers. This continued even into college. If it weren't for my mother, I have no idea where I would be or whom I would be. She couldn't protect us from his ugly words or his physical abuse that made you feel as though you were stupid, ugly, and worthless. But she tried to reframe his words and make his words less powerful, and combine those with hugs and kisses to make the tears less salty. Overtime, I was able to stand up to him. And, for the next half of my life, all I have done and do is fight with him and defend myself from the continued jabs. I am an adult, and he is an aged soul. Yet, I still fall victim to the flames of his pain and suffering. That's what makes all of this very difficult. I've spent a better part of my life wishing my dad never went into combat. But if he never did, if he had gone to college and pursued a career in engineering as he wanted, would I be who I am now? We will never know . . . .

—*Adult Veteran-by-Proxy*

The resilient proxy exhibiting self-efficacy is one who demonstrates a belief that they are able to cope with any situation or challenge and affect the outcome of their situation and their future (Bandura, 1991; Kelly, 2006). Self-efficacy constitutes belief in one's problem-solving skills; scholastic, health, vocational, and civic literacy skills to affect outcomes; self-instruction and self-development to influence outcomes to influence well-being; locus of control or expectancy of success; and persistence in the face of adversity (Bandura, 1991).

Self-regulation is one's influence and control (not the belief) over one's thoughts, actions, and feelings to affect an immediate or distal outcome in one's environment and for one's self (Bandura, 1991; Huebner et al., 2007; Perrier et al., 2010). So much of self-regulation depends on an individual exercising personal power. A self-regulated individual is one who is autonomous, able to delay gratification with minimal impulsivity; able to set goals and meet those goals through self-monitoring; able to self-reflect and demonstrate self-valuation that is positive and self-fulfilling (Bandura, 1991; Mmari et al., 2009).

Finally, social relatedness refers to an individual's ability to connect with others, to love and be loved, and to care for and be cared about (Bollinger & Palkovitz, 2003; Clough, 2006; Mmari et al., 2009; Waters et al., 2000). Social relatedness is influenced early by the primary attachments of the individual, and constitutes the social networks of an individual, one's readiness to interact with and within the environment across social groups, and one's affiliative skills to adequately satisfy one's need to belong (Kelly, 2006; Kobak & Sceery, 1988; Waters et al., 2000). Social relatedness enables an individual to cope with life stressors and promote physical, emotional, and social well-being in the face of adversity, challenges, and risk factors.

When resiliency is part of the continuum, self-efficacy, self-regulation, and social relatedness are thought to be enhanced to diminish the harmful effects of secondary traumatic stress, ambiguous loss, and insecure attachment.

KEY ELEMENTS TO AMENDING THE LOSS

The emotional involvement of the parental figure remains one of the important factors in the development of a maturing child across the life span. More importantly, when trauma is an element of this relationship, parental involvement and responsiveness are key to the maturing child's ability to *right* or amend the loss suffered as a result of secondary traumatic stress, ambiguous loss, and insecure attachment, especially in the cases of the combat-related proxies.

With the relationship between the combat veteran and the veteran-by-proxy child, traumatic stress significantly decreases levels of trust, feelings of safety, misperceptions of power, and diminishes esteem as well as the prospects of intimacy (Chartrand & Siegel, 2007; Dekel & Goldblatt, 2008; Lincoln et al., 2008; Motta et al., 1997). Further, the transmission of traumatic stress increases the likelihood of secondary traumatic stress in the veteran-by-proxy child, and increases the likelihood of the veteran-by-proxy experiencing numbing, anxiety and depression, hypervigilance, dissociation, and academic/vocational underachievement (Dekel & Monson, 2010; Motta et al., 1997).

To guard against these symptoms, and secondary traumatic stress, ambiguous loss and insecure attachment decreasing one's self-efficacy, self-regulation and social relatedness, specific protective factors for the proxy child's must be strengthened to ensure healthy outcomes.

Promoting Resilience to Amend Loss

Resilience is an individual's ability to recover, adjust, and adapt in situations where adversity or challenges are present (Fraser et al., 1999; Greene & Livingston, 2002). When individuals (i.e., children, adolescents, adults) exhibit moderately high to high levels of resilience, they are more likely to present with good outcomes and successes even in the presence of significant risks (Greene & Livingston, 2002). In families where risk factors are present, such as traumatic stress, resilience is further promoted through strong parent–child relations; family support programs; and early identification initiatives of at-risk families (Chartrand & Siegel, 2007; Dekel & Monson, 2010; Erbes et al., 2007; Fraser et al., 1999; Huebner et al., 2007; Kelly, 2006; Lincoln et al., 2008; Mmari et al., 2009).

Parents are significant to diminishing or perpetuating risk for their children. In fact, resilience is enhanced when the emotional distance between parent and child is diminished (Chartrand & Siegel, 2007; Dekel & Monson, 2010; Fraser et al., 1999; Kelly, 2006). For the veteran-by-proxy, their parents' primary trauma, their use of aggression and physical violence against family members, and even their alcohol and substance use increase the level of risk to the proxy beyond the risk factors of secondary trauma, ambiguous loss, and insecure attachment (Dekel & Monson, 2010; Fraser et al., 1999). When parents are consistently involved in the life and activities of their child (i.e., the veteran-by-proxy child), and take a more active and inspired role in their child's achievements and expectations, not only is the child more likely to exhibit resilience, but also more likely to demonstrate higher levels of self-efficacy, self-regulation, and social relatedness (Kelly, 2006).

Dekel and Monson (2010) recommended strengthening the parent–child relationship, as the family environment evolves when the combat veteran parent returns from deployment. As such, the return of veteran parent does not have to be void of parenting interventions and supports that re-acclimate the combat veteran to the overt and implicit nuances of parental role, emotional support, and engagement in the community that was once known to the combat veteran and did not lack certainty (Dekel & Monson, 2010; Lincoln et al., 2008). While the presence of PTSD can impair the parents' ability to redevelop a strong relationship with the proxy and facilitate the proxy's secure attachment, research shows that early identification of the veteran's ability to reconnect to family members is key to identifying veterans' "success at maintaining and preserving healthy relations in their families" (Dekel & Monson, 2010, p. 308).

Further, family functioning and communication are also critical to enhancing resilience within the proxy, as families are the primary agents of socialization for human behavior and human development (Huebner et al., 2007; Kelly, 2006). For combat veteran families, risk is heightened when violence and abusive communication recur frequently (Huebner et al., 2007; Lincoln et al., 2008). Further, the uncertainties that accompany ambiguous loss are significantly increased due to the unpredictability of the combat veteran's poor communication patterns, social withdrawal from family functions and rituals, and impulsivity when making decisions affecting the family (Chartrand & Siegel, 2007; Huebner et al., 2007; Landau, 2007; Lincoln et al., 2008). However, when veteran families participate in positive daily rituals that accentuate stability and security in society, and provides the proxy with healthy boundaries, the child is more likely to present as resilient with higher levels of self-efficacy, self-regulation, and social relatedness (Dekel & Monson, 2010; Huebner et al., 2007; Lincoln et al., 2008; Mmari et al., 2009). Lincoln et al. (2008) suggest that families need to be supported through the readjustment phase to identify possible and unanticipated difficulties arising in the family system. The focus of this intervention is to diminish vulnerabilities and heighten success in communication, and mediating internal conflicts and concerns (Lincoln et al., 2008; Weiss & Berger, 2010).

Finally, intervention and support ensure service outreach and planning with families and children of returning combat veterans to identify and respond early to the negative effects of secondary trauma stress (Erbes et al., 2007; Mmari et al., 2009; Weiss & Berger, 2010). Whether a Family Strengthening Model, or a family-version of the Warrior Resiliency Training model using Rational Emotive Behavior Therapy (REBT) (Jarrett, 2008), outreach and service planning must seek to facilitate the child's mastery over the effects of the secondary trauma and address the realities of the relationship with their veteran parent (Collins & Kennedy, 2008; Erbes et al., 2007; Landau, 2007; Paschall, Ringwalt, & Flewelling, 2003). The focus of these interventions is to lower aggression and poor impulse control, increase abilities to interact with peers and other social networks, and most importantly, learn how to cope while rebuilding a relationship with their combat veteran parent (Collins & Kennedy, 2008; Erbes et al., 2007; Jarrett, 2008; Lincoln et al., 2008; Mmari et al., 2009).

Interventions structured on enhancing resilience, and strengthening the veteran-by-proxy child's relationship with the combat veteran parent are essential. Although the proxy child may never be able to alter their perception of the loss of the parent they knew or thought they knew, with outreach and interventions structured on enhancing resilience to affect self-efficacy, self-regulation, and social relatedness the child is less likely to question their value in society.

CONCLUSION

Veterans-by-proxy carry the weight of an uncontrollable and volatile environment that threatens their actual and perceived well-being as well as their level of resilience. The combat veterans' visible and non-visible wounds and experienced traumas significantly affect the well-being of the veteran-by-proxy. In fact, research shows it is the veteran-by-proxy more so that lends the veteran cognitive, emotional and behavioral support at the expense of the proxy's psychological self. As the veteran-by-proxy fills the combat veteran's emotional void, the proxy is left with the responsibility of amending the loss of self and repairing the damage through resilient adjustment and adaptation to the combat veteran's transmitted PTSD.

It is not enough to wait until issues emerge to intervene on behalf of veterans' families. It is critical that we identify needs early to ensure that within veteran families the parents are able to exhibit a strong responsiveness and attunement to children to ensure the secondary traumatic stress and its subsequent factors are diminished over time. By promoting a stable relationship with the veteran parent and giving the parent the tools to emotionally and psychologically reengage with their child postcombat, combat veteran parents are able to emotionally, physically, and financially invest their time, energy, and resources in their child and the veteran-by-proxy is no longer at a need to amend the loss of self, as the self is integrated.

REFERENCES

Ainsworth, M. (1973). The development of infant-mother attachment. In J. L. Gewirtz (Ed.), *Attachment and dependency*. Washington, DC: V. H. Winston.

American Psychological Association. (2007). *The psychological needs of U.S. military service members and their families: A preliminary report.* Washington, DC: Author. Retrieved from http://www.apa.org/pubs/info/reports/military-deployment-summary.pdf

Bandura, A. (1991). Social cognition: Theory of self-regulation. *Organizational Behavior & Human Decision Process, 50,* 248–287.

Beckham, J., Braxton, L., Kudler, H., Feldman, M., Lytle, B., & Palmer, S. (1997). Minnesota multiphasic personality inventory profiles of Vietnam combat veterans with posttraumatic stress disorder and their children. *Journal of Clinical Psychology, 53,* 847–852.

Benjamin, J. (2006). Crash: What we do when we cannot touch. *Psychoanalytic Dialogues, 16*(4), 377–385.

Bissell, T. C. (2007). *The father of all things: A marine, his son and the legacy of Vietnam.* New York, NY: Pantheon Books.

Bollinger, B., & Palkovitz, R. (2003). The relationship between expressions of spiritual faith and parental involvement in three groups of fathers. *The Journal of Men's Studies, 11*(2), 117–129.

Boss, P. (2007). Ambiguous loss theory: Challenges for scholars and practitioners. *Family Relations, 56,* 105–111.

Bowlby, J. (1982a). *Attachment and loss: Attachment* (Vol. 1). New York, NY: Basic Books.

Bowlby, J. (1982b). Attachment & loss: Retrospect and prospect. *American Journal of Orthopsychiatry, 52*(4), 664–678.

Bridges, L., Connell, J., & Belsky, J. (1988). Similarities and differences in infant-mother and infant-father interaction in the strange situation: A component process analysis. *Developmental Psychology, 24*(1), 92–100.

Chartrand, M., & Siegel, B. (2007). At war in Iraq and Afghanistan: Children in US military families. *Ambulatory Pediatrics, 7*(1), 1–2.

Christiansen, S. L., & Palkovitz, R. (2001). Why the "good provider" role still matters: Providing as a form of paternal involvement. *Journal of Family Issues, 22*(1), 84–106.

Clough, W. R. (2006). To be loved and to love. *Journal of Psychology and Theology, 34*(1), 25–31.

Collins, R. C., & Kennedy, M. C. (2008). Serving families who have served: Providing family therapy and support in interdisciplinary poly-trauma rehabilitation. *Journal of Clinical Psychology: In Session, 64*(8), 993–1003.

Corwyn, R. F., & Bradley, R. H. (1999). Determinants of paternal and maternal investment in children. *Infant Mental Health Journal, 20*(3), 238–256.

Crittenden, P. J. (2000). A dynamic-maturational exploration of the meaning of security and adaptation: Empirical, cultural and theoretical consider-ations. In P. M. Crittenden & A. H. Claussen (Eds.), *The organization of attachment relationships: Maturation, culture and context.* New York, NY: Cambridge University Press.

Daud, A., Skoglund, E., & Rydelius, P. A. (2005). Children in families of torture victims: Transgenerational transmission of parents' traumatic experiences to their children. *International Journal of Social Welfare, 14,* 23–32.

Dekel, R., & Goldblatt, H. (2008). Is there intergenerational transmission of trauma? The case of combat veterans' children. *American Journal of Orthopsychiatry, 71*(3), 281–289.

Dekel, R., & Monson, C. M. (2010). Military-related post-traumatic stress disorder and family relations: Current knowledge and future directions. *Aggression and Violent Behavior, 15,* 303–309.

Department of Defense. (2008). Military Spouses Day (Washington, D.C.), *As Delivered by Secretary of Defense Robert M. Gates, Washington, D.C., Tuesday, May 06, 2008.* Office of the Assistant Secretary of Defense (Public Affairs), U.S. Department of Defense. Retrieved from http://www.defense.gov/speeches/speech.aspx?speechid=1236.

Dollahite, D. C., & Hawkins, A. J. (1998). A conceptual ethic of generative fathering. *Journal of Men's Studies, 7*(1), 109–132.

Erbes, C. R., Polusny, M. A., Dieperink, M., Kattar, K., Leskela, J., & Curry, K. (2007). Care for returning service members: Providing mental health care for military service members returning from Iraq and Afghanistan. *Minnesota Psychologist,* November, 2007, 5–8.

Figley, C. R. (Ed.). (1995). *Compassion fatigue: Secondary traumatic stress disorder in those who treat traumatized.* New York: Routledge.

Flake, E. M., Davis, B. E., Johnson, P. L., & Middleton, L. S. (2009). The psychosocial effects of deployment on military children. *Journal of Developmental Behavioral Pediatrics, 30*(4), 271–278.

Fonagy, P. (1997). Attachment, the development of the self, and its pathology in personality disorders. In C. Maffei, J. Derksen, & H. Groen (Eds.), *Treatment of personality disorders.* New York: Plenum Press.

Fraser, M. W., Richman, J. M., & Galinsky, M. J. (1999). Risk, protection and resilience: Toward a conceptual framework for social work practice. *Social Work Research, 23,* 129–208.

Greene, R., & Livingston, N. C. (2002). A social construct. In R. R. Greene (Ed.), *Resiliency: An integrated approach to practice, policy and research* (pp. 63–94). Washington, DC: NASW Press.

Huebner, A. J., Mancini, J. A., Wilcox, R. M., Grass, S. R., & Grass, G. A. (2007). Parental deployment and youth in military families: Exploring uncertainty and ambiguous loss. *Family Relations, 56,* 112–122.

Jarrett, Maj. T. (2008, July–September). Warrior resilience training in operation Iraqi freedom: Combining rational emotive behavior therapy, resiliency and positive psychology. *The Army Medical Department Journal,* 32–38.

Kelly, D. (2006). Parents' influence on youths' civic behaviors: The civic context of the caregiving environment. *Families in Society, 87*(3), 447–455.

Kelly, D. (2008, Winter). Severe sexual maltreatment & social inclusion: A case study on insecure attachment. *Journal of Pastoral Counseling,* 79–92.

Kobak, R. R., & Sceery, A. (1988). Attachment in late adolescence: Working models, affect regulation and representations of self and others. *Child Development, 59,* 135–146.

Lamberg, L. (2008). Redeployments strain military families. *Journal of the American Medical Association, 300*(6), 644.

Landau, J. (2007). Enhancing resilience: Families and communities as agents for change. *Family Process, 46*(3), 351–365.

Levy, T. J., & Orlans, M. (1998). *Attachment, trauma and healing: Understanding and treating attachment disorder in children and families.* Washington, DC: CWLA Press.

Lewis, M., Feiring, C., & Rosenthal, S. (2000). Attachment over time. *Child Development, 71*(3), 707–720.

Lincoln, A., Swift, E., & Shorteno-Fraser, M. (2008). Psychological adjustment and treatment of children and families with parents deployed in military combat. *Journal of Clinical Psychology, 64*(8), 984–992.

McCann, I. L., & Perlman, A. (1990). Vicarious traumatization: A framework for understanding the psychological effects of working with victims. *Journal of Traumatic Stress, 3*(1), 131–149.

Mmari, K., Roche, K. M., Sudhinaraset, M., & Blum, R. (2009). When a parent goes off to war: Exploring the issues faced by adolescents and their families. *Youth & Society, 40*(4), 455–475.

Motta, R. W., Joseph, J. M., Rose, R. D., Suozzi, J. M., & Leiderman, L. J. (1997). Secondary trauma: Assessing intergenerational transmission of war experiences with a modified Stroop procedures. *Journal of Clinical Psychology, 53*(8), 895–903.

Nelson, B. S., & Wright, D. W. (1996). Understanding and treating posttraumatic stress disorder symptoms in female partners of veterans with PTSD. *Journal of Marital and Family Therapy, 22*(4), 455–467.

Parson, J., Kehle, T. J., & Owen, S. V. (1990). Incidences of behavior problems among children of Vietnam veterans. *School Psychology International, 11,* 253–259.

Paschall, M. J., Ringwalt, C. L., & Flewelling, R. L. (2003). Effects of parenting, father absence and affiliation with delinquent peers on delinquent behavior among African American male adolescents. *Adolescence, 38*(149), 15–33.

Perrier, C. P. K., Boucher, R., Etchegary, H., Sadava, S. W., & Molnar, D. S. (2010). The overlapping contributions of attachment orientation and social support in predicting life-events distress. *Canadian Journal of Behavioural Science, 42*(2), 71–79.

Pruett, D. D. (1997). How men and children affect each other's development. Edited from *Zero to Three Journal, 18*(1). Retrieved October 27, 2006, from www.zerotothree.org/fathers.html

Rosenheck, R., & Fontana, A. (1998a). Transgenerational effects of abusive violence on the children of Vietnam combat veterans. *Journal of Traumatic Stress, 11,* 731–741.

Rosenheck, R., & Nathan, P. (1985). Secondary traumatization in the children of Vietnam veterans with post-traumatic stress disorder. *Hospital and Community Psychology, 36*(5), 538–539.

Walker, J. (2008). Communication and social work from an attachment perspective. *Journal of Social Work Practice, 22*(1), 5–13.

Waters, E., Weinfield, N. S., & Hamilton, C. E. (2000). The stability of attachment security from infancy to adolescence and early adulthood: General discussion. *Child Development, 71*(3), 703–706.

Weiss, T., & Berger, R. (2010). *Posttraumatic growth and culturally competent practice: Lessons learned from around the globe.* Hoboken, NJ: John Wiley & Sons, Inc.

Part II

OUTREACH AND PRACTICE WITH SPECIALIZED COMMUNITIES

Sydney Howe-Barksdale and William Valente

As the Military becomes more welcoming of diversity, society faces the challenge of offering appropriate services to each branch represented in the Armed Forces today, both active and reserve. The men and women returning from combat return stateside with challenges that negatively affect transition and reintegration.

Part II of *Treating Young Veterans* examines the barriers faced by veterans of specialized communities as they reintegrate into civilian life. Coming home to Atlanta, Georgia is different from coming home to a small town in Connecticut in terms of culture, community support, and access to services. Donna Caplin and Katharine Kranz Lewis report on the unique experiences of 14 returning veterans as they engage with family, college life, social isolation, work, and mental health issues. In the following chapter, the experiences of veterans who return to the streets instead of a home, whether immediately or after a period of time, are observed by Wesley Kasprow and Robert Rosenheck. After providing a detailed demographic analysis, the authors offer an examination of the mental health and substance abuse issues this population faces.

Godfrey Gregg and Jamila Miah look at the toll of combat stress and military sexual trauma on female veterans and propose a phenomenological model for treatment. Experience of life in and after the Military is often different for veterans and their spouses, depending on factors such as gender and type of military service. These factors, and how the health care system impacts them, are presented by Kristy Straits-Tröster, Jennifer Gierisch, Patrick Calhoun, Jennifer Strauss, Corrine Voils, and Harold Kudler. Exposure to toxic substances, sexual harassment and trauma, stigma in civilian life, coordination of childcare for spouses living alone, and ramifications of getting needed mental health services on career advancement and how these issues are more relevant to specific groups are examined in this chapter.

The Armed Services strive to de-individualize soldiers to encourage cohesion, hierarchy, teamwork, and efficacy. Nevertheless, veterans do not shed their gender, culture, race, socioeconomic status, or place of origin upon entry into the Armed Services and these identity markers reassert themselves, often dramatically, as veterans attempt to reintegrate into civilian life. Effective supportive and treatment services are necessary to address the individual needs of every veteran by recognizing their strengths and differences.

6

COMING HOME: EXAMINING THE HOMECOMING EXPERIENCES OF YOUNG VETERANS

Donna Caplin and Katharine Kranz Lewis

But the thing I had to give up, it's that I miss who I was.

STUDY PARTICIPANT WHO RESPONDED ABOUT THE "PROFOUND
PERSONAL SACRIFICE [HE] MADE" SERVING IN IRAQ

Social support is an integral factor in the ability of traumatized veterans to assimilate back into their communities (Bolton, Litz, Glenn, Orsillo, & Roemer, 2002; Friedman, 2004, 2005; Solomon & Mikulincer, 1990, p. 251). Creating environments that are supportive to returning veterans and their loved ones is essential to the success of reintegration postdeployment (Friedman, 2005, p. 1287; Solomon & Mikulincer, 1990, pp. 251–254). [The] "Homecoming reception is relevant to a soldiers' attempt to legitimize and validate his or her actions and sacrifices made during a mission" (Bolton et al., 2002, p. 241). Connecticut war veterans return from tours of duty in Iraq and Afghanistan often after extended and multiple deployments. The deployments themselves are marred with great severity of violence and chaos in the conflicts over extended and recurrent periods of time. When exiting their active duty status, enlisted military, career military, military reservists, and National Guardsmen and women may have diverse homecoming experiences, which can impact a veteran's access to important services for their mental, physical, and emotional well-being. These homecoming experiences are influenced by one's personal interactions in civilian contexts, as well as limited access to clinical programs that increase gaps in treatment (Department of Defense [DOD], 2007).

These treatment service gaps create missed opportunities for young veterans and their families to receive health education, veteran benefit information, and support services as they reintegrate into their community. Historically, veterans, particularly Vietnam veterans, suffering from war-related psychological sequelae were diagnosed with posttraumatic stress disorder (PTSD) (National Center for PTSD, 2009; Pearrow & Cosgrove, 2009, pp. 77–78). Vietnam veterans, specifically, were the subjects of many studies that looked at the comorbidities associated with PTSD, including long-term social maladjustment that continues for some survivors to this day. As with the Vietnam Era, gaps in treatment services during homecoming are a public health concern.

> War is a public health catastrophe because the aftermath of war extends beyond the individual survivor to the family and community. [The ramifications of war] may be felt through generations, and they pose public health needs often not readily discernible. The numerous behavioral problems associated with PTSD can have devastating effects on spouses, children, and other family members, further strengthening the need for preventive public health strategies.
>
> —*Foreman and Havas, 1990, p. 172*

The homecoming reception involves veterans' ability to address their diagnostic issues (e.g., PTSD; traumatic brain injury (TBI); loss of limb/s; etc.) while managing factors that further increase risk factors for feelings of loss and alienation. These risk factors include minority status, experiences before and after deployment, depression, anger, and lack of perceived social support (Wiblemo, 2005). PTSD, alone, is a more comprehensive diagnosis and its multiple dimensions can make the homecoming process for veterans a daunting experience, especially when existing with other factors such as substance abuse, cognitive and memory deficits, occupational instability, marital problems and divorces, family discord and violence, homelessness, and incarceration (Scully, 2005).

In a large study of several thousand predeployment (2530) and postdeployment (3671) active military personnel from Operation Iraqi Freedom/Operation Enduring Freedom (OIF/OEF), concerns about the stigma of a mental health disorder and other barriers to treatment were twice as high among those most in need of mental health services (Hoge et al., 2004, pp. 19–21). In another study of over 9000 subjects screened for mental health disorders, the authors concluded subthreshold PTSD (i.e., below the criteria for a PTSD diagnosis) was significantly associated with a higher risk for suicidal ideation (Marshall et al., 2001, p. 1471). Additionally, in a qualitative study of suspected risk factors for suicide among a sample of OIF/OEF veterans who sought mental health care, avoidance behavior or habituation to pain, perceiving self as a burden, and failure to establish a sense of belonging at home and in the community were common (Brenner et al., 2008).

THEORETICAL FRAMEWORK

The Conservation of Resources Theory (COR) (Hobfoll & Schumm, 2002) has valuable applications for studying combat veterans. COR theory looks at the environment as the context within which resource gains and losses and the resulting impact on individuals are experienced. In stressed individuals, especially individuals stressed by war trauma, this theory emphasizes that health promotion efforts should focus on improving environmental factors that facilitate resource gains, such as gains in family relations, gains in healthy relations with intimate partners, strong work roles, and other supportive social systems that facilitate healthy reintegration into society (Hobfall & Schumm, 2002).

As these themes suggest, traumatized veterans reintegrating into civilian society can exhibit behaviors that put them at risk of alienating those closest to them, possibly resulting in a loss or reduction of resources (Ray & Vanstone, 2009). Through the lens of COR Theory, war veterans with limited social connections will have a more difficult readjustment to civilian life, which may impact physical well-being, employment, and community involvement. These elements relate to veterans' social supports. "Social support ... is a buffer against psychological stressors" (Martin, Ghahramanlou-Holloway, Tucciarone, 2009, p. 105). It allows veterans and their families to perceive themselves as members of a, and to feel a sense of, community. Applying COR Theory, it is proposed that veteran-recommended programs and support services can offset resource losses including those losses emerging from war trauma and long separations, and assist veterans in recovering from war trauma, while facilitating social connections with their families and communities.

METHOD

This qualitative research study describes Connecticut veterans' adjustment to life postdeployment to Iraq (OIF) and Afghanistan (OEF), and their special challenges in maintaining relationships, as well as their knowledge about supportive services that ease transition to civilian life. The study gathers information on the life of returning combat veterans as they struggle to adapt to their roles of spouse, parent, child, employee, student, and community resident.

Target Population

The target population was OIF and OEF veterans at risk of developing PTSD and related mental health problems, who reside in the state of Connecticut. Connecticut is a small eastern coastline state with nearly 3.5 million people, and the state has many manufacturers who provide supplies and equipment to the Military, including aircraft engines, helicopters, and nuclear submarines (State of Connecticut, 2009). However, Connecticut is home to only one U.S. Military base, the Naval Submarine Base in New London (Military.com, 2009). Because of this situation, soldiers must train at other large military bases prior to deployment to Iraq and Afghanistan. Connecticut military troops can be sent to bases far from home both before and after OIF/OEF tours, increasing the frequency and length of separation from family and friends. Relational stresses for returning veterans compounded by traumatic war experiences and long separations can create special challenges in maintaining family relationships and reestablishing community connections. Fourteen participants agreed to contribute their reflections to the study.

The Study Questionnaire

Guided by Interpretive Phenomenological Analysis (IPA) as the framework for obtaining and interpreting qualitative research (Brocki & Weardon, 2006; Nel, 2006; Ray & Vanstone, 2009; Smith, Flowers, Osborn, 1997), this study was conducted using a 14-question, semistructured interview developed by the primary researcher (Table 6.1: Interview Questions)[1]. The questionnaire was intended to create

---

[1]Interview data was captured using both digital and analog recorders; researcher notes were used during and, occasionally, after the interview as a backup source of data to record important observations and comments both during the interview and outside of the recording. While some technical aspects of collecting the recorded data were problematic early in the study, the majority of the interviews were captured in their entirety. Three of the participants asked during the interview to have the recorder turned off for a period to discuss sensitive topics with the researcher, but allowed note-taking. Several of the study subjects voluntarily participated in discussions with the researcher following the interview if time allowed, and important dialogue was sometimes captured in notes by the researcher during or following the discussions. All but one of the participants completed the full interview, with the incomplete interview due to the participant's work responsibilities. Participants were told that the interviews would take about 1–2 hours, with the actual interview time ranging from approximately 45 minutes to as long as 2 hours. Coding the interview data, and choosing an experienced medical

TABLE 6.1 Interview questions (Caplin, 2008)

The qualitative interview included the following questions:

1. How have you adjusted to life in the United States since you returned from duty in Iraq or Afghanistan?
2. How have your family members adjusted to your homecoming and readjustment? Have these relationships changed since you last spent significant time together? If so, how have they changed?
3. How did you keep in contact with your family and friends while you were deployed?
4. If you have children (or are coparenting unrelated children): What are their ages? How has each of the children reacted to your homecoming and reintegration period? Is there anything that you think has helped the children adjust successfully to living with you again after such a separation? Have your children had any new issues such as sleep problems, academic changes, or difficulty getting along with siblings or friends? Any other issues?
5. Are there any particular persons or activities that have helped with your readjustment to civilian life?
6. Who, if anyone, do you confide in about your war experiences?
7. If you or a friend were having difficulty adjusting after returning home, where would you go for assistance?
8. Are you able to communicate regularly with the "buddies" from your combat unit? Do any of these "buddies" live close enough to see on a regular basis? How do you communicate with them? Are these contacts helpful to you as you return to civilian life?
9. Do you belong to any formal or informal groups related to your military experience?
10. What suggestions do you have for programs that might alleviate stress for OIF/OEF veterans returning to families and communities? What are your preferences for education regarding post-traumatic stress disorder, or other mental health topics? What other topics might interest you?
11. The Department of Defense does not currently share information about returning enlisted and career military making it difficult for outreach personnel to contact these persons for activities that might help in the readjustment period. What do you think is the best way to reach OIF/OEF veterans and their families so that programming can be aimed at their special needs? Would you want to be contacted about available outreach programs?

(Continued)

---

transcriptionist familiar with issues of confidentiality who agreed to discuss the project data only with the researchers protected confidentiality of the study subjects. The secondary researcher and the transcriptionist had no contact with the participants. At the conclusion of the interview session, all participants received a letter thanking them for their participation, which included written contact information for Connecticut veteran mental health resources, brochures about veteran PTSD, and other mental health disorders, and the researchers' contact information, along with a $25 grocery gift certificate for participating.

TABLE 6.1 *Continued*

The qualitative interview included the following questions:

12. Have you attended any programs for veterans since your return home? What programs? Where were the programs? Who was invited? Were the programs helpful to you or your family? Were the programs convenient for you?
13. Have you had any education about PTSD or other mental health disorders? If yes, how was it presented? Was the program helpful? Have you been screened for PTSD? If yes, where and when? What setting?
14. Is there anything else you would like to discuss about your experiences? Do you have any questions about the study or anything else?

Note. This study was completed as part of a graduate requirement. Donna Caplin graduated from the University of Hartford with a Master of Science in Nursing degree in May 2009. Ms. Caplin presented this research at the Force Health Protection Conference in Albuquerque, New Mexico, August 2009, and in April 2010 at a Connecticut Sigma Theta Tau Research Conference. Ms Caplin is presently adjunct faculty at the University of Connecticut School of Nursing. Dr. Kathryn Kranz Lewis is Assistant Professor at the University of Hartford with emphasis on public health, and is the Executive Director of the Connecticut Public Health Policy Institute. Dr. Lewis worked in the acute care setting at Bellevue Hospital and in the Department of Public Health, Bureau of School Health, in New York City. Before coming to the University of Hartford, she was a research associate with the Massachusetts Health Policy Forum in Waltham, MA. Ms. Caplin and coauthor Dr. Katherine Kranz-Lewis, and other nurse colleagues, presented a paper titled "Sharing Knowledge, Creating Alliances—Crossing Borders to Improve Public Health" at the American Public Health Conference in San Diego, CA, 2008.

dialog about the special challenges that OIF/OEF veterans face following deployment, and to discover coping strategies and support systems that promote successful transition and reintegration. The qualitative section of the interview questionnaire can be reviewed in Table 6.1.

Additionally written demographic and quantitative data were obtained from each subject, including but not limited to age, sex, and marital status; home of record; military branch; number of tours of duty in Iraq and/or Afghanistan; and length of OIF/OEF tour(s) in months as well as length of time (in months) at home following most recent OIF/OEF deployment and following previous deployments. Participants were instructed that they could stop the interview at any time, or choose to skip any questions for any reason at any time. The quantitative data were aggregated to study the complex issues of military separations from family, friends, and communities and possibly discover some insights about transitioning home that are unique to Connecticut.

No interview sessions were discontinued due to subject distress, although one 43-year-old career officer cried after the interview was completed, and stated:

> This was the first time I have talked to anyone about this ... I am on Nexium twice a day because I keep it inside ... I have an ulcer.

—Research sample

The study subjects were all Connecticut veterans of OIF/OEF, and comprised 13 men and one woman aged 22–58 years, at varying stages of civilian reintegration spanning from five months to nearly five years (i.e., 55 months). Ethnic/racial diversity was minimal, with one Hispanic subject among the predominately Caucasian sample. Veteran participants were from rural and small towns, large towns, and one from a large city. Military branches represented include the Army, Navy, Air Force, and Marines. Six of 14 veterans had multiple deployments in OIF/OEF, and two others had previous military deployments, one each to Bosnia and the Gulf War. Eight deployments were 12 months or longer (four at 12 months; two at 15 months; one at 14 months; one at 13 months), with 14 veterans reporting OIF/OEF exposure ranging from 3 to 27 months in total.

One veteran was concerned about sharing military information but reported that he had spent 3 months in Iraq and had several OIF deployments to Kuwait and two southern U.S. military bases. One subject has been medically retired, and one was refused later redeployment with his unit due to his injuries but remains in the Marine Reserves. Seven participants are still serving in Guard or Reserve capacities and could be eligible for future OIF/OEF tours, including one full-time career soldier.

With regard to their physical or mental health, some of the participants volunteered information not included in the questionnaire. Three of the participants reported combat-related TBI, with two of those three reporting persistent severe headaches. Three of the participants (including one with TBI) stated that they had PTSD, with two of the three receiving treatment for their diagnosis. In addition, other mental health issues reported by participants included alcohol abuse among six participants during and after the early months following homecoming and two participants reporting emotional numbness. Five veterans reported flashbacks that caused them to react as if still deployed, three experienced road rage, and five had angry outbursts, and two experienced homicidal thoughts. One participant reported several episodes of intimate partner violence and other violent acts that resulted in at least two arrests.

Veterans are employed in law enforcement (e.g. state and local police), direct care in a halfway house for ex-convicts, health care in hospitals, mental health programs (e.g. Vet Center, Connecticut Military Support Program), career military (full time, Connecticut National Guard, Reserves), financial services, and retail sales. Five veterans are attending college and three named nursing, radiology, and criminal justice as their majors. The youngest veteran interviewed is seeking work in a local police department two months after separating from the Military.

FINDINGS AND ANALYSIS

Homecoming experiences of veterans can have some influence on veterans' ability to transition and reintegrate into civilian contexts. The following results[2] describe the homecoming experiences in relation to military friendships; personal relationships with civilians; VA issues; housing and employment issues; community involvement; and mental health screening and education.

Military Friendships

Participants offered that they are most comfortable talking to other veterans about their war experiences, and most were able to identify one or more close military "buddies." The relationships with these "buddies" were described as being very important, with the most common reason that "buddies" understand what each other have been through. One young veteran discussed being with his Army Reserves unit after returning home:

> You get there and you tell your war stories and vent. I guess it's sort of like counseling. You can't talk to civilians about that sort of stuff because they don't understand . . .

[2]Response bias in the interview data is a concern, as this study relies on the ability of the participants to give honest insight into the issues surrounding reintegration. It is possible that some participants may have held back important information due to expressed concern about privacy. Several of the veterans expressed that they met with the researcher only because the contact person was familiar and trustworthy. Participants' fears of being perceived as weak and concerns about combat operations security and military-related reputations may have also impacted these data. The study was conducted in an academic setting, independent of the military or Veterans' Administration, to mitigate the impact of researcher bias and promote participant comfort in telling their personal stories.

A trauma nurse and military officer described her Iraq experience as *"landing on the moon."* She spoke of two military nurse mentors who guided her through her transition after coming home from a combat hospital in Iraq. She spoke of them visiting, taking her to a quiet restaurant, and reported that they took her out the day before she returned to work as a civilian. She reports that these two nurses, along with a supportive daughter, and several work colleagues, have been an integral part of her successful transition home.

Participants who identified themselves as officers expressed more reluctance to talk about upsetting war memories due to their supervisor status, their feeling of responsibility for their subordinates (i.e., *"I'm the rock"*), and the inability to talk to superior officers for fear of losing promotional opportunities. One officer, who was immersed in Iraqi culture while training Iraqi soldiers, spoke of a colleague who had a similar position:

I felt the only person I could talk to was him.

Four participants expressed a desire to go back to serve with their unit and talked about missing the camaraderie, the "black and white" nature of military missions versus the many "gray areas" that cause stress at home (e.g., child care choices; money management; employment changes). In addition, participants also mentioned missing "being in shape," and sometimes feeling an obligation to help combat-related friends who are still in the war theater. A Gulf War veteran who also served a total of 27 months across two tours in Iraq explained that he volunteered for repeat tours because his "buddies depended on him," and he wanted to "finish the job" started in the Gulf War.

Several of the studied veterans described military friends as best friends, and in many cases relayed that this "buddy" or "buddies" were the only people with whom they could share their war stories and have that narrative appreciated, understood, and valued. Even though many "buddies" are scattered out of state and even overseas, including Massachusetts, Rhode Island, New York, Pennsylvania, Kansas, California, Hawaii, and Iraq, participants use phone and electronic resources to keep in touch with these important contacts. Veterans who reported that they were actively engaged with their Guard or Reserve units seemed to enjoy the regular contact and some admitted benefiting from the frequent socialization.

Access and attachment to a group of "buddies" have much to do with group identification and attachment. Group identification requires an internalization of the norms and values of the ethnic, social, or cultural group (in the case of the veteran, a "patriotic vocational group" and even heritage rooted in the U.S. Constitution and American cultural identity), as well as an emotional attachment to the group with a sense of individual sacrifice (Brook, Balka, Brook, Win, Gursen, 1998; Brook, Whiteman, Balka, Win, Gursen, 1998; Phinney, Cantu, & Kurtz, 1997). As veterans form their military group identity early in their career or deployment, they attempt to balance group identification needs with a personal desire for a positive relationship with the larger society (Phinney et al., 1997). When this balance in group identification is not achieved, even veterans may experience feelings of alienation, anxiety, depression, or loss of identity.

Personal Relationships

Participants who served early in the OIF/OEF wars had limited communication with friends and family during deployment. Those in later tours described an improved ability to use e-mail and phones to regularly communicate with these important contacts. Parents spoke of helping children with homework while away, even in combat zones. Many felt the increased connection, even electronic, helped them stay closer to family and friends, and eased their transition home. Participants identified common stressors in the period immediately following homecoming; including spouse role reversals, parental hovering, and the feeling that home life had become exclusive and went on without them, becoming reacquainted with their now older children, and financial issues and loss of economic power in home decision-making. Many felt lonely without their military buddies, and lost without the routine of military life. Some had grown apart or become disconnected from friends and family members, and felt isolated among previous civilian coworkers and other civilians who were perceived to care little about the wars or the sacrifices made by veterans and their families.

Further, long separations from family and friends to attend to their recurring and extended OIF/OEF tours were the norm for some participants. One veteran, now divorced, explained that due to the long separations, he only knew his young wife when they were on vacation. The lack of large combat training facilities in Connecticut resulted in deployments to many other military bases pre- and post-OIF/OEF tours where families could not reasonably visit on a regular basis. Additionally, 10 of 14 were sent far away from Connecticut to military bases in North Carolina, Georgia, Florida, Wisconsin, Texas, California, and Hawaii. Two veterans identified their female spouses as having a particularly difficult time adjusting to the long separations.

A newly married female spouse (no children) was angry and alone after suddenly moving to Connecticut from Massachusetts just prior to her spouse leaving for a second Iraq deployment. Another female spouse with two children also struggled with loneliness and anger about her husbands' frequent deployments. The veteran of this spouse recalled that family support sessions were available to his family, but they were in a southern state. Due to demands of work and family, these programs were too far away to be of assistance. One subject summed up the difficulty for returning OIF/OEF veterans in the following statement:

> At first everybody says welcome back, it's a big party. And then all of a sudden the umbilical cord is cut and you're on your own and you have to stand on your own two feet. A lot of guys drink. I know a lot of divorces because of the booze. Financial issues, because you get behind on bills. Stress is put on the marriage. And let's face it, these guys are gone and the spouse is left with the kids, the bills are piling up, never mind taking care of the house. These guys come back and it's all falling apart. Never mind the deal with Iraq, they are losing their jobs full time because employers can't keep supporting them, and let them go and their home lives are falling apart. So where are you supposed to go?

Seven participants were married at the time of the study, and three veteran participants reported divorcing spouses: two immediately following their tours in Iraq; and one during his tour of duty. These divorces were reported as causative factors in housing insecurity for these three veterans, with one living in a hotel for a short time after returning home, and another returning to Connecticut to live with his parents (which he described as a "step back"). The other veteran impacted by divorce moved in with a new girlfriend and their blended families. Another participant stated that he and his fiancée separated soon after he returned from Iraq, but they married following a long period of separation.

One particular veteran, who reported PTSD, came home to a young wife who had been unfaithful during his deployment. The subsequent divorce created a serious family rift due to his parents' religious views against divorce. Rejection by his ex-military father was especially difficult and prompted a violent emotional reaction:

> I just wanted to destroy him, knock him out. I don't know if I would have been able to stop if I had ... that was the turning point for my family because they realized ... that the divorce wasn't because of

me ... I think I was manifesting the pain and anger and that was the first time I realized that, OK, I am not right upstairs.

Connecticut appears to lack the family support programs available near large military training facilities, as well as the surrounding community:

> ... It is very difficult as a reservist, being pulled out of a place you know, with no support in the immediate vicinity. I know my wife and kids felt alone without any help. ... Living up north, there's not a lot of military compared to down south. Down south it's almost every other person is in the military. Up north, when I go to drill in my uniform, people stare at me ...

One veteran, who reported 80–100 firefights over a 12-month period, recalled several dangerous episodes of physical abuse that he attributed to the effects of PTSD and TBI. These episodes included waking in the act of choking his wife, setting fire outside a bathroom where his wife had barricaded herself during one of his violent episodes, and choking a store clerk for talking on a cell phone while he waited for service.

This veteran stated that he has severed many key family relationships after experiencing rejection (father and other family members) and has had several arrests for violent episodes and reckless driving. He is presently receiving mental health services and medical treatment for serious combat injuries (including PTSD and TBI) that occurred when Iraqi insurgents targeted him for assassination. His ability to relate to the researcher was impaired as he was continually scanning the interview location with his eyes during the session, and reported that the researcher's hand gestures made him very anxious. Although he is attending school, he expressed dissatisfaction with his work in the financial sector and reports his overall health as poor. He and his wife do not plan on having children because of his violent behavior. In addition, he and his wife were evicted from his home due to the above-mentioned arson.

Military/VA Issues

A common theme that emerged from the study was distrust of the military and the VA system. Two participants learned about extended tours from sources outside the military establishment. One was sent to Iraq involuntarily near the end of his enlistment (after already serving a tour in Afghanistan) and then had this tour extended, saying:

> ... I found out it was extended, I found out through my wife who was back in New Hampshire. How could she know before I did?

Another veteran, a marine sniper who served in Iraq, had negative stories about health care in the VA system:

> ... I lost some hearing in Iraq during a fire fight and I had a long battle with trying to get at least a disability for it. They wouldn't approve it. They denied me. They said it was because I was a cop that I lost the hearing, because of shooting without ear protection and stuff. And I wasn't even a cop when I put in the claim.

He further stated:

> [t]here are records that are lost of my prior military and stuff. And they tell me I have to find it. That's impossible. You really cannot find your own records ... Every time I go get a shot; I have to get all the shots all over again. I started getting irritated.

The veterans described significant disparities in type and amount of mental health services offered after deployment within various branches of the service. One reservist who sought treatment for PTSD was denied disability benefits. He has chosen not to pursue this issue due to concern that he would be denied a future bid for employment with a federal law enforcement agency. A Marine veteran with TBI, PTSD, and other physical injuries was expected to self-refer for follow-up care after discharge from Quantico, even though he did not have the mental acuity to assess his own needs and follow up with his own care. In contrast, the youngest veteran in the study who reported he had seen little or no action during his 13-month deployment to Iraq, had a mandatory, one-on-one mental health screening session with a Navy psychologist upon his return. A young Army infantry veteran reported that he was screened in a room with *"500 people."* Veteran participants working in state and local police departments reported access to free police department-based counseling services, and have a psychological evaluation as part of preemployment screening for the police department.

Five participants, who described themselves as officers, discussed their reluctance to access military or VA resources if they had need of mental health services due to concerns about privacy and career advancement. However, four of these officers did express willingness to refer subordinates to military/VA care. But veterans' willingness to access or accept important mental health services may also be limited by mistrust, stigma, and fear of confidentiality breach. One officer reported that a subordinate combat veteran was discharged for substance abuse and mental health issues after refusing treatment, and within one week he had reportedly died.

Housing and Employment

Housing and employment were significant stressors for this group of veterans. Six of the participants had housing concerns or crises due to failed relationships; family rejection; violent episodes which caused one eviction; and in two cases, low income.

According to the National Coalition for Homeless Veterans (NCHV, 2009):

> OIF/OEF veterans are entitled to return to their pre-deployment jobs and pay scale under Uniformed Services Employment and Reemployment Rights Act (USERRA, 2009) protection after their discharge, but increasingly many jobs are disappearing because of layoffs and business failures [along with the economic climate]. Veterans who cannot find other employment quickly are in imminent danger of becoming dependent on shared living arrangements or becoming homeless.

For one of the youngest participants who entered the Army immediately after high school, his deployments (6 months in Afghanistan and 15 months in Iraq) kept him away from home for almost 4 years. Having married between these tours, he and his wife moved to his wife's home in New Hampshire after discharge, where he received an offer to work at the Naval Shipyard. Because his marriage dissolved he returned home to his parents which he described as "a step back." He talked about having "nothing in common" with most of his old friends, which provided limited opportunities for shared housing. In less than a year since his return to the east coast, he had lived in three residences and is living with an older sister.

Nine of the 14 participants are gainfully employed in civilian occupations that have allowed them to assimilate their military skills into the civilian setting. For this group, these particular skills ease transition back and forth between military and civilian life and enhance employment opportunities. Three veterans in the study who are police officers talked about the transferability of combat skills to police work, the support of other war veterans in the workplace, and their positive feelings of acceptance in the police community and organizations. This may explain why five participants are employed in or pursuing careers in law enforcement.

The health care system is another area where the participants are finding or continuing civilian employment. A trauma nurse is continuing her work after a nine-month tour in Iraq. She reports that her hospital colleagues have been very supportive, and she is using the nursing and leadership skills she acquired from the military as a civilian employee. One veteran is pursuing a career in radiology, and another in nursing. A fourth veteran who was in a leadership position in a combat hospital is currently a surgical technician.

Community Involvement

Most participants reported that they are not interested in the Veterans of Foreign Wars (VFW) and other related organizations because the majority of veteran members served in the Vietnam War. However, two stated they are members of the VFW. Two veterans reported that a new organization, the Iraq and Afghanistan Veterans of America (IAVA) makes it easier for OIF/OEF veterans to form support networks, possibly because of their youthfulness. A Marine veteran reported that the Marines have a large network, and web sites for communicating with each other, including IAVA.

> Guys don't want to go to the VFW, American Legion, DAV because it's not our generation.

Several veterans attending college expressed difficulty "fitting in" with college peers. Among the six participants attending college, two offered that they do not wear any identifying military items on campus that would make them vulnerable to antiwar comments or probing questions about their combat experiences. In other words, they hide their veteran status and military identity.

> I have no identification anywhere on me, that I was a soldier... Because it's the same way when everybody asks you, "oh you were in Iraq?" You have to tell them, "yea I was." [They'll say] "Well how was it?" And then they automatically cut you off and they tell you their ending. So, after falling into that trap a few times, and

realizing that nobody has a good opinion [of my experiences in Iraq], everybody who is 17, 18, never worked a day in their life, they seem to have everything squared away. .... [Just] don't wear anything to shows you were a soldier.

Hiding one's identity as a veteran is a reality for the veterans in this study. Veterans felt scattered across Connecticut and other states from the "brethren" in their units; socially separated from civilians in their communities and on college campuses; and upset by antiwar sentiments expressed by family members, friends, college peers and throughout the media. Veterans felt they came home "alone" and without "fanfare" or recognition by their communities. After the connectedness of military life, there was little face-to-face social networking among most of the participants, their families and with local veteran organizations, creating gaps in social support.

Mental Health Screening and Education

Mental health screening and mental health services are available to veterans immediately following their military assignments and throughout their veteran status (Center for Public Policy & Social Research, 2008; DOD, 2008). However, many of the study participants reported conditions that inhibited their reporting of mental health symptoms following the end of deployments. Veterans in this study experienced a lack of privacy during mental health screening postdeployment, with most screenings occurring in large groups. One participant even reported that they were told to "*raise their hand*" before the large group if they had mental health issues.

Further, veterans in this study expressed a lack of interest in the screening process as many reported that they "just wanted to go home to their families." Some also admitted that they did not report mental health symptoms for fear of having their homecoming delayed. In addition, screenings in groups of mixed-rank personnel left veterans fearful of disclosure that could significantly affect career opportunities when higher-ranking officer(s) were in the large screening group, and were also concerned about showing weakness, especially among career officers.

Even more significant for these veterans was concern about being discharged from the military or passed over for promotion after being diagnosed with a mental health issue. A few participants were rejected by family members and military peers after being diagnosed with a mental disorder. Social and vocational peer rejection was devastating to some of these study participants. This may explain why some participants reported they would more likely seek treatment for mental health issues outside the VA system.

Most of the participants found the large group debriefing sessions immediately after return from OIF/OEF not helpful, and resented the delay in seeing their families. Some reported that they just filled in the boxes on the health survey without admitting to any problems. If this behavior is as prevalent among returning soldiers as it was in this research study, then mental health survey results obtained immediately postdeployment may be very misleading.

According to the Center for Public Policy & Social Research (2008) analyses, many veterans needing mental health services tend to look beyond the VA because they either have employer-sponsored health insurance, or they see the VA hospitals/clinics as extensions of the military bureaucracy they perceive as untrustworthy. Some veterans also have concerns about the stigma associated with the diagnostic label of mental illness and how it may affect their benefits.

> If I did have some issues, I really wouldn't want to go through the unit. I felt better even going to the [local] Vet Center ... That's like personal business. You don't want anybody knowing about it.

Another significant barrier to VA care mentioned by some participants was the lack of flexibility in VA clinic and pharmacy hours, which open from 8 a.m. to 4 p.m. Considering the competing demands of family, work, and school that participants juggle in their lives after such long absences, the clinic and pharmacy hours seemed unrealistic and too rigid. These issues, combined with the work of Dr. Charles Hoge and colleagues about the reluctance of veterans with mental health symptoms to seek care, illustrate the difficulties faced by researchers to accurately measure the impact of PTSD in OIF/OEF veterans and provide appropriate services after homecoming (Hoge, Castro, Messer, McGurk, Cotting, Koffman, 2004; Milliken, Auchterlonie, Hoge, 2007).

Some of the participants' suggestions for programming and education to assist veterans with transition and reintegration into civilian communities are:

1. Pre- and postdeployment family counseling in the same setting, so that the veteran and their family can sustain an established bond with practitioners.
2. Mandatory sessions with a mental health worker post-deployment.

3. Rank-specific group screening/debriefing sessions to ensure outreach efficacy to the population of veterans.
4. Reducing stigma surrounding PTSD and mental illness by allowing the veteran to go home to their families prior to debriefing and health screenings, and providing group therapy with only 4–5 OIF/OEF veterans.

Several participants also suggested mentoring by military peers and PTSD education before and after deployment to decrease the likelihood of significant crises during the returning veterans' transition and reintegration.

DISCUSSION

Social isolation and disconnection occurring when partners, family members, friends, coworkers, and academic peers reject the returning veteran, or when the veteran perceives a lack of support or understanding in these important relationships is the predominant theme emerging from the study. The demise or deterioration of these relationships and connections is a significant source of stress for the participants. For several participants, this deterioration negatively affected their ability to positively reintegrate into civilian life and find a place in their community. This is illustrated in the responses of participants, such as:

> For a long time I felt like I didn't belong in Iraq, I didn't belong in the United States, I didn't belong to my family, I didn't belong where I worked.
>
> ... We kind of were separating even before I got home. That was a hard spot.
>
> There are a couple of family members who had very strong anti-war, and also probably their own anxiety. They didn't really acknowledge my return. Just kind of, "Oh, you're back".
>
> —*Rejection, Isolation & Disconnection*

Difficulties in reestablishing relationships and subsequent divorce are at the top of loss issues emerging for veterans within this study. Three of the 14 participants dealt with divorce surrounding their deployment, with many of the other participants struggling to reestablish relationships with spouses, intimate partners, children, family, and friends. While divorce rates have not spiked for military personnel since 2001 (Karney & Crown, 2007), there remains a strong perception that marital ties are more likely to be dissolved postdeployment. In this study, relationship demise was more prevalent among young participants, but not among older participants with more established relationships.

The isolation preceded by, and concurrent with, rejection makes sustaining relationships with "buddies" and reestablishing relationships with families problematic. Connecticut veterans, in this study, were sometimes far away from their closest friends or "military buddies," who they reported to be an essential source of support during transition from soldier to civilian postdeployment. Further, participants were emotionally traumatized as they watched the demise of relationships and rejection by intimate partners, family, and close friends, for which they were not prepared. Finally, inconsistent, inadequate, or inaccurate postdeployment screening for PTSD and other mental health disorders, often due to respondents not reporting symptoms, appeared to impact and affect the participant's ability to reestablish relationships during homecoming.

Thus, long separations with minimal breaks before and after OIF/ OEF deployments and multiple extended tours in war zones created significant challenges for veterans to overcome. These challenges include readjusting to managing household duties, parenting now older children and missing developmental milestones, and being able to reconnect intimately with spouses, parents, or close civilian friends. Social isolation is severe enough to impact some veterans' daily life.

The recurrent themes of rejection, social isolation, and social disconnections among participants through their homecoming experiences, are supported by research highlighting the difficulties that traumatized military veterans can have when trying to reconnect with their families, friends, and communities (Center for Public Policy and Social Research, 2008; Rand Center for Military Policy and Health Research, 2008, p. 30). In particular, PTSD-related rejection by key family figures and friends is also sobering. It is clear from the narratives that families need to be supportive and educated about the readjustment phase after combat deployment, and learn strategies to cope as caregivers when veterans return home and exhibit mental health symptoms.

This study revealed challenges and opportunities in networking, education about PTSD and mental health disorders postdeployment, mental health services and veteran benefits, and family education and support services that can ease the stress for military families. Distrust of the military and VA system, fear of stigma, fear of being perceived as weak, and fear about the loss of promotional opportunities represent barriers to mental health care among this studied group.

Since several of the participants admitted that they would be unlikely to use Military/VA resources for mental health concerns, it is unknown how many veterans may turn to familiar primary care settings or how many private primary care providers have received relevant training about veteran mental health issues (DOD, 2007, p. 28). This presents an opportunity for Military agencies to educate community providers about identifying at-risk veterans and providing them with appropriate resources. Community organizations already committed to the welfare of area residents can be a valuable resource for veterans returning home. Communities have valuable resources to prevent and address problems associated with PTSD in war veterans, including broken families, substance abuse, joblessness, and homelessness. Housing insecurity, for example, affected participants stressed by divorce, rejection, and low income. One veteran with violent outbursts was evicted from his apartment. Having access to temporary housing in a familiar setting until they are able to secure employment and permanent housing is an essential protective element for veterans returning home.

These outcomes mirror the findings of the Connecticut Veterans Needs Assessment (2008) that concluded having private health insurance, distrust of the Military, concerns about confidentiality and stigma surrounding mental health diagnoses cause many veterans to seek mental health care outside the VA (Center for Public Policy and Social Research, 2008). Lack of knowledge about Connecticut VA centers and the state-funded Military Support Program (MSP, 2009) may also prevent veterans from seeking assistance with mental health issues in settings that might be more comfortable for them.

We propose that using community resources to reduce the impact of a disease by identifying the population at risk, providing education, outreach programs, and early intervention is essential to optimal well-being of combat veterans. Predeployment programs that familiarize veterans and families with veteran providers prior to service might improve utilization of mental health services, and prevent some of the adjustment stresses and disconnections among veterans and their loved ones during and beyond the veterans' return home.

Many new resources are now available to returning OIF/OEF veterans online. One training program for transitioning veterans called BATTLEMIND (Walter Reed Army Institute of Research (WRAIR), 2009) has been adopted by the Military to help soldiers, families, and providers deal with mental health issues surrounding military deployments. Also, information about PTSD is prevalent on military websites, and organizations affiliated with military service, including several new sites for veterans of Iraq and Afghanistan. There has been as explosion of mental health educational resources for these veterans on the Internet. Prior to this research conducted in 2008–2009, these types of resources were fewer and far less organized and yielded no resources that could be used by minors of families impacted by OIF/OEF deployments. In fact, veteran children and teens are now the focus of some mental health educational resources on the Internet.

CONCLUSION

The need to explore life after combat for these veterans is essential to understanding their struggles and successes. Overcoming reluctance to self-identify as OIF/OEF veterans in the community may require novel means to communicate with this growing population of OIF/ OEF veterans. This may necessitate utilizing resources like Facebook, Twitter, cell phone text messaging, and other electronic networks. Further, as many veterans take advantage of college opportunities under the GI Bill, campuses might institute support networks to welcome these transitioning civilians. Connecticut's state colleges are working to establish veteran "Oasis Centers" to provide separate spaces for veterans to network and study, as well as receive support to integrate into the traditional learning settings.

Replicating this research study in other states may reveal regional differences in the support services and networks available to OIF/ OEF veterans as they return from deployment. Including military personnel and families in program planning is an important element in developing effective PTSD prevention strategies. It is hoped that this study will inform and help communities plan and develop programs that assist OIF/OEF veterans and their loved ones cope with the transition to civilian life after deployment. We expect a better understanding of the phenomena that put this population at risk for mental health disorders, maladjustment, and the associated social implications.

REFERENCES

Bolton, E., Litz, B., Glenn, M., Orsillo, S., & Roemer, L. (2002). The impact of homecoming reception on the adaptation of peacekeepers following deployment. *Military Psychology, 14*(3), 247–248.

Brenner, L., Gutierrez, P., Cornette, M., Betthauser, L., Bahraini, N., & Staves, P. (2008). A qualitative study of potential suicide risk factors in returning combat veterans. *Journal of Mental Health Counseling, 30*(3), 216–223.

Brocki, J., & Weardon, A. (2006). A critical evaluation of the use of interpretive phenomenological analysis (IPA) in health psychology. *Psychology and Health, 21*(1), 87–108.

Brook, J. S., Balka, E. B., Brook, D. W., Win, P. T., & Gursen, M. D. (1998). Drug use among African Americans: Ethnic identity as a protective factor. *Psychological Reports, 83*, 1427–1446.

Brook, J. S., Whiteman, M., Balka, E. B., Win, P. T., & Gursen, M. D. (1998). Drug use among Puerto Ricans: Ethnic identity as a protective factor. *Hispanic Journal of Behavioral Science, 20*(2), 241–254.

Center for Public Policy and Social Research. (2008). *Connecticut Veterans Needs Assessment: The OEF/OIF project final report, October 1, 2008.* Central Connecticut State University, M. B. Goldstein, & J. Malley, Principal Investigators. Retrieved from the Connecticut Department of Veterans' Affairs (CTVA) website November 17, 2009, http://www.ct.gov/ctva/cwp/view.asp?a=3780&q=432910

Connecticut Military Support Program. (2009). *About the Connecticut Military Support Program (MSP): Support for our troops and their families.* Retrieved from the official state of Connecticut website (CT.gov) December 4, 2009, http://www.ct.gov/msp/cwp/view.asp?a=2926&Q=335690&mspNav=

Department of Defense Task Force on Mental Health (DOD). (2007). *An achievable vision.* Report from the Defense Health Board Task Force on Mental Health, Falls Church, VA.

Foreman, S., & Havas, S. (1990). Massachusetts post-traumatic stress disorder program: A public health treatment model for Vietnam veterans. *Public Health Report, 105*(2), 172–179.

Friedman, M. (2004). Acknowledging the psychiatric cost of war. *New England Journal of Medicine, 351*(1), 75–77.

Friedman, M. (2005). Veterans' mental health in the wake of war. *New England Journal of Medicine, 352*(13), 1287–1290.

Hobfall, S., & Schumm, J. (2002). Conservation of resources theory: Application to public health promotion. In R. DiClemente, R. Crosby, & M. Kegler (Eds.), *Emerging theories in health promotion practice and research* (pp. 285–312). San Francisco, CA: John Wiley and Sons, Inc.

Hoge, C., Castro, C., Messer, S., McGurk, D., Cotting, D., & Koffman, R. (2004). Combat duty in Iraq and Afghanistan, mental health problems, and barriers to care. *The New England Journal of Medicine, 351*(1), 13–22.

Karney, B. R., & Crown, J. S. (2007). *Families under stress: An assessment of data, theory, and research on marriage and divorce in the military.* Rand National Defense Research Institute, RAND Corporation.

Marshall, R., Olfson, M., Hellman, F., Blanco, C., Guardino, M., & Struening, E. (2001). Comorbidity, impairment, and suicidality in subthreshold PTSD. *American Journal of Psychiatry, 158*, 1467–1473.

Martin, J., Ghahramanlou-Holloway, M., Lou, K., & Tucciarone, P. (2009). A comparative review of U.S. military and civilian suicide behavior: Implications for OIF/OEF suicide prevention efforts. *Journal of Mental Health Counseling, 31*(2), 101–118.

Milliken, C., Auchterlonie, J., & Hoge, C. (2007). Longitudinal assessment of mental health problems among active and reserve component soldiers returning from the Iraq War. *Journal of the American Medical Association, 298*(18), 2146–2147.

Military.com. (2009). *Installation guide.* Retrieved November 17, 2009, from http://benefits.military.com/misc/installations/Browse_Location.jsp

National Coalition for Homeless Veterans. (2009). *Veteran Homelessness Prevention Program.* Retrieved November 17, 2009, from http://www.nchv.org/news_article.cfm?id=515

National Center for PTSD. (2009). *Findings from the National Vietnam Veterans' Readjustment Study.* (Price, J.) Retrieved November 16, 2009, from http://www.ptsd.va.gov/professional/pages/vietnam-vets-study.asp

Nel, P. (2006). Trainee perspectives on their family therapy training. *Journal of Family Therapy, 28,* 307–328.

Pearrow, M., & Cosgrove, L. (2009). The aftermath of combat-related PTSD: Toward an understanding of transgenerational trauma. *Communication Disorders Quarterly, 30*(2), 77–82.

Phinney, J. S., Cantu, C. L., & Kurtz, D. A. (1997). Ethnic and American identity as predictors of self-esteem among African American, Latino, and White adolescents. *Journal of Youth and Adolescence, 26*(2), 165–185.

Rand Center for Military Policy and Health Research. (2008). *Invisible Wounds of War: Summary of recommendations for addressing psychological and cognitive injuries.* Rand Corporation, 2008. ISBN#978-0-8330-4453-2. Retrieved November 15, 2009, from http://www.rand.org/pubs/monographs/ 2008/ RAND_MG720.1.pdf

Ray, S., & Vanstone, M. (2009). The impact of PTSD on veterans' family relationships: An interpretive phenomenological inquiry. *International Journal of Nursing Studies, 46,* 838–847.

Scully, J. (2005). *Statement of the American Psychiatric Association on posttraumatic stress disorder (PTSD) to the House Committee on Veterans' Affairs, July 26, 2005.* Retrieved from EBSCO Host database, military and government collection, November 16, 2007, and updated link November 15, 2009, http:// veterans.house.gov/hearings/schedule109/jul05/7-27-05f/apa.html

Smith, J. A., Flowers, P., & Osborn, M. (1997). Interpretive phenomenological analysis and the psychology of health and illness. In L.Yardley (Ed.), *Material discourses in health and illness* (pp. 68–91, chap. 4). New York: Routledge.

Solomon, Z., & Mikulincer, M. (1990). Life events and combat-related posttraumatic stress disorder: The intervening role of locus of control and social support. *Military Psychology, 2*(4), 251–254.

State of Connecticut. (2009). *About Connecticut.* Retrieved November 17, 2009, from http://www.ct.gov/ctportal/cwp/view.asp?a=843&q=246434#DES

Uniformed Services Employment and Reemployment Rights Act of 1994. (2009). *USERRA Fact Sheet*. Retrieved November 17, 2009, from http://www.esgr.org/userrathelaw.asp

Walter Reed Army Institute of Research. (2009). *Battlemind: Armor for your mind*. Developed by the Land Combat Study Team (POC: Castro, C.). Retrieved December 8, 2009, from https://www.battlemind.army.mil/index.html. [Brochure *Battlemind Training I* with contact information retrieved December 8, 2009, from http://www.ptsd.ne.gov/pdfs/WRAIR-battlemind-training-Brochure.pdf].

Wiblemo, C., Deputy Director Veterans' Affairs, Rehabilitation Division. (2005). *Post-traumatic stress disorder and traumatic brain injury*. Congressional testimony on House Veterans Affairs, Subcommittee on Health. Retrieved from the EBSCO Host database, military and government collection, November 11, 2007.

7

Beyond Words: Homeless Veterans Who Served in Iraq and Afghanistan

Wesley Kasprow and Robert Rosenheck

The oldest and strongest traditions of veterans care are based on the conviction that no civilized nation will turn its back on the poor, sick and homeless former soldiers who once relinquished civilian freedoms to serve their country.

—Progress report on the Veterans Administration Program for Homeless Chronically Mentally Ill Veterans, October 22, 1987

By June 2009, over 1 million veterans had served in the conflicts in Operation Iraqi Freedom in Iraq (OIF), and Operation Enduring Freedom in Afghanistan (OEF). About 40% had enrolled to receive health care services from the Department of Veterans Affairs (VA), a level of enrollment that is appreciably higher than seen in other eras (Seal et al., 2009). Several recent studies have documented the high prevalence of psychological problems of these returning veterans (e.g., Burnam, Meredith, Tanilian, & Jaycox, 2009) with one study showing that 37% of OEF/OIF veterans using VA health care between 2002 and 2008 received a mental health diagnosis (Seal et al., 2009).

Considerably less information has been available about homelessness among veterans returning from OEF and OIF, although concern about increasing numbers of homeless veterans is widespread in the media and some advocates anticipate a "tsunami" of homelessness as veterans return from the Middle East (Eckholm, 2007).

Since 1987, the VA has developed an integrated network of services and programs designed to address the treatment, rehabilitation, and residential needs of homeless veterans. A key component of these services is community-based outreach. Typically, clients of VA homeless services programs are on average 50 years old and have been separated from the military for over a decade on average prior to their first episode of homelessness (Kasprow, Rosenheck, DiLella, Cavallaro, & Harelik, 2009; Mares & Rosenheck, 2004). One might not expect a high level of homelessness or use of VA homeless services by veterans returning from OEF and OIF. However, historic precedents may not apply to the newest generation of war zone veterans, who are the first group of veterans of the All Volunteer Force (AVF) to face extended war zone service. VA homeless programs have been monitoring the number of homeless program clients who report service in OEF/OIF since the fiscal year of 2005. While constituting a small portion of the veterans seen in the program, the number has been increasing steadily.

The purposes of the present study are: (1) to estimate the proportion of OEF/OIF veterans who have presented to the VA homeless programs homeless and compare it to with the proportion of OEF/OIF veterans in the general population to evaluate whether OEF/OIF veterans are accessing homeless services at expected or greater than expected rates; and, (2) characterize OEF/OIF veterans contacted by VA homeless outreach programs in comparison with veterans of other service eras in the general population.

METHODS

The following describes the methods used to estimate the proportion of OEF/OIF veterans accessing homeless services and characterize those veterans contacted by outreach programs.

Proportion of OEF/OIF Veterans in the National Veteran Population

OEF/OIF veterans (numerator) included individuals who had separated from military service in OEF or OIF between October 1, 2001 and May 1, 2007. Total counts within age categories were obtained from VA administrative data (VISN Support Service Center, 2007). An estimate of the number of U.S. veterans from all service eras (denominator) by age category was obtained from a VA database called "VetPop 2007" (National Center for Veterans Analysis and Statistics, 2007). This estimate was based on 2000 U.S. census data, projected for 2006.

Proportion of OEF/OIF Veterans Among VA Homeless Program Clients

Since 1987, VA's Health Care for Homeless Veterans (HCHV) program has provided community outreach, assessment and referral services, and time-limited residential treatment to homeless veterans across the nation. The sample of homeless veterans included all HCHV program clients for whom an intake assessment interview was conducted between October 1, 2004 and June 30, 2007. If a client had more than one interview during that time, the most recent interview was used.

A homeless veteran was identified as serving in OEF/OIF if: (1) he or she reported service in the theater of operations for the wars in Afghanistan or Iraq during the VA homeless program intake interview and (2) the veteran's Social Security Number was matched in the OEF/OIF Roster database identifying veterans who had separated from military service in OEF or OIF between October 1, 2001 and December 31, 2006 and were enrolled for VHA health care (VA National Data Systems, 2007).

VA Homeless Program Intake Interview

Intake interviews with homeless veterans entering the HCHV program were conducted by trained program clinicians (predominantly social workers and nurses) during outreach visits in community locations (e.g., shelters, soup kitchens) or following a referral to a VA medical center. Specific measures were taken to insure privacy and confidentiality. A typical interview lasted 20 minutes, with additional time taken by the clinician following the interview to identify preliminary diagnoses.

The interview gathered self-report data in several areas including demographic characteristics, military history, current residential and employment situations, and medical and psychiatric problems. It also included a section to record clinical psychiatric diagnoses based on *DSM-IV* (American Psychiatric Association, 1994) criteria. These diagnoses were derived from unstructured assessments, and were therefore based on clinical judgment. The following measures were used in the current analyses.

Demographics

All information in this section came from the veteran's self-report. Demographic information included veteran ethnicity (White, Black, Hispanic, Other), sex, age, and marital status. Military history information included service era (ranging from pre-World War II to Persian Gulf) and whether the veteran had been exposed to fire in a combat zone. Service in the theater of operations of several military conflicts, including the wars in Afghanistan and Iraq, was specifically assessed. Information on residence and income included type of residence at the time of interview, receipt of public support payments, usual employment pattern for the past three years and number of days worked in the 30 days preceding the interview.

Preliminary Diagnoses of Substance Abuse and Psychiatric Problems

Interviewers used veteran responses on the intake interview, additional clinical notes, and contacts with staff members familiar with the veteran to identify preliminary diagnoses of substance abuse and psychiatric problems. These were recorded on the intake interview form. The current analyses focused on alcohol abuse/dependency, drug abuse/dependency, affective disorder, schizophrenia or other psychotic disorder, and combat-related posttraumatic stress disorder (PTSD).

Data Analysis

The proportion of OEF/OIF veterans in the VA homeless program was compared to the proportion of OEF/OIF veterans in the general veteran population by a series of 2 (OEF/OIF vs. other) $\times 2$ (homeless vs. nonhomeless) contingency table analyses (Selvin, 1991). A separate analysis was conducted for each of six age categories and the overall sample.

In addition, comparisons between OEF/OIF homeless veterans and other VA homeless program clients less than the age of 65 (the maximum age of homeless OEF/OIF veterans) on several demographic and clinical characteristics were conducted through a multivariable general estimating equation (GEE) model of group membership (OEF/OIF vs. other) controlling for program location. Veteran characteristics that were significant at $p < 0.001$ were retained in the final model.

RESULTS

The following presents results of the analysis of OEF/OIF veterans who are homeless.

Relative Proportion of OEF/OIF Veterans Within VA Homeless Programs

Table 7.1 lists the number of OEF/OIF and other veterans by age category within both the nonhomeless and homeless groups. The odds ratios (and 95% confidence intervals) for presentation to the VA

TABLE 7.1 Relative proportion of OEF/OIF veterans within VA homeless programs[a]

Age	Not Homeless Other[b]	OEF/OIF	Homeless Other	OEF/OIF	Odds Ratio	95% CI
20–24	230,000	102,189	254	251	2.22	1.87–2.65
25–34	1,218,000	368,328	2341	488	0.69	0.63–0.76
35–44	2,703,000	172,396	11,628	212	0.29	0.25–0.33
45–54	3,713,000	90,442	36,256	77	0.09	0.07–0.11
55–64	6,001,000	20,611	18,916	7	0.11	0.05–0.23
65–74	4,305,000	230	3310	0	NA	NA
Overall	18,170,000	754,196	72,705	1035	0.39	0.36–0.42

[a]In accordance with instructions from National Center for Veterans Analysis and Statistics, estimates of veterans in the general population are rounded to the nearest 1000.
[b]Veterans who report no service in OEF/OIF.

homeless program among OEF/OIF veterans are also listed for each age category and overall. These results indicate that OEF/OIF veterans are seen in the VA homeless program at lower than expected numbers in all age categories except for the under-25-year-old category. Veterans in that youngest age category are more than twice as likely to be seen in the VA homeless program than would be expected from the proportion of OEF/OIF veterans in the general population, although it is uncertain how robust this finding is given the small numbers of homeless veterans in this age group.

Characteristics of OEF/OIF VA Homeless Program Clients

Table 7.2 displays demographic and clinical characteristics of OEF/OIF veterans seen in the HCHV program. Demographically, the OEF/OIF group is younger, has a higher percentage of female and Hispanic veterans and is less likely to be divorced or separated. More OEF/OIF veterans reported full-time employment or military service as their usual employment pattern in the last three years, while fewer reported being disabled or retired. More OEF/OIF veterans also reported receipt of VA benefits for *service connected* psychiatric or other conditions. Despite these differences, the percentage of OEF/OIF veterans who reported having received less than $500 within the past 30 days was about the same as non-OEF/OIF veterans.

The recent experience of homelessness was somewhat less extensive among OEF/OIF veterans than among other homeless veterans. OEF/OIF veterans spent fewer days homeless and more days housed

TABLE 7.2 Characteristics of OEF/OIF and other VA homeless program clients

	Other (n = 69,848)		OEF/OIF (n = 1035)	
	N	m (±SD) or %	N	m (±SD) or %
Age		50.4 (±8.1)		30.9 (±8.1)
Female	2908	4.1	137	13.2
Black	32,504	46.5	359	34.7
Hispanic	3631	5.2	121	11.7
White	31,634	45.3	492	47.5
Other	1858	2.7	61	6.0
Married	4321	6.2	142	13.7
Divorced, separated, widowed	42,716	61.2	357	34.5
Never married	20,138	28.9	531	51.3
Usual employment status, past 3 years				
Full time	21,657	31.0	558	53.9
Part time	10,681	15.3	109	10.5
Military	56	0.1	82	7.9
Disabled/Retired	18,333	26.2	61	5.9
Unemployed	18,406	26.4	205	19.8
Days worked in 30 days		3.1 (±6.9)		5.0 (±8.6)
Income (past 30 days) less than $500	40,717	58.3	640	61.8
Service Connected, psychiatric	3722	5.3	107	10.3
Service Connected, other	9271	13.3	188	18.2
Housing status (past 30 days)				
Days housed		11.0 (±12.8)		17.4 (±13.1)
Days homeless		13.3 (±13.2)		7.7 (±11.3)
Days institutional settings		5.6 (±10.4)		4.9 (±9.8)
Chronically homeless	23,744	34.0	150	14.5
Reports combat participation	11,515	16.5	703	67.9
Alcohol abuse/dependency	37,869	54.2	404	39.0
Drug abuse/dependency	33,522	48.0	293	28.3
Schizophrenia or other psychotic	8091	11.6	78	7.5
Affective	29,612	42.4	408	39.4
Combat PTSD	6121	8.8	449	43.4
Any serious mental illness diagnosis[a]	36,598	52.4	671	64.8
Concurrent SA and SMI	26,270	37.6	338	32.7
Non-OEF/OIF veterans at sites that saw no OEF/OIF veterans have been excluded from this table				

[a]At least one of the following diagnoses: Schizophrenia or other psychotic disorder; affective disorder, combat PTSD.

in the 30 days prior to entry into the HCHV program. A lower percentage of veterans in the OEF/OIF group met the HUD definition of chronic homelessness (homeless for at least one year or experiencing more than three episodes of homelessness within the past three years).

Clinically, fewer OEF/OIF veterans were given provisional diagnoses at intake of alcohol dependency, drug dependency, schizophrenia, or other psychotic disorders. However, a provisional diagnosis of combat-related PTSD was substantially higher in this group. It should also be noted that self-report of participation in combat was much more frequent for OEF/OIF veterans.

In order to characterize differences at intake between OEF/OIF and non-OEF/OIF homeless veterans controlling for correlations among the variables described above, a multivariable GEE model of group membership was conducted. Only significant variables ($p < 0.001$) were retained in the model. The results of the model are shown in Table 7.3.

The results of the multivariable model showed that OEF/OIF veterans were younger and more likely to be married. They were more likely to report recent employment in the military and less likely to report being unemployed or disabled/retired and less likely to have been homeless for more than one year at the time of entry into the HCHV program. OEF/OIF veterans were almost ten times more likely to report participation in combat. The only differences that

TABLE 7.3 Multivariable analysis of characteristics of OEF/OIF and other VA homeless program clients

Variable	B	SE(B)	Z	p	OR	95% CI
Age	−0.211	0.005	−39.92	<0.0001	0.81	0.80–0.82
Married	0.628	0.126	4.97	<0.0001	1.87	1.46–2.40
Never married	0.157	0.087	1.81	0.0703	1.17	0.99–1.39
Military employment	2.021	0.298	6.78	<0.0001	7.55	4.21–13.54
Disabled/retired	−0.735	0.171	−4.29	<0.0001	0.48	0.34–0.67
Unemployed	−0.138	0.091	−1.52	0.128	0.87	0.73–1.04
Homeless more than 1 year	−0.404	0.119	−3.40	0.0007	0.67	0.53–0.84
Reports combat participation	2.257	0.097	23.21	<0.0001	9.56	7.90–11.57
Drug dependency/abuse	−0.754	0.105	−7.18	<0.0001	0.47	0.38–0.58
Schizophrenia/other psychotic disorder	−0.626	0.137	−4.56	<0.0001	0.53	0.41–0.70
Combat-related PTSD	1.297	0.099	13.17	<0.0001	3.66	3.02–4.44

were seen on preliminary diagnoses in the multivariable model were a lower likelihood of being diagnosed with drug abuse/dependency or schizophrenia/other psychotic disorder and a much higher likelihood of being diagnosed with combat-related PTSD.

DISCUSSION

The purpose of the current study was to assess whether OEF/OIF veterans were represented in a service-seeking homeless population at levels consistent with or greater than, their presence in the general veteran population. OEF/OIF veterans were underrepresented at all age categories except for the youngest (under the age of 25) category, where presentation to the homeless program was more than twice the expected number, although the small numbers of veterans in this age group leaves important measurement uncertainty about this estimate. While quite small in actual numbers, VA homeless programs will need to develop ways of assisting this new group of veterans.

The results of the multivariable analysis show that even controlling for the substantial age differences between OEF/OIF and other homeless veterans in VA programs, there are still substantial differences between these groups. The most salient characteristics of OEF/OIF veterans are greater rates of participation in combat and an increased likelihood of receiving a preliminary diagnosis of combat-related PTSD. While that diagnosis presents a serious clinical challenge, OEF/OIF veterans have notable strengths that may facilitate their participation in treatment. Findings demonstrate that OEF/OIF veterans are less likely to have been unemployed or disabled at the time of entry into VA homeless programs. Further, they are less likely to have been homeless for longer than one year, and they are more likely to be married. These findings are also consistent with those of a national study of OIF/OEF veterans seeking VA treatment for PTSD that also found numerous positive prognostic indicators in this generation of veterans, especially as compared to veterans with PTSD related to the Vietnam conflict (Fontana & Rosenheck, 2008). Thus, identifying veterans' social supports and incorporating them in treatment plans are important steps in working with young veterans who are homeless.

The high prevalence of PTSD among OEF/OIF VA homeless program clients is consistent with other studies of OEF/OIF veterans who use VA health care. For example, Seal et al. (2009) found that

21% of OEF/OIF veterans who used VA health care between 2002 and 2008 had a diagnosis of PTSD. Additionally, among veterans who were in the regular military (rather than National Guard or Reserve), PTSD was highest in veterans under the age of 25.

It should be noted that the findings here pertain only to the treatment-seeking veterans encountered by VA homeless programs and may not be generalized to OEF/OIF homeless veterans who are not engaged in VA services. Moreover, the data presented here are based on the initial assessments of the VA homeless outreach program. The clinical picture presented by these veterans may change over the course of treatment.

These results show that returning OEF/OIF veterans do access VA homeless program services and will likely require modifications to existing services due to differences in age and clinical characteristics. Further research on long-term VA service of these homeless program clients should be pursued.

CONCLUSION

There are no words to express the pain of knowing that homelessness and the marginalization that accompanies this existence are realities for many veterans who have given much of themselves through their role in military service. As previously stated, OEF/OIF veterans have significant strengths that may sustain their active participation in treatment services related to homelessness and other clinical issues that may be presented. Thus, it is critical that veterans' protective factors, such as their family resources and employment resources (actual and potential), be part of service delivery planning to ensure optimal outcomes that are in themselves, beyond words.

REFERENCES

American Psychiatric Association. (1994). *Diagnostic and statistical manual of mental disorders* (4th ed.). Washington, DC: Author.

Burnam, A. M., Meredith, L. S., Tanilian, T., & Jaycox, L. H. (2009). Mental health care for Iraq and Afghanistan war veterans: Meeting combat-related mental health needs requires broad reform of services that looks beyond the veterans health administration. *Health Affairs, 28,* 771–782.

Eckholm, E. (2007). Surge seen in number of homeless veterans. *New York Times,* November 8, 2007. Retrieved October 1, 2009, from http://www.nytimes.com/2007/11/08/us/08vets.html.

Fontana, A., & Rosenheck, R. A. (2008). Treatment-seeking veterans of Iraq and Afghanistan: Comparison with veterans of previous wars. *Journal of Nervous and Mental Disease, 196,* 513–521.

Kasprow, W. J., Rosenheck, R. A., DiLella, D., Cavallaro, L., & Harelik, N. (2009). *Health care for homeless veterans programs: Twenty-second annual report.* West Haven, CT: Northeast Program Evaluation Center.

Mares, A. S., & Rosenheck, R. A. (2004). Perceived relationship between military service and homelessness among homeless veterans with mental illness. *Journal of Nervous and Mental Disease, 192,* 715–719.

National Center for Veterans Analysis and Statistics. (2007). *VETPOP 2007 online database* [http://www1.va.gov/vetdata/page.cfm?pg=15].

Phoenix VA Healthcare System. (2009/2010). *Addressing the Homelessness in the Veteran Population, A PowerPoint Presentation.* Retrieved February 28, 2011, http://gocyf.az.gov/SAP/documents/2009AZSAC/B_AddressHomeless-VetPop/AddressHomelessVetPopMichealLeon.ppt

Seal, K. H., Metzler, T. J., Gima, K. S., Berenthal, D., Maguen, S., & Marmar, C. R. (2009). Trends and risk factors for mental health diagnoses among Iraq and Afghanistan veterans using Department of Veterans Affairs Health Care 2002–2008. *American Journal of Public Health, 99,* 1651–1658.

Selvin, S. (1991). *Statistical analysis of epidemiological data.* New York: Oxford University Press.

VA National Data Systems. (2007). OEF/OIF Roster (rmtprd.med.sas.oefoif.roster) [internal VA online database]. Department of Veterans Affairs.

VISN Support Service Center. (2007). OEF/OIF basic demographic briefing book [internal VA online database]. Department of Veteran Affairs.

8

Tragedy, Loss, and Triumph After Combat: A Portrait of Young Women Veteran Survivors of Sexual and Combat Trauma

Godfrey Gregg and Jamila S. Miah

> *O, thus be it ever, where freeman shall standbetween their loved homes and the war's desolation!... Then conquer we must, when our cause it is just, and this be our motto, In God is our trust (Key, 1814).*

As a soldier in the U.S. Army, you are tasked with upholding the Constitution and protecting America's freedoms. Soldiers live the *Seven Core Army Values* every day (www.goarmy.com).

Loyalty: Bear true faith and allegiance to the U.S. Constitution, the Army, your unit and other Soldiers ....

Duty: Fulfill your obligations ....

Respect: ... And self-respect is a vital ingredient with the Army value of respect, which results from knowing you have put forth your best effort ...

Selfless Service: Put the welfare of the Nation, the Army and your subordinates before your own. Selfless service is larger than just one person ....

Honor: Live up to Army values ... of respect, duty, loyalty, selfless service, integrity and personal courage in everything you do.

Integrity: Do what's right, legally and morally. Integrity is a quality you develop by adhering to moral principles ....

Personal courage: Face fear, danger or adversity (physical or moral) ....

Since its birth and throughout its history, Americans have been called upon to serve and protect their republic. From the fortifications at West Point, Bunker Hill, and Tripoli to the heaths and beaches at Gettysburg, Antietam, and Normandy, Americans have continuously made the ultimate sacrifice on behalf of their country.

The United States is currently engaged in a war which has two fronts: Iraq (OIF) and Afghanistan (OEF). More than 2 million Americans have served in these conflicts since they commenced as early as 2003 and more than 220,000 or 11% of the combat personnel have been females (Alvarez, 2009). Because of insurgencies in Iraq and other environmental factors (i.e., Islamic traditions) senior officers have been forced to augment gender restrictions. Female officers routinely patrol neighborhoods and have assumed other duties such the interrogation and physical searching of civilians, particularly female civilians. Concomitant with the changes in these duties have been the increased dangers faced by female military personnel. Comparable to their male counterparts, female soldiers have been exposed to all facets of combat: multiple deployments, extended tours of duty, environmental hazards, loss of friends, and mental and physical traumas (Alvarez, 2009; Myers, 2009).

These are multiple biopsychosocial–spiritual stressors encountered by female veterans between the ages of 18 and 35 years of age who have been recently deployed to Iraq and/or Afghanistan. The writers sought to discover and explore how issues of tragedy and loss impacted the lives of female military personnel during their active tours of duties and subsequently upon their return to a new construction of civilian life, and how these female veterans were able to triumph over traumatic experiences associated with their military history.

TRAUMA AND LOSS FROM COMBAT

Although women routinely assisted on the battlefields during the Civil War, it was not until the establishment in 1901 of the Army Nurse Corp that their services were officially organized (Chaumba & Bride, 2010; Perlin, Mather, & Turner, 2005; Wing et al., 2000). Currently, women are the fastest growing segment in the military, comprising approximately 15% of all active military personnel; approximately 11% of the active forces in Afghanistan and Iraq; and approximately 1.7 million or 7% of the total veteran population (25 million) with one out of every seven female veterans under the age of 50 (Washington, Kleimann, Michelini, Kleimann, & Canning, 2007).

The increasing numbers of female military personnel has presented the Department of Veterans Affairs (VA) with numerous challenges both in the active theaters overseas and throughout its medical facilities in the United States. In the active theaters it is estimated that approximately 23–30% of female military personnel will encounter military sexual trauma (MST) and/or attempted MST (Campbell & Raja, 2005; Valente & Wight, 2007). Moreover, despite efforts to thwart this activity, MST has not abated (Alvarez, 2009; Campbell & Raja, 2005; Kelly et al., 2008; Myers, 2009). Additionally, MST which occurs during active service leads to a 59% higher risk of psychological/mental health problems among female military personnel/veterans (Chaumba & Bride, 2010; Seal et al., 2009; Williamson & Mulhall, 2009).

Although no one returns to civilian life unchanged, female veterans, most notably those who served Iraq and/or Afghanistan, are exhibiting greater difficulty adapting to new civilian life. Research indicates that female veterans who were repeatedly exposed to noncombat related violence (i.e., sexual assault and/or rape) were more likely to demonstrate impaired physical and emotional functioning, necessitating higher medical visits than those who were not subjected to these repeated threats (Himmelfarb et al., 2006; Sadler et al., 2004). In light of the aforementioned statistics concerning MST, it should not surprise that female veterans encounter greater risks for developing PTSD (Chaumba & Bride, 2010).

Overall, impaired functioning, chronic unemployment, poor interpersonal relationships and divorce and homelessness, along with Axis I diagnoses of clinical depression, anxiety disorders, substance dependence/abuse accompanying suicide are the phenomena seen increasingly among female personnel with a combination of MST and combat stress (Fairweather, 2006; Gamache, Rosenheck, & Tessler, 2003; Hoge et al., 2004; Okie, 2005; Schnurr & Lunney, 2008; Williamson & Mulhall, 2009). In addition, longer tours, multiple deployments, shorter periods at home (dwell time), and intensified traumatic injuries (Hoge et al., 2004; Williamson & Mulhall, 2009) increase the likelihood of MST/combat stress-related PTSD.

MST, Combat Stress, and PTSD

According to the Department of Defense (DOD), MST, an umbrella term for sexual harassment and sexual assault, is defined as unwanted verbal and physical contact of a sexual nature which occurs in a military environment (Chaumba & Bride, 2010; Sadler, Booth, Mengeling, & Doebbeling, 2004; Suris & Lind, 2008; Zinzow, Grubaugh, Monnier, Suffoletta-Maierie, & Frueh, 2007). Nationally, sexual harassment and sexual assault account for more than 60% of nonfatal workplace violence toward American women (Sadler et al., 2004). Furthermore, this violence is most prominent in male-dominated milieus: fire department, law enforcement, law firms, medicine, and military settings (Chaumba & Bride, 2010; Sadler et al., 2004; Suris & Lind, 2008; Zinzow et al., 2007).

MST emerges as the most deleterious of interpersonal stressor/jeopardy encountered by women in the military (Campbell & Raja, 2005; Suris & Lind, 2008; Yaeger, Himmelfarb, Cammack, & Mintz, 2006; Zinzow et al., 2007). Some research suggests that current rates of MST range from 30% to 70% of women in combat (Campbell & Raja, 2005; Zinzow et al., 2007). Female veterans state that incidences of harassment and/or assault were further detrimental because of imposed silences— making formal complaints would negatively impact careers within and beyond the military (Campbell & Raja, 2005; Yaeger et al., 2006).

Combat stress emerges from being shot at, receiving injuries, witnessing injuries and death, killing another, handling dead bodies, substandard and/or chaotic living arrangements, hazardous materials, and shattered morale (Castro & McGurk, 2007; Chaumba & Bride, 2010; Hoge et al., 2004). Further, length of deployment and uncertain deployment schedules heighten the level of combat stress due to the uncertainty of discontinuing one's deployment and proximity to fatal threats associated with combat (Castro & McGurk, 2007; Hoge et al., 2004). Combat stress is not gender specific. However, when MST is combined with combat stress, they pose highly significant risk factors for PTSD.

Posttraumatic stress disorder (PTSD) affects 15–24% of individuals who are exposed to traumatic events, with women twice as likely as men to develop PTSD (Simmons & Granvold, 2005). The physical violence, coercion, threats, intimidation, isolation, and emotional or sexual abuse associated with MST amplify combat-related stress and exposure (Valente & Wright, 2007). MST is akin to domestic violence, with MST, during active duty, leading to a 59% higher risk of psychological and mental health problems (i.e., chronic breast pain, irritable bowel syndrome, painful digestion, chronic fatigue, or decreased libido) (Gilhooly, Ottenweller, Lange, Tiersky, & Natelson, 2001; Johnson et al., 2006; Melby, 2008; Savas et al., 2009; Williamson & Mulhall, 2009) and subsequent need for treatment among female personnel.

The female service members who are deployed currently are exposed to combat-related trauma, as well as sexual trauma. Women in combat are also receiving PTSD diagnoses at the same rate as men who are returning from Iraq and Afghanistan (Lapierre, Schwegler, & LaBauve, 2007; Rundell, 2006). MST may be the principal determinant of PTSD, and when combined with combat stress the functioning of the female is impaired.

> I stay in what I call my little cocoon. When I say that my family understands I don't want to go anywhere.
>
> —*Women in Their Own Words, 2009*

MST carries a social stigma and self-blame, and is associated with a variety of mental health conditions such as anxiety disorder, dissociative disorders, substance abuse disorders, depression, and personality disorder (Haskell, et al., 2008; Hyun, Pavao, & Kimerling, 2009). In a study conducted by Murdoch, Pryor, Polusny, and Gackstetter (2007) it was evident that both men and women who were exposed to sexual stressors reported a higher incidence of psychiatric distress such as depression and anxiety as well as poorer social and emotional functioning.

The military itself is a patriarchal society and has its own set of rules and is isolated from most of the civilian community. The military training is based on principles such as camaraderie, unity, and uniformity as even depicted in the *Seven Core Army Values*. According to Hoppen (2006), MST takes place not only during war time but also during peace time. However, when the MST occurs in combat the fracture to the personhood of the woman may be irrevocably altered for a long period of time.

For example, during combat, a female service member may have been raped by her commanding officer and then has to see him daily, and continue to take orders from him. These orders are integral to the health, safety, and well-being of the unit. Further, the predatory abuser has control over her career. Female service members are dependent on their predatory abusers for basic necessities such as medical and or psychiatric care. In a sea of enemy combatants who will kill or capture and torture the female soldier because she is an American warrior, the choice for these women is to either continue being victimized or sacrifice everything—career, stability and security of the unit, and their physical and mental health, to avoid further trauma (Fratangelo, 2007). MST is a blatant breach of trust, betrayal and security to all soldiers, and destroys cohesion and camaraderie and fuels PTSD (Friedman, 2006).

Wounds, Scars, and the Return Home

Suris, Lind, Kashner, Borman, and Petty (2004) reported that in their study, 270 women veterans were surveyed to examine sexual assault, risk of PTSD, health care utilization, and cost of care. The results of the study showed that 64.1% of the women reported a positive history of sexual assault either in the military, in civilian life and or during childhood.

Female veterans with a prior history of assault are at a higher risk for substance abuse problems, suicidal ideations, and/or attempts. Further, they are at even greater risk of poor social relations which negatively impact the conditions of family, friends, and social networks.[1]

> I get really tense around groups of kids. If I had my gun, maybe it would be better. It would give me control. It's my security blanket.
>
> —*Women in Their Own Words, 2009*

Further, invisible wounds from MST and combat-related stressors jeopardize parent–child relationships and intimate partner relationships. Berz Taft, Watkins, and Monson (2008) in their study of Vietnam female veterans who were also biological mothers defined parenting satisfaction as: effectiveness and a sense pleasure in the parent–child relationship. Their study concluded that symptoms of PTSD, specifically hyperarousal, were associated with decreased parenting satisfaction among female veterans while avoidance and numbing symptoms were associated with male veterans.

> I feel like I'm robbing him of being a good mother. I don't want to embarrass him; I don't want to go to one of his football games someday and be a mother that flips out.
>
> —*Women in Their Own Words, 2009*

Moreover, findings concluded that hyperarousal resulted in harsher punishments toward the children which in turn increased

---

[1]Some research shows that the prevalence of completed rapes in an active duty sample is 1% and or all types of unwanted sexual contact is reportedly 21% (Himmelfarb et al., 2006). Some of the speculation between the discrepancies in the numbers may be due to the fact that female active duty service members are more reluctant to disclose because of concerns that the assault may be known to their colleagues. The other reason may be that the samples used for the previous studies were from a clinical sample at Veterans Affairs and therefore higher rates of abuse were found. It is also noteworthy that female army soldiers have a higher rate of childhood sexual trauma compared to nonmilitary women, with military women with early childhood trauma are more likely to experience rape more often than those who have no prior history (Himmelfarb et al., 2006).

negative behaviors among them (Williamson & Mulhall, 2009). Cotten, Skinner, and Sullivan (2000) reached similar findings in their study of Vietnam and Persian Gulf War female veterans. Additionally, this study concluded that a significant percentage of returning female veterans, notably those from lower socioeconomic levels and lower levels of education, experienced difficulty expressing their emotions to significant others (i.e., family and friends).

Psychological and neurological wounds that are visible and nonvisible, and associated with multiple deployments and combat stress (i.e., PTSD and TBI), have contributed to harmful effects on the spousal system. Williamson and Mulhall (2009) stated that although the divorce rate among military personnel is not drastically higher than that of the civilian population, the statistics are disconcerting when examined by gender: marriages of women in the military are three times as likely to fail when compared to their male counterparts. According to Melby (2008) contrary to previous opinions, TBI does not induce hypersexual arousal; rather, research indicates that there is a drastic decrease in libidinal urges.

> My husband kept saying, Angie, it does not make a good wife to just do the dishes and make dinner. I didn't understand what he was talking about. My emotions were so numb that I couldn't be intimate. I was still in soldier mode ... when it came to closeness or intimate feelings, there was nothing.
>
> —*Women in Their Own Words, 2009*

MST in the combat arena has a devastating impact on female service members, making the need for treatment obvious. These women have unique mental health needs and require specialized programs (Hoff & Rosenheck, 1998). There are many forms of treatment that can be used for female victims of PTSD as a result of MST; however, we propose a model that includes Cognitive Behavioral Therapy (CBT), an evidence-based treatment along with the Recovery model of care. This is blending the two emerging approaches of treatment. The scientific, objective, evidence-based approach emphasizes external scientific reality, whereas the recovery model stresses the importance of the subjective, phenomenological experience. This may pose as a conflict under various circumstances, however, as clinicians we are treating individuals and we should be able to make choices based on both factual scientific information as well as values.

TRIUMPH AFTER COMBAT:
THE PHENOMENOLOGICAL MODEL

Theories and models regarding observed human behavior are to be value free and anchored in logical positivism—distinct separation between the observed and the observer/practitioner (Swigonski, 1994).

> A profession whose hallmark is a commitment to enhancing clients' dignity and worth must question approaches to research in which the activities reduce clients to mere objects of observation and manipulation.
>
> —*Swigonski, 1994, p. 389*

Swigonski's (1994) words are significant, and since the 1960s, the voices of American women have increasingly demanded recognition and inclusion regarding implementation of policies and programs that affect their well-being, development, and social growth (Enns, 2010; Nes & Iadicola, 1989; Swigonski, 1994). Essential to this dynamic is the Feminist Standpoint Perspective.

Contrary to logical positivism, Feminist Standpoint posits that the lived experiences of marginalized/oppressed individuals and groups have value, thus, their voices warrant our focus. Standpoint refers to the social location which an individual occupies; and from this standpoint that the individual (i.e., female military personnel/veterans) formulates her perspective as reality. Fundamental in understanding her standpoint is awareness and acceptance that she does not have the same perspectives of reality as members of the dominant class structure (i.e., male military personnel/veterans) (Swigonski, 1994). However, survival in the environment mandates the female military personnel/veterans understand reality from the perspectives of the dominant group as well as their own perspectives. Hence, female military personnel/veterans are required to maintain a *double consciousness* or an awareness of the dominant culture's perspective and their own perspective (DuBois, 1903; Swigonski, 1994).

The theory of "double- consciousness" is not a new phenomenon and complements the Feminist Standpoint. DuBois (1903) stated the American [Black] is always looking at himself through the eyes of others (particularly *White* America); he is always measuring his soul by a tape of a world which looks at him both with contempt and pity. Consequently, the history of the American [Black] is one of continual strife; this continual strife is to merge his double self into a better and more authentic self (DuBois, 1903) deemed acceptable to *White* America.

Similarly, female military personnel/veterans must employ a double consciousness and merge their self into a more acceptable self for the male-dominated military and veterans' institutions. Combined with combat exposure and MST, there is even greater need to elevate the more marginalized perspective as the new, authentic reality.

A Case Profile

A female veteran was brought in by her family for treatment at our facility. She had been experiencing symptoms of PTSD, Major Depression and homelessness. She was also a survivor of military sexual trauma. She had been suffering from nightmares from the sexual assault she suffered while in the military. She was depressed and was severely traumatized by the event. The military had made her feel less than human, she said. Being discharged from the military also proved that she was no longer able to perform as a soldier. Beliefs such as "I can never do anything" and "I am a failure" stemmed from her experience in the Military. She continued to feel that she had let the Marine Corps down. However, upon challenging that thought she was able to realize that it was the Marine Corps that had let her down. She was disillusioned with the Marine Corps because they were "not dignified, strong and caring towards their own soldiers, which is what they claimed to be." During her treatment she was asked to challenge her thought of "I am a failure" by taking a look at her life and achievements before the Corps and while in the Corps prior to the sexual assault. This was one way she used in order to not allow the predator and the Corps control her thoughts.

Cognitive Behavioral Therapy

Cognitive Behavioral Theory (CBT) is based on the cognitive model which is described as the way we perceive situations influences how we feel emotionally. It is ideal to support female personnel and veterans' perspectives because the theoretical assumption behind CBT is that behavioral change is mediated by the person's cognitive events. CBT also teaches individuals to identify distressing situations and how their thinking becomes distorted as a result. Aaron Beck (1979) theorized that people who are depressed think in a negative way because their thinking is biased toward negative interpretations. Negative schemas are formed due to stressful life events. Thus, the theory predicts that when an individual is faced with a similar situation later in life the negative schema that was learned earlier is then activated (Beck Rush, Shaw, & Emery, 1979).

The notion of schemas allows a CBT therapist to get a better understanding of the individual, and helps them to change their way of thinking, and consequently their negative behavior. The cognitive triad as described by Beck et al. (1979) is a very important concept because the framework makes negative behaviors and thinking more manageable for the individual and gives them some hope that their condition is not their fault. Beck et al. (1979) describes "Depressongenic Assumptions" as faulty beliefs that the individual develops over the years and are learned. This is where the schema formation takes place. The individual may develop the faulty beliefs in their childhood from attitudes and opinions of their loved ones. It is very important to identify these beliefs because individuals with depression tend to have patterns of beliefs such as acceptance/rejection, failure/success, gain/loss, and so on (Beck et al., 1979).

CBT allows female personnel/veterans to triumph over the losses from combat by helping them grasp why they are not able to function like they used to prior to the traumatic events and the onset of their depressive and/or PTSD symptoms. Some may view it as pathologizing the female veteran; however, this phenomenon gives them hope in terms of resolving and overcoming trauma through their treatment. Further, the therapist is able to provide hope by conceptualizing depression and/or PTSD as medical illnesses and as highly treatable and educating the female veteran about the symptoms in order to reduce or prevent future relapses.

Recovery Model

The Recovery Model is built on the premises that individuals can and do recover from major mental illness; and that they have the dignity and the right to failure. The Recovery Model emphasizes the principle of choice, skill-building, self-determination, empowerment, peer support, and also the recovery of social roles (Deegan, 1996). It also suggests that individuals with mental illness can be rehabilitated back into the society and make a recovery which does not necessarily require a complete relief of symptoms. The Recovery Model treats the whole person and not just the illness. One of the principles of recovery is that the client is not the illness and there is more to an individual than just a diagnosis (DeSisto, Harding, McCormick, Ashikaga, & Gautum,

1995). This is ideal for female personnel/veterans who may feel a void of meaning, purpose, and optimal functionality postcombat or deployment. The Recovery Model involves the development of new meaning and purpose in one's life as one learns to grow beyond the catastrophic effects of one's trauma (Frederick, Stanley, Kress, & Vogel-Scibilia, 2001; Walker, 2006).

The Recovery Model recognizes the double standard that the society has regarding marginalized individuals with mental illness as opposed to one who is part of the dominant group with a mental illness or who does not have a mental health diagnosis. The Recovery Model, particularly for female personnel/veterans, is promoted by minimizing paternalism and allowing survivors of MST the dignity of risk, the right to learn, and the opportunity to grow through failure as well as success. Female service members are mothers, sisters, and wives, and are expected to fulfill these roles immediately after returning from active duty. The battle to recover *the self* begins when female personnel/veterans return home. Not only have they had to endure multiple traumas such as: combat and loss of friends, they may have also been victims of MST. In such instances, if they are labeled with a mental health diagnosis they are being re-victimized. If the valued social role has been disrupted as a result of the illness, role recovery becomes an important focus of rehabilitation and self-directed recovery (Deegan, 1993; Jacobson & Greenley, 2001).

Female veterans need to be treated with utmost respect and therapists need to be cognizant of the fact that they may have been victims of multiple traumas both pre- and postmilitary. They need to feel safe and should be given the choice of having a female clinician who has sensitivity to survivors of MST. This is the beginning of making an individual feel that they have some control and/or choice in their treatment, which is consistent with the Recovery Model of care. If the veteran is too fragile or symptomatic, such as being tearful, experiencing increased depressive symptoms, hyper-vigilance, increased anxiety, she may probably need to be stabilized on medication prior to being exposed to any form of psychotherapy. As clinicians we need to understand that these women have come from an environment of rules and orders taking orders and may transfer the perceived paternalistic culture of the military onto the treatment modality.

The Recovery Model strongly suggests a structured partnership, which means that the clinician is not dictating treatment, is partnering with the veteran, and treating the veteran as the expert of her own life experiences/symptoms. Choices such as group therapy, creative arts therapy, and individual therapy should be offered so the veteran can decide which form of treatment to utilize. In addition, introducing veterans to nonmedication alternatives, such as deep-breathing exercises, meditation, and other stress reducing coping strategies is an integral part of the treatment. Female veterans can also benefit from information about family and community education programs to facilitate the resuming of their civilian roles. Thus, creating a wellness plan is crucial because it allows the individual to develop their own "wellness toolbox," have a daily maintenance plan, list their cognitive and emotional triggers, identify their early warning signs, and have available a crisis plan or a behavioral advance directive with their clinician (Copeland, 2010). This process encourages the female veteran to have the confidence necessary to overcome the helplessness she may have felt in the past.

Further, female veterans may come with irrational beliefs such as "I am unlovable," "I am a failure," and "I can never do anything right." These cognitive distortions are negative overgeneralizations. A common statement among women veterans is "the military broke me" and it is meant both physically and psychiatrically. Female veterans may come in for treatment for various reasons such as depression, homelessness, relationship issues, and/or are brought in by frustrated family members.

When we look at the profile of the female veteran in the previous section, she needed a safe environment and also needed to be educated on Major Depression and PTSD. She had been blaming herself for what had happened and was happening to her. A few things made the difference. Changing her living environment helped, she felt supported and cared for by the clinical staff. Being in group therapy also made her feel that she was not the only one suffering from depression. By changing her thoughts and coming to understand that she was a survivor of MST and it was not her fault, her mood became less labile. Her emotions and cognitions were intertwined. It was evident that her negative thoughts did not cause the sad emotions all the time. Her sad emotions also led to negative thoughts.

Initially, the treatment just focused on teaching her the coping skills to deal with her affect. She completed her CBT worksheets identifying her negative thoughts, feelings, and behaviors religiously, and was very interested in learning coping skills. She began the session by reporting her mood on a scale of 1–10. Midway through the course of treatment a change took place; the veteran began to have her own agenda items for the sessions. She would identify what she wanted to cover in the sessions and it would be in order of importance.

By doing so, she was feeling empowered and more in control. She was no longer helpless and or hopeless. She was making progress and the worksheets showed her that her emotions were less intense and her thought processes were changing. As the treatment went on, she was less tearful, no longer disheveled. She smiled more often and began to do more art work. She was also looked forward to going back to college to get her Bachelor's Degree in Arts.

CONCLUSION

CBT, along with the Recovery Model, is one of the best forms of treatment for female veteran survivors of MST because it addresses core beliefs and the automatic negative thoughts that influence depressive symptomatology along with PTSD symptoms. Further, the therapeutic relationship is crucial as the Recovery Model approach aids the female veteran survivor in controlling the direction of treatment.

Focusing on the health of female veteran survivors of MST requires that health care professionals design and implement gender-specific programs (Washington, 2004; Yano et al., 2006). These programs must take into account the lived experiences of this heterogeneous group, validate their varied experiences, and include their voices in the design and implementation of current programs, and in the research on future policies and interventions (Chaumba & Bride, 2010; Washington, 2004; Wing et al., 2000; Yano et al., 2006). Furthermore, all policies and programs must address challenges and risks encountered by female military personnel whether their status is active, reserve, or veteran.

It is not enough to treat female veterans as though their issues are similar to that of their male counterparts. Triumph after combat must also take into consideration the realities of traumatic losses associated with combating enemies within the safe and secure structures of the military milieu they are honored to serve.

REFERENCES

Alvarez, L. (2009, August 16). G.I. Jane stealthily breaks the combat barrier: Women at arms. *The New York Times*, A1, A4.

Beck, A., Rush, J., Shaw, B. F., & Emery, G. (1979). *Cognitive therapy of depression.* New York: Guilford Press.

Being a soldier/Living the Army values. Retrieved September 9, 2010, from http:// (physical and moral)www.goarmy.com

Berz, J., Taft, C., Watkins, L., & Monson, C. (2008). Associations between PTSD and parenting satisfaction in a female veteran sample. *Journal of Psychological Trauma, 7*(1), 37–45.

Campbell, R., & Raja, S. (2005). The sexual assault and secondary victimization of female veterans: Help-seeking experiences with military and civilian social systems. *Psychology of Women Quarterly, 29*, 97–106.

Castro, C. A., & McGurk, D. (2007). The intensity of combat and behavioral health status. *Traumatology, 13*(4), 6–23.

Chaumba, J., & Bride, B. (2010). Trauma experiences and posttraumatic stress disorder among women in the United States military. *Social Work in Mental Health, 8*, 280–303.

Copeland, M. E. (2010). *Recovery and wellness: Transforming ourselves and our services.* Presented at Transforming Day Treatment Centers Into Psychosocial Rehabilitation and Recovery Centers; Facilitating Community Integration. Washington, DC.

Cotten, S., Skinner, K., & Sullivan, L. (2000). Social support among women veterans. *Journal of Women and Aging, 12*(1/2), 39–62.

Deegan, P. E. (1993). Recovering our sense of value after being labeled mentally ill. *Journal of Psychosocial Nursing, 31*(4), 7–11.

Deegan, P. E. (1996). Recovery as a journey of the heart. *Psychiatric Rehabilitation Journal, 19*, 91–97.

DeSisto, M. J., Harding, C. M., McCormick, R. V., Ashikaga, T., & Gautum, S. (1995). The Maine–Vermont three decades studies of serious mental illness: Longitudinal course of comparisons. *British Journal of Psychiatry, 167*, 338–342.

DuBois, W. (1903) *The souls of Black folk.* New York: Barnes and Nobles.

Enns, C. (2010). Locational feminisms and feminist social identity analysis. *Professional Psychology: Research and Practice, 41*(4), 333–339.

Fairweather, A. (2006, December 7). Risk and protective factors for homelessness among OIF/OEF veterans [Iraq Veterans Project]. *Swords to Plowshares,* 1–8.

Fratangelo, D. (2007). *Military sexual trauma—The new face of PTSD.* Retrieved from http://www.msnbc.msn.com/id/18494197

Frederick, J. F., Stanley, J., Kress, K., & Vogel-Scibilia, S. (2001). Integrating evidence-based practices and the recovery model. *Psychiatric Services, 52*, 1462–1468.

Friedman, M. J. (2006). Posttraumatic stress disorder among military returnees from Afghanistan and Iraq. *American Journal of Psychiatry, 163*(4), 586–593.

Gamache, G., Rosenheck, R., & Tessler, R. (2003). Overrepresentation of women veterans among homeless women. *American Journal of Public Health, 93*(7), 1132–1136.

Gilhooly, P., Ottenweller, J., Lange, G., Tiersky, L., & Natelson, B. (2001). Chronic fatigue and sexual dysfunction in female Gulf war veterans. *Journal of Sex and Marital Therapy, 27*, 483–487.

Haskell, S., Papas, S., Heapy, A., Reid, M., & Kerns, R. (2008). The association of sexual trauma with persistent pain in a sample of women veterans receiving primary care. *Pain Medicine, 9*(6), 710–717.

Himmelfarb, N., Yaeger, D., & Mintz, J. (2006). Posttraumatic stress disorder in female veterans with military and civilian sexual trauma. *Journal of Traumatic Stress, 19*, 837–846.

Hoff, R. A., & Rosenheck, R. A. (1998). Female veterans' use of Veterans Affairs health care services. *Medical Care, 36*(7), 1114–1119.

Hoge, C., Castro, C., Messer, S., McGurk, D., Cotting, D., & Koffman, R. (2004). Combat duty in Iraq and Afghanistan, mental health problems, and barriers to care. *New England Journal of Medicine, 351*(1), 13–22.

Hoppen, J. (2006). Women in the military: Who's got your back? *Off Our Backs: The Feminist News Journal.* Retrieved from http://www.offourbacks.org/ WomMilBack.htm

Hyun, J. K., Pavao, J., & Kimerling, R. (2009). Military sexual trauma. *PTSD Research Quarterly, 20*(2).

Jacobson, N., & Greenley, D. (2001). What is recovery? A conceptual model and explication. *Psychiatric Services, 52*(4), 482–485.

Johnson, K., Bradley, K., Bush, K., Gardella, C., Dobie, D., & Laya, M. (2006). Frequency of mastalgia among women veterans: Association with psychiatric conditions and unexplained pain syndromes. *Journal of General Internal Medicine, 21*, 570–575.

Kelly, M., Vogt, D., Scheiderer, B., Ouimette, P., Daley, J., & Wolfe, J. (2008). Effects of military trauma exposure on women veterans' use and perceptions of veterans health administration care. *Journal of General Internal Medicine, 23*(6), 741–747.

Key, F. S. (1814). *The Star Spangled Banner.* Retrieved November 3, 2009, from http://www.kids.niehs.nih.gov/lyrics/spangle.htm

Lapierre, C. B., Schwegler, A. F., & LaBauve, B. J. (2007). Posttraumatic stress and depressive symptoms in soldiers returning from combat operations in Iraq and Afghanistan. *Journal of Traumatic Stress, 20*(6), 933–943.

Melby, T. (2008). Regaining intimacy after war. *Contemporary Sexuality, 42*(10), 3–5.

Murdoch, M., Pryor, J. B., Polusny, M. A., & Gackstetter, G. D. (2007). Function and psychiatric symptoms among military men and women exposed to sexual stressors. *Military Medicine, 172*(7), 718–725.

Myers, S. L. (2009, August 17). Living and fighting alongside men, and fitting in. *The New York Times,* A1, A6.

Nes, I., & Iadicola, P. (1989). Toward a definition of feminist social work: A comparison of liberal, radical, and socialist models. *Social Work, 34*(1), 12–21.

Okie, S. (2005). Traumatic brain injury in the war zone. *The New England Journal of Medicine, 352*(20), 2043–2047.

Perlin, J., Mather, S., & Turner, C. (2005). Women in the military: New perspectives, new science. *Journal of Women's Health, 14*(9), 861–862.

Rundell, J. R. (2006). Demographics of and diagnoses in operation enduring freedom and operation Iraqi freedom personnel who were psychiatrically evacuated from the theatre of operations. *General Hospital Psychiatry, 28*, 352–356.

Sadler, A., Booth, B., Mengeling, M., & Doebbeling, B. (2004). Life span and repeated violence against women during military service: Effects on health status and outpatient utilization. *Journal of Women's Health, 13*(7), 799–811.

Savas, L., White, D., Wieman, M., Dacis, K., Fitzgerald, S., Laday-Smith, S. et al. (2009). Irritable bowel syndrome and dyspepsia among women veterans: Prevalence and association with psychological distress. *Alimentary Pharmacology & Therapeutics, 29*(1), 115–125.

Schnurr, P., & Lunney, C. (2008). Exploration of gender differences in how quality of life relates to posttraumatic stress disorder in male and female veterans. *Journal of Rehabilitation Research & Development, 45*(3), 383–394.

Seal, K., Metzler, T., Gima, K., Bertenhal, D., Maguen, S., & Marmar, C. (2009). Trends and risk factors for mental health diagnoses among Iraq and Afghanistan veterans using Department of Veterans Affairs Health Care, 2002–2008. *American Journal of Public Health, 99*(9), 1651–1658.

Simmons, C. A., & Granvold, D. K. (2005). A cognitive model to explain gender differences in rate of PTSD diagnosis. *Brief Treatment and Crisis Intervention, 5*(3), 290–299.

Suris, A., & Lind, L. (2008). Military sexual trauma: A review of prevalence and associated health consequences in veterans. *Trauma, Violence, & Abuse, 9*(4), 250–269.

Suris, A., Lind, L., Kashner, M., Borman, P., & Petty, F. (2004). Sexual assault in women veterans: An examination of PTSD risk, healthcare utilization, and cost of care. *Psychosomatic Medicine, 66*, 749–756.

Swigonski, M. (1994). The logic of feminist standpoint theory for social work research. *Social Work, 39*(4), 387–393.

Valente, S., & Wight, C. (2007). Military sexual trauma: Violence and sexual abuse. *Military Medicine, 172*(3), 259–265.

Walker, M. T. (2006). The social construction of mental illness and its implications for the Recovery Model. *The International Journal of Psychosocial Rehabilitation, 10*(1), 71–87.

Washington, D. (2004). Challenges to studying and delivering care to special populations: The example of women veterans. *Journal of Rehabilitation Research & Development, 41*(2), vi–ix.

Washington, D., Kleimann, S., Michelini, A., Kleimann, K., & Canning, M. (2007). Women veterans' perceptions and decision-making about veterans affairs health care. *Military Medicine, 172*, 812–817.

Williamson, V., & Mulhall, E. (2009). Invisible wounds: Psychological and neurological injuries confront a new generation of veterans. *Iraq and Afghanistan Veterans of America*, 1–23.

Wing, D., Oertle, J., Cabioc, A., Evans, C., Smith, D., & Stangeby, B. (2000). A student directed community project to support sexually abused women veterans suffering from post-traumatic stress disorder. *Public Health Nursing, 17*(4), 239–246.

Women in Their Own Words. (2009). *The New York Times.* Retrieved October 30, 2009, from http://www.nytimes.com/slideshow/2009/10/30/us/1101TRAUMA

Yaeger, D., Himmelfarb, N., Cammack, A., & Mintz, J. (2006). DSM-IV diagnosed posttraumatic stress disorder in women veterans with and without military sexual trauma. *Journal of General Internal Medicine, 21,* S65–S69.

Yano, E., Bastion, L., Frayne, S., Howell, A., Lipson, L., McGlynn, G. et al. (2006). Towards a VA women's health research agenda: Setting evidence-based priorities to improve the health and health care of women veterans. *Journal of General Internal Medicine, 21,* S93–S101.

Zinzow, H., Grubaugh, A., Monnier, J., Suffoletta-Maierie, S., & Frueh, B. (2007). Trauma among female veterans: A critical review. *Trauma, Violence, & Abuse, 8*(4), 384–400.

9

LIVING IN TRANSITION: YOUNG VETERANS' HEALTH AND THE POSTDEPLOYMENT SHIFT TO FAMILY LIFE[1]

Kristy Straits-Tröster, Jennifer M. Gierisch, Patrick S. Calhoun, Jennifer L. Strauss, Corrine Voils, and Harold Kudler

Moderator: Anything else you want to say for the record? Get on the tape so it gets transcribed and people will read? . . . .
Participant: Anybody who ever gets out of the Army, especially from a war, everybody just needs someone to listen to them, actually care what they're saying. Instead of just a mile of paper, pushing them through . . . that would be nice.

—*Exchange between Focus Group Moderator and a Former Active Duty Soldier*

Over 1.7 million Americans have served in the all-volunteer U.S. fighting forces since 2002. Over 75% of U.S. troops have experienced two or more deployments to Afghanistan in support of Operation Enduring Freedom (OEF) or Iraq in support of Operation Iraqi Freedom (OIF). Prolonged and/or multiple deployments and combat exposure have profound impact on veterans and their families as they transition to civilian life at home and in their communities.

Military service members face significant readjustment challenges and health concerns when they return from deployment to a combat area of operations or retire from military service. Although over half of OEF/OIF forces eligible for Department of Veterans Affairs (VA) health care have accessed services, many eligible combat veterans have not yet utilized this benefit (VHA, 2010). Data about the subgroup of OEF/OIF veterans who have accessed VA care have been gleaned

[1]This material is based upon work supported in part by the VA Mid-Atlantic Mental Illness Research, Education, & Clinical Center and by Department of Veterans Affairs, Veterans Health Administration, Office of Research and Development, and Health Services Research and Development. The views expressed in this chapter are those of the authors and do not necessarily represent the views of the Department of Veterans Affairs or the United States government. The authors have no competing interests.

from prior, quantitative medical record reviews focused on the prevalence of health and mental health problems and patterns of health services use. For example, VA medical records indicate that musculoskeletal disorders were the most commonly diagnosed physical health complaints associated with VA health care visits of OEF/OIF veterans (VHA, 2010). This likely reflects the physical health risks associated with duties during deployment, such as carrying heavy gear and body armor over long distances and uneven terrain, and represents chronic pain conditions associated with injuries and wear and tear on joints such as knees, ankles, and backs. Physical injuries incurred during deployment may impact readjustment to civilian life.

Mental health disorders are the second most common group of diagnoses associated with OEF/OIF veterans' VA health care visits; depression, posttraumatic stress disorder (PTSD), and other anxiety disorders are the most prevalent (Seal, Bertenthal, Miner, Sen, & Marmar, 2007; Seal et al., 2009). About a quarter of OEF/OIF veterans seen in VA facilities before October 2005 received a mental health diagnosis, and veterans aged 18–24 were at greater risk compared to veterans over 40 (Seal et al., 2007). More recent studies indicate that the proportion of OEF/OIF veterans who received a mental health diagnosis at VA facilities rose to 35% in 2008 (Cohen et al., 2009). Thus, there appears to be a temporal increase in reported mental health problems following deployment to current conflicts in Iraq and Afghanistan (Seal et al., 2009). How these mental health concerns affect the newest cohort of veterans and their families as they reconnect at home, school or work, however, is largely unknown.

The impact of traumatic stress associated with combat duty on family support and functioning was identified by the National Vietnam Veterans Readjustment Study (NVVRS), a retrospective examination of long-term adjustment of Vietnam-era veterans that included assessment of family difficulties (Kulka et al., 1990). In addition to individual struggles with depression, anxiety, and alcohol use, a subset of Vietnam veterans reported readjustment problems with broad effects within their family, social, and professional lives, including occupational instability, marital conflicts, and family problems. As compared to those without PTSD, the NVVRS found that veterans with PTSD reported significantly higher rates of marital, parental, and other family adjustment problems including violence (Kulka et al., 1990).

The experiences of OEF/OIF veterans may be similar to other cohorts of combat veterans. However, the full range of health and readjustment concerns of OEF/OIF veterans and their families have only recently begun to be examined. For example, spouses of deployed OEF/ OIF service members experienced rates of mental health problems similar to that of soldiers (Eaton et al., 2008). Spouses were less concerned, however, about the social implications or stigma around seeking help than were their military partners. Nearly 75% of OEF/ OIF veterans referred for behavioral health evaluations at one VA medical center reported one or more family problems during the previous week (Sayers, Farrow, Ross, & Oslin, 2009), including feeling like a guest in one's home (41%), being unsure about one's family role (37%), and not feeling warm toward one's children or noticing their children acting afraid (25%). Family problems may not be routinely assessed in health care settings yet may have tremendous impact on postdeployment health and trauma recovery.

Medical record review and routine clinical assessment of veterans seeking treatment are important first steps toward characterizing the needs and guiding development of quality health care, patient-centered support services, and relevant research for this cohort of veterans. Diagnostic and utilization data, however, cannot contextualize the development and persistence of distress for veterans and their family members. Neither can these retrospective strategies elicit direct input from OEF/ OIF veteran health care consumers and their families regarding preferences for health care delivery.

METHOD

Qualitative methods offer the opportunity to probe these issues in depth and explore views and perspectives through the lens of those most affected, including VA users and those not currently accessing VA services (Berkowitz, 1996). Accordingly, we conducted a qualitative study examining health concerns, family and civilian transition issues, satisfaction with and barriers to VA health care, and support among OEF/ OIF veterans and their spouses.

Recruitment and Group Procedures

Eligible participants living within a 60-minute drive of a large VA medical center in the Southeastern United States were identified from a random sample of 800 OEF/OIF veterans, obtained through a data use agreement with the VA Office of Public Health and Environmental Hazards. These data were obtained as part of an OEF/OIF needs assessment conducted for the Mid-Atlantic Region's Mental Illness Research, Education and Clinical Center focused on postdeployment mental health. Eligible veteran participants had returned from deployment and either remained in the National Guard/Reserves or had separated from military service, according to the Defense Manpower Data Center. Participants were recruited from the extracted sample of OEF/OIF veterans by telephone about one week after the mailing of an advance letter sent to alert the veteran to the subsequent recruitment telephone call. Six focus groups with 10–12 participants each were conducted over three days in October, 2006 ($n = 66$). All participants were paid $100 to reimburse them for their time, travel, and child care expenses. Veterans ($n = 54$) were recruited to these focus groups, stratified by gender and military duty status: two male Active Duty but separated groups; two male National Guard/Reserves groups; and one female veteran group with varied duty status. We also conducted one focus group with nonveteran female spouses ($n = 12$).

A moderator led each discussion using a semistructured interview guide. The two-page interview guide was divided into four sections, each structured to tap a major topic of interest (e.g., postdeployment health concerns, preference for VA services). Each section included both open-ended, general questions developed to encourage general discussion, as well as direct, closed questions developed to gather specific information. Table 9.1 summarizes the major content areas of the interview guide. Copies of the interview guide are available upon request from the first author. All discussions were audiotaped and transcribed. The Institutional Review Board at the VA Medical Center in Durham, North Carolina approved this research.

Analysis

We used manifest content analysis, which provided a topical survey of findings (Sandelowski & Barroso, 2003). Topical surveys are obtained from highly structured interviews that permit counting to determine the frequency of occurrence of an experience across cases. (In this study, cases are focus groups.) Topical surveys are useful when the research purpose is to explore the universe of responses to a given topic (e.g., health concerns during deployment). Two team members (JMG, CIV) generated one or more descriptive labels (codes) for each speaker turn. Codes were compared, the coding scheme was finalized through discussion, and then the coding scheme was applied to all transcripts by one team member (JMG).

To examine possible differences in the variables identified in the analysis, we created a code-by-group matrix, which allowed us to

TABLE 9.1 OEF/OIF veteran topical survey code by group type matrix

Code	Male Active Duty Veterans[a]	Male Reserve and National Guard Veterans[a]	Female Veterans	Veteran Wives
Issues and health concerns during deployment				
Unsanitary living conditions	X	X	X	
Air quality	X	X	X	
Disease exposure		X	X	
Chemical exposure	X	X	X	
Joint pain		X		
Dehydration		X		
Respiratory illnesses	X	X	X	
Dysentery	X	X	X	
Mistrust of chemoprophylaxis	X	X	X	
Side effects of chemoprophylaxis	X	X	X	
Lack of communication with home	X	X	X	X
Suicidal ideation	X			
Fear of death			X	
Sexual assault			X	
Child care issues				X
Postdeployment issues and health concerns				
Trouble with sleep	X	X	X	X
Knee and joint pain	X	X	X	X
Hearing loss	X	X	X	
Dry skin issues	X	X		
Respiratory trouble	X	X	X	
Digestive problems	X		X	
Weight management	X	X	X	X
High blood pressure		X		
Hair loss		X	X	
Sexual disinterest			X	
Alcohol abuse	X	X		
Potential long-term effects of chemical exposures	X	X	X	X
Exaggerated startle responses	X	X		
Long-term side effects of chemoprophylaxis administered during deployment	X	X	X	
Hypervigilance	X	X		

(Continued)

TABLE 9.1 *Continued*

Code	Male Active Duty Veterans[a]	Male Reserve and National Guard Veterans[a]	Female Veterans	Veteran Wives
Difficulty with irritability and anger	X	X	X	X
Trouble transitioning to civilian life	X	X	X	X
Family discord due to shifting family roles	X	X		X
Antisocial attitudes and behaviors	X	X	X	X
Hypersocial behaviors			X	
Depression	X	X		
Memory loss	X	X	X	
Concentration problems		X	X	
Claustrophobia		X		
Emotional distress from watching media coverage of war	X	X		
Overprotection of family members			X	X
VA Medical Center service needs for OEF/OIF veterans				
Information about VA benefits	X	X	X	X
Joint and back pain services	X		X	
Sleep disorder services	X	X	X	X
Weight management	X	X	X	X
Dental care	X		X	
Wellness services			X	
Information for veterans and families on normal readjustment problems after deployment	X	X	X	X
Career counseling	X	X	X	X
Financial counseling	X	X	X	
General psychological services	X	X	X	X
Stress management	X	X	X	X
Anger management	X	X	X	X
Tobacco abuse treatment	X	X	X	X
Alcohol abuse treatment	X	X	X	X

(*Continued*)

TABLE 9.1 *Continued*

Code	Male Active Duty Veterans[a]	Male Reserve and National Guard Veterans[a]	Female Veterans	Veteran Wives
Barriers to seeking care for postdeployment issues				
Military career repercussion of seeking services		X	X	
Take care of problems on their own	X	X		X
Normalizing their experience	X	X	X	X
Stigma of seeking health services	X	X	X	X
Difficult to access services at the VA	X	X	X	X
Overwhelmed with transitions to civilian life			X	
Feeling others are in greater need of services	X		X	

[a]We conducted two groups of these service member types.

determine whether some experiences were present, for example, among National Guard/Reservists but not among veterans of active duty. We organized the matrix into four areas based on the structure of the interview guide: health concerns during deployment, postdeployment health concerns, VA medical center service needs for OEF/OIF veterans, and barriers to seeking care for postdeployment issues. The findings were organized by higher order themes or topics that emerged from the data under each section of the interview guide. Within each topic we indicated whether the findings were present among all groups or only among a subset of groups.

RESULTS

All veteran participants reported having been deployed to Iraq and/or Afghanistan, with some additionally deployed to Kuwait. Most had returned from their last deployment in 2004 or 2005 and the mean time since last deployment was 27 months (SD = 11). Use of VA health care was reported by 23 of the 54 veterans (43%), a proportion similar to that of OEF/OIF veterans using VA health care nationally at the time of this study. Table 9.1 presents the code-by-group type matrix results. Key findings according to the four major areas of interest in the interview guide are summarized below.

Health Concerns During Deployment

When asked to enumerate their concerns while deployed, all veteran groups expressed concern about health problems resulting from exposure to chemicals, air quality (e.g., sand, smoke from burn pits) and unsanitary living conditions (e.g., contaminated food and water). Dysentery and respiratory complications (e.g., lung infections, dry/persistent cough) were commonly reported illnesses among OEF/OIF veterans. All veteran groups expressed concern about medication side effects (e.g., sleeplessness, diarrhea) and mistrust about chemoprophylaxis administered during mobilization and while in the OEF/OIF theater. The National Guard/Reservists groups also reported problems with knee and joint pain during deployment.

All veteran groups mentioned lack of regular communication with loved ones back home as an additional stressor while deployed. National Guard/Reservist groups also felt that their loved ones did not have access to the same formal or informal social supports during their deployment as did active duty family members. Spouses of National Guard/Reservists echoed social support concerns, especially when they did not live close to a military base.

Each type of group experienced unique stressors as well as combat exposures. For example, the female veteran group expressed concerns about sexual harassment and assault and reported combat-related fear of death. Active duty veteran groups listed problems with suicidal ideation while deployed. The veteran spouses group expressed stressors related to child care, such as dealing with family crises alone and needing to stop working outside the home while their husbands were deployed in order to take care of their children.

Postdeployment Health Concerns and Problems

Veteran groups expressed a variety of postdeployment health concerns. As one veteran of the National Guard/Reserves group noted,

> I feel like it took years off my life. I don't know if I'll get over it, but it felt like just being over there for that period of time, I came back more unhealthy.

Common physical complaints were chronic joint pain, hearing loss, respiratory issues, and weight management issues. Male active duty veterans and National Guard/Reservists groups reported ongoing skin problems not reported in the female veteran group. Both male and female veteran groups expressed concern over the potential long-term side effects of chemoprophylaxis, such as vaccines for malaria and anthrax. The male veteran group expressed specific concerns about the potential effects of chemoprophylaxis on their future fertility. Another prominent concern, across genders, was difficulty with increased use of alcohol.

Many veterans expressed a need for a transition period in order to decompress from OEF/OIF deployment. As one female veteran stated,

> I think there is a healing time. For me, [it was] six months. I had healed a lot in six months ... I think gradually you sort of heal yourself and part of that for me was called like "hibernating" because I was on all the time, never had any time off so I like needed to hibernate.

During this decompression from deployment transition, veterans experienced many emotional and mental health issues. Difficulty with irritability and anger was a major problem expressed by all OEF/OIF combat veteran groups. As one male active duty veteran stated:

> I believe a lot of people have a lot of problems with what they saw [during deployment], and not knowing how to get the anger out of them because what is the first thing we use? We use anger. We used being scared. We use it as adrenaline to push a fight or do what we've got to do. And when you get home, you can't go to Wal-Mart and push that anger at Wal-Mart and if you do, the cops get called and then you get arrested or something.

Problems with anger dysregulation and irritability expressed in all groups affected veterans' family relationships. As one male National Guard/Reservist group member expressed,

> ... my wife, she'll say one thing and all of a sudden I'm flying off the bat at her ... I get upset and holler at her and she turns her head and I see tears running down the side of her face because I'm hollering for no good reason, just because she ticked me off!

Difficulties with anger control were present for the female veteran group as well. As one female veteran stated,

> I had this anger problem [after returning from deployment], the least little bitty thing I would be ready to snap . . . I've been on an emotional rollercoaster since I got back.

Some veterans reported that their anger issues had resulted in their getting involved in the criminal justice system,

> . . . ever since I've been back I have a real short temper. And I've had a problem, I've gotten arrested a couple of times over it and I never had a problem before I joined the Army. Real short temper.

Sleep problems were expressed by all returning OEF/OIF veteran groups. Some active duty veterans stated that their sleep difficulties affected their relationships with their wives. As one veteran stated,

> I had problems sleeping with my wife because at night I just, crazy reactions, you know, all through the night. And I was waking her and so I slept in the living room for about three to four months. I think because I done that, I've never really gotten that close back with my spouse. I never really bonded back to where we were before I went on tour.

All male veteran groups expressed issues with hypervigilance. As one active duty veteran stated,

> I don't sleep. I hear everything outside. I can hear noises through the house. I always tell my wife . . . that you don't have to worry about nothing, nothing coming in [the house] because I hear it before they do anything.

Hypervigilant behaviors extended into everyday activities. For example, some male veteran groups expressed the need to be in control within their environments, such as sitting in particular places while dining out so they would have a good view of their surroundings. Also all male veteran groups enumerated exaggerated startle responses to noise (e.g., jumpiness) since returning from deployment.

Across veteran groups, members stated they wanted to withdraw from social settings, including family interactions, upon returning home from OEF/OIF deployment. One member of a National Guard/Reservist group summed up the feeling echoed by many when he stated,

> When I got back, everybody is happy for you to be back and they rush
> around you and they want to spend time and I'm just saying, 'Just
> leave me alone.'

Other veteran groups reported struggling with trying to reintegrate
into civilian life but still trying to avoid situations involving crowds and
noise,

> I'm a student, I go to school so I would go early and stay late just in
> the library where it is quiet. I went deer hunting a ton last year and
> didn't kill a single thing, just sat up there because there is peace
> and quiet.

Transition to civilian life was further complicated by cognitive
problems. All veteran groups enumerated issues with loss of concentration and lapses in memory since returning home which were problematic during their postdeployment transition period. Male veteran
groups stated they experienced emotional distress from watching
media coverage of the war and depression since returning from
deployment.

All veteran groups expressed feelings of not being able to turn off
their military mindset, which complicated interactions with civilians.
As one National Guard/Reservist stated,

> When I have to deal with people, it annoys me. I think they should
> understand me and they don't . . . you talk to a civilian and you
> expect them to think the same way you do. I tell my wife that I just
> can't tolerate civilians anymore.

The veteran spouse group also reported trouble transitioning to
civilian life. As one wife stated,

> I felt like there were so many resources in the Army . . . and then you
> get out and it's kind of like you're thrown to the wolves . . . the civilian
> world is a whole different world!

Postdeployment shifts from military roles and responsibilities to
civilian and family issues were difficulties expressed in all veteran
groups. As one Reservist recounted,

> . . . [During deployment] you've got a purpose. You wake up in the
> morning; you know what you're going to do. There's a real focus
> on what you've got to do and that's really, for some of us, for a lot

of us, easy! And now you come home and try to remember if you paid your electric bill on time and the water bill and the momma and the kids have all been taken care of ... I think that transition is a little bit awkward.

Spouses and male veteran groups also indicated that long deployments caused family roles and responsibilities to shift (e.g., family money issues, discipline of children), which resulted in family discord upon demobilization. The female veteran group uniquely expressed a lack of sexual interest, yet also reported needing to be around people "all the time" and feeling "overprotective" of their children.

Veterans' Preferences for Types of VA Services

When asked directly which services VA Medical Centers should provide to returning OEF/OIF veterans, many listed suggestions were endorsed and other ideas were offered. These included providing information for family members about postdeployment adjustment problems and offering counseling for career, financial management, and benefits assistance. All veteran and spouse groups felt that the VA should offer services to help this cohort of veterans better manage postdeployment stress, anger issues, sleep problems, tobacco use, alcohol misuse, and concerns about possible chemical exposures during deployment. All OEF/OIF veteran groups expressed confusion about their eligibility for VA benefits and how "service connection" was determined.

Barriers to Seeking Care for Postdeployment Issues

When asked why some veterans do not seek help for their health concerns and related issues through VA Medical Centers, both male and female veteran groups stated that they and other veterans they know did not feel that they have problems; they attribute their issues as "normal stuff" associated with military service. The female spouse group reiterated their impression that their husbands did not recognize that they had any problems. As one veteran's wife stated,

I think when you're dealing with it for so long it becomes normal. And they you don't realize how abnormal it is until you're out of that atmosphere ... compared to the civilian world, he didn't realize how un-normal so much stuff was, what happened when he was over there.

Members of the female veterans group indicated that they did not seek VA services because they felt overwhelmed by the transition back to civilian life. As one female veteran summarized,

> I haven't gone to the VA ... I have enough dealing with just getting back into life and where I'm going to live and all those things. It was just too much getting back.

When veterans did recognize service-related problems, especially mental health issues, male active duty and National Guard/Reservist groups reported that they preferred to take care of problems on their own. Female spouses affirmed that their veteran husbands did not seek help because they were "taught to suck it up" in the military and these attitudes and behaviors persisted into civilian life. Active duty and female veteran groups also stated that they did not seek services because they felt less deserving than veterans with worse problems. All groups stated that it was difficult to access services at the VA due to long waits for appointments and confusion about benefits.

Across all groups, concerns about stigma associated with mental health issues also inhibited use of VA services. As one male active duty veteran recounted,

> While I was in the Army, growing up in the Army, I looked down upon people who went to mental health. I always thought they were weak. I thought, 'Why are you going to the psychiatrist every day man? Are you kind of suicidal? Do I need to watch you?' But after my experiences, I had to go there myself and get help finally myself.

National Guard/Reservist groups also affirmed concern about possible repercussions of seeking health services on future military promotions if they wanted to continue serving. As one National Guardsman stated,

> There is a stigma attached to it [mental health services]. If you tell them you're dealing with some anger or some panic attack issues, they might be kind of concerned with hanging around or wanting to do a mission with you later on.

Suggestions for reducing barriers to health/mental health care included streamlining access to care such as reducing wait times for appointments; offering more assistance to "get through the maze" of enrolling for benefits; having caring, informed health care providers and telephone support; offering evening and weekend clinics; considering "peer support" options; and integrating physical and mental health treatment to reduce embarrassment and stigma associated with receiving specialty treatment for psychological concerns. All groups suggested fostering an approach that focused more on normal adjustment and less on "fixing" the veteran, without using terms that might connote weakness such as "disease" or "disorder."

DISCUSSION

This study elicited the perspectives of OEF/OIF veterans and their spouses as they transitioned to civilian life after deployment. Overall, our findings suggest a myriad of health concerns and a need for education and outreach to engage veterans and their families in patient-centered health care and clarify benefits eligibility. Although some experiences were not reported by all groups, we noted considerable overlap of health concerns and readjustment problems described by male and female veterans from both active duty and Reserve component military units. Health concerns expressed were comparable to those identified among OEF/OIF veterans assessed at the War Related Illness and Injury Study Center-New Jersey during a similar time period (Helmer et al., 2007). Concerns about environmental exposures due to burn pits, potential airborne chemicals, and chemoprophylaxis were similar to those expressed by veterans of the Persian Gulf War (Kang, Li, Mahan, Eisen, & Engel, 2009). Although postdeployment musculoskeletal pain was reported among all the veteran groups, only National Guard/Reservists reported problems with knee and joint pain during deployment, perhaps related to older age among these personnel. Chronic pain issues, related to minor acute injuries associated with routine military duty as well as more severe injuries associated with polytrauma, are likely to continue to be a treatment focus for this cohort of veterans as they age (Clark, Bair, Buckenmaier, Gironda, & Walker, 2007; Gironda, Clark, Massengale, & Walker, 2006).

All veteran and spouse groups reported concerns about lack of communication with loved ones while deployed. Prolonged separation due to training and deployment has been associated with decreased intimacy and increased family conflict, including domestic violence (Sayers et al., 2009) and increased behavioral problems among children of deployed parents (Flake, Davis, Johnson, & Middleton, 2009). Male and female veteran groups described difficulty engaging with their children postdeployment and, in some cases, feeling excessively protective of them.

Although the group of female spouses reported concerns about their service members' limited home communication, they reported few specific health concerns for their partner during deployment, perhaps partly as a consequence of the limited communication or the service members' efforts to not worry their spouses. However, spouses did report veteran health problems following their return home, including problems with sleep, joint pain, and weight management. Because the veteran groups articulated many more health concerns during and after deployment than the spouse group recalled, it is possible that service members did not disclose these issues to their families.

Indeed, most of the veteran health problems reported by spouses upon postdeployment were observable, such as trouble with sleep. Spouses may not have been as attuned to veterans' less visible problems (e.g., respiration, digestion, hearing). It is also possible that spouses may have enumerated only the most pressing postdeployment health concurs that affected family discord. Engaging families in recovery from trauma is effective but underutilized (Glynn, Cohen, Dixon, & Niv, 2006; Sherman, Faruque, & Foley, 2005). The discrepancy between veterans' problems and spouses' awareness of them may be another barrier to health care access.

The female veteran group uniquely reported concern about sexual assault and fear of death. Although both men and women may experience military sexual trauma (MST), rates of MST and related PTSD are disproportionately high among women veterans (Frayne et al., 1999; Yaeger, Himmelfarb, Cammack, & Mintz, 2006). Other negative outcomes associated with MST in women include heightened risk for major depression, substance abuse, suicidality, and domestic violence (Butterfield, McIntyre, Stechuchak, Nanda, & Bastian, 1998; Hankin et al., 1999). Sexual trauma is also associated with increased health care visits, service use and costs, and decreased health status functioning and health-related quality of life (Frayne et al., 1999; Kelly, Tyrka, Price, & Carpenter, 2008; Kimerling, Clum, & Wolfe, 2000; Kimerling, Gima, Smith, Street, & Frayne, 2007; Wagner, Wolfe, Rotnitsky, Proctor, & Erickson, 2000). Thus, sexual assault is an important consideration for routine assessment of all veterans, particularly women who may present with complex clinical complaints. The experience of sexual assault or harassment while deployed is also likely to impact reintegration into relationships upon return.

Women veterans' perceived risk of being killed despite not technically being deployed in a combat role likely reflects the many varied duties of female service members in the GWOT. Within our women veterans' focus group, several women served as military police and in military intelligence and encountered many dangerous situations. More recently, women have been placed with Marines and Special Forces units to provide culturally sensitive body searches of Islamic women. These duties have brought female military personnel into close combat situations. Finally, data from the NVVRS study suggest that the perception of being at risk of being killed may be a more potent predictor of PTSD among women than among men, regardless of their actual exposure to enemy combat (King, King, Gudanowski, & Vreven, 1995).

Health Care Service Needs and Barriers

The widespread prevalence of concern about anger dysregulation among veterans indicates a particularly important issue to address as returning service members transition to their homes and communities. Frustration with civilian inefficiencies and family roles were cited as triggers for angry outbursts and barriers to resuming relations with families. In combination with problems associated with alcohol use, impulsive anger may result in clashes with the criminal justice system. Early anger dysregulation intervention may help to redirect the veteran to mental health/readjustment services. Several states are piloting jail diversion programs for OEF/OIF veterans who present as new offenders and are willing to access mental health treatment in lieu of jail time for minor offenses (Frisman & Griffin-Fennell, 2009). Across all focus groups in this study there was consensus that OEF/OIF veterans need access to treatments for anger, stress management, alcohol, and tobacco use, suggesting openness to pursuing these services.

Veteran and spouse groups made several suggestions for reducing stigma associated with seeking counseling or other mental health care, such as clarifying benefits eligibility and including family members in educational efforts on readjustment issues. Subsequent to the time these focus groups were conducted, VA has initiated several programs consistent with these suggestions, including piloting integrated care Post-Deployment Health Clinics, partnering with Department of Defense and Vet Center staff to formally reach out to service members and their families before and after deployment, and developing high-quality, informational websites with links to crisis ser- vices and updated social networking communications (http://www. oefoif.va.gov/). Within the last year, multiagency collaboration through the Defense Centers of Excellence for Psychological Health and Traumatic Brain Injury produced an informative, attractive portal to information designed to promote the processes of building resilience, facilitating recovery, and supporting reintegration of returning service members, veterans, and their families (www.realwarriors.net).

Study Strengths

Our findings augment current knowledge about the health concerns of returning veterans, largely gathered through routine clinical screenings and medical records reviews. These qualitative findings provide a snapshot of perceived health care needs and barriers to care through the eyes of this newest cohort of combat veterans. The inclusion of an all-female veteran group and a female spouse group provided unique information and perspectives that might not have been voiced in more heterogeneous groups. Creation of separate groups for active duty and reserve component military personnel facilitated comparisons between these military units, whose resources and deployment patterns may vary considerably from each other. Random selection of eligible participants provided unique opportunities to elicit input from both help-seeking veterans and those who had not yet accessed VA health care, which may better represent the views of OEF/OIF veterans within this region at the time of the study.

Limitations

These findings were obtained in the fall of 2006 and are based on the experiences of veterans who had last returned from deployment between 2004 and 2005, less than half way through the war's current duration. As the war has progressed, the threat of chemical exposure has become less salient than the threat of blast exposure associated with improvised explosive devices (IEDs) and related combat (Taber, Warden, & Hurley, 2006). These results may not generalize to the cohort of combat veterans more recently separated from military service who experienced different health threats. Study participants were recruited from a single region in North Carolina, a military population-dense state, and therefore these results may not represent the concerns, needs, and preferences of all OEF/OIF veterans.

CONCLUSION

This qualitative study identified key health and mental health problems experienced by Active Duty and National Guard/Reservist veterans who had been deployed to Iraq and/or Afghanistan, including those already receiving VA care (43%) and those who had not yet accessed VA (57%). As most returning military personnel will not seek services through VA, both community and VA providers should be aware of key postdeployment issues identified by OEF/OIF veterans and their families. As the war continues, the health and mental health needs of returning combat veterans and their families must drive the development and delivery of effective support and clinical interventions. All veteran and spouse groups expressed interest in a variety of mental health and wellness services, suggesting that there is an opportunity for early intervention and perhaps prevention of chronic health/mental health problems associated with past wars.

REFERENCES

Berkowitz, S. (1996). Using qualitative and mixed method approaches. In R. Reviere (Ed.), *Needs assessment: A creative and practical guide for social scientists* (pp. 53–70). Washington, DC: Taylor & Francis.

Butterfield, M. I., McIntyre, L. M., Stechuchak, K. M., Nanda, K., & Bastian, L. (1998). Mental disorder symptoms in veteran women: Impact of physical and sexual assault. *Journal of the American Medical Women's Association, 53,* 198–200.

Clark, M. E., Bair, M. J., Buckenmaier, C. C., 3RD, Gironda, R. J., & Walker, R. L. (2007). Pain and combat injuries in soldiers returning from operations enduring freedom and Iraqi freedom: Implications for research and practice. *Journal of Rehabilitation Research and Development, 44*(2), 179–194.

Cohen, B. E., Gima, K., Bertenthal, D., Kim, S., Marmar, C. R., & Seal, K. H. (2009). Mental health diagnoses and utilization of VA non-mental health medical services among returning Iraq and Afghanistan veterans. *Journal of General Internal Medicine, 25*(1), 18–24.

Eaton, K. M., Hoge, C. W., Messer, S. C., Whitt, A. A., Cabrera, O. A., McGurk, D., Cox, A., & Castro, C. A. (2008). Prevalence of mental health problems, treatment need, and barriers to care among primary care-seeking spouses of military service members involved in Iraq and Afghanistan deployments. *Military Medicine,* Retrieved November 7, 2009, from http://www.ncbi.nlm.nih.gov/pubmed/19055177, *173*(11), 1051–1056.

Flake, E. M., Davis, B. E., Johnson, P. L., & Middleton, L. S. (2009). The psychosocial effects of deployment on military children. *Journal of Developmental and Behavioral Pediatrics, 30*(4), 271–278.

Frayne, S. M., Skinner, K. M., Sullivan, L. M., Tripp, T. J., Hankin, C. S., Kressin, N. R. et al. (1999). Medical profile of women veterans administration outpatients who report a history of sexual assault occurring while in the military. *Journal of Womens Health Gender Based Medicine, 8*(6), 835–845.

Frisman, L. K., & Griffin-Fennell, F. (2009). Suicide and incarcerated veterans— Don't wait for the numbers. *Journal of the American Academy of Psychiatry Law, 37*(1), 92–94.

Gironda, R. J., Clark, M. E., Massengale, J. P., & Walker, R. L. (2006). Pain among veterans of operations enduring freedom and Iraqi freedom. *Pain, 7*(4), 339–343.

Glynn, S. M., Cohen, A. N., Dixon, L. B., & Niv, N. (2006). The potential impact of the recovery movement on family interventions for schizophrenia: Opportunities and obstacles. *Schizophrenia Bulletin, 32*(3), 451–463.

Hankin, C. S., Skinner, K. M., Sullivan, L. M., Miller, D. R., Frayne, S., & Tripp, T. J. (1999). Prevalence of depressive and alcohol abuse symptoms among women VA outpatients who report experiencing sexual assault while in the military. *Journal of Traumatic Stress, 12*(4), 601–612.

Helmer, D. A., Rossignol, M., Blatt, M., Agarwal, R., Teichman, R., & Lange, G. (2007). Health and exposure concerns of veterans deployed to Iraq and Afghanistan. *Journal of Occupational and Environmental Medicine, 49*(5), 475–480.

Kang, H. K., Li, B., Mahan, C. M., Eisen, S. A., & Engel, C. C. (2009). Health of US veterans of 1991 Gulf War: A follow-up survey in 10 years. *Journal of Occupational and Environmental Medicine, 51*(4), 401–410.

Kelly, M. M., Tyrka, A. R., Price, L. H., & Carpenter, L. L. (2008). Sex differences in the use of coping strategies: Predictors of anxiety and depressive symptoms. *Depression and Anxiety, 25*(10), 839–846.

Kimerling, R., Clum, G. A., & Wolfe, J. (2000). Relationships among trauma exposure, chronic posttraumatic stress disorder symptoms, and self-reported health in women: Replication and extension. *Journal of Traumatic Stress, 13*(1), 115–128.

Kimerling, R., Gima, K., Smith, M. W., Street, A., & Frayne, S. (2007). The Veterans Health Administration and military sexual trauma. *American Journal of Public Health, 97*(12), 2160–2166.

King, D. W., King, L. A., Gudanowski, D. M., & Vreven, D. L. (1995). Alternative representations of war zone stressors: Relationships to posttraumatic stress disorder in male and female Vietnam veterans. *Journal of Abnormal Psychology, 104*(1), 184–195.

Kulka, R., Schlenger, W. E., Fairbank, J. A., Hough, R. L., Jordan, B. K., Marmar, C. R. et al. (1990). *Trauma and the Vietnam war generation: Report of findings from the national Vietnam veterans readjustment study* (Vol. 2). New York: Brunner/Mazel.

Sandelowski, M., & Barroso, J. (2003). Classifying the findings in qualitative studies. *Qualitative Health Research, 13*(7), 905–923.

Sayers, S. L., Farrow, V. A., Ross, J., & Oslin, D. W. (2009). Family problems among recently returned military veterans referred for a mental health evaluation. *Journal of Clinical Psychiatry, 70*(2), 163–170.

Seal, K. H., Bertenthal, D., Miner, C. R., Sen, S., & Marmar, C. (2007). Bringing the war back home: Mental health disorders among 103,788 US veterans returning from Iraq and Afghanistan seen at Department of Veterans Affairs facilities. *Archives of Internal Medicine, 167*(5), 476–482.

Seal, K. H., Metzler, T. J., Gima, K. S., Bertenthal, D., Maguen, S., & Marmar, C. R. (2009). Trends and risk factors for mental health diagnoses among Iraq and Afghanistan veterans using Department of Veterans Affairs health care, 2002–2008. *American Journal of Public Health, 99*(9), 1651–1658.

Sherman, M. D., Faruque, H. D., & Foley, D. D. (2005). Family participation in the treatment of persons with serious mental illness. *Psychiatric Services, 56*(12), 1624–1625.

Taber, K. H., Warden, D. L., & Hurley, R. A. (2006). Blast-related traumatic brain injury: What is known? *Journal of Neuropsychiatry and Clinical Neurosciences, 18*(2), 141–145.

VHA Office of Public Health and Environmental Hazards. (2010) Analysis of VA Health Care Utilization among Operation Enduring Freedom (OEF) and Operation Iraqi Freedom (OIF) Veterans, December 2010.

Wagner, A. W., Wolfe, J., Rotnitsky, A., Proctor, S. P., & Erickson, D. J. (2000). An investigation of the impact of posttraumatic stress disorder on physical health. *Journal of Traumatic Stress, 13*(1), 41–55.

Yaeger, D., Himmelfarb, N., Cammack, A., & Mintz, J. (2006). DSM-IV diagnosed posttraumatic stress disorder in women veterans with and without military sexual trauma. *Journal of General Internal Medicine, 21*(Suppl. 3), S65–S69.

Part III

ADVOCACY PRACTICE TO PROMOTE YOUNG VETERANS' WELL-BEING

David Gitelson and William Valente

F or significant and lasting change to occur in the scope and quality of services offered to veterans, change needs to happen to policy, programs, and services. It is only through the continuing hard work of mental health professionals, activists, politicians, veterans, and civilians that these changes will take place.

In Part III of *Treating Young Veterans*, the authors tackle macrolevel issues, specifically, how to push for advancement through policy, programs, initiatives, and institutional change. Education is an essential building block in the construction of change. In the first chapter of Part III, Christina Harnett and Lt. Col. Michael Gafney describe the landscape facing veterans upon reintegration and examine specific ways the government is addressing reintegration. A major challenge in reintegration is employment. Veterans need employment as well as the mental and physical well-being necessary to maintain employment while juggling the responsibilities of everyday life, which requires skills very different from those honed in combat. In the following chapter, Christina Harnett and Joan DeSimone look at employment issues and how the challenges of civilian worklife are drastically different from the challenges of combat life.

Providing services is not just the right thing to do for veterans who have served the country, it also makes fiscal and practical sense. Justin Holbrook, in the next chapter, reviews the benefits to creating and expanding legal systems that emphasize treatment and rehabilitation to work with veterans who have committed crimes. David Gitelson reports on an outreach project in which social workers from the VA educated First Responders on best practices in working with combat veterans in civilian life. In the final chapter, Thomas Reed examines how the VA claims system works or does not work while presenting a civilian call-to-arms to overhaul antiquated procedures.

Through studying what is currently offered, the authors of Part III of *Treating Young Veterans* recognize and identify programs and systems that work and ones that fail. Identifying gaps is the first step in exploring what can be done and the contributors and editoral staff of this book hope it will be done.

10

ENSURING EQUALITY AFTER THE WAR FOR THE NATIONAL GUARD AND RESERVE FORCES: REVISITING THE YELLOW RIBBON INITIATIVE

Christina Harnett and Lieutenant Colonel Michael Gafney

A PROLOGUE

"You know you never defeated us on the battlefield," said the American colonel. The North Vietnamese colonel pondered this remark a moment. "That may be so," he replied, "but it is also irrelevant."[1]

Yet again has the United States and its military seemed to have confused winning battles with winning the war. In the case of returning Reserve Component (RC) combat veterans, we won the battle. We successfully trained them during their Reserve careers, sharpened their skills and battle drills to deploy them, used (and sometimes expended) them on the battlefield and brought them back home. Yet we, as a nation refuse to pay the price to win the war.

For these young men and women Reservists, winning the war means being able to successfully return to their former lives. They do not live on or around a military post. Their families and/or loved ones do not live in a supportive community with others who share their experiences. They do not work daily in the military milieu with others who have had the same experiences of war and confront the same demons on a daily basis. No, when Reservists return, they take off the uniform and return to their original civilian role. They continue to live in the shadow world of a citizen soldier. Neither full-time soldier

---

[1] Conversation in Hanoi, April 25, 1975 between Colonel Harry, Summers, Jr, the Chief, Negotiations Division, U.S. Delegation, Four Party Joint Military Team and Colonel Tu, Chief, North Vietnamese (DRV) Delegation in Summers, H. G., Jr (1995). *On strategy: A critical analysis of the Vietnam War* (p. 2). Novato, CA: Presidio Press.

nor full-time civilian, they juggle two diametrically opposed lives and drag their families and loved ones along on an odyssey they did not plan for and probably do not understand.

Like most people, they envision a Reservist as a one weekend a month and two weeks in the summer part-time soldier. This patriotic eccentricity can be tolerated. Except that now we expect them to train longer and harder. We expect their employer to be more tolerant (of their absence). We expect all of this with limited explanation. We expect them all to understand when we completely change the contract with the Reservist from what was essentially a "weekend warrior" to full-time soldier. This change means their loved one or employee leaves home over and over to perform a mission that used to belong only to full-time Active Duty personnel.

To do this, we must ensure that our Reservists meet the standards of their Active Component counterparts. In the case of the U.S. Army, we have a long and successful history of training soldiers to go to war. We simply extend this training to the Reserve and National Guard as they prepare to deploy to war. By the end of that training we have brought these men and women to the level of readiness where we expect them to kill another human being without conscious thought or reflection. Or as the Marines call it—muscle memory.

We expect and they, to their great credit, will act to protect themselves and others from harm by the enemy. To do this, they may be required to kill their enemy. Not "neutralize" not "take out" not "eliminate," but "kill" their enemy. What we teach is for them to shoulder their rifle, look down the barrel, aim at the center of mass, pull the trigger, feel the recoil on their shoulder, smell the burned powder, and kill another human being. In the time it has taken to pull the trigger, we have turned upside down a lifetime of Judeo-Christian teaching. Then before they even have a chance to reflect on their action, their peers begin to congratulate them on that success. They may offer thanks for saving their lives. We may even reward them with a medal or commendation. Regardless of the method, we reinforce the idea that they have done the "right thing." That killing another human being was the right thing to do. And we continue to reinforce that idea throughout their time in theater. Then, one day it is time to come home.

Unlike WWII where it was many months before a soldier was able to return home, and unlike Korea where air-travel took days to get home with many stops, or return home was by ship, the return home from Iraq or Afghanistan is more akin to Vietnam. It can be only 300 hours from the time our Reservist is in theater on guard for a firefight, ambush or IED to when he/she is in civilian clothes wandering the streets of their hometown. Not the months they spent getting ready for combat, but hours with almost no preparation for being a civilian once again.

One of the first questions a returning Reservist is asked by those at home is, "Did you kill anybody?" And it may well be at this point that our Reservist confronts for the first time his/her feelings of having killed someone. Not only must they confront this reality but as a Reservist they probably do it completely alone, isolated from their fellow soldiers, and with people who may not be supportive (or understanding). Unlike their Active Duty counterpart, the RC Service member has returned to the civilian world full of people with no understanding of the war, the horrors faced by the individual soldier, the conditions in which the soldier lived, the pressures to accomplish the mission or the camaraderie that only exists among those who have faced death together. Yet the soldier may be judged as he/she stands alone without the support of his/her peers. Theirs is the reality facing returning Reservists.

By engaging Afghanistan and Iraq in combat, we have embarked on a 70–80-year odyssey to provide care for our veterans for the rest of their lives. Unfortunately this cost was never factored in to the cost of the war. It is, however, the cost "of doing business" and unless it is paid, we will fail the men and women who have sacrificed so much to protect this country. Until we are willing to pay this cost to return our RC women and men to their civilian lives, we will, ultimately, lose the war.

INTRODUCTION

This is the first time at a national level that the military has engaged a process to integrate service members and their families into active components and community systems to promote prevention, support and reintegration of a population. The effort crosses all demographics including rural and urban areas and socioeconomic levels and promotes a holistic concept involving the individual, family and their community. This endeavor is supported by modern technological innovations for information-sharing, outreach and interpersonal interventions in a truly holistic approach. It is the first time a proactive system has been designed, implemented and

given the financial resources to promote wellness and resiliency
within the population it is designed to serve[2].

In the traumatic aftermath of the terrorist attacks of September 11, 2001,
the United States Government initiated the Global War on Terror
(GWOT). This included three strategic military initiatives: Operation
Enduring Freedom (OEF) directed at Afghanistan, Operation Iraqi
Freedom (OIF) which launched a military invasion of Iraq in 2003,
and Operation Noble Eagle (ONE) whose mission was to provide
increased protection for overseas military bases and other homeland
security initiatives (Belasco, 2009). Since September 2010, OIF has
been renamed as Operation New Dawn (OND). The subsequent
tsunami of deployment and post-deployment veterans' issues has
forever reshaped the nature and meaning of military service; it is "the
road less traveled for members of America's all-volunteer Armed
Forces" (Bowen & Martin, 2011, p. 3). For the first time in history, the
National Guard has become an operational reserve when it was
previously a strategic reserve.

This chapter's focus is on the unique characteristics of the RC that
put them at particular risk for deployment and postdeployment adjustment issues especially when returning home to family, work, and community after deployment, and on a nationally mandated Deployment
Cycle Support (DCS) program for the RC. This was implemented as a
health promotion strategy to address the disparities that are unique to
the reservists' experience of combat and reintegration. To this end, the
development and implementation of the Maryland National Guard
Yellow Ribbon Reintegration Program will be reviewed.

The GWOT has several unique features that distinguish it from other
conflicts in which our country has engaged over the last 50 years. First,
the nature of military operations has changed. The norm of service
is marked by multiple and/or extended deployments with shorter
respite periods between deployments (Tanielian, Jaycox, Adamson, &
Metscher, 2008). Second, as opposed to more conventional wars, OIF
and OEF have no clear "safe zones" and every location has the potential
to become a battlefield leaving military personnel at continuous risk of
injury or death (Katz, Bloor, Cojucar, & Draper, 2007; Manderscheid,
2007) and in a potential state of heightened anxiety. "Soldiers and
Marines on patrol are under constant threat from improvised explosive
devices (IEDs), snipers, and the grinding tension between terror and
tedium" (Lafferty, Alford, Davis, & O'Connor, 2008, p. 3).

---

[2]Observation by a former Mental Health Advisor to the Department of Defense on the Deployment
Cycle Support initiative.

Third, the ratio of wounded to killed service members is the highest in our history due to improvements in military medicine and technical advances in personal protective equipment, and military health care is focusing more intently on the nature of brain trauma and its psychiatric sequelae resulting from blast injuries in combat (Tanielian et al., 2008). Fourth, despite medical advances for physical injuries, psychological injuries resulting from combat have soared and approximately one-third of returning veterans self-report symptoms indicative of posttraumatic stress disorder (PTSD) (Manderscheid, 2007). Finally, the RC is experiencing its highest level of deployment in the last 50 years as the United States attempts to sustain its first prolonged conflict with an all-volunteer force (Sollinger, Fisher, & Metscher, 2008).

THE MANPOWER OF THE GUARD FORCES

The wars in Iraq and Afghanistan have endured longer and proven more intransigent than either the government or citizens anticipated. Greater numbers of RC service members are being deployed to war zones for extended periods and multiple tours. Table 10.1 displays the total deployment figures for all military personnel engaged in the current conflicts through February of 2009. As may be seen, the total number of service members deployed in these conflicts is over 1.8 million, and of these, approximately 28% were in the RC. When multiple deployments are considered, almost 27% of RC forces have deployed for more than one tour of duty. Finally, both National Guard and Reserve personnel comprise nearly 26% of total deployment events on file[3] covering this period. Thus as GWOT swelled, the U.S. military's reliance on the individual Reservist or National Guards-man as an operational force member grew stronger to meet staffing demands. As of this date, RC personnel represent nearly one-third of all service members deployed in GWOT and similarly almost one-third of the military strength called up for multiple tours.

   In addition to the costs of military staffing demands, as may be seen in Table 10.2, a second cost of GWOT is the human toll extracted in lives and war injuries. Since the beginning of these efforts, over 5000 lives have been lost in the OEF and OIF conflicts. Of those, 993 were RC service members. These losses sustained by RC constitute 18% of the total service members lost to combat or combat-related injuries. When

---

[3]A deployment event is one service member deploying one time.

TABLE 10.1 Total deployed military personnel and percent of total deployed personnel by service for OEF and OIF conflicts as of February 2009[a]

Service	Total Deployment Events on the File	Number of Members With Only One Deployment	Number of Members With More Than One Deployment	Total Number of Members Ever Deployed	Percent of Total Number of Members Ever Deployed
Army Active Duty	916,139	341,645	234,035	575,680	30.41
Army National Guard	289,983	186,490	46,261	232,751	12.29
Army Reserve	160,360	95,423	28,020	123,443	6.52
Army Total	1,366,482	623,558	308,316	931,874	49.22
Navy Active Duty	495,815	190,709	122,826	313,535	16.56
Navy Reserve	48,783	24,628	8,362	32,990	1.74
Navy Total	544,598	215,337	131,188	346,525	18.30
Marine Corps Active Duty	330,202	112,852	93,442	206,294	10.90
Marine Corps Reserve	41,923	31,078	5,066	36,144	1.91
Marine Corps Total	372,125	143,930	98,508	242,438	12.81
Air Force Active Duty	481,092	145,892	120,583	266,475	14.07
Air National Guard	134,492	32,116	32,748	64,864	3.43
Air Force Reserve	97,042	19,240	18,328	37,568	1.98
Air Force Total	712,626	197,248	171,659	368,907	19.49
DoD Active Duty Total	2,223,248	791,098	570,886	1,361,984	71.94
DoD National Guard Total	424,475	218,606	79,009	297,615	15.72
DoD Reserve Total	348,108	170,369	59,776	230,145	12.16
DoD Total	2,995,831	1,180,073	709,671	1,889,744	99.81
Coast Guard Active Duty	4,091	2,797	520	3,317	0.18
Coast Guard Reserve	246	209	14	223	0.01
Coast Guard Total	4,337	3,006	534	3,540	0.19
Active Duty Total	2,227,339	793,895	571,406	1,365,301	72.11
National Guard Total	424,475	218,606	79,009	297,615	15.72
Reserve Total	348,354	170,578	59,790	230,368	12.17
Total	3,000,168	1,183,079	710,205	1,893,284	100.00

[a]Source: Department of Defense Office of Public Communication. CTS Deployment File Baseline Report (Contingency tracking system), February 2009.

TABLE 10.2 Casualty totals by service component for OIF and OEF conflicts October 7, 2001, through October 12, 2010[a]

Casualty Type	Army			Navy		Marines		Air Force		
	USA	ARNG	USAR	USN	USNR	USMC	USMCR	USAF	ANG	USAFR
OIF Totals	18,931	4,612	1,909	614	127	8,456	1,193	416	60	24
OIF Hostile death	2,000	365	173	47	18	725	126	29	0	0
OIF Nonhostile death	491	130	73	32	6	158	13	15	2	5
OIF WIA	16,440	4,117	1,663	535	103	7,573	1,054	372	58	19
OEF Totals	5,349	1,032	224	223	8	2,520	84	226	13	7
OEF Hostile death	583	104	26	36	4	191	10	28	1	1
OEF Nonhostile death	149	33	23	26	0	47	4	24	1	1
OEF WIA	4,617	895	175	161	4	2,282	70	174	11	5
OIF/OEF Total Fatalities	3223	632	295	141	28	1121	153	96	4	7
Percent of Total Fatalities for all Services	56.5%	11.1%	5.2%	2.5.7%	.49%	19.7%	2.7%	1.7%	>0.01%	0.12%

Total Fatalities Across All Services = 5700. USA = Army Active; ARNG = Army National Guard; OIF = Operation Iraqi Freedom; OEF = Operation Enduring Freedom; WIA = Wounded in Action. USAR = Army Reserve; USN = Navy Active; USNR = Navy Reserve; USMC = Marine Corps Active; USMCR = Marine Corps Reserve; USAF = Air Force Active; ANG = Air National Guard; USAFR = Air Force Reserve.

[a]*Source:* Defense Manpower Data Center. Retrieved October 13, 2010, from http://siadapp.dmdc.osd.mil/personnel/CASUALTY/gwot_component.pdf

considering "wounded in action" (WIA) rates for these conflicts, Reservists incurred 20% of all injuries reported by the military for the duration of both operations. As of March 2009, approximately 34,000 military members have been wounded in action in OIF/OEF conflicts (Department of Defense (DoD), 2009).

According to a 2008 DoD Report for the period 2003–2007, almost 44,000 military patients had been diagnosed with traumatic brain injury (TBI) as a consequence of combat; the Military Health System estimates that it has spent approximately $100 million on direct/purchased care for victims of TBI and another $10.1 million on related prescriptions. Rates of PTSD for this period are reported to have been almost 40,000 cases with an estimated $63.8 million expended on direct/purchased care and another $13.1 million on associated prescription costs. These health care expenditures do not include future costs of health care or associated costs of postdeployment loss of earnings due to combat-related disabilities; nor can they capture the psychosocial costs of deployment to the individual, the family, or the community.

The fiscal costs of GWOT are staggering and growing. Belasco (2009) reports that as of June 2009 Congress has approved approximately $944 billion to cover a wide range of related costs including those for "military operations, base security, reconstruction, foreign aid, embassy costs, and veterans' health care for the three operations initiated since the 9/11 attacks" (Belasco, 2009, p. i). The total appropriation of funds was differentially allocated in the following manner: 72% ($683 billion) to Iraq, 24% ($227 billion) to Afghanistan, 3% ($29 billion) to security enhancements, and 1% ($5 billion) of funds were unallocated. The cumulative total spending expected through fiscal year 2010 is over $1 trillion with OIF's and OEF's spending increasing to 97% of the cumulative total war funding (Belasco, 2009).

At present, there is growing national attention as to the long-term deployment health consequences for GWOT veterans (Smith et al., 2008) as well as factors mediating successful reintegration of deployed military. Such concern has renewed research interest in the consequences of wartime experience on our nation's military and military families (Lapierre, Schwegler, & LaBauve, 2007).

While it is true that many veterans return home and successfully reintegrate without difficulty, many also bring with them a range of significant behavioral health issues (House Veterans' Affairs Committee, 2009), and with each redeployment the stress is intensified for the veteran and members of his/her social world, having serious implications for adjustment and functioning postwar (House Veterans'

Affairs Committee, 2009). These issues have wide-reaching implications for personal adjustment, family dynamics, social relationships, and employment-related dimensions. In short, deployment experiences have far-reaching and long-term consequences for military members and other members of the civilian world in which they live and work. GWOT has inaugurated an era of unprecedented attention to the psychological consequences of combat deployments; behavioral health issues manifest the potential to outpace rates of combat injuries (Sammons & Batten, 2008).

The psychological impact of deployment in war time has been empirically well established. Recent studies have demonstrated clear evidence that troops who have been exposed to the extreme and unpredictable violence of OIF and OEF sustain higher rates of physical injuries with psychological sequelae and higher rates of psychological injuries as a direct consequence of deployment experiences (Seal, Bertenthal, Miner, Sen, & Marmar, 2007; Smith et al., 2008). For example, a 2007 study revealed that more than one in three veterans who have served in these war zones are suffering from a variety of conditions, including PTSD, anxiety, depression, substance abuse disorder, and other mental health conditions (Seal et al., 2007).

Along a similar vein, a study conducted by Smith et al. (2008) using self-report data from a longitudinal study of both Active and RCs found a threefold increase in new onset PTSD symptoms among deployed soldiers having combat exposure as contrasted against nondeployers. The authors speculate that such factors as the intensity and unpredictability of urban combat, the constant threat of roadside bombs, multiple and extended deployments, and the difficulty associated with distinguishing allies from enemies may all contribute to exceedingly high levels of stress and the potential for long-term health consequences. Likewise, Lapierre et al. (2007) found among Army veterans returning from OIF/OEF deployments, that approximately 44% self-reported "clinically significant" symptoms of depression, PTSD, or both syndromes. Because the wars in Afghanistan and Iraq are different from other conflicts, these distinctions clearly impact both the nature of the deployment experience and the challenges associated with reintegration into interpersonal relationships, and family and community life after deployment (Manderscheid, 2007). Lastly, a clear understanding of the direct impact of deployment on behavioral health in general is made all the more complex by the potential intermittent presence and absence of symptoms in some disorders (Karney, Ramchand, Osilla, Caldarone, & Burns, 2008).

Two "signature injuries" of OIF and OEF are PTSD and TBI (DoD, 2007) and the two conditions may share a direct relationship (Hoge et al., 2008) with a span of influence that is disruptive to both personal and intrapersonal functioning. For instance, PTSD has been associated with both an increased risk for suicidal ideation among veterans (Pietrzak et al., 2010) and negative behaviors in intimate relationships including physical and psychological abuse (Monson, Taft, & Fredman, 2009).

Moreover, children of veterans suffering from PTSD are at higher risk for psychiatric and academic difficulties (House Veterans' Affairs Committee, 2009). Furthermore, RC service members with repeated deployments report higher rates of somatic complaints as well as more symptoms of depression and PTSD than first deployers (Polusny et al., 2009). Despite this, little longitudinal research has been conducted on military trauma to fully understand its impact on postdeployment mental health issues and adjustment (Litz, 2007).

One recent study that does shed some light on the impact of repeated deployments on both physical and behavioral health, as well as redeployment fitness, was conducted using a large sample of National Guard members. When soldiers with at least one OIF/OEF deployment were compared to those without the deployment experience, they were three times more likely to be identified as having PTSD and major depression and twice as likely to report conditions of chronic pain (Kline et al., 2010). Currently, the long-term deployment consequences of cognitive and behavioral health problems and their wide-ranging impact on all spheres of a veteran's functioning are not well-understood (Karney et al., 2008) but research on Vietnam veterans with severe PTSD has documented its negative influence on employment (Smith, Schnurr, & Rosenheck, 2005).

A problem of relatively recent origin that is also receiving increased scrutiny is the rate of military sexual trauma (MST) reported among female soldiers serving in OIF/OEF conflicts. According to Katz et al. (2007), females constituted 10.5% of the troops deployed in OIF/OEF by 2007, and for the first time in history, are serving in combat. Katz et al. (2007) further note that female veterans are one of the fastest-growing segments of new service users at VA health facilities. In their sample of female soldiers seeking treatment at a VA facility, 56% reported MST which included "sexual harassment, unwanted physical advances, and/or attempted or completed sexual assault" and that these women had greater emotional symptomatology and difficulty adjusting to civilian life than women without MST (Katz et al., 2007, p. 243). They maintain their findings parallel to those of other national studies. As of February 2009, 214, 266 female service members deployed in GWOT (DoD, 2009).

In an attempt to provide early identification and intervention of behavioral health issues, the DoD instituted the use of a Post-Deployment Health Assessment (PDHA) upon a soldier's return from OIF/OEF. The assessment is administered at the demobilization station and is designed to screen for physical and behavioral health-related concerns. It consists of a self-report questionnaire with items including demographics and physical health/behavioral health symptoms that may be related to deployment. A health care practitioner reviews the form with the soldier, asks additional questions, conducts a brief interview, and provides information regarding care options. Critics using the procedure have charged that the PDHA was an ineffective tool in screening for behavioral health concerns and it underestimated rates of combat-related symptoms because many disorders might have been missed due to the early administration of the tool.

Subsequent to the initiation of the PDHA, the DoD instituted a Post-Deployment Health Reassessment (PDHRA) to be administered within 3–6 months after a soldier returned from deployment (Milliken, Auchterlonie, & Hoge, 2007). In a study conducted by Milliken et al. (2007) to test the efficacy of the PDHRA to screen for mental health disorders at a later period, researchers compared PDHA and PDHRA data obtained from a large sample of AC and RC soldiers who served in OIF. As hypothesized, soldiers reported more mental health symptoms on the PDHRA than on the PDHA and were referred for care at higher rates. It is significant to note that the highest rate of increase for concerns expressed by respondents on the PDHRA evaluation included those centering on interpersonal conflicts, followed by an increased rate of symptoms related to PTSD.

Taken together, the authors argue that there exists a large need for clinical care among veterans several months following return from combat. These findings lend validity to an earlier study that found 35% of OIF veterans sought mental health care during the year following homecoming (Hoge, Auchterloine, & Milliken, 2006). Increasing the validity of behavioral health screening efforts has also been directed toward the use of standardized screening tools for assessing behavioral health problems among soldiers in active combat. Felker, Hawkins, Dobie, Gutierrez, and McFall (2008) tested the feasibility of utilizing standardized mental health screening instruments to assess behavioral health symptoms among soldiers presenting at a U.S. military hospital in Kuwait. This investigation substantiated the utility of such instruments for screening purposes and revealed significant levels of emotional distress and functional impairment in over half of the soldiers screened. These investigators identified 19% of the sample as having PTSD-related symptoms, 35% evidenced symptoms related to major depression, and 11% manifested severe alcohol misuse. Additionally, a disproportionate rate of female soldiers (27%) seeking care led them to suggest that female soldiers might represent a group at-risk for elevated rates of behavioral health issues among soldiers in combat. Collectively, these studies demonstrate that increasing the validity and timing of assessment results in better identification of those in need of immediate intervention or of those at risk for behavioral dysfunctions.

Suicide and suicide attempts among military personnel, both in deployed and nondeployed members of all services, has been and continues to be a major health concern for our country at this time. As early as 2008, a trend of increasing suicide rates was noted by the Army, many of these resulting from relationship difficulties with no premorbid history of behavioral health issues in the majority of cases (Army Behavioral Health Technology Office, 2008). A 28-year high for suicide among Army active duty soldiers was reached in 2008 and that trend continued over the subsequent 4 years (Kuehn, 2009). Consequently, initiatives have increased through health promotion and intervention efforts across the entire deployment cycle targeting a reduction in military deaths.

For instance, in 2009, in response to both AC and RC rates, the Army inaugurated the Suicide Prevention Task Force which designed and implemented the "Army Campaign Plan for Health Promotion, Risk Reduction and Suicide Prevention." This campaign was designed to implement rapid changes to policies and programs in an effort to stem the rising tide of suicides. Recently, a report released by the National Guard Bureau on cumulative suicide rates for National Guard personnel from 2007 through August 27, 2010 revealed the following. Through that period, 236 suicides were confirmed with another 11 cases pending. As of August 27, 2010, 70 suicides were confirmed with another 11 pending. The confirmed total of 70 exceeded the rates for the previous 3-year period, which were 59, 56, and 62, respectively. The majority of victims were white males in the early stages of service. Of those suicides occurring among members who had deployed (percentage of totals is not identified in the report) the event occurred beyond one year postdeployment. Associated risk factors are identified as substance abuse issues, significant relationship issues, and financial/occupational issues (National Guard Bureau, 2010).

In addition to a risk for increased rates of behavioral health disorders in returning military personnel, there are also barriers to receiving behavioral health care and a fear of stigmatization among military members (Hoge et al., 2004; Pietrzak, Johnson, Goldstein, Malley, & Southwick, 2009; Smith et al., 2008). Forces creating barriers to care have been identified as gap factors such as financial and structural elements of a health system and personal and social factors which include both personal beliefs and values as well as military culture (Burnam et al., 2008). These barriers to care continue to be addressed to date.

Finally, GWOT deployments affect families and the community. It has been reported that almost 2 million children have experienced the absence of a parent due to deployment (Flake, Davis, Johnson, & Middleton, 2009). In 2007 alone, an estimated 700,000 children had one parent absent through deployment (APA, 2007); as of 2008, active duty members had approximately 1.2 million dependents below the age of 25 (Lamberg, 2008). According to a quadrennial quality of life report issued in 2008 by the DoD (2009), the AC and their family members totaled 3.24 million members, while the RC accounted for 1.95 million persons. On a different level, it has been posited that over 57.6 million Americans are directly affected as a consequence OIF/OEF deployments (Koppes, 2010). Deployment in service to one's country brings with it potential risks for personal and sweeping public-health-related issues.

National Guard and Reserve Culture

According to Griffith (2009), "evolving threats to U.S. national security have necessitated changes in the missions, structure, and organization of reserve forces" (p. 1). Consequently, the National Guard is being transformed into an "operational force" which is frequently deployed overseas, whereas prior to GWOT, they were primarily involved in domestic state issues (Commission on the National Guard and Reserve, 2008). Their initial use in the federal service was to provide a strategic reserve activated by the President in response to a national emergency. This trend toward relying heavily on the RC as an operational rather than strategic force has led to the largest deployment of RC troops in the last 50 years (National Governor's Association, 2007).

> The military's growing commitment to the Total Force Policy, at a time when reserve forces are being pressed into repeated deployments to Afghanistan and Iraq, ... has placed unprecedented strain on reservists and their families. (Library of Congress, 2007, p. 25).

While all deployed personnel, both Active and Reserve, experience challenges in "coming home" to family, work and the community, combat veterans of the National Guard and Reserve Forces confront additional challenges not faced by the AC. To fully understand this, as well as the critical importance of the reintegration movement to the RC, it is important for the reader to have a clear understanding of the basic differences between Active and RCs. Table 10.3 delineates these points of difference and graphically depicts various general distinctions between the Active and Reserves Components along various dimensions across the deployment cycle; the latter is important because it demonstrates the changes experienced by RC service members as they mobilize, deploy, and return home (see Table 10.3). Even within the RC, the reader will note that there are distinctions between the National Guard and other organization and the other RC service members.

RC members navigate the complexities of both civilian and military worlds and there are distinct elements of their cultures that make deployment and reintegration a more complex issue in some ways than for those with full time military status. Reservists are frequently referred to as "Weekend Warriors" or "Citizen Soldiers," meaning they do not have a central identity as "military"; rather, their primary identity is as a civilian (Manderscheid, 2007) and they move between these worlds following deployment (McNutt, 2005).

Reservists typically drill one weekend a month and serve two weeks a year on active duty. While both the AC and the other Reserve Forces function under Title 10 U. S. Code federalizing them, the National Guard operates under Title 32 and is a state-level military organization, while the other RC personnel are Title 10 although on reserve status. Under Presidential authority, these troops may become federalized through Title 10 to meet national needs as in the current deployments.

Before deployment, AC members live and work on military posts or in nearby military communities. RC forces on the other hand, live and work in civilian communities either in or outside the state location of their military organization; and, it is not uncommon for RC members to live long distances from their home military installations, possibly "50–100 miles from their unit of assignment" (Griffith, 2010, p. 199). When deployed, RC service members leave family and loved ones (who may previously have had no understanding of military culture and may not want to be a part of military culture), employers, and educational career paths; AC members leave families who have had

TABLE 10.3 Selected points of difference between National Guard and Reserve Forces as compared to Active Military Forces

	Dimensions of Deployment Cycle Differences					
	Predeployment Phase		Deployment Phase		Postdeployment Phase	
	Active Forces	National Guard and Reserves	Active Forces	National Guard and Reserves	Active Forces	National Guard and Reserves
Legal/Military status	Title 10	Titles 32	Title 10	Title 10	Title 10	Titles 32
Employment	Military	Civilian/Part-time military	Military	Military	Military	Civilian/Part-time military
	Military	Civilian/Part-time military	Military	Military	Military	Civilian/Part-time military
Residence	Post/Military community	Home state/neighboring state community	Post/Military community	Post/Military community	Post/Military community	Home state/neighboring state community
Method of mobilization	Unit	Individual service member/unit	–	–	–	–
Method of demobilization	–	–	–	–	Unit discharged to home base	Individuals discharged to home state/neighboring state communities
Health care	Military health care	Private insurance/none	Military health care	Military health care	Military health care	Limited military health care/private insurance/none

(Continued)

TABLE 10.3 *Continued*

Dimensions of Deployment Cycle Differences

	Predeployment Phase		Deployment Phase		Postdeployment Phase	
	Active Forces	National Guard and Reserves	Active Forces	National Guard and Reserves	Active Forces	National Guard and Reserves
Access to health care	On base/allied military medical facilities	Community private practitioners	—	—	On base/allied military medical facilities	Limited access allied military medical facilities/community private practitioners
Health care venue	On duty	Personal/Employer time	On duty	On duty	On duty	Personal/Employer time
Support mechanisms	Military community and family	Family and community	Military community and family	Military community and family	Military community and family	Family and community

the benefit of living in and being immersed into a military culture. Another distinction exists between the two groups in that the AC typically deploys in units, whereas the RC may deploy as individuals or as units and merge into already existing units in theater.

Prior to deployment, the RC receives health care in the civilian community through private practitioners using privately held insurance, possibly subsidized through civilian employers. Sadly, in some cases, members may not have health care insurance at all. AC members are insured through the military and receive an array of health-related services on base or through allied military medical facilities. Another difference exists as to when medical care is given and under what circumstances. AC members may attend appointments on duty time, while RC members may have to arrange employment leave or seek care around their civilian work schedule.

Finally, predeployment, although both groups find social support within their immediate families, the AC has the advantage of being embedded in a military community in which members provide support and information among members. The RC member and family do not benefit from this shared culture and employers may not necessarily be supportive of the requirements of the Reservist's military organization given the disruptive influence and strain the interruption in employment may cause the civilian employer.

Nevertheless, when National Guard soldiers and other Reservists return to demobilization sites back in this country, the earlier distinctions become apparent again, and may have significant consequences for postdeployment functioning of members, families, and communities. Typically, after a three-day interval at the demobilization site, units of RC members are discharged back into their civilian communities which may be scattered across states, while the AC unit is discharged back to their posts and military communities.

Many Reservists choose to return immediately to their civilian employers postdeployment, while others take time off to rest and engage with families. Some begin the search for civilian employment. During this time immediately following demobilization, the RC is covered for a brief period by military health care plans and has limited access to military medical facilities. Following this period if employed, they typically return to their private insurance plans and schedule medical appointments around work confines.

The next time Reservists come together as a military cohort following the deployment experience is the first reintegration event held at 30 days which is described later. Consequently, direct military peer support may be unavailable until that time and between future reintegration events and drill weekends. The latter factors may complicate the reintegration process for members by disrupting the continuum of social support and the continuity of care for both psychological and physical health issues (Lafferty et al., 2008). As one enlisted soldier observed, "the VA will treat you for life for a line of duty issue. The problem is, you need to live near one."

> The needs of the National Guard and Reserves are different ... we don't live on posts and most of us don't live near a post or base or any of those things and there are different needs ... many times the mother services really don't have a good handle on what a Reservist or National Guardist is[4].

Reserve troops confront unique challenges when deployed abroad and upon returning home. Typically, these members are married and employed. The average age of Reservist GWOT veterans is 36.2 years compared to the AC component in which almost half of the members are under 25 years of age (DoD, 2007). Given the important economic, familial and social roles these RC members fill, prolonged tours of duty in theater may create severe strain on the service member, his/her family and communities. In addition to the physical and psychological costs of deployment, reintegration into the home community also presents challenges in terms of finances and reemployment (National Governor's Association, 2007) and there are approximately 3 million family members directly impacted by deployment of the RC (Committee on House Veteran Affairs, Subcommittee on Health, 2008).

The tolls of war not only include the direct physical and psychological costs to the individual service member, but they also significantly influence the Reservists' successful reentry into civilian life. Reentry health status directly impacts family and interpersonal functioning as well as behavior at work and in the community.

> I've been back a month. Two weeks ago, I just got a job at ___. The other day, I went into the office to pick-up my pay check wearing my gun. The payroll lady called the manager. He took me in his office and asked if I had PTSD. Then he fired me. Can you believe that? Just for wearing my gun. I wasn't in the store- I just went into

---

[4]Observation by an Army Reserve Officer.

the office. I don't know what his problem was but I'm p−−− off. Now, I have to find another job[5].

THE YELLOW RIBBON REINTEGRATION PROGRAM

Attempting to address the mounting problems faced by Reserve and National Guard troops under their unprecedented role as an operational force, President Bush signed into law as part of the Defense Authorization Act of 2008 (P.L. 110–181) the Yellow Ribbon Reintegration Program. This mandated the establishment of a Yellow Ribbon Reintegration Program (P.L. 110–181). In addition to amending policies on Guard and Reserve affairs, the law directed the Secretary of Defense to establish a national combat veteran reintegration program to provide service members and families information, services and referral, and outreach activities throughout the entire deployment cycle.

The measure was initially intended to serve National Guard and Reserve members and families and was depicted as a "national combat reintegration program"; indeed, the title alone connoted that it was a program targeting the homecoming of veterans. The title, however, may be considered somewhat of a misnomer as the actual law dictates specific content and services for military and family members across the entire deployment cycle and is not restricted solely to the reintegration phase of military service.

This national initiative was designed to foster the emotional and physical well-being of all constituents involved by serving as a vehicle for resources delivered at the federal, state, and local levels. The facilitation of access to an array of services was conceptualized to occur by creating community, state, and federal partnerships. The latter would serve as active participants in health promotion by providing readiness activities and services for Reservists and families throughout all four phases of the deployment cycle: (1) Predeployment, (2) Deployment, (3) Demobilization, and (4) Postdeployment-Reconstitution (see policy attached).

In a directive memorandum issued in July 2008, the Under Secretary of Defense for Personnel and Readiness (2008) issued a statement on the policies, procedures, and responsibilities for specific implementation of the Yellow Reintegration Program for joint deployment and support of all parties involved. This memorandum established the

---

[5]Young National Guard veteran upon return from Afghanistan.

Joint Family Resource Center for the organization of resources in every state. In a further specification, it noted that support services would be provided for National Guard and Reserve service members and family members to include "spouses, children, parents, grandparents, siblings and/or significant others" (Under Secretary of Defense for Personnel and Readiness, 2008, p. 2). The inclusion of family members and significant others in the program was considered to be an important element in ameliorating the impact of military deployment stressors, including family separation on families and other support system persons (Under Secretary of Defense for Personnel and Readiness, 2008).

As outlined in the memorandum, each phase of the deployment cycle contains specific events and activities to assist in providing education and services for mitigating the impact of deployment on all units, families, and communities. The various phases of deployment cycle support dictated by the memorandum are graphically represented for the National Guard in Figures 10.1 through 10.4 as "Before, During, and After Deployment," "Before Deployment," "During Deployment," and "After Deployment" and engage soldiers, families, employers, and community in a holistic fashion. Each segment contains distinctive elements that may initiate and end in a particular phase, bridge from one phase into the next, or be threaded throughout multiple cycles. The initiation of phasic tasks is based on a timeline of military preparation for predeployment, deployment, and postdeployment activities (see Figures 10.1 through 10.4).

Before Deployment: Focuses on the provision of education to promote military readiness in units, families, and communities to withstand the stress of combat deployment and family separation. These activities and events cover a spectrum of themes. Some of these include: development of family care plans, family counseling, an introduction to VA benefits and support, financial counseling, legal readiness, sexual assault prevention and awareness, community outreach, employer support of the Guard and Reserve, child custody arrangements, an introduction to Tricare and MilitaryOneSource, and marriage enrichment to name a few (see Figure 10.2). **During Deployment:** Activities are offered to families through affiliation with organizations at the state and local level such as National Guard and Reserve State Family Programs, State Veterans Affairs Offices, veterans' service organizations, State Departments of Health and Human Services, and local universities and colleges. Offerings for this phase might include review of legal documents, spouse/family member employment and employer support, combat and operational stress prevention and

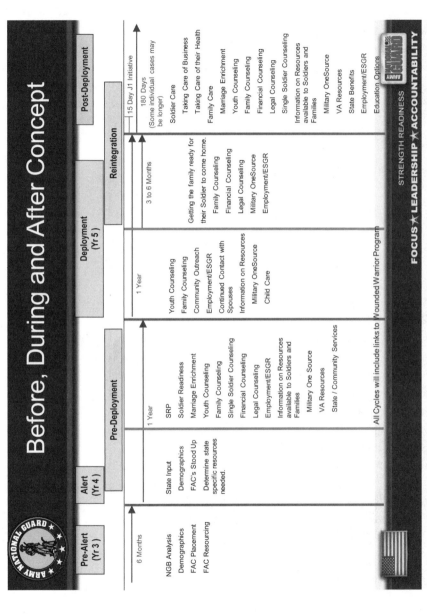

FIGURE 10.1 Army National Guard Yellow Ribbon deployment cycle support system. *Source:* Thede, E. (2007). *National Guard Bureau Briefing on the Army National Guard Yellow Ribbon Program.* Washington, DC: National Guard Bureau.

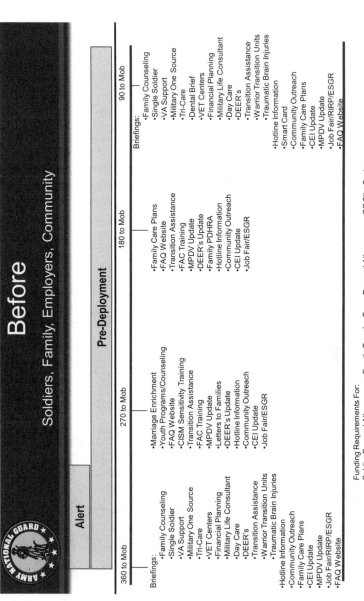

FIGURE 10.2 Components of the predeployment phase of the deployment cycle support system. *Source:* Thede, E. (2007). *National Guard Bureau Briefing on the Army National Guard Yellow Ribbon Program.* Washington, DC: National Guard Bureau.

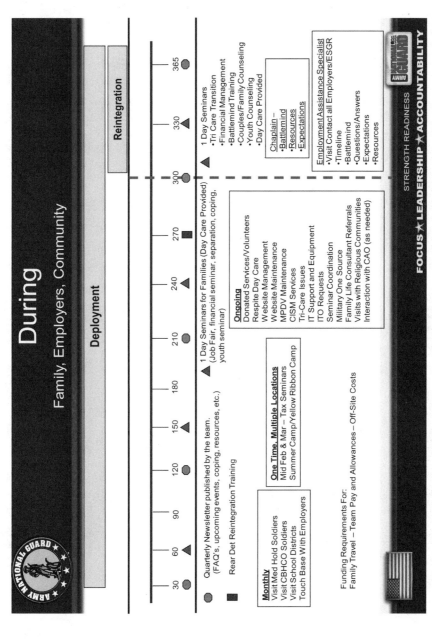

FIGURE 10.3 Components of the deployment phase of the deployment cycle support system. *Source:* Thede, E. (2007). *National Guard Bureau Briefing on the Army National Guard Yellow Ribbon Program.* Washington, DC: National Guard Bureau.

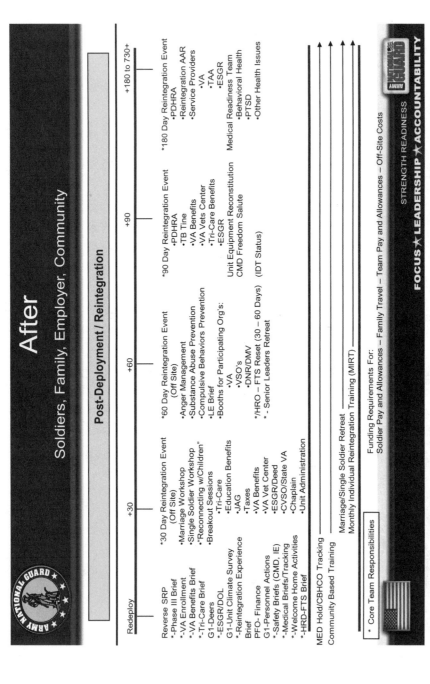

FIGURE 10.4 Components of the postdeployment phase of the deployment cycle support system. *Source:* Thede, E. (2007). *National Guard Bureau Briefing on the Army National Guard Yellow Ribbon Program.* Washington, DC: National Guard Bureau.

SEC. 582. YELLOW RIBBON REINTEGRATION PROGRAM

The Secretary of Defense shall establish a national combat veteran reintegration program to provide National Guard and Reserve members and their families with sufficient information, services, referral, and proactive outreach opportunities throughout the entire deployment cycle. This program shall be known as the Yellow Ribbon Reintegration Program ...

The Yellow Ribbon Reintegration Program shall consist of informational events and activities for members of the RCs of the Armed Forces, their families, and community members to facilitate access to services supporting their health and well-being through the four phases of the deployment cycle: (1) Predeployment, (2) Deployment, (3) Demobilization, (4) Post-deployment-Reconstitution ... The Secretary shall designate the Under Secretary of Defense for Personnel and Readiness as the Department of Defense executive agent for the Yellow Ribbon Reintegration Program ...

The Under Secretary of Defense for Personnel and Readiness shall establish the Office for Reintegration Programs within the Office of the Secretary of Defense. The office shall administer all reintegration programs in coordination with State National Guard organizations. The office shall be responsible for coordination with existing National Guard and Reserve family and support programs. The Directors of the Army National Guard and Air National Guard and the Chiefs of the Army Reserve, Marine Corps Reserve, Navy Reserve, and Air Force Reserve may appoint liaison officers to coordinate with the permanent office staff.

The office may also enter into partnerships with other public entities, including the Department of Health and Human Services, Substance Abuse and the Mental Health Services Administration, for access to necessary substance abuse and mental health treatment services from local State-licensed service providers. (HR 4986, 120-121).

management for families, religious community support, educational involvements, and outreach to employers (see Figure 10.3).

After Deployment: Initial reintegration services begin for the soldiers at demobilization stations or within the first few days at the home station. The event held at this time is designed to give them the critical information they will need during their first 30–45 days at home while they are on leave. Later events occur during the next 180 days following their return to home station and focus on reconnecting soldiers with their families, employers, and communities through the provision of information and access to resources designed to facilitate successful reintegration. Activities not completed during the initial reintegration activity at demobilization are the beginning points for this phase. Such tasks include service member record processing, enrollment in the VA and VSO's, veteran's counseling center/ military career counseling, and briefings to include TRICARE, ESGR/ DOL, financial assistance, safety, and medical issues. It also includes welcome-home activities. The directive further mandates that State National Guard and Reserve commands host reintegration events at approximately 30-, 60-, and 90-day intervals following demobilization and that family members be encouraged to attend 30- and 60-day events. The first event focuses on reconnecting the veteran with his/ her family or significant others. This initial family reintegration event highlights benefits and resources and provides a forum for participants to address negative behaviors related to the stresses of combat, stresses related to trauma, transition challenges, educational issues, and other nonmilitary-related concerns (Under Secretary of Defense for Personnel and Readiness, 2008) (see Figure 10.4).

In addition to break-out sessions addressing TRICARE, financial planning, educational benefits, VA benefits, legal information, and other resources, the 30-day event features workshops on marriage, single soldiers, female soldiers, reconnecting with children, and mental health-related issues. It may also include job fairs and career coaching as well as the presence of chaplains and other faith-based representatives and unit administrators to address issues of concern to service members (Under Secretary of Defense for Personnel and Readiness, 2008) (see Figure 10.4).

The next event focuses on the veteran and his/her interaction with the community and features workshops addressing anger management, substance abuse prevention, and the prevention of compulsive behaviors. In addition, the resources provided at the first event are also featured (see Figure 10.4). During the final event, service members receive the PDHRA and other medical interventions as well as continuing support from resources outlined earlier. At about this time, the Command will schedule a Command Freedom Salute, Welcome Home Warrior-Citizen, and other such warrior recognition programs. (Under Secretary of Defense for Personnel and Readiness, 2008) (see Figure 10.4).

The Maryland Yellow Ribbon Reintegration Program

The Maryland National Guard (MDNG) has emerged as a leader in efforts to mitigate the difficulties veterans and their families experience upon return from a combat zone. As early as 2006, initiatives were developed for soldiers engaged in OEF and OIF conflicts and their families. The 2006 Maryland legislative session mandated scholarships, death benefits, outreach and advocacy for service members and their families through the State Department of Veterans Affairs. It also fostered the establishment of a Task Force to Study State Assistance to Veterans as means of providing aid and support to these soldiers and families impacted by engagement in those conflicts (National Governors Association, 2007). In addition, the Governor of Maryland provided additional funding for reintegration initiatives from state funds, in recognition of the need to help Maryland OIF/OEF veterans despite the lack of federal funding for reintegration efforts. All of these Maryland strides predate the DoD mandate for state-level Yellow Ribbon Reintegration Programs.

With early recognition that the National Guard and Reserve troops returning from GWOT were displaying increased rates of postdeployment issues, the MDNG has assumed a proactive role in the development and delivery of a comprehensive program to boost retention of its citizen soldiers and to assist them in a successful transition throughout the deployment cycle. Nationally, the first program, "Beyond the Yellow Ribbon," was begun by the Minnesota National Guard in 2005, at the direction of the Minnesota Adjutant General. Guided by the Minnesota example, the Maryland program adopted the concept of requiring troops to attend a series of events at intervals upon their return to the homeland from a deployment. While the Maryland system employed the general framework of the Minnesota program, the Maryland Reintegration Program gradually evolved over time and developed its own program identity.

The Maryland initiative was inaugurated in October 2007, under the direction of the Adjutant General of the Maryland National Guard who authorized the development of a model program for all members of the Maryland Army National Guard (MDARNG) preparing for, transitioning to, and returning from military service in GWOT. Furthermore, since 2006 the MDARNG had also begun the procedure of administering the PDHRA scale to all returning troops days after demobilization. Maryland's early program was already designed to be delivered along a continuum from predeployment through postdeployment phases. The "Maryland Model," as it has come to be known is designed to meet the mandate to assist citizen soldiers and their families in successfully coping with the challenges of deployment and homecoming along a psychosocial continuum. To date, over 2000 National Guard members have participated in the Yellow Ribbon

Reintegration Program. Approximately, 800 other program participants have included spouses, domestic partners, parents, children, and friends. Despite being in a relationship however, some soldiers often attend the events alone. At a recent event when one soldier was asked if his wife was in attendance he responded, "No, she's sick of this crap. She's tired of hearing about it."

In the early stages of Maryland's Yellow Ribbon Program, the content and presentations at the events (workshops such as Reconnecting with Children, Anger Management, etc.) were developed by licensed, volunteer mental health care providers who had worked with the National Guard Family Readiness Groups. As the numbers of troops deploying and returning from Iraq and Afghanistan increased, other agencies such as the Maryland Defense Force, which had overseen the administration of the PDHRA prior to the inception of the reintegration events, as well as the Maryland Department of Veterans Affairs and the Veterans Administration Hospital in Baltimore provided additional mental health professionals.

The Maryland Model Structure

The current Maryland Model is consistent with the fundamental constitution of the national directive which was federally mandated and discussed earlier. It employs components specifically designed to assist service members and their families in successful adaptation to active military service, and to aid the same in the transition to civilian life. It is a holistic approach to health promotion, as directed by the national mandate, incorporating primary, secondary, and tertiary prevention strategies. This graduated step-up/step-down program consists of elements that parallel the entire deployment cycle outlined earlier. Specifically, this section will describe the activities and structure of the Postdeployment aspect of reintegration which consists of four phases: Phase 1: Demobilization, Phase 2: 30-Day Event, Phase 3: 60-Day Event, and Phase 4: 90-Day Event.

There are several features of the Maryland Model that may distinguish it from other programs. First, reintegration events are held at hotels throughout the state or at the Baltimore Convention Center; the locale and venue are determined by the unit returning, venue availability and the number of participants. The soldier is strongly encouraged to have family members and significant others accompany him or her to the event. Overnight accommodations with participants arriving the night before the event are typically provided at the venue, and child care is available for parents. Second, although sessions were originally developed and designed to be delivered by licensed behavioral health professionals through PowerPoint instruction, early participant feedback reshaped the approach to an interactive model. All behavioral health sessions are facilitated by two professionals so that one is always available to gauge participant reaction and respond to any immediate needs that may arise. Third, the curriculum is dynamic and shifts to reflect topics addressing the current needs of veterans and their families and from time to time it will include modules addressing specific audience demographics (e.g., units experiencing combat-related casualties). Fourth, participant groups other than the general session are intentionally limited to approximately 20 persons, consequently depending on the number of attendees, the number of classes offered on a topic will increase/decrease accordingly. This then, drives the fluctuation in the numbers of behavioral health and military staffing required for each event. Finally, a concerted effort has been made to recruit behavioral health specialists who have an understanding and appreciation of the culture of the RC. To promote military cultural competence of civilian staff, ongoing opportunities for exposure to, and engagement with, aspects of military work and life have been promoted and facilitated through events and continuing education activities.

Typically, two weeks prior to an event a briefing is held via conference call with military and civilian staff to discuss the upcoming event, the nature of the unit(s) attending, and staffing. It is during this conference that event details are finalized. The morning of the event just prior to implementation, all staff meet to review any interim changes to the program. At the conclusion of every event, a general After Action Report (AAR) meeting is held with staff to discuss observations of all aspects of the event and to generate feedback/recommendations for future events. It is during this time that suggested revisions for policies, procedures, curricular content, or instructional strategies are generated. It is a time for military and civilian staff to provide insights from two different perspectives on the success of that aspect of program implementation.

The "advanced" courses build on topics introduced in Phase 2 (see Table 10.4) and provide opportunities for reflection of experiences since the last event. Similar to Phase 2, Phase 3 includes multiple modules as described in Table 10.5. In addition to these modules,

TABLE 10.4 Curriculum for phase 2 reintegration program

Module	Audience	Focus
General Session Module	All	The general session includes a briefing by the Officer in Charge of Reintegration or Reintegration Operations Officer that orients the participants to the schedule of activities and resources available throughout the day. It also provides information regarding the rationale for the required and elective modules in the teaching curriculum. Finally, the group is addressed by the Unit Commander and Command Staff.
Paths to Resilience	All	Investigates the nature of resilience and factors associated with building or maintaining resilience. The unit includes a review of the nature of the stress response and its impact on emotional, cognitive and physical functioning, common postdeployment stressors, and strategies for building resilience.
Relationships I (formerly "Making Marriage Work")	Required for married soldiers or partners in long-term relationship	Explores common issues with spouses and significant others and topics related to children for returning soldiers. The module presents multiples strategies for coping with marital/relational and child-related issues.
Reconnecting with Children	Required for soldiers with children	General recommendations are provided for coping with a host of deployment-related issues children may experience. A strategy included here is the communication of feelings. In addition, signs indicating the need for potential counseling intervention are presented in a developmental context. Referral information is presented.
Single Soldiers' Challenges	Required for single soldiers	The purpose is to inform soldiers of the potential postdeployment-related challenges, and to provide effective management strategies and an overview of symptoms of persistent distress, and referral information.
Anger Management	Required for all	Covers the nature of anger, recognizing anger, appropriate versus inappropriate expressions of anger, steps in managing anger as well as professional referral information.

Title	Status	Description
Law Enforcement Perspectives for Veterans	Required for all	Presented by law enforcement professional with behavioral health background. Oriented to typical law enforcement interactions with veterans and suggestions for avoiding problems during reintegration.
Female Soldier Issues	Required for female soldiers	Content focuses on gender-specific issues and challenges of being a female soldier.
TRICARE Insurance	Elective	Discusses what TRICARE benefits are available to demobilized veterans and their families, and where and how to get help with TRICARE-related questions.
Military Onesource	Elective	Introduces the Military Onesource organization and its functions. Describes free counseling services and the resources, expertise and materials offered pro bono to military families.
Department of Veterans Affairs	Elective	The Veterans Benefits Administration (VBA) and Veterans Health Administration (VHA) are defined and the scope of their activities specified. In addition, resources available through organizations and accessibility are discussed.
Returning to Work: U.S. Department of Labor	Elective	Presents services available through the Department of Labor in assisting veterans with finding work. In addition, highlights soldiers' reemployment rights and responsibilities as Guardsmen or Reservists under the "Uniformed Services Employment/Reemployment Rights Act."
Financial Planning	Elective	Assists soldiers with all elements of financial planning and fiscal challenges resulting from deployment.
Successful Job Techniques: U.S. Department of Labor	Elective	Reviews approaches for successful job searches including presentation of self and skill/talent identification.
The Successful Resume: U.S. Department of Labor	Elective	Reviews the key elements of successful resume writing, the importance of the resume, and how potential employers use the resume to assess fit of potential applicants.

TABLE 10.5 Curriculum for phase 3 reintegration program

Module	Audience	Focus
General Session Module	All	Includes a briefing by the Reintegration Director or Reintegration Operations Officer that orients the participants to the schedule of activities and resources available throughout the day. It also provides information regarding the rationale for the required and elective modules in the teaching curriculum. Finally, the group is addressed by the Unit Commander and Command Staff.
Applied Resilience II	All	Reviews material presented in Phase II Resilience module such as the nature of the stress response, the impact of stress on physiological, cognitive and emotional functioning, and the nature of resilience and its factors. It also focuses on building resilience skills through a combination of the following activities: positive coping exercise, thought/feeling/behavior exercise, cognitive restructuring exercises, and deep breathing.
Feeling a Part After Being Apart: Changing Views of Self, Others, and the World	All	Normalizes the experience of having altered views/perceptions toward self, others, and the world after returning from combat. Some common views of returning veterans are reviewed and ways of identifying and challenging distorted thinking are taught. Finally, the module presents tips on being supportive for partners, family members, and friends as well as suggestions for the soldier in responding to questions about combat experience and sharing information.

The Female Soldier	Required for female soldiers	Explores the changing roles of females in combat, the impact of mobilization cycles, and common reactions during postdeployment. In addition, the module provides information on the impact of stress on physical and emotional functioning, active coping strategies and information regarding VA Center referrals and programs.
Substance Abuse	Required for all	Discusses identification of alcohol abuse problems. Module also contains brief CAGE questionnaire, discussion of reasons for drinking, symptoms of alcoholism and common questions and answers related to alcoholism and problem drinking.
Spousal/Significant Other Awareness Group	Spouses and significant others only/Elective	Offered as a discussion group identifying issues and common themes in reuniting with loved ones as well strategies for successful interactions and problem-solving. Provides a forum for the sharing of common concerns and experiences.
Relationships II (Work, Family and Community Relationships)	Required all	Builds upon the earlier workshop focusing on significant issues in relationships and methods for achieving/ maintaining healthy interactions
Anger Management: Resetting Your Battlemind	Required	Covers the nature of anger, recognizing anger, appropriate versus inappropriate expressions of anger, steps in managing anger as well as professional referral information

vendors/presenters from Phase 2 as well as community organizations are present at tables throughout the event to answer questions or inquiries from participants; this includes the reappearance of a Veterans' Administration representative to discuss the support services offered through that organization (Veterans' Benefits Administration, 2011).

> I didn't think this was going to be useful. But, now I see it really is important. It really is helpful.[6]

Since the inception of the present model, both qualitative and quantitative self-report program evaluation data of the psycho-educational components and overall program event quality indicate that the program is favorably received by both soldiers and their significant others. These data provide useful information about a participant's perception of specific events, in particular and the overall event, in general. Although they say relatively little regarding the effectiveness of the reintegration program, they have provided valuable data identifying which segments needed revision or deletion.

These program evaluation data relate directly to the quality of activities presented within an immediate event but do not reflect more objective measures of program outcomes such as rates of physical/behavioral health complaints, rates of psychiatric disorders related to deployment, family dynamics, and educational issues. Nor do they shed light on public health concerns such as rates of domestic violence, suicide, and alcohol-related crime statistics. While Yellow Ribbon Programs are being implemented nationwide, to date, there are no empirical studies demonstrating their effectiveness in achieving the goals originally outlined in the National Defense Authorization Act of 2008.

Challenges of Implementing Maryland's Model

There are many complexities associated with bringing to life the federally mandated Yellow Ribbon Reintegration Program. Issues from fiscal and physical resources, to staffing, to the engagement of commanders around the importance of the issue, all complicate implementation. The second author of this chapter has had direct leadership responsibility for the development and implementation of Maryland's program since its inception. In order to capture his unique perspective regarding

---

[6]National Guard veteran soldier responding at the end of a session incorporating peer-to-peer support.

the experience and to illuminate some of the challenges just mentioned, a transcription of a conversation between both authors is presented (see Authors' Dialogue).

CONCLUSION

GWOT has shaped our new reality of a veteran's homecoming. Once the excitement of homecoming subsides within the first few days and weeks of return for the service member and his/her family, commonly referred to as the "honeymoon period," the real work of reintegration begins for all parties involved: veterans, families, friends, and communities. This work attempted to provide the reader with an understanding of our government's response to the current realities of our service members' experiences when deploying and reintegrating into a civilian world.

The Yellow Ribbon Reintegration Program, as a deployment cycle support mechanism for health promotion and prevention of health/behavioral health issues, is a significant step in ensuring wellness for our nation's citizenry and for protecting the constant readiness of our military services. However, it is also a new and relatively young program. There are some recommendations that the present review and our experiences in reintegration suggest.

While the Defense Authorization Act of 2008 provides a specific directive for evaluation, to date and to the knowledge of the present authors, there are no empirical studies to support the effectiveness of the Yellow Ribbon Program in achieving its goals. Most of the information providing support is based on anecdotal reports or changes in trends that are attributed to aspects of the program. Consequently, funding is needed to develop longitudinal, multisite research initiatives that specifically target programmatic outcomes. These research ventures should be coordinated across programs and results used to generate empirical "best practices" and drive evidence-based program changes. This recommendation is consistent with Griffith's (2010) call for program evaluation and systematic review of program implementation and programmatic outcomes.

Research findings and statistics on veteran suicides tell us that the program timeline is too short to be of full benefit to veterans and their families. Problems and medical/behavioral health symptoms may not be present initially at homecoming. In fact, they may not present until almost a year after the veteran arrives home, in some cases. It is critical that the program model be extended to include a one-year postmobilization event so that soldiers and families may come together to address adjustment issues and challenges that have resulted from deployment.

If the holistic approach of the Yellow Ribbon initiative is to be most beneficial and sustained into the future, there must be active engagement of constituencies at the local, state, and federal levels. Outreach programs and partnerships for information-sharing and skill-building are required along health/behavioral health, education, and employment lines in order to coordinate existing efforts and to generate needed ones. An example of this form of community collaboration and outreach may be found in the MDNG's *Forums on Veterans' Reintegration* issues which consisted of three events targeting engagement of educators, employers, and health/behavioral health providers from across the state of Maryland around veterans' needs.[7] Partnerships such as this actively engage all stakeholders and increase capacity for effectively meeting deployment-related issues.

Finally, there is a pervasive need to directly and actively engage military leadership at all levels around the importance of deployment cycle support to the service member, the family, the community, and the military. Without leadership support, these stakeholders are all at risk of experiencing the unfettered consequences of deployment that may extend for generations.

> In the old days, Desert Storm, we got a flier on the airplane because our engines were having problems and they said "here's how you do it." The second one coming back from Heidelberg during 9/11 and going into the zone for Bosnia—came back, turned my gear in, got on a plane and flew home and went back to work five days later. The first one cost me a marriage ... As we learned from Viet Nam, when you don't do it (reintegration support), you have long-term mental health and community issues that have now gone into second generation effects that we're seeing in our clinics- third generation effects, fourth generation effects. So, from a cost-effective means, yes. It is very cost-effective to handle it now than 20–30 years later, "a" "b"—it's the right thing to do morally. It's also our obligation to our soldiers who defend our rights and our lifestyle to do this for them ... Why would you not? Because, we are taking

---

[7]Full details of the events as well as videos of presentations and other resources are available at http://www.towson.edu/nationalguardexpo/index.asp.

people from our culture into an extremely different culture who have a totally different base belief system and asking the veterans to come back home having experienced that difference. There's many, many levels here . . . just being deployed alone, when you come home you are different.[8]

REFERENCES

American Psychological Association. (2007). *The psychological needs of U.S. military service members and their families: A preliminary report.* Washington, DC: Author. Retrieved from http://www.apa.org/pubs/info/reports/military-deployment-summary.pdf

Army Behavioral Health Technology Office, Suicide Risk Management and Surveillance Office. (2008). *Army Suicide Event Report (ASER), Calendar Year 2007.* U.S. Army, Tacoma, Washington.

Belasco, A. (2009). *The cost of Iraq, Afghanistan, and other Global War on Terrorism operations since 9/11.* Washington, DC: Congressional Research Service.

Bowen, G. L., & Martin, J. A. (2011). The resiliency model of role performance for service members, veterans, and their families. *Journal of Human Behavior in the Social Environment,* (in press).

Burnam, M. A., Meredith, L. S., Helmus, T. C., Burns, R., Cox, R. A., D'Amico, E. et al. (2008). Systems of care: Challenges and opportunities to improve access to high-quality care. In T. Tanielian & L. Jaycox (Eds.), *Invisible wounds of war: Psychological and cognitive injuries, their consequences, and services to assist recovery.* Washington, DC: RAND Corporation.

Commission on the National Guard and Reserve. (2008). *Transforming the National Guard and Reserves into a 21st century operational force: Final Report,* January 2008. Washington, D.C.: U. S. Congress.

Committee on House Veteran Affairs Subcommittee on Health. (2008). *Family Mental Health Assistance FDCH Congressional Testimony/Statement of Stacey Bannerman,* February 2008. Retrieved July 11, 2008. Retrieved from http://veterans.house.gov/Media/File/110/02-28-08H/110-73transcriptH02-28-08.htm

Defense Manpower Data Center. (2009). *CTS deployment file baseline report as of February 28, 2009.* Provided by the Office of the Assistant Secretary of Defense for Public Affairs, Office of Public Communication.

Department of Defense (DoD). (2009). *Report of the Second Quadrennial Quality of Life Review.* Office of the Deputy Under Secretary of Defense (Military Community and Family Policy). Retrieved from http://cs.mhf.dod.mil/content/dav/mhf/QOL-library/PDF/MHF/QOL%20Resources/Reports/Quadrennial%20Quality%20of%20Life%20Review%202009.pdf

---

[8]Army Reserve Officer discussing homecoming prior to development of reintegration programs.

Department of Defense, Operation Iraqi Freedom and Operation Enduring Freedom Casualty Status Fatalities of as May 11, 2010. Retrieved November 5, 2010 from http://www.defense.gov/news/casualty.pdf

Department of Defense Task Force on Mental Health. (2007). *An achievable vision: Report of the Department of Defense Task Force on Mental Health.* Falls Church, VA: Defense Health Board.

Department of Defense, United States Military Casualty Statistics: Operation Iraqi Freedom and Operation Enduring Freedom (March 25, 2009). Congressional Research Service, Washington, DC.

Department of Defense, United States Military Casualty Statistics. (2010). *Casualties by Military Service Component, October 7, 2001, through May 1, 2010.* Retrieved May 11, 2010, from http://siadapp.dmdc.osd.mil/personnel/CASUALTY/castop.htm

Department of Defense, Office of the Deputy Secretary of Defense/Military Community and Family Policy. (2005). *2005 Demographics report.* Washington, DC.

Department of Defense, Office of the Undersecretary of Defense for Personnel and Readiness. (2008). Directive-Type Memorandum (DTM) 08-029. *Implementation of the Yellow Ribbon Reintegration Program* (pp. 1–15). Retrieved August 1, 2008, from www.dtic.mil/whs/directives/corres/dir3.html

Felker, B., Hawkins, E., Dobie, D., Gutierrez, J., & McFall, M. (2008). Characteristics of deployed Operation Iraqi Freedom military personnel who seek mental health care. *Military Medicine, 173*(2), 155–158.

Flake, E. M., Davis, B. E., Johnson, P. L., & Middleton, L. S. (2009). The psychosocial effects of deployment on military children. *Journal of Developmental Behavioral Pediatrics, 30*(4), 271–278. Retrieved from http://journals.lww.com/jrnldbp/Citation/2009/08000/The_Psychosocial_Effects_of_Deployment_on_Military.1.aspx

Griffith, J. (2009). Contradictory and complementary identities of U.S. Army reservists: A historical perspective. *Armed Forces and Society, 20*(10), 1–23.

Griffith, J. (2010). Citizens coping as soldiers: A review of deployment stress symptoms among reservists. *Military Psychology, 22,* 176–206.

Hoge, C. W., Auchterloine, J. L., & Milliken, C. S. (2006). Mental health problems, use of mental health services and attrition from military service after returning from deployment to Iraq or Afghanistan. *Journal of the American Medical Association, 295,* 1023–1032.

Hoge, C. W., Castro, C. A., Messer, S. C., McGurk, D., Cotting, D. I., & Koffman, R. L. (2004). Combat duty in Iraq and Afghanistan, mental health problems, and barriers to care. *New England Journal of Medicine, 351*(1), 13–22.

Hoge, C. W., McGurk, D., Thomas, J. L., Cox, A. L., Engel, C. C., & Castro, C. A. (2008). Mild traumatic brain injury in U.S. soldiers returning from Iraq. *New England Journal of Medicine, 358,* 453–463.

House of Representatives. (2007). Defense Authorization Act of 2008. Washington, DC: U.S. Government Printing Office. *Congressional Record*

(H14495-15204), H.R. 1585. Public Law 110–181. http://dx.doi.org/10.1080/08995601003638967

House Veterans' Affairs Committee. (2009). *Assessing combat exposure and post-traumatic stress disorder in troops and estimating the costs to society: Implications from the RAND Invisible Wounds of War Study.* Testimony of Terri Tanielian (March 2009) before Subcommittee on Disability Assistance and Memorial Affairs, Washington, DC.

Karney, B. R., Ramchand, R., Osilla, K. C., Caldarone, L. B., & Burns, R. M. (2008). Predicting the immediate and long-term consequences of post-traumatic stress disorder, depression, and traumatic brain injury in veterans of Operation Enduring Freedom and Operation Iraqi Freedom. In T. Tanielian & L. Jaycox (Eds.), *Invisible wounds of war: Psychological and cognitive injuries, their consequences, and services to assist recovery.* Washington, DC: RAND Corporation.

Katz, L. S., Bloor, L. E., Cojucar, G., & Draper, T. (2007). Women who served in Iraq seeking mental health services: Relationship between military sexual trauma, symptoms, and readjustment. *Psychological Services, 4*(4), 239–249.

Kline, A., Falca-Dodson, M., Sussner, B., Ciccone, D. S., Chandler, H., Callahan, L. et al. (2010). Effects of repeated deployment to Iraq and Afghanistan on the health of New Jersey Army National Guard troops: Implications for military readiness. *American Journal of Public Health, 100*(2), 276–282.

Koppes, L. (2010). *The hidden casualties of war: Promoting healing and resiliency for U.S. service members and their families—A two day symposium* [PPT]. Retrieved from http://uwf.edu/cap/HCW/brief/KoppesBrief.pps

Kuehn, B. M. (2009). Soldier suicide rates continue to rise: Military, scientists work to stem the tide. *Journal of the American Medical Association, 301*(11), 1111–1113. Retrieved November 5, 2009, from http://jama.ama-assn.org/cgi/content/full/301/11/1111

Lafferty, C. L., Alford, K. L., Davis, M. K., & O'Connor, R. (2008). "Did you shoot anyone?": A practitioner's guide to combat veteran workplace and classroom reintegration. *Advanced Management Journal, 73*(4), 4–11.

Lamberg, L. (2008). Redeployments strain military families. *Journal of the American Medical Association, 300*(6), 644.

Lapierre, C. B., Schwegler, A. F., & LaBauve, B. J. (2007). Posttraumatic stress and depression symptoms in soldiers returning from combat operations in Iraq and Afghanistan. *Journal of Traumatic Stress, 20*(6), 933–943.

Library of Congress, Federal Research Division. (2007). *Historical attempts to reorganize the reserve components.* Washington, DC: Author.

Litz, B. T. (2007). Research on the impact of military trauma: Current status and future directions. *Military Psychology, 2007, 19*(3), 217–238.

Manderscheid, R. W. (2007). Helping veterans return: Community, family, and job. *Archives of Psychiatric Nursing, 21*(2), 122–124.

McNutt, J. M. (2005). Work adjustment of returning Army reservists: The effect of deployment and organizational support. *Dissertation Abstracts International-B 66*/04, p. 2293, Oct 2005. Retrieved August 18, 2010, from http://proquest.umi.com/pqdlink?did=913530251&Fmt=2&clintid=79356& RQT=309&VName=PQD

Milliken, C. S., Auchterlonie, J. L., & Hoge, C. W. (2007). Longitudinal assessment of mental health problems among active and reserve component soldiers returning from the Iraq war. *Journal of the American Medical Association, 298*(18), 2141–2148.

Monson, C. M., Taft, C. T., & Fredman, S. J. (2009). Military-related PTSD and intimate relationships: From description to theory-driven research and intervention development. *Clinical Psychology Review, 29,* 707–714.

National Defense Authorization Act for Fiscal Year 2008, Pub. L. No.110–181; 122 Stat. 122 (2008).

National Governor's Association Center for Best Practices, Social, Economic and Workforce Programs Division. (2007, October). *State programs to facilitate the reintegration of National Guard troops returning from deployment* (pp. 1–29). Retrieved June 18, 2008, from www.nga.org/portal/ site/nga

National Guard Bureau. (2010). *Year to date suicides: 2007–2010.* Briefing released September 2010. Washington, DC: National Guard Bureau.

Pietrzak, R. H., Goldstein, M. B., Malley, J. C., Rivers, A. J., Johnson, D. C., & Southwick, S. S. (2010). Risk and protective factors associated with suicidal ideation in veterans of Operations Enduring Freedom and Iraqi Freedom. *Journal of Affective Disorders, 123,* 102–107.

Pietrzak, R. H., Johnson, D. C., Goldstein, M. B., Malley, J. C., & Southwick, S. M. (2009). Perceived stigma and barriers to mental health care utilization among OEF-OIF veterans. *Psychiatric Services, 60*(8), 1118–1122.

Polusny, M. A., Erbes, C. R., Arbisi, P. A., Thuras, P., Kehle, S. M., Rath, M. et al. (2009). Impact of prior Operation Enduring Freedom/Operation Iraqi Freedom combat duty on mental health in a predeployment cohort of National Guard soldiers. *Military Medicine, 174*(4), 353–357.

Sammons, M. T., & Batten, S. V. (2008). Psychological services for returning veterans and their families: Evolving conceptualizations of the sequelae of war-zone experiences. *Journal of Clinical Psychology: In Session, 64*(8), 921–927.

Seal, K. H., Bertenthal, D., Miner, C., Sen, S., & Marmar, C. (2007). Bringing the war back home: Mental health disorders among 103,788 U.S. veterans returning from Iraq and Afghanistan seen at Department of Veterans Affairs facilities. *Archives of Internal Medicine, 167*(5), 476–482.

Smith, M. W., Schnurr, P. P., & Rosenheck, R. M. (2005). Employment outcomes and PTSD symptom severity. *Mental Health Services Research, 7*(2), 89–101.

Smith, T. C., Ryan, M. A., Wingard, D. L., Slymen, D. J., Sallis, J. F., & Kritz-Silverstein, D. (2008). New onset and persistent symptoms of posttraumatic stress disorder self reported after deployment and combat exposures: Prospective population based US military cohort study. *British Medical Journal, 336*(7640), 336–371.

Sollinger, J. M., Fisher, G., & Metscher, K. N. (2008). The wars in Afghanistan and Iraq: An overview. In T. Tanielian & L. Jaycox (Eds.), *Invisible wounds of war* (pp. 19–31). Santa Monica, CA: RAND Corporation.

Tanielian, T., Jaycox, L. H., Adamson, D. M., & Metscher, K. N. (2008). Introduction. In T. Tanielian & L. Jaycox (Eds.), *Invisible wounds of war* (pp. 3–15). Santa Monica, CA: RAND Corporation.

Thede, E. (2007). *Army National Guard Yellow Ribbon Program*. Washington, DC: National Guard Bureau. Retrieved from www.ausa.org/programs/familyprograms/AnnualMeetingActivities/previous/Documents/2007FF_BeyondtheYellowRibbon.pdf

Veterans Benefits Administration. (2011). Retrieved from http://www.vba.va.gov/VBA/

THE YELLOW RIBBON INITIATIVE

The Authors' Dialogue

Dr. Harnett: Colonel Gafney, you have been involved in Maryland's Yellow Ribbon Program since its beginning. Would you talk about some of the challenges you've experienced in implementing it over the years?

LTC Gafney: As an organization, our biggest problem is getting hotels and hotel spaces because one of the things hotels want is sixty days notice on who's coming, how many rooms are you going to buy, who's going to be in what rooms—those kind of things. They want a list and they want to lock-in a price and the number of rooms by then. What happens with us and I'm sure it happens with others is that the units don't know who's going to come. The list does not have high priority with the units therefore they really don't do any organization and we are often changing the number of people, the number of attendees, the number of rooms, the number of children right up to a matter of days before an event. Because again, the units don't provide us the information because they don't see it as important. Oftentimes, Commanders provide no command support. They see this as something "Why is this something we have to do this?" So, the problem is finding a hotel or organization that will work with you up to that point. Otherwise we will find that we are paying for many hotel rooms we didn't use. So, command emphasis is a huge problem because commanders don't want to do it. They see it as taking the time away from other training and they don't see any point

Dr. Harnett: What about soldier attitude?

LTC Gafney: Soldier attitude. If soldiers are not ordered to these events, they will not come. They see it as a waste of their time. They've done what they want to do. They don't feel they need it. They don't see any requirement to do it. They don't see how it benefits them. That's a different attitude when families come because oftentimes family members nudge soldiers during a class or point out to them that whatever behavior is being talked about is something that they, the soldiers, are doing or their engaging in whether it's overuse of alcohol, whether it's it how they treat the family, whether it's how they withdraw from the family, whatever it is, the families see the problems the soldiers never do. So when we get families, we get a much more involved soldier in the event as opposed to the soldier just sitting back passively listening and not taking part.

The other thing we stopped using is powerpoint presentations. Soldiers all hate powerpoints. They have had them since day 1. It's commonly known as "death by powerpoint." We use small groups—20–30 people maximum. Two teachers in a class so we can facilitate conversation while the other person observes the group and tries to involve people who may not be involved. And we use licensed, professional staff to do this. We don't use volunteers who are nonprofessional. We do not use other soldiers to do this. We don't use contractors. The staff is all professional because if in fact we are going to have these soldiers come by and only be seen for three events, 30 and 60 days with family and 90 days for a PDHRA, then we want to maximize the skilled eyes we have looking at a soldier. It doesn't help to have some volunteer or some contractor up there reading a powerpoint when the soldier isn't engaged, isn't part of it and not taking part- and have what can be disruptive or antisocial behavior be looked at as a symptom of something deeper. So with professional people, they can look, they can modify the class on a moment's notice to take into account the way a conversation is going. If you have somebody just reading off powerpoint presentation, they're not prepared to deviate from that presentation and generally, don't have the skills to address soldier/family problems that may present that are not part of a powerpoint presentation. So, we feel it important to have trained eyes looking at soldiers if we only have two times we can see them.

Dr. Harnett: Would you address the issue of leadership?

LTC Gafney: To make these things work, the leadership has to be proactive, involved and advocate for the program from the commander all the way down. If there's a break in the leadership chain, whether it's the commander, brigade commander, battalion commander, company commander, platoon leader, squad leader, section leader, if the command breaks down at any one of those points, then the whole program doesn't work. You could have the best intentions by the highest leaders, the Adjutant General could have the best intentions to make it work but if somebody's squad leader says, "this is a waste of time and I don't care if you show up or not" that's what a soldier will do—not show up. So, it takes an unbroken leadership chain from top to bottom to make this work.

SELECTED RESOURCES

American Psychological Association
www.apa.org

Center for the Study of Traumatic Stress
http://centerforthestudyoftraumaticstress.org/

Defense Centers of Excellence for Psychological Health and Traumatic Brain Injury
http://www.dcoe.health.mil/

Guard and Reserve Deployment: Guides and Resources
http://www.military.com/benefits/resources/deployment/guides-and-resources-for-guard-and-reserve

Maryland Defense Force
http://mddf.maryland.gov/

Maryland National Guard
http://www.md.ngb.army.mil/

Military Child Education Coalition
http://www.militarychild.org/

National Committee for Employer Support of the Guard and Reserve
http://www.military.com/benefits/legal-matters/userra/employer-support-of-guard-and-reserve

National Guard Bureau
www.ngb.army.mil/

Office of the Assistant Secretary of Defense for Reserve Affairs
http://ra.defense.gov/

Our Military Kids
http://www.ourmilitarykids.org/

Towson University
http://www.towson.edu/

U.S. Department of Defense
http://www.defense.gov/

U.S. Department of Defense, Deployment Health Clinical Center/Reservist Resource Center
http://www.pdhealth.mil/reservist/default.asp

United States Department of Veterans Affairs
http://www.oefoif.va.gov/

11

MANAGING THE RETURN TO THE WORKPLACE: RESERVISTS NAVIGATING THE STORMY SEAS OF THE HOMELAND

Christina Harnett and Joan DeSimone

The extraordinary selfless service of these magnificent citizen soldiers demands that we honor our legal and solemn obligation to make the transition from military service back to citizen in the workplace as seamless and as smooth as possible. They earned the right and deserve no less.

—Lieutenant General (Ret.) H. Steven Blum Former Chief,
National Guard Bureau and Former Deputy Commander of the
United States Northern Command (USNORTHCOM), October 28, 2010

Work represents the lifeblood of people.

D. L. BLUSTEIN (2008)

Two worlds, military and civilian, are spanned by members of the young veterans' universe who serve in the reserve components of our modern military system. The complexity of the elements of the War on Terror parallels the demands and challenges the veterans of our armed forces confront upon returning home and resettling into family, community, and workplace. Cultural disparities, shifts in economic forces, changes in business, and the veteran's "new normal" perspective influence family, community, and employment relationships; and, never before in the history of modern warfare, has a veteran confronted more complex employment challenges in returning home and resuming civilian status. Unlike the homecoming of yesteryear, today's "yellow ribbon welcome" begins a complex journey of readjustment to work identity, technological advances, an economic tsunami, and a home culture that has shifted. Change entire clause to read "Reservists, who exit the civilian world and reenter after combat, are a little understood segment of the American society;" the reintegration workplace challenges they face are not well-known by researchers nor the general public. This work is an attempt to shed light on the complexity of employment issues confronting these "weekend warriors" upon homecoming and reintegration to the workplace. Recommendations to facilitate this process are generated for Reservists, employers, and the military service branches.

According to the Bureau of Labor Statistics, U.S. Department of Labor (2010), the unemployment rate for veterans in the Gulf II era was 10.2% in 2009. Younger veterans (aged 18–24) were unemployed at a rate of 21.1% or 65,000 persons in 2009, while their older cohorts (aged 25–34) experienced a rate of 10.6% unemployment affecting over 100,000 individuals (U.S. Department of Labor, 2010). These statistics indicate a growing need to more fully comprehend the reintegration experience as it relates to reemployment, and a return to social roles, responsibilities, and routines (Faber, Willerton, Clymer, MacDermid, & Weiss, 2008) and existing research suggests several employment-related conditions and labor market outcomes may be affected by a service member's experience of combat and absence from the work force.

Managing the return of combat veterans to the workplace is rapidly becoming more commonplace today. This is especially true if the service member is an armed forces Reservist despite age, employment trajectory, career tenure, or previous civilian position within a company. Such a strategy derives from the confluence of three forces: the reality of war and its combat consequences of separation from civilian life, the nature of work caused by shifts in globalization amid rapidly shifting social and economic forces of the 21st century (Blustein, 2008), and the current limits of available labor opportunities. The physical and psychological costs of combat from the Global War on Terror (GWOT) operations across the globe have extracted unparalleled tolls on our veterans challenging, and in many cases compromising, successful reunification to their civilian and work life worlds. The long-term personal and societal costs of deployment-related cognitive and psychological injuries manifest themselves in scenarios of homelessness, domestic violence, reduced productivity, suicide, familial strain, and diminished quality of life (Tanielian, Jaycox, Adamson, & Metscher, 2008).

According to Kanter (1999), the central feature of our current job market rests on a flow of information, people, and capital; "intangible information-centered assets such as proprietary technologies, brands, workforce skills, and strategic relationships, appear to matter more than tangible assets" (Kanter, 1999, p. 9). In fact, those people who produce knowledge (knowledge workers) or process data (data workers), comprised 52% of the U.S. labor force in 2000 demonstrating that "... we have moved from a society in which we work with our hands to one in which we work with our mind" (Wolff, 2005, p. 38). Standardization, automation, and instant communication further contribute to the rapidly shifting landscape of employment as workers are exposed to changes in the nature of work not seen since the industrial revolution (Harvey, 2002). Given the rapid shifts in both technology and information, veterans absent from the civilian work world for extended periods of time may find themselves as strangers in a strange land trying to navigate the unpredictable and stormy seas of the American labor force.

Research has informed our understanding of the reintegration challenges of the active services, and anecdotal information exists for all service members on their deployment cycle experiences (Klerman, Loughran, & Martin, 2005; Manderscheid, 2007; Military.com, 2007). However, a relative paucity of research exists on the conditions and experiences of "citizen soldiers" or Reserve Component (RC)[1] (Tanielian, Jaycox, Schell, Marshall, & Vaiana, 2008), particularly when they demobilize and merge back into their citizen work roles (Colonel (Ret.) R. Schnell, personal communication, October 28, 2010.) While a great deal is known about employment issues for traditional military members who are discharged into civilian life, little is known about the challenges faced by members of the National Guard and Reserve Forces[2] and their reentry work stressors despite reports of employer support waning (Commission on the National Guard and Reserves, 2008; McNutt, 2005).

Members of the reserve forces move between civilian status to military status and back following deployment (McNutt, 2005). Compared to their active military peers, they tend to be older and are more likely established in a career; unlike active military, Reservists rely on civilian employers as their primary source of income and gain supplemental income through their part-time military affiliation (Griffith, 2010). For the most part, returning active military members transition into active military status at home, living in or near military installations that

---

[1] The Reserve Component (RC) of the armed forces includes: Army National Guard, Air Force Reserve, Air National Guard, Army Reserve, Navy Reserve, Marine Corps Reserve, and the Coast Guard Reserve.

[2] Throughout the chapter, the term "Reserve Forces" or "Reserve Component" will be used to include members of the National Guard as well as other Reserve Force branches of the military.

provide for an array of medical and psychosocial needs. The various service branches provide transition and employment counseling for those separating from military service. Reserve members have a strong affiliation to their units. But, unlike their active colleagues who live and work within a military community, reserve members may have only episodic (i.e., monthly drills and summer trainings) contact with their military peers when not deployed. For them, affiliation is strongest with their civilian worlds, and reintegration presents more challenges than for members of the active services (Manderscheid, 2007).

The reintegration process is made more complicated by the fact that Reservists may be deployed as individuals, in teams, or by whole units. Consequently, postdeployment support and continuity of care for both physical and psychological issues are split among several facilitators: the home unit, the active unit with which they served, and civilian health and behavioral health providers (Lafferty, Alford, Davis, & O'Connor, 2008). Problems are compounded by the fact that geographically, reserve members' homes are dispersed widely throughout a state or states making casual contact with fellow Reserve unit members unlikely. Furthermore, Reservists do not usually live in close proximity to their military units (Griffith, 2010).

Like all veterans, Reservists may face difficulty in trying to cope with intrapersonal and interpersonal changes that have resulted from the deployment experience. Regrettably, few studies have investigated the relationship between deployment stressors and health outcomes for this population (LaBash, Vogt, King, & King, 2007). However, one of these studies, a longitudinal investigation of both active and reserve soldiers, revealed that Reservists reported higher rates of behavioral health issues and were referred for behavioral health interventions at higher rates than active service colleagues when screened after several months of returning home (Milliken, Auchterlonie, & Hoge, 2007). This indicates intrapersonal changes were present during the reintegration process, potentially contributing to the strain of returning home. As one Reservist reflected, the deployment world changed him, while his civilian social support world seemed to have been frozen in time.

> When I returned a year later and rekindled relationships with friends, girlfriends, and family, something was different. My friends seemed to be almost as I had left them—living at home—scrounging money to do things- living very much in the moment ... and much like me a year earlier, had not a clue as to what else was going on in the world.

> I had just spent a year overseas ... on my own, away from everything I knew .... Of course, they were still my friends and family and I loved them the same, but I had been hardened as a person.

Homecoming observations, such as the one noted above, under-score the intrapersonal and interpersonal dynamics that complicate a warrior's reentry into civilian society. This reaction may be reciprocal, and in family interactions "in many instances, a traumatized soldier is greeting a traumatized family, and neither is recognizing the other" (Hutchinson & Banks-Williams, as cited in Bowling & Sherman, 2008, p. 451).

> ... military spouses and children informally carry the rank of their spouse or parent, which includes guidelines for behavior and pressure to conform. It is widely believed that service members' career advancement can be adversely affected by the behavior of their family members (Albano, 2002). For example, officers' inability to handle their family problems could be generalized to their ability to handle difficulties within their unit and bring into question their leadership competence. The dynamic of reconnecting with family and friends occurs in the face of occupational ambiguities.
>
> —*Drummet, Coleman, and Cable, 2003, p. 279*

The dynamic of reconnecting with family and friends occurs in the face of occupational ambiguities.

THE CONCEPT OF OCCUPATIONAL AMBIGUITIES

There are a myriad of postcombat perspectives, attitudes and issues that affect occupational options and employment reintegration among the National Guard and Reserve Forces. Paralleling the movements of members in other services after war, some Reserve Force veterans return to civilian work seeking career advancement and striving to parlay new skills learned during deployment (Doyle & Peterson, 2005; Manderscheid, 2007; Tanielian et al., 2008). On the other hand, unlike their active military peers, Reserve Force members may resume employment in the same career and in the same company as mandated by law. Yet, in today's economy, some veterans return to find their previous employer no longer exists, and others return to their previous circumstance of unemployment satisfied with a current status quo of high unemployment (Department of Labor, 2010).

Moreover, others have the perception they never left the civilian workforce to deploy; rather, they used advanced modern technology to "telecommute" from the combat zone to the homeland.

Given the shift in the nature of war, the alteration of Reservists' military status from strategic to operational forces, the alteration in our country's economy, and the rapidly expanding technological innovations in commerce and global business, our Guard and Reserve veterans face unparalleled reintegration stressors—among which factors related to work, identity, and financial concerns play pivotal roles. Among the members of this military stratum, there appears to be a belief that society-at-large is relatively uninformed as to the unique role they play in the military and the resultant reintegration challenges they influence for returning soldiers, especially reservists. As a National Guard officer observed,

> Reservists believe that their culture, the role they play in the military, and the challenges they face when they return home is little understood by the American mainstream.

This discord in civilian society's understanding of the role they play in securing reintegration for returning soldiers creates many ambiguities, especially occupational ambiguities. In order to close this gap of misperceptions and facilitate better understanding the phenomenological underpinnings of the transition to civilian employee experienced by *citizen soldiers*, the authors provide observations by Reservists, and include in this text pilot data derived from focus groups and interviews with returning National Guardsmen.[3] Considered collectively, these sources will address the current state of workplace reintegration issues for Reservists and form the basis for our charge to increase scholarship in this area. There is an urgent need for employment strategies on the part of the veteran. Specific recommendations for facilitating workplace success are generated for both the repatriate and the employer.

> ... work is a central aspect of life; indeed, the struggle to earn one's livelihood represents perhaps the most consistent and profound way in which individuals interface with their social, economic and political contexts ... Working represents the lifeblood of people, whose hopes and dreams are tied to the activities that they engage in to make a living. When working is going well, people may be

---

[3]This research was approved by the Institutional Review Board of the Johns Hopkins University.

able to enjoy a great deal of psychological health and vigor; however, when work is not available and when it is a source of denigration, tedium, and despair, it can represent the bane of their existence

—*Blustein, 2008, p. 237*

It is not feasible to fully understand the complexities impinging on Reservists as they encounter the reality of transition to their former home culture without placing this shift in context.

War and Its Consequences of the Return to Work

As of February of 2009, over 1,893,284 million service members have been deployed in Operation Iraqi Freedom (OIF) and Operation Enduring Freedom (OEF). Of the total number of military deployed, 297,615 of these were National Guard members and 230,145 were Reserve members (Defense Manpower Data Center, 2009). Many of the Reserve members had multiple deployments. Reserve forces appear to bear a significant amount of the burden of war, as according to U.S. Military Casualty Statistics, more than 50% of war casualties were those sustained by Reserve forces (House Committee on Veterans' Affairs, 2008).

The wars in Afghanistan and Iraq are different from other wars in which the United States has been engaged and consequently, they extract different tolls from our service members (Tanielian & Jaycox, 2008). These differences impact not only the deployment experience but also ways in which the veteran must adjust upon homecoming. Some of these distinctions include: a prolonged tour of duty (some members serving more than 2 years) and multiple deployments, a lack of clear battle and safe zones increasing the level of personal risk, and a combination of active and reserve military serving as operational forces (House Committee on Veterans' Affairs, 2008; Lafferty et al., 2008; Manderscheid, 2007). Taken together, these forces impact the risk and stress levels for our military personnel and complicate reintegration for both active and reserve forces (Manderscheid, 2007). As soldiers leave the military, they bring home with them the mental and physical wounds of their wartime experiences (Hoge et al., 2008; Lafferty et al., 2008). But most importantly, they carry these burdens into a labor market they hope will exist for them and into positions that may create tension between job demands and familial roles and responsibilities (Greenhaus & Beutell, 1985).

While many service members will return from combat without difficulties and will adapt successfully, many veterans return with significant behavioral health issues (House Veterans' Affairs Committee, 2009). Sammons and Batten (2008) maintain that GWOT brings with it unprecedented attention to the psychological costs of combat and a potential for psychological morbidity to far supersede rates of combat injuries. The Department of Defense (DOD) has identified two "signature injuries" of the OEF/OIF conflicts, posttraumatic stress disorder (PTSD) and traumatic brain injury (DOD, 2007).

However, according to Litz (2007), little longitudinal research has been focused on military trauma from an epidemiologic perspective despite the fact that postdeployment mental health disorders are an important public health issue as well as a potential lifelong combat legacy. A recent study of 2543 National Guards members investigating the effects of repeated deployments on health found that soldiers with at least one OIF/OEF deployment were three times more likely to have positive screens for symptoms of PTSD and major depression, twice as likely to report conditions of chronic pain, and at least 90% more likely to score below the average norm for the population-at-large on physical functioning as compared to nondeployed soldiers (Kline et al., 2010).

PTSD in veterans has been associated with increased risk for suicidal ideation (Pietrzak et al., 2010) and negative conditions in intimate relationships such as dissatisfaction, decreased intimacy and psychological and physical abuse (Monson, Taft, & Fredman, 2009). Combat-related behavioral health conditions impact marriages and children of members diagnosed with PTSD are at higher risk for academic and psychiatric problems (House Veterans' Affairs Committee, 2009). Suicide by both deployed and nondeployed service members has become an issue of dramatic concern in the current conflicts for all armed forces (DOD, 2010). For example, suicide rates among Army active duty soldiers in 2008 marked a 28-year high and a development that continued in a 4-year upward trend (Kuehn, 2009). Consequently, in response to the alarming rates of suicide in both active and reserve members, in 2009, the Army commissioned the Suicide Prevention Task Force, which in turn developed and implemented the Army Campaign Plan for Health Promotion, Risk Reduction and Suicide Prevention as a means of delivering rapid changes in policies and programs (U.S. Army, 2010).

The challenge of predicting the cognitive and mental health consequences of deployment is complicated by the waxing and waning of problems and symptoms and the differential impact of these outcomes of combat in the short- and long term. Consequently, the global impact of these conditions on new veterans and their families cannot be understood in the absence of longitudinal empirical investigations (Karney, Ramchand, Osilla, Caldarone, & Burns, 2008). However, research on Vietnam era veterans with PTSD suggests a negative outcome for employment circumstances of current veterans suffering from more severe levels of these and other social and emotional disorders. For instance, among Vietnam veterans receiving treatment at a VA facility for severe or very severe PTSD, Smith, Schnurr, and Rosenheck (2005) found symptom severity negatively correlated with part-time and full-time employment; as the severity of PTSD symptoms increased, the probability of either full or part-time employment decreased for these veterans.

Combat has far-reaching consequences also affecting families and the community-at-large. Approximately 2 million children have been impacted by the loss of a parent to deployment (Flake, Davis, Johnson, & Middleton, 2009); in 2007, it was estimated that 700,000 American children experienced the deployment of at least one parent (APA, 2007). As revealed by a quadrennial quality-of-life report issued by the DOD (2009) in 2008, there were 3.24 million active duty and family members in the armed forces and 1.95 million Reservists and family members. Of these, 55% were married active duty members and almost half of the National Guard and Reserve force members were married. At that time, the active duty component alone was estimated to have 1.2 million dependent children, and as of June 2008, over the course of military deployments, an armed forces member left behind a family member in over 1,000,000 deployments. On a broader scale, it has been estimated that more than 57.6 million people in this country are affected as a consequence of service members' deployments to Iraq and Afghanistan (Koppes, 2010). Thus, deployments have far-reaching consequences with direct effects extending beyond deployed families and into the employment sector where the need to provide for families is heightened upon return from combat.

The Reserve Culture and the Return to Work

In order to fully comprehend the plight of Reservists as they attempt to regain civilian status, it is important to understand the basic culture of the reservist component. Members of the National Guard and Reserve forces bridge both worlds and carry dual identities as citizens and warriors. These *citizen-soldiers* or *weekend warriors*, as they have come to be known, are typically employed in full-time positions and careers in the civilian world until summoned to the service of our country. When called, young men and women leave families, relationships, jobs, careers, educational pursuits, and the community behind. The impact of this departure and deployment experience on them and their biopsychosocial ecosystems may be minimal or it may be profound.

Research indicates they may be less well-prepared to deal with the separation from family than their active duty counterparts who typically experience multiple separations from home during their military careers (Vogt, Samper, King, King, & Martin, 2008). Reserve force members return to families who may have little understanding of military culture, and to communities who may view them as active military as well as to employers who expect them to "pick-up where they left off" prior to deployment.

Manderscheid (2007) observes that OIF and OEF are significantly different conflicts from American conventional wars of the past. He notes four distinctions in this regard. First, in past wars, a tour of duty was relatively short, but it is not unusual today to find reservists who have already served more than two years. Second, earlier wars were relatively conventional with clear geographical boundaries and clear battle and safe zone demarcations. In current conflicts, no safe zones exist and all warriors are exposed to continuous threats to survival and consequently, must remain intensely and constantly vigilant. Third, formerly soldiers were drafted and came with strong civilian support. Now, military human resources are drawn from volunteers, reservists, or career military, who have a range of mixed expectations about adjustments to both warfare and return to civilian life. Additionally, there is mixed public sentiment regarding current conflicts, and members of the civilian community may not be as supportive of the warrior's service as one may expect. These wars pose a variety of challenges that may result in increased psychological and physicals risks to combatants including enemies who cannot be immediately discriminated from civilians nor readily confronted, the unpredictable use of improvised explosive device (IEDs), and the assignment to active combat zones that allow for little respite from heightened threat (Sammons & Batten, 2008).

In 1916, the National Defense Act established both the National Guard with its dual state-federal status and what later emerged as the Army Reserve. Typically, the Reservist's commitment was confined to monthly trainings/drills with a consecutive two-week period of annual duty training in summer. However, deployments under the Total Force Concept of 1970 in response to events of the first Gulf War transformed the Army Reserve from a "static force used to deter threats" to "a dynamic force that had to be mobilized and deployed for effective military operations"; gradually, world events and military policy caused a focus on shifting the Reservist's identity from "weekend warriors" to "soldier warriors" paralleling the increased reliance on them for military conflicts (Griffith, 2009, pp. 12–13). Their special status as part-time warriors has earned them the moniker of "transmigrant" meaning "some combination of plural membership in social groups or social networks, cultural identities reaching across and linking people and institutions . . ." (Lomsky-Feder, Gazit, & Ben-Ari, 2008, p. 598).

Today's GWOT has resulted in both extended military actions and stabilization efforts relying heavily on both Guard (Keohane, 2007) and Reserve components. This shift in mission from strategic reserve to operational force for the Guard

> will challenge the traditions of the citizen soldier as never before. The one weekend a month and two weeks each summer paradigm instituted as part of the National Defense Act of 1916 and promulgated for the past 90 years, has been shattered.
>
> —*Keohane, 2007, p. 6*

The same is assumed for other reserve component forces with similar populations. Now, our Reserve and National Guard soldiers constitute approximately 1 million of the troops currently serving in the U.S. military. Forty percent of the troops serving in Iraq are members of the RC and they may be activated in service for as long as two years (Center for the Study of Traumatic Stress, 2009) and many members may anticipate more frequent and longer deployments with shorter rest periods in between tours (Tanielian et al., 2008) to reconnect with families. This shift is forcing a reconceptualization of the nature and demands placed upon citizen soldiers, their families, and their employers.

According to Keohane (2007), increased reliance on the National Guard will directly impact the level of support from employers of those service members. Keohane (2007) notes that even under the old paradigm of monthly drills and a two-week summer commitment, military and employer demands often clashed but were resolved in a collaborative, informal manner. However, in more recent times, there is evidence to suggest reluctance on the part of the employer to engage and retain personnel who admit that they are members of the Guard. Keohane (2007) notes that factors such as "open-ended," multiple, and the unpredictable timing of deployments will "ultimately damage the employability" of Guard service members.

The reality of lengthy, repeated deployments caused by a protracted GWOT has resulted in both existing and potential reservists revising their expectations on the likelihood of deployment (Klerman et al., 2005). Each time reservists are calledup and careers stalled, there is concern by reservists of the window of opportunity closing on promotions and other employment-related opportunities (La Bash, Vogt, King, & King, 2009) or as observed by 28% of activated Reservists in a RAND report—they may experience some earnings loss with deployment (Klerman et al., 2005). Given the economic realities of our times, there is a consistent concern that there may be no job upon homecoming.

Perhaps, career and financial concerns contribute to turnover in choosing to terminate status as a military member, especially under conditions of lengthy deployments for those with larger civilian salaries or those who are self-employed (Klerman et al., 2005). As noted in a study of Army Reserve deployments for the period 2003–2008 comprising approximately 40,000 positions, between 40% and 50% were "new arrivals" (Lippiatt & Polich, 2010). Furthermore, 25–40% of soldiers assigned to a unit one year prior to mobilization, terminated military service during the following year (Lippiatt & Polich, 2010). This loss of personnel is a DOD concern as it reflects unit instability and the loss of potentially valuable job skills prized by the military (Klerman et al., 2005).

Reentry Into the Workforce

Historically, a guiding assumption of our American culture has been that every veteran desires, and has a right to, work. Indeed, this belief is the foundation of national, community and personal outreach efforts to aid veterans in finding meaningful employment throughout the modern history of this country. Soldiers' wartime experiences, both pre- and postdeployment, have been captured in research studies and in personal stories. Glimpses of varied perspectives for all American veterans of all wars may be found in personal narratives, correspondence, and visual materials preserved through the Veterans History Project of the American Folklife Center at the Library of Congress (American Folklife Center, 2010).

Paralleling the current state of military warfare, the issues and factors involved in the successful reintegration of warriors into the postdeployment work environments are dynamic and complex. Moreover, the manner in which the various military services prepare its veterans for this reentry is dictated by the philosophies and cultures of each of those services, as well as by law. Members of the active military (e.g., Navy, Army, Air Force, etc.) end their careers in search of new jobs after having served a specific enlistment period. In addition to an employment search, Reserve Forces may also face a daunting challenge of reentering a former position after a departure caused by a *call up* for deployment. Recently, the latter situation has been made more challenging because of the transition of Reserve Forces into an operational force; multiple deployments have caused multiple leaves of absence from the workplace. Thus, where active duty personnel have a consistent employment profile, Reservists' employment profiles are staggered with missing periods from the civilian workforce that must be explained to an uninformed civilian employer.

An early attempt to provide assistance to veterans is found in one employment initiative. The Uniformed Services Employment and Reemployment Rights Act of 1994 (USERRA) was legislated in order to protect the employment rights of members of the RC thereby ensuring adequate military staffing levels and aiding the DOD in its retention and recruitment efforts. It

> guarantees the rights of reservists to be reemployed by their civilian employer after serving on active duty, prohibits employers from discriminating against individuals in any aspect of employment because of their service in the reserves, and mandates some continuation of benefits to reservists who have been activated.
>
> —*CBO Testimony, 2007, pp. 1,2*

In addition to USERRA regulations governing a reservists' postdeployment return to work, a national organization under the DOD titled Employer Support of the Guard and Reserve (ESGR), was founded in 1972. The mission of the volunteer organization is to gain support from employers as well as the community to ensure readiness and stability of Reserve members. This mission targets cooperation and collaboration between members of the RC and their employers by recognizing employers who have provided outstanding support to reservists, by increasing awareness of USERRA, and by assisting in the resolution of conflicts deriving from the employee's military commitment. Because the RC is now part of the Total Force strategy of our national defense, the ESGR's 56 field committees exist throughout the United States in each state, the District of Columbia, Guam, Puerto Rico, the Virgin Islands, and Europe to promote employer compliance with existing employment laws, and thus protecting the rights of Reservists. For the fiscal year 2009, ESGR volunteers briefed 443,833 service members and 162,849 employers. In addition to providing direct support to both Guard Reserve members and employers, the ESGR website provides a host of prospective resources for all concerned with the successful reentry of veterans into various occupational fields (Employer Support of the Guard and Reserve, 2010). However, "... so many Americans have toggled between military service and civilian work through the Afghan and Iraq wars, the strain on them and their employers has tested the laws meant to make sure they can double as workers and troops" (Kansas City Star, 2009).

In response to increasing demands placed on Reservist veterans upon reintegration, the "Yellow Ribbon Reintegration Program" (YRRP) component of the Defense Authorization Act of 2008 (P.L. 110–181) was passed by Congress and signed by President Bush in December of 2007 (House of Representatives, 2007). This legislation mandates a continuum of support for both soldier and family across the entire deployment cycle. It dictates that

> The Secretary of Defense shall establish a national combat veteran reintegration program to provide National Guard and Reserve members and their families with sufficient information, services, referral, and proactive outreach opportunities throughout the entire deployment cycle ... Program shall consist of informational events and activities for members of the reserve components of the Armed Forces, their families, and community members to facilitate access to services supporting their health and well-being ... Information sessions shall utilize State National Guard and Reserve resources in coordination with the Employer Support of Guard and Reserve Office, Transition Assistance Advisors, and the State Family Programs Director ... As part of the Yellow Ribbon Reintegration Program, the Office for Reintegration Programs may develop programs of outreach to members of the Armed Forces and their family members to educate such members and their family members about the assistance and services available to them under the Yellow Ribbon Reintegration Program. Such assistance and services may include ... employment assistance.
>
> —HR 4986, pp. 121–123

Originally, this act was designated for State National Guard and Reserve organizations who, unlike their active military counterparts, have a dual status of *citizen-soldiers* as noted previously and who transition rapidly from military to civilian status when called to active duty. The YRRP provides multiple forms of social support, educational outreach and intervention to aid the veteran's transition back to family, workplace, and community.

Reintegration assistance is targeted toward helping the soldier adjust to the reality of intrapersonal and interpersonal changes accompanying reentry to civilian life and provides an array of support services to accomplish its mission. Yet, part of reintegration is in obtaining and sustaining employment in the civilian community, especially for the *weekend warrior* with the staggered employment profile.

National level engagement by civilians and military members around the employment issue is seen in the initiation of a recent, large survey of approximately 5000 respondents sponsored by a civilian organization, Military.com, an online quasi-military organization. The results of their online, nonrandom sample survey (Military. com, 2010) reveal several employment issues confronting returning military personnel—the most significant of which is the employer/ employee relationship. Their data suggest a "profound disconnect" between employers and returning veterans moving back into the workforce. Approximately 61% of employers surveyed did not understand job qualifications of veterans, and another 64% of the veterans believed they needed additional help in making a successful transition to the workforce. Transitioning service members, on the other hand, felt illprepared to translate their military skills into civilian work skills (66%) and over half of the respondents were unsure how to network their skills in a professional manner (57%). Finally, at least one-third of employers surveyed were unfamiliar with USERRA (Military.com, 2007), which stipulates that an employer must rehire a veteran into the same job that was left for deployment or offer the veteran an equivalent one.

The role of the employment organization in facilitating the veteran's return to civilian employment has been demonstrated to be of significant influence on work adjustment and satisfaction with the organization (McNutt, 2005). McNutt (2005) has argued that despite deployment in numbers equal to that of active military, most literature found on Army reserve personnel tends to be clinical in theme addressing topics such as PTSD, psychological and social consequences of deployment, and other markers of psychological distress. Little attention has been given to the role employment organizations play in mitigating the effects of deployment and to the impact of organizational support on reintegration to the workplace.

A recent survey conducted by the Society for Human Resource Management (SHRM) (2010) presents a view from the manager's perspective on employment reintegration issues and efforts made on the part of management to assist the veteran. For example, in a sample of 429 randomly selected human resource professionals, 52% reported being somewhat familiar with USERRA regulations (an increase of 6% over 2003), while 29% were somewhat or extremely familiar with ESGR (an increase of 2% over 2003). Furthermore, 53% reported hiring veterans in full-time, part-time or temporary positions over the last 3 years, and 50% of respondents stated that their organizations made direct efforts to recruit and hire veterans; 11% whose companies had not hired veterans made specific attempts to attract and hire them.

The SHRM (2010) survey provides additional information regarding support services offered to Guard and Reserve veterans and family members during deployment and upon reintegration to the workplace. For instance, 63% of employers provided a health insurance extension to family members during deployment, while 47% provided the same extension to the service member. Employers are also managing the reintegration with employee assistance program resources (66%), providing remedial "catch-up skills" (58%), allowing flexible work arrangements (48%), and providing recognition for military service (44%).

Employers have also experienced a range of challenges in losing a worker to deployment. Uncertainty as to the length of absence was the most common concern for managers (74%), while the burden on remaining employees to fill the gap (51%) and recruiting temporary employees to fill the open job (44%) were also common concerns. Few managers (13%) were concerned about cultural or psychological issues or the need for alternative work arrangements for members of their workforce who were returning veterans (Society for Human Resource Management, 2010). While the veteran may find it difficult to translate his/her military skills into civilian employment language, a sample of over 2600 managers and human resource professionals who responded to an online CareerBuilder survey believe that it is critical for the veteran to market their military experience and accomplishments in seeking employment. They viewed specific characteristics associated with military service as critical to the job search of returning veterans, especially reservists:

1. disciplined approach to work,
2. ability for teamwork,
3. leadership, respect and integrity,
4. ability to perform under stressful conditions, and
5. problem-solving skills (CareerBuilder, 2009).

The reality of the returning soldier's loss of military role and function (i.e., membership in a particular social context), and reacceptance of his/her civilian group identity/shared membership is particularly significant to the reintegration experience. Therefore, the importance of the employer/employee relationship, which allows for financial, as well as social independence, is central to the reintegration process and the successful reengagement of the individual as he/she reorients toward a meaningful existence within the context of social roles and responsibilities.

THE STUDY

In developing background research for this chapter, the present authors initiated a qualitative investigation of employment issues and challenges among current National Guard veterans; pilot data on two small samples of National Guard members are presented below.[4] Using focus groups as recommended by Manderscheid (2007), National Guard soldiers volunteered to discuss their workplace reintegration issues. Questions guiding this research are designed to elicit the veteran's perspective on factors that are perceived to facilitate or impede successful reentry into work life and career. Three main questions guide our investigation:

1. What are the dynamics involved in the reintegration experience?
2. What are the relationships among those dynamics?
3. How can we use this knowledge to further the acceleration of a successful reintegration experience as it pertains to the work life of returning veterans?

---

[4]This research was approved by the Institutional Review Board of the Johns Hopkins University.

Although results are based on a very limited, convenience sample, preliminary findings were elicited from veterans between the ages of 18 and 35 years of age, returning home within the last two months from deployment, who completed the Reintegration Work Attitudes, Issues and Challenges Questionnaire (RWAIC) and participated in focus groups facilitated by the current authors (see Appendix).

As may be seen in the Appendix, the RWAIC consists of demographic information which includes traditional variables as well as variables related to military status and experiences (e.g., service affiliation, number of deployments, and length of time since returning from combat). In addition, the RWAIC consists of seven forced-choice items requiring a "yes" or "no" response. These items tap work-related attitudes, issues and experiences. If a respondent marked "yes" in response to a question, he/she was asked for further clarifying information. Following completion of the RWAIC, a facilitated group discussion reviewed each question in the instrument. National Guard members were encouraged to share insights on their experiences and the facilitators probed responses for further information or relevance to the topic. This methodology resulted in an experiential descriptive of reentry into the world of civilian work and the supports and impediments to a successful reintegration.

Table 11.1 contains demographic information on the two small samples of National Guard Service members who agreed to participate in the qualitative research project (see Table 11.1). As may be seen, the total sample size was 19 (males = 16; females = 3) with disproportionately few female reporting. The average age of male participants was 28.7 years with a range of 27–54 years. Alternatively, females had a higher mean age of 41.6 years and a range of 39–46 years. Of the total sample, 7 members were single, 11 were married, and 1 was divorced.

TABLE 11.1 Demographic characteristics of National Guard sample by gender

Gender	Male $N = 16$	Female $N = 3$
Mean age	29.7 years	41.6 years
Age range	21–54 years	39–46 years
Marital status		
Single	7	–
Married	8	3
Divorced	1	–

TABLE 11.2 **Number of deployments and employment status by gender**

Gender	Male	Female
Number of deployments	21	3
Employment status		
Employed	9	3
Unemployed	5	–
Not reporting	2	–

Table 11.2 demonstrates the trend toward multiple deployments among National Guard soldiers (see Table 11.2). Although each of the 19 participants reported deploying at least once, 5 reported deploying twice, and soldiers with multiple deployments tended to be older (age range = 39–46 years). This table also reflects a dim picture of the current economic reality of unemployment among returning veterans. Of the 19 participants, 12 were currently employed, 5 reported being unemployed, and 2 failed to respond to the item. Even within this small sample, 26% of the veterans were without full-time employment. Their age range was 22–45 years with the average age for unemployment of 30.6 years.

A review of written responses to questions in the RWAIC as well as verbal comments during group discussions provided insights into personal perspectives on postdeployment work reentry. When asked "Has your attitude toward the type of work you do changed as a result of your return or reentry?" One soldier responding affirmatively commented, "I can do something more important," while another "wanted more responsibility" after returning. An expansion on this comment is found in his remarks during our discussion.

> When I got back from the war and went back to work, I didn't feel I was being challenged. I felt I could contribute a lot more, so I ended up asking for and getting more responsibility—a greater workload. But now, I was getting eight hours of work done in half the time.

A third soldier found himself to be "more focused" on workplace tasks but another struggled with the relative unimportance of his civilian job as compared to his military skills and occupation during deployment. Collectively, these comments reveal the underlying theme of a shift in perspective following deployment that is common among National Guard members returning to citizen status. Quite simply, the job they held in the military may have been of higher status than their civilian position, or they have undergone a personal transformation and the former job is no longer a good fit for their interests or talents, or it is not as exciting or stimulating as the deployment experience. There may have been a shift in personal values as exemplified by the statement of a soldier, who had served in military intelligence. "Once I came back from deployment and sat in front of my computer, I was bored. I wanted my life to mean something."[5]

The second question on the RWAIC asked, "Has your attitude toward the workplace changed as a result of your return or reentry?" reveals attitudinal shifts among respondents toward the civilian work and workplace. Affirmative responses resulted in the following comments by soldiers: "I notice now that most people in my workplace think and act for themselves, not as a team." I am "somewhat less concerned with urgency of tasks that need to be completed on the civilian job"; "I see things differently." These statements reveal the cognitive set or perspective that a citizen soldier develops through the deployment experience and which lingers upon return to civilian life.

"What work related challenges have you experienced as a result of your return from combat?" led to a variety of responses illustrating the diversity of veteran reemployment experiences from confronting new computer technology to dealing with increased work demands under a workforce reduction. One soldier found "updates and workplace changes" to be challenging, while another cited a "loss of patience with incompetence, mistakes." For one person (a full-time member of the National Guard), changing units after deployment led to a "different attitude toward leadership who has not deployed to a combat zone." Another person transitioning to a new job and career felt her new position required "a lot of learning." Finally, one soldier observed, "People don't know how to make you feel welcomed and we don't know what the work challenges are to better prepare ourselves to reintegrate back to work."

When asked "what skills do you, or did you, need to develop to ease your reintegration or return to the workplace?" and a related question "what can management do to support your full engagement back into the workplace?" responses indicated a need for "retraining" and "computer skills" as well as an array of suggested and/or implemented management initiatives. One soldier commented, "In my situation, my

---

[5]This comment was made during a reintegration training; the soldier was employed as a civilian intelligence analyst at a federal agency.

supervisor had me retrain alongside others in my position. It lasted for about a week and a half to two weeks. It helped me ease back in easily." Another stated, "They gave training" and suggested a "meet and greet two week honeymoon period to adjust." A third reported "my supervisor took it into his own hands to inform me of changes and integrated this into the first few weeks of returning to work." Two soldiers encouraged management to "talk to them . . . (because) each return is different for each person." "Be supportive in terms of understanding that there are many things to take care of when you get back—even after 60, 90 days—I felt rushed back to work." Finally, a last contributor remarked, "there's no kind of formal reorientation or no formal kind of retraining. You're told—just come on back."

The last RWAIC item to be reviewed is question 11—"Please identify what you consider to be the greatest single barrier to successful reintegration in the workplace." Respondents addressed this item from two perspectives: job-related challenges and more personal appeals for understanding of the reintegration experience and the importance of returning to work for the individual. Examples of the former include, "catching up on updates, new processes, etc. . . . , " "changes in policies (union, state, and federal)," and the importance of a "good management team." One soldier provided a unique glimpse into the unique nature of workplace reintegration issues confronting members of the National Guard.

> Returning to the workforce is challenging for soldiers that lost their jobs prior to deployment. Before I could return to the workforce, I had to submit several job applications while overseas. In addition I had to do telephone interviews in order to secure a position. Finding the job is harder than what we face returning to the workforce.

The second category of responses to the item addressed the temporal dimension of reintegration—"Time. You must have time to reintegrate" and the "time lost associating with coworkers." In addition, a need for belongingness or "trying to fit in someplace, to feel valued and appreciated" or that one is "making a contribution" to the work and the workplace were also noted.

Taken together, insights garnered from this very limited initial sample of respondents provide a starting point from which to better understand the Reserve Force perspective on coming home and resuming a civilian existence as a productive member of society. These interviews with returning combat veterans reveal several reemployment circumstances and challenges that lend validity to the limited research and anecdotal evidence that exist, but they need to be more fully articulated and explored in order to better understand the young veteran's experience of the reintegration process. More research is needed to determine the effect of the veteran's prior employment history on his/her employment reintegration status and experience. A more comprehensive understanding of employment variables and employer dispositions as they are perceived through the eyes of the veteran, would aid in the development of workplace programs and policies which could further the successful acceleration of the returning soldier's full reintegration back to civilian life. The remainder of this chapter explores concepts that may further our understanding of this phenomenon and management traditions and perspectives that may increase the frustration of veterans and thwart efforts toward achieving a satisfying reintegration.

DISCUSSION

A recognition of the employer's central role as a reintegration facilitator is critical in preparing employees for both deployment and post-deployment work-related issues. Expectations of job productivity, work significance, task accomplishment, employee relations, and self-management are far too often accompanied by the experience of frustration, failure, exclusion, and resentment on both the part of the employee as well as the employer. Moreover, veterans may return to a workplace to find unanticipated changes that require an adjustment in expectations. Civilian peers may have been promoted or left the company while the veteran returns to the exact same job (Manderscheid, 2007). At present, organizations such as the Society for Human Resources have not identified or advocated for policies that would ease the anxiety inherent on the parts of employer and employee both pre- and postdeployment. Only recently, are national organizations confronting the new reality of employees with dual work commitments: civilian and military (J. Moran, personal communication, April 1, 2010).

As revealed in responses to the RWAIC, the individual soldier's return to work seems to be a critical component of his/her return to a social identity that embodies social routines, roles and responsibilities (Faber et al., 2008), in addition to being known as a "workplace warrior." In a relatively new paradigm, it appears to be the responsibility of the civilian community, particularly the employer, to be the catalyst of the returning civilian soldier's reintegration into the social dynamics of the workplace, if this reintegration experience is to be successful.

Due to the interconnected challenges of moving between and among the worlds of war, work, and a changing personal identity, these three components may make reintegration less of the traditionally understood transitional process and more of a transformative one—carrying with it ramifications for reentry into former or new jobs. The reintegration process crosses boundaries between military and civilian identity, between work and warrior identity, and between self and social identity, having components of each within both worlds, making the boundaries less distinct and more blurred and permeable, as the returning soldiers have reported. Boss (2007) refers to "boundary ambiguity" within the family as a way to describe the dynamics of who is in and who is out, and who is performing what roles and tasks within the system. This "ambiguous absence and ambiguous presence" (Faber et al., 2008) is a characteristic which can be applied to the workplace as well as to the family, due to the fluidity of the transitions from military deployment to civilian reintegration. Along with "boundary ambiguity," is the concept of "ambiguous loss," or as Boss (2007) defines it, "a loss that remains unclear . . . when families are separated by military deployment, they of course hope to be reunited again but also know that they will never be the same as they were before the separation" (Boss, 2007, p. 105).

There is also a shift in the nature of work, the workplace, and the employee/employer relationship within the organizational management system. Management practices themselves are undergoing their own transitions, based on the "Millennial Generation's" expectations "regarding job content, training, career development, and financial rewards" (De Hauw & De Vos, 2010, p. 301). These expectations also parallel the workplace changes in employment demographics, technology enhancements, talent and succession management, and the advent of virtual workplaces, emphasizing a better balance between work and life goals. In these contemporary work places, employees struggle to balance professional priorities and personal time, both of which involve tasks and responsibilities.

Employers struggle to balance work productivity and employee motivation through alternative, innovative, and entrepreneurial workplace practices, such as flextime, job sharing, and telecommuting, in addition to the more traditional approaches of job enlargement, job rotation, and job enrichment (Robbins, 2003). One seasoned employee in the current study reported that he simply "telecommuted" to his civilian job from his military deployment in Afghanistan, and lost no time or experienced any perceived separation from his civilian work while deployed. This is indeed a new phenomenon indicative of a changing workplace, changing technology, changing expectations of a younger workforce, and a change in the nature of war with soldiers "telecommuting" to the workplace during rest periods in order to stay in touch with employers and associates and oversee the management of projects. Telecommuting may be viewed as a virtual continuation of civilian employment—thus upon physical reentry into the workplace, no psychological adjustment is needed.

Some dynamics serving as potential impediments to full reintegration into the workplace include the civilian disorientation or fog of uncertainty that accompanies the returning soldier's life circumstances in general, in addition to the anxiety of anticipating the impending interactions with former supervisors, peers, and/or friends in the workplace. It is important to note that in general, stress reactions may accompany the returning veteran's reunion with his/her family. Drummet et al. (2003) have explored the stress of returning military personnel and their findings emphasize the unique, and often repeated stressors, caused by multiple military and/or civilian relocations and subsequent reorganizations of family life during reunions. This is often accompanied by further stress due to the return to civilian work and reconnecting with multiple persons who present varying reactions to both the veteran's combat experience and the reengagement of the former employee.

Additionally, time has not stood still for anyone. There are unanticipated changes in workplace assignments, duties, roles, and technical applications that will not be familiar to the returning soldier, even if attempts have been made to keep the deployed soldier up-to-date with this information. Civilians encountering returning combat veterans often note "a change" in the disposition or personality of the former employee; this "difference" may make co-workers less likely to interact with them in the workplace. Coworker's expectations of the returning individual are based on past predeployment work history and are now altered by the veteran's experience of deployment, lack of work and workplace routine and familiarity, and the accompanying anxiety of both the employee's and coworker's anticipation of blending back into the workplace environment. Due to frequent references and dramatic portrayals sensationalized in the news, there may exist a bias in the perception of the general public that all veterans returning from combat are experiencing some form of PTSD. Therefore, coworkers might expect that the person will be different and minimize contact or withdraw completely from the returning veteran. From the veteran's perspective, this withdrawal of social support may lead to increased anxiety in work performance and in workplace interactions.

Some returning young veterans have reported feelings of apprehension about adjusting to former peer and supervisory relationships in the workplace. The reality of unit cohesion and warzone camaraderie ends when a soldier returns to civilian life. Some veterans experience this as a lack of support and care, team bonding, or even affection, in the civilian workplace. There is the risk, as one veteran observed, of being a "stranger in a strange land," with the young veterans attempting to reintegrate into a civilian workplace that may seem distant, boring, and unfamiliar after the constant vigilance, survival, and defensive challenges of combat.

Developmentally, one of the most significant markers in the life of an adult is employment, and the concept of work is one of the cornerstones of Western societies (Settersten, 2004). It is an accepted, unspoken, social contract that, between the ages of 18 and 65 years or until retirement, most adults will engage in employment of some type. Work is a social interaction among adults. When a previously employed returning soldier is not reemployed or reengaged in the work environment, there is little social connectivity as a civilian, and little psychological connectivity with their previous social role as an employed, responsible adult. If the returning soldier was not previously employed, then work presents an opportunity to be socially connected to other adults in a meaningful way.

Transition to civilian work is complex and multifaceted, and is experienced differently depending on the civilian soldier's unique circumstances and prior employment history. However, as the returning soldier transitions through the reintegration experience, there is an accompanying change in the perception of their civilian status, roles, and responsibilities, "none of which seems to matter to anyone" as one National Guardsman observed, along with a challenge to their self-perceived personal identity—"who am I, worker or warrior?"

Reemployment may be the reengagement of civilian role management, daily workday routine management, and present reality management. Stated differently, the experience of reintegration may be the reinvention or return of the civilian social identity within the changing dynamics of the family's circumstances and changing context of the workplace. Research indicates management must be sensitive to strain occurring between roles and provide a spectrum of resources to reduce conflict between work and family, thus facilitating a stronger work–family balance (Cinamon & Rich, 2010; Voydanoff, 2004). One young female Guard member in the current study reported being unable to accept the seeming meaninglessness of a civilian existence that centered around the work one performs, and so she consequently returned full-time to the military, where she repositioned her career within a command position and was fully engaged in significant mission-critical deployment.

The shift in service deployments reveals a new circumstance for the veteran; the citizen soldier must cross the boundaries of war-fighter to citizen-worker multiple times. Each time is different but also seemingly similar. For the returning combat veteran the world of work has shifted. It is reported that returning to the workplace is routine, boring, and meaningless after living in a hyper-vigilant, mission-critical environment for months, if not years, at a time. At times, the transition from soldier to civilian happens in less than a week, hardly time for the psychological, let alone physical, reentry into the social order. Bridges' (2009) model of transitions seems particularly appropriate in these circumstances.

Returning combat veterans do not automatically return to functioning successfully as civilians. They are warriors leaving the war zone to return home. They have become accustomed to a management style indicted by clear lines of communication through the chain of command, and clear expectations of goal achievement through the accomplishment of mission-critical events. They have worked in a chain of command within the logic of circumstances; their technical expertise and personal mindfulness and responsibility for their actions helping them to survive. They are highly functioning adults, both competent and courageous, and expected to be regarded thusly. One former young combat veteran, working within the transit industry and referenced above, expressed his frustration upon returning to the workplace:

> I returned as a self-motivated, highly skilled, productive mechanic, where I was asked by my civilian co-workers to stop being so darn productive. They indicated that I was creating management expectations that their production level was to equal mine, and even surpass it, because I was adjusting to new equipment purchased during my deployment. Even my supervisor was uncomfortable because he was used to micromanaging, and I was usually ahead

of schedule, so I became frustrating to him because I was self-motivated. In fact, I discovered I was a model employee, because I was just doing what I thought was my duty, but the others thought that I was trying to be better than them. They finally made me the supervisor just to get me out of the trenches, and busy with more administrative work, so that I wouldn't interfere with what they considered standard operating procedure in terms of productivity. It was very frustrating to me because people didn't like me either as a worker or as a supervisor.

Civilian supervisors often do not appreciate that, for the returning veteran, there is a difference in self-motivation, a military standard of productivity, and perceptions of duty and responsibility in a military mission-critical environment in which one is expected to work to full capacity in a highly stressful, potentially deadly combat zone, each and every day, whether on duty or not. Somehow, even in civilian mission-critical industries, the same vigilance, standards of both numerical quantity and/or qualitative excellence in productivity, and the management chain of command, are not as easily understood or accepted by workers. Civilian workplaces are quite different from the war zone experience of the combat veteran. The warrior may return to a work environment that stands in stark contrast to that of the military one.

More research is needed to investigate the dynamics of young veterans returning home and to the work force amid the storm and stress of multiples changes, to more fully comprehend the reintegration experience from the returning soldier's perspective, and from the employer's perspective. The following questions warrant further empirical investigation.

1. Just what does it mean to have a lengthy leave of absence employee on deployment several times, or a partially absent deployed employee telecommuting through time and space, while actively living and working in a war zone?
2. How do the organization, supervisor, and coworkers adjust to this phantom employee?
3. Does this herald a new trend in the workplace pushing the boundaries of telecommuting to an unknown border?
4. How best might the various military services prepare their charges to resume their adult civilian lives?

5. How do employers capture the work ethic, commitment and new skill sets of these returning young soldiers reinvesting their energy into a noncritical work routine?
6. How does the soldier identify, translate, and market "war skills" into "peacetime skills" in a rapidly shifting landscape of economic circumstances?
7. Will the workplace allow the "new civilian" to adapt to his/her "new normal" in a supportive, yet understanding manner while surrendering their warrior identity to a meaningful civilian existence?

Multiple deployments are an increasing phenomenon, affecting both the military and civilian worlds of work and the worker, personal, and social identity. One's social identity is a complex amalgamation of one's membership in "communities, families, neighborhoods, work teams, and various other forms of social group" (Haslam, Jetten, Postmes, & Haslam, 2009, p. 1).

It would be of significant social benefit to learn more about how to successfully accelerate the cyclic experience of readiness, deployment, and reintegration.

CONCLUSION

The review of the literature, collection of focus group responses and comments made during the focus group discussions as well as anecdotal information offered in support of this manuscript, all lead to the generation of recommendations for the veteran, management, and the military and policy-makers of this country. Since the modern era of the military and geopolitical conflicts is upon us, they are our "new normal." Consequently, efforts must be made by all stakeholders, soldiers, armed forces, employers and other community members to assist veterans in reestablishing themselves as productive members of our civilian society.

The work we do often defines who we are . . . It provides one of our most important identities by directing our lives in certain directions rather than others (Peterson 2006, p. 286). Employers must see the returning combat veteran differently. No matter when or how the civilian soldier left their place of employment, they are now returning home as a seasoned warrior who has survived the test of war. They are accomplished and heroic, having left home, work and country to respond to the call of duty to serve their country and promote democratic principles. They are mission-minded and principle-driven, trained as leaders and able to mobilize teams to action. They are different and employers should not underestimate their ability to perform or the skill sets they bring to meet work challenges. For example most recently, their skills and strategies at "extreme negotiations" have been identified as having great relevance to modern business (Weiss, Donigian, & Hughes, 2010).

One approach to managing the return of combat veterans to the workforce that is especially useful for repatriates returning to work is a model proposed by Chari (2008). This transition management model, based on the work of Watkins, is designed to increase success in transitional acceleration, facilitate the employee's mastery of the learning curve, and set the stage for further development in the future. According to Chari (2008), it is an antidote to the "Darwinian leadership model of survival of the fittest." This proposed paradigm includes several basic points; four of these generic suggestions are especially relevant to any veteran facing reintegration to a new workplace or to one who is assuming a new role within an organization. Given the additional adjustment stressors of the reintegration transition, we recommend:

1. *Become more self-aware.* In this regard, employees are reminded to actively/consciously manage the techniques used to secure success; do not assume that "tried and true" techniques used in the past will continue to garner success. Evaluate relative strengths and weaknesses with an eye toward self-development and improvement of skills needed in the present position (Chari, 2008). As mentioned earlier, veterans come to the workplace with an array of new skills gained through military service. The challenge lies in identifying and using those skills in a new setting, learning new skills and in recognizing and refining skills that are not necessarily strengths.

2. *Invest in systematic and specific learning.* Entering a new organization or position may make one feel overwhelmed when confronted with new policies, procedures, culture or new stratum of culture, and people. Establish what is essential to learn and determine the most efficient way of doing so (Chari, 2008). In the case of a new company, actively learn the culture and history of the organization; this helps avoid alienating others through missteps, misjudgments or unwarranted assumptions

regarding cultural values, mission, and so on. If one is a returning employee, the veteran must actively readjust to the civilian culture and routines of the organization by actively seeking out a mentor and to facilitate adjustment to new changes in policies, personnel, procedures, and so on.

3. *Manage key relationships.* In order to develop or reestablish productive working relationships with supervisors, have early (and ongoing) conversations regarding expectations, style, resources, and personal development. This allows for the management of the supervisor's expectations for performance (Chari, 2008).

4. *Create coalitions.* Influence those outside of your immediate sphere of influence. It is important to make a conscious effort to identify those people in the work environment who are key to your success and to successfully influence them (Chari, 2008) to support your professional development.

Finally, veterans are encouraged to:

5. *Develop short- and long-term goals for a career path.* Careers and career success must be actively managed. By setting goals and objectives in order to meet career aspirations, the veteran continues to make progress with a mission focus.

The Center for the Study of Traumatic Stress has established a health promotion campaign to improve the quality of workplace reentry for returning Guard and Reserve veterans titled "Courage to Care." An informational worksheet has been developed as part an outreach effort to help educators, health providers and employers better understand the psychological and emotional issues facing veterans in transitioning from active duty into the workforce in their former or new jobs. Some general recommendations for preparing the workplace include:

1. Dispelling myths regarding maladjustment or changes in personality by encouraging a positive climate and positive, supportive collegial relationships.

2. Fostering respect and reintegration through a discussion with employees about their concerns related to the service member's return and the planning of a welcoming event.

3. Preparing the transition for the returning veteran and employee who held the position during the deployment period.

Preparations for workplace reentry begin with renegotiation and realignment of responsibilities and roles for the former employee as well as preparing him/her for any changes that have occurred during the absence; the employee who held the position in the veteran's absence is expected to also undergo a transition adjustment and should be prepared for the veteran's return. The provision of job-related training in new management policies or in new technology is important as is planning for special accommodations needed for veterans who return with war-related injuries. Finally, it is recommended that confidentiality in employee assistance programs be reinforced with an accompanying explanation of how to access needed services; this is especially important for those returning after intense combat and for whom stress may be ongoing (Center for the Study of Traumatic Stress, 2009).

A second point of intervention in the health promotion campaign noted above is in its heightened awareness of postdeployment issues and recommendations for managers and supervisors of RC veterans to view return and reentry as a process during which a series of phases or issues is likely to unfold as the service members adjusts. This "workplace reintegration roadmap for managers" maintains that anticipation, homecoming, coping with change, a range of reactions and successful readjustment may all be part of a veteran's attempt to cope with the transition to civilian worker.

- First, regarding anticipation of the return to work, providing relevant workplace information (personnel changes, policy changes, workload information, or any workplace changes occurring during the absence) in a supportive and thoughtful manner will aid in dispelling any undue anxiety.
- Second, some form of celebration will serve to communicate appreciation for the veteran's service to country. Also, as the "honeymoon" period of returning home wanes, the employee may experience some normal disappointments.
- Third, veteran's reactions to deployment vary. Some return to work and naturally reassume their former role without excessive stress, while others experience the change as highly stressful. In either case, the manager is advised to provide structure in the workplace by providing opportunities for education and training, thus facilitating a sense of accomplishment, and to recognize the new skills, teamwork, and problem-solving strategies the veteran has honed during deployment.

- Fourth, some soldiers may miss the intensity experienced during deployment in returning to civilian work and they may be hesitant to discuss this disappointment or perceived lack of fit. It is important to address the confidentiality of employee assistance programs as well as the varied services they provide.
- Fifth, it is important to remember that work provides meaning and fulfillment in one's life. It is one of the most important aspects of reintegration. Incorporating the suggested strategies will benefit the soldier and the homecoming efforts on behalf of the organization, management, and fellow workers will be highly appreciated by the veteran (Center for the Study of Traumatic Stress, 2009).

Employers attracting and hiring new veteran employees would benefit by following some of the suggestions outlined above as well by familiarizing themselves with the USERRA regulations governing the hiring of Reserve members. Moreover, a familiarity with the role of the ESGR in providing support and resources to both employee and employer will help aid in successful recruitment and retention of Reservists.

While it cannot be disputed that the American military has made great strides in promoting the wellness of the veteran and family members upon homecoming through efforts such as deployment cycle support programs, much is yet to be learned from the experiences of the Reservists as they attempt to return to the civilian world of employment. Consequently, a greater focus on the experiences and perceptions of "citizen-military" would lead to better transition assistance. Greater funding for empirical investigations and increased attention to career development, educational assistance, and career exploration would significantly contribute to this initiative.

As lengthy multiple deployments become the expected norm of Guard and Reservists, the traditional civilian career ladder will not be climbed in the traditional manner by reserve members. Alternate career paths need to be created by military career counselors in partnership with civilian human resource professionals. Only through community–military partnerships can young veterans transfer deployment experience into work experience relevant to today's labor market demands and needs. It is the role of the military to foster these partnerships, and the role of the civilian community to embrace these opportunities.

As stated at the beginning of this chapter, veterans embody the life-blood of our nation and as such should be valued in all areas of society, including labor.

REFERENCES

American Folklife Center/Library of Congress. (2010). *Veterans History Project.* Retrieved July 3, 2010, from http://.loc.gov/vets/about.html

American Psychological Association. (2007). *The psychological needs of U.S. military service members and their families: A preliminary report.* Washington, DC: Author. Retrieved from http://www.apa.org/pubs/info/reports/military-deployment-summary.pdf

Blustein, D. L. (2008). The role of work in psychological health and well-being: A conceptual, historical, and public policy perspective. *American Psychologist, 63*(4), 228–240.

Boss, P. (2007). Ambigious loss theory: Challenges for scholars and practitioners. *Family Relations, 56*(2), 105–110.

Bowling, U. B., & Sherman, M. D. (2008). Welcoming them home: Supporting service members and their families in navigating the tasks of reintegration. *Professional Psychology: Research and Practice, 39*(4), 451–458.

Bridges, W. (2009). *Managing transitions: Making the most of change.* Reading, MA: Perseus Publishing Group.

CareerBuilder. (2009). *Employers targeting U.S. veterans for hiring, new Career-Builder survey finds.* Retrieved September 2, 2010, from http://www.careerbuilder.com/share/aboutus/pressreleasesdetail.aspx?id=pr523&sd=9/10/2009&ed=12/31/2009

Center for the Study of Traumatic Stress, Uniformed Services University of the Health Science. (2009). *Courage to care: Helping National Guard and Reserve reenter the workplace.* Retrieved from http://www.cstsonline.org/csts_items/CTC_helping_national_guard_reserve_reenter_ workplace.pdf

Chari, S. (2008). Handling career role transitions with confidence. *The International Journal of Clinical Leadership, 16,* 109–114.

Cinamon, R. G., & Rich, Y. (2010). Work family relations: Antecedents and outcomes. *Journal of Career Assessment, 18*(1), 59–70.

Congressional Budget Office. (May 17, 2007). *The effects of reserve call-ups on civilian employers. Testimony of Heidi Golding* (pp. 1–5). Washington, DC: Congressional Budget Office. Retrieved from http://www.cbo.gov/ftpdocs/63xx/doc6351/05-11-Reserves.pdf

Commission on the National Guard and Reserve. (2008). Transforming the National Guard and Reserves into a 21st Century Operational Force: Final Report, January 2008, Washington, D.C.: U. S. Congress.

Defense Manpower Data Center. (2009). *CTS deployment file baseline report as of February 28, 2009.* Provided by the Office of the Assistant Secretary of Defense for Public Affairs, Office of Public Communication.

Department of Defense (DOD). (2007). *An achievable vision: Report of the Department of Defense Task Force on Mental Health.* Falls Church, VA: Defense Health Board. Retrieved from http://www.health.mil/dhb/mhtf/MHTF-Report-Final.pdf

Department of Defense (DOD). (2009a). *U.S. Military Casualty Statistics.* (Current as of March 20, 2009.) Retrieved from http://www.fas.org/sgp/crs/natsec/RS22452.pdf

Department of Defense (DOD). (2009b). *Report of the Second Quadrennial Quality of Life Review.* Office of the Deputy Under Secretary of Defense (Military Community and Family Policy). Retrieved from http://cs.mhf.dod.mil/content/dav/mhf/QOL-library/PDF/MHF/QOL%20Resources/Reports/ Quadrennial%20Quality%20of%20Life%20Review% 202009.pdf

Department of Defense (DOD). (2010). The challenge and the promise: Strengthening the force, preventing suicide and saving lives. *Final report of the Department of Defense Task Force on the Prevention of Suicide by Members of the Armed Forces.* Retrieved from http://www.health.mil/dhb/downloads/Suicide%20Prevention%20Task%20Force%20report% 2008- 21-10_V4_RLN.pdf

De Hauw, S., & De Vos, A. (2010). Millennials' career perspective and psychological contract expectations: Does the recession lead to lowered expectations? *Journal of Business and Psychology, 25,* 293–302.

Doyle, M. E., & Peterson, K. A. (2005). Re-entry and reintegration: Returning home after combat. *Psychiatric Quarterly, 76*(4), 361–370.

Drummet, A. R., Coleman, M., & Cable, S. (2003). Military families under stress: Implications for family life education. *Family Relations, 52*(3), 279–287.

Employer Support of the Guard and Reserve. (2010). Retrieved September 2, 2010, from http://www.esgr.org/Site/Home/tabid/55/Default.aspxtrieved

Faber, A., Willerton, E., Clymer, S. R., MacDermid, S. M., & Weiss, H. M. (2008). Ambiguous absence, ambiguous presence: A qualitative study of military reserve families in war time. *Journal of Family Psychology, 22*(2), 222–230.

Flake, E. M., Davis, B. E., Johnson, P. L., & Middleton, L. S. (2009). The psychosocial effects of deployment on military children. *Journal of Developmental Behavioral Pediatrics, 30*(4), 271–278. Retrieved from http://journals.lww.com/jrnldbp/Citation/2009/08000/The_Psychosocial_Effects_of_Deployment_on_Military.1.aspx

Greenhaus, J. H., & Beutell, N. J. (1985). Sources of conflict between work and family roles. *Academy of Management Review, 10*(1), 76–88.

Griffith, J. (2009). Contradictory and complementary identities of U.S. Army Reservists: A historical perspective. *Armed Forces and Society, 20*(10), 1–23.

Griffith, J. (2010). Citizens coping as soldiers: A review of deployment stress symptoms among reservists. *Military Psychology, 22*(2), 176–206.

Harvey, J. H. (2002). *Perspectives on loss and trauma.* Thousand Oaks, CA: Sage Publications, Inc.

Haslam, A. A., Jetten, J., Postmes, T., & Haslam, C. (2009). Social identity, health, and well: An emerging agenda for applied psychology. *Applied Psychology, 58*(1), 1–23.

Hoge, C. W., McGurk, D., Thomas, J. L., Cox, A. L., Engel, C. C., & Castro, C. A. (2008). Mild traumatic brain injury in U.S. soldiers returning from Iraq. *New England Journal of Medicine, 358*, 453–463.

House Committee on Veteran's Affairs, Subcommittee on Health. (2008). *Statement of Mental Health America.* Retrieved from http://veterans.house. gov/hearings/Testimony.aspx?TID=42018&Newsid=177&Name Mental Health America

House of Representatives. 2007 *Defense Authorization Act of 2008.* Washington, DC: U.S. Government Printing Office. *Congressional Record* (H14495– 15204), H.R. 1585. Public Law 110–181. Retrieved from http://dx.doi. org/10.1080/08995601003638967

House Veterans' Affairs Committee. (2009). *Assessing combat exposure and post-traumatic stress disorder in troops and estimating the costs to society: Implications from the RAND invisible Wounds of War Study.* Testimony of Terri Tanielian (March 2009) before Subcommittee on Disability Assistance and Memorial Affairs, Washington, DC.

Kanter, R. M. (1999). Change is everyone's job: Managing the extended enterprise in a globally-connected world. *Organizational Dynamics, 28*, 7–23.

Kansas City Star. (2009, May 9). Returning reservists find military duty clashes with job protection.

Karney, B. R., Ramchand, R., Osilla, K. C., Caldarone, L. B., & Burns, R. M. (2008). Predicting the immediate and long-term consequences of posttraumatic stress disorder, depression, and traumatic brain injury in veterans of Operation Enduring Freedom and Operation Iraqi Freedom. In T. Tanielian & L. Jaycox (Eds.), *Invisible wounds of war: Psychological and cognitive injuries, their consequences, and services to assist recovery.* Washington, DC: RAND Corporation.

Keohane, C. J. (2007). *Transforming the guard: Construct and challenges for the operational reserve* (pp. 1–23). Carlisle Barracks, PA, U.S. Army War College, March 30, 2007. Retrieved from http://www.dtic.mil/cgi-bin/GetTRDoc? Location=U2&doc=GetTRDoc.pdf&AD=ADA469684

Kuehn, B. M. (2009). Soldier suicide rates continue to rise: Military, scientists work to stem the tide. *Journal of the American Medical Association, 301*(11), 1111–1113. Retrieved November 5, 2009, from http://jama.ama-assn. org/cgi/content/full/301/11/1111.

Klerman, J. A., Loughran, D. S., & Martin, C. (2005). *Early results on activations and the earnings of reservists. RAND Technical Report* (pp. x–xiii). Washington, DC: RAND Corporation. Retrieved from http://www.rand. org/pubs/technical_reports/2005/RAND_TR274.sum.pdf

Kline, A., Falca-Dodson, M., Sussner, B., Ciccone, D. S., Chandler, H., Callahan, L. et al. (2010). Effects of repeated deployment to Iraq and Afghanistan on the health of New Jersey Army National Guard troops: Implications for military readiness. *American Journal of Public Health, 100*(2), 276–282.

Koppes, L. (2010). *The hidden casualties of war: Promoting healing and resiliency for U.S. service members and their families—a two day symposium* [PPT]. Retrieved from http://uwf.edu/cap/HCW/brief/KoppesBrief.pps

La Bash, H. A., Vogt, D. S., King, L. A., & King, D. W. (2009). Deployment stressors of the Iraq war: Insights from the mainstream media. *Journal of Interpersonal Violence, 24*(2), 231–258.

Lafferty, C. L., Alford, K. L., Davis, M. K., & O'Connor, R. (2008). "Did you shoot anyone?": A practitioner's guide to combat veteran workplace and classroom reintegration. *Advanced Management Journal, 73*(4), 4–11.

Lippiatt, T. F., & Polich, J. M. (2010). *Reserve component unit stability: Effects on deployability and training* (pp. 1–71). Washington, DC: RAND Corporation. Retrieved from http://www.litagion.com/pubs/monographs/2010/RAND_MG954.pdf

Litz, B. T. (2007). Research on the impact of military trauma: Current status and future directions. *Military Psychology, 19*(3), 217–238.

Lomsky-Feder, E., Gazit, N., & Ben-Ari, E. (2008). Reserve soldiers as transmigrants. *Armed Forces and Society, 34*(4), 593–614.

Manderscheid, R. W. (2007). Helping veterans return: Community, family, and job. *Archives of Psychiatric Nursing, 21*(2), 122–124.

McNutt, J. M. (2005). Work adjustment of returning Army reservists: The effect of deployment and organizational support. *Dissertation Abstracts International-B 66*/04, p. 2293, October 2005. Retrieved August 18, 2010, from http://proquest.umi.com/pqdlink?did=913530251&Fmt=2&clintid=79356&RQT=309&VName=PQD

Military.com. (2010). *About us.* Retrieved July 3, 2010, from http://www.military.com/aboutus/aboutushome.htm

Milliken, C. S., Auchterionie, M. S., & Hoge, C. W. (2007). Longitudinal assessment of mental health problems among active and reserve component soldiers returning from the Iraq war. *Journal of the American Medical Association, 298*(18), 2141–2148.

Monson, C. M., Taft, C. T., & Fredman, S. J. (2009). Military-related PTSD and intimate relationships: From description to theory-driven research and intervention development. *Clinical Psychology Review, 29*, 707–714.

Peterson, C. (2006). *A primer in positive psychology.* New York: Oxford University Press.

Pietrzak, R. H., Goldstein, M. B., Malley, J. C., Rivers, A. J., Johnson, D. C., & Southwick, S. S. (2010). Risk and protective factors associated with suicidal ideation in veterans of Operations Enduring Freedom and Iraqi Freedom. *Journal of Affective Disorders, 123*, 102–107.

Robbins, S. P. (2003). *Organizational behavior* (13th ed.). Englewood Cliffs, NJ: Pearson Education.

Sammons, M. T., & Batten, S. V. (2008). Psychological services for returning veterans and their families: Evolving conceptualizations of the sequelae of war-zone experiences. *Journal of Clinical Psychology: In Session, 64*(8), 921–927.

Settersten, R. A., Jr. (2004). Social policy and the transition to adulthood: Toward stronger institutions and individual capacities. In R. A. Settersten, Jr., F. F. Furstenberg, Jr., & R. G. Rumbaut (Eds.), *On the frontier of adulthood: Theory, research, and public policy.* Chicago: University of Chicago Press.

Smith, M. W., Schnurr, P. P., & Rosenheck, R. M. (2005). Employment outcomes and PTSD symptom severity. *Mental Health Services Research, 7*(2), 89–101.

Society for Human Resource Management. (2010). *SHRM poll: Employing military personnel and recruiting veterans—Attitudes and practices.* Retrieved September, 2, 2010, from http://www.shrm.org/Research SurveyFindings/Articles/pages/EmployingMilitaryPersonnelRecruiting Veterans.aspx

Tanielian, T., & Jaycox, L. (Eds.). (2008). *Invisible wounds of war: Psychological and cognitive injuries, their consequences, and services to assist recovery.* Washington, DC: RAND Corporation.

Tanielian, T., Jaycox, L. H., Adamson, D. M., & Metscher, K. N. (2008). Introduction. In T. Tanielian, & L. Jaycox (Eds.), *Invisible wounds of war: Psychological and cognitive injuries, their consequences, and services to assist recovery.* Washington, DC: RAND Corporation.

U.S. Army. (2010). *Health promotion and risk reduction suicide prevention report 2010.* Retrieved September 1, 2010, from http://www.army. mil/-news/2010/07/28/42934-army-health-promotion-risk-reduction-and-suicide-prevention-report/index.html

U.S. Department of Labor, Bureau of Labor Statistics. (2010). *Employment situation of veterans—2009* (USDL-10-0285). Washington, DC: Government Printing Service. Retrieved August 13, 2010. http://www.bls.gov/

Vogt, D. S., Samper, R. E., King, D. W., King, L. A., & Martin, J. A. (2008). Deployment stressors and posttraumatic stress symptomatology: Comparing active duty and National Guard/Reserve personnel from Gulf War I. *Journal of Traumatic Stress, 21*(1), 66–74.

Voydanoff, P. (2004). The effects of work demands and resources on work-to-family conflict and facilitation. *Journal of Marriage and Family, 66,* 398–412.

Weiss, J., Donigian, A., & Hughes, J. (2010). Extreme negotiations. *Harvard Business Review, 88*(11), 66–75.

Wolff, E. N. (2005). The growth of information workers: In the U.S. economy. *Communications of the ACM, 48*(10), 37–42.

APPENDIX

Reintegration Work Attitudes, Issues, and Challenges Questionnaire

Copyright DeSimone, J. and Harnett, C., 2010

Demographic Information

Age: _____   Rank: _____   Number of deployments: ____

Gender: Female ____   Male ____

Marital status: Married ____ Single ____ Divorced ____ Separated ____
    Widowed ____ Domestic Partnership ____

Number of weeks or months returned from deployment: ____ weeks ____
    months

Please check your Service
    Affiliation: National Guard _____   Reserve _____

Please check the appropriate
    response: Unemployed _____   Employed _____
               Laid-Off _____

Instructions: Before we begin the focus group process, we ask that you read each of the questions below and record any responses that easily come to mind. Skip any items that do not apply to you.

1. Has your attitude toward the **type of work** you do changed as a result of your return or reentry?   Yes___ No ___
    If **yes**, how?
2. Has your attitude toward the **workplace** changed as a result of your return or reentry?
    Yes___ No ___
    If **yes**, how?
3. Have you changed **positions** in your organization as a result of your deployment?
    Yes ___ No ___
    If **yes**, from what to what?
4. Have you changed careers as a result of your deployment? Yes ___ No ___
    If **yes**, from what to what?

5. Have you changed organizations as a result of your deployment? Yes ___ No ___
   If **yes**, from what to what?
6. What work related challenges have you experienced as a result of your return from combat? **Please list any that you have identified.**
7. Has your relationship with your supervisor changed as a result of your deployment?
   Yes___ No ___
   If **yes**, how and in what ways?
8. Has the way you relate to your coworkers changed as a result of your deployment?
   Yes ___ No ___
9. What skills do you, or did you, need to develop to ease your reintegration or return to the workplace? Please list all.
10. What can management do to support your full engagement back into the workplace?
11. Please identify what you consider to be the **greatest single barrier** to successful reintegration in the workplace.
12. Is there anything that **we have not asked you** that you believe is important for us to know in terms of better understanding the challenges facing veterans reintegrating into the workforce?

Thank you for your responses. These data will be used to inform a book chapter and develop a survey to investigate returning young veterans attitudes, issues, and challenges in reentering the workforce.

12

VETERANS' COURTS AND CRIMINAL RESPONSIBILITY: A PROBLEM-SOLVING HISTORY AND APPROACH TO THE LIMINALITY OF COMBAT TRAUMA

Justin Holbrook

In January 2010, Britten Walker was arrested after assaulting a federal police officer and a doctor at the Department of Veterans Affairs (VA) Medical Facility in Buffalo, New York. A 32-year-old veteran who had served three combat tours in Iraq and Afghanistan, Walker committed the assaults after threatening to kill a VA worker, bomb several television stations, and bomb cars on the New York State Thruway. "The VA is totally unequipped to handle all the soldiers who are coming back from Iraq and Afghanistan and need help," Walker angrily told reporters when he first appeared in court on federal charges stemming from the assault and threats. "This has been devastating on me and my family. ... I'm sick of America right now."[1] According to Walker's family, the young veteran had no intention of hurting anyone when he boiled over at the VA. "He suffers from [post-traumatic stress disorder], and he needs help," Walker's twin brother told reporters. "For some reason, he hasn't been able to make a connection with the counselors at the VA in Buffalo."[2]

Facing federal felony charges, Walker's case was assigned to U.S. Magistrate Judge Jeremiah McCarthy. Instead of immediately scheduling the case for trial, Judge McCarthy took the unusual step of appointing a psychiatrist to evaluate Walker for combat-related trauma.[3] After reading the psychiatrist's report, the judge released Walker from jail to attend a 30-day treatment program for veterans suffering from post-traumatic stress disorder (PTSD).[4] Once Walker successfully completed the program, the judge turned Walker over to family members on the condition that he attend an outpatient mental health program until the conclusion of his case.[5] "I'm sure you're not going to let yourself or them down, is that correct?"[6] McCarthy asked Walker. "That is correct, your honor," Walker politely answered.[7]

Five months later, Walker's case became the first of its kind in the country to be transferred from federal court to a local veteran's treatment court for final adjudication. After carefully orchestrating the arrangement between the U.S. Attorney's Office, the U.S. Office of Probation & Pretrial Services, the local veterans court, Walker's defense attorney, and veterans advocates, Judge McCarthy dismissed Walker's case without prejudice to allow it to be heard by the Buffalo Veterans' Treatment Court, a division of Buffalo City Court.[8] The focus of everyone involved, Walker's defense attorney said, was to help the veteran receive the psychiatric counseling he needed.[9] The prosecuting attorney agreed, telling reporters, "We are seeking a better way to provide justice to those veterans who, despite the sacrifices they made for our country, sadly find that they have brought the war home with them."[10]

For those involved in veterans' advocacy and treatment, Walker's case is significant for a number of reasons. First, his is the first criminal case nationwide to be transferred from federal court to a local veterans' treatment court where the goal is to treat—rather than simply punish—those facing the liminal effects of military combat. Walker's case may be seen as a key performance indicator of the broadening acceptance of veterans' courts and the success with which they are viewed. Second, the case reignites the still unsettled controversy over whether problem-solving courts generally, and veterans' courts specifically, unfairly shift the focus of justice away from the retributive interests of victims to the rehabilitative interests of perpetrators. One can imagine, for example, the victims whom Walker threatened objecting to dismissal of his case without a finding of guilty and imposition of an appropriate sentence. Third, Walker's case serves as a signal reminder to all justice system stakeholders, including parties, judges, attorneys, and treatment professionals, of the potential benefits of sidestepping courtroom adversity in favor of a coordinated effort that seeks to ameliorate victim concerns while advancing treatment opportunities for veterans suffering from combat-related trauma.

This chapter explores these issues in light of the development of veterans' treatment courts around the country. As a backdrop, attention is first given to the history of combat-related trauma as a medical and psychological condition requiring specialized diagnosis. The chapter then reviews combat-related trauma within the social context of criminal responsibility, exploring case law from the years following World

War I through the Supreme Court's 2009 decision in *Porter v. McCollum*.[11] The recent initiative to create specialized problem-solving courts for veterans is then discussed, as well as the tenet methodologies employed by most veterans' courts. Drawing lessons from the long history of combat-related trauma in the United States, the chapter concludes by advocating for increased trial court use of treatment methodologies designed to assist traumatized veterans facing criminal prosecution.

COMBAT TRAUMA AND THE LIMINAL EFFECTS OF WAR: A HISTORY

Although known by various names, accounts of combat trauma extend into the mists of mythology, literature, and history.[12] In Homer's *Odyssey*, Odysseus returns home from the Trojan wars to find himself in a country he does not recognize. Confused, he asks the goddess Athene, "What land is this, what neighborhood is it, what people live here?"[13] In Shakespeare's *Henry IV*, Lady Percy worries over her husband's "thick-eyed musings and cursed melancholy" after he returns home from a bloody battle. "In thy faint slumbers I by thee have watch'd," she tells him, "and heard thee murmur tales of iron wars[.]"[14] Psychologists reviewing historical records have discovered PTSD-like symptoms in such historical figures as Alexander the Great (356–323 B.C.), Captain James Cook (1728–1779), and Florence Nightingale (1820–1910), each of whom was exposed to combat or death.[15]

In the modern era, serious inquiry into the relationship between postcombat behavior and combat trauma began in the late 18th century when Dr. Benjamin Rush, widely considered to be the father of American psychiatry, observed in 1786 that soldiers of the Revolutionary War "who enjoyed health during a campaign, were often seized with fevers upon return to the *Vita Mollis* at their respective homes."[16] Civil War-era physicians made similar observations, diagnosing what today arguably would be considered PTSD as "nostalgia" or "soldier's heart" in a statistically significant number of cases.[17] For example, during the first year of the civil war, doctors reported 5213 cases of "nostalgia," a rate of 2.34 cases per 1000 soldiers.[18] During the second year of the war, the rate rose to 3.3 per 1000.[19] In the years after the Civil War's conclusion, Dr. James Mendes DaCosta studied a group of veterans who presented as physically sound but nevertheless "complained of palpitations, increased pain in the cardiac region, tachy-cardia, cardiac uneasiness, headache, dimness of vision, and giddi-ness."[20] Describing the condition as a "disturbance of the sympathetic nervous system," Dr. DaCosta labeled it "irritable heart," a term later used interchangeably with the eponymous diagnosis "DaCosta syn-drome."[21] At the same time, European physicians were observing similar symptoms—called "Swiss disease"—among Swiss soldiers who had experienced combat conditions in Europe.[22]

From Soldier's Heart to Shell Shock

By World War I, doctors had begun drawing distinct connections between combat activity and postcombat behavior, though medical investigation remained largely focused on physiological symptoms. British physicians speculated that "muscular exertion" was the primary cause of "soldier's heart," and the cohort of conditions linked to "soldier's heart" and "DaCosta syndrome" began to be called "effort syndrome" in the popular literature.[23] Others, noting both the psychological and physiological elements of the condition, labeled it "neurocirculatory asthenia."[24] The genesis of the condition remained indeterminate, however, with one commentator admitting as late as 1942 that "it is generally agreed that the cause of soldier's heart is obscure."[25]

Simultaneously with these developments, which primarily focused on physiological etiology, another branch of trauma-related inquiry arose as a result of the concussive explosions experienced by soldiers during World War I.[26] Experts initially believed the "shell shock" exhib-ited by such soldiers resulted from small cerebral hemorrhages.[27] As evidence, doctors pointed to the presence of blood in the spinal fluid of some patients.[28] Opinions changed, however, when soldiers who had not been exposed to concussive airblasts presented with similar symptoms, and doctors ascribed a psychopathological cause rooted in identifiable personality predispositions.[29] Both "soldier's heart" and "shell shock" were "marked by breathlessness and nervous instability, were less common in men previously accustomed to active, outdoor work, and regularly called into question the possibility of malinger-ing."[30] Even in light of these similar symptoms, the conditions remained diagnostically unique, as did the manner in which the diagnoses were received.[31] Perhaps because of the negative bias then existent toward psychology generally, diagnoses of "shell shock"—or "combat neuro-sis" as it also was called—were "often equated with malingering or cowardice," while diagnoses of "soldier's heart" received more sympathetic consideration due to their supposed physiological connection.[32] As with the Civil War, cases of "shell shock" among soldiers were significant. By 1916, an estimated 40% of British casualties were related to "shell shock," with some 80,000 British soldiers treated by the British Army Medical Service for the condition and nearly 200,000 soldiers discharged.[33]

Despite the experience of World War I, by the onset of World War II neither medical practitioners nor military authorities had definitively linked the trauma of combat with the postcombat behaviors observed in veterans. Rather, experts remained convinced that "shell shock" and "soldier's heart" stemmed from personality traits exacerbated by exposure to combat rather than combat itself.[34] Hoping to screen out enlistees exhibiting such traits, U.S. military authorities rejected 1.6 million of 20 million draftees during World War II for psychological reasons, a rejection rate 7.6 times that of World War I.[35] Similarly, soldiers who made it through the screening process but suffered from postcombat trauma were discharged at a rate five times that of World War I.[36]

As the number of discharges exceeded the number of enlistees, the military revised its policy and, by 1943, attempted to treat men suffering from such "combat exhaustion" with rest, food, and sleep rather than discharge.[37] The goal was to return fatigued soldiers to the battlefront as quickly as possible.[38] Notably, the number of casualties reportedly associated with combat trauma escalated during World War II.[39] In 1944, the rate of soldiers admitted to overseas hospitals for psychological conditions was 47 per 1000. Other estimates place the overall incident rate of psychological casualties at nearly 114 per 1000.[40]

By the time of the Korean conflict, medical and military authorities had established a set of treatment protocols for "combat exhaustion" requiring temporary hospitalization with eventual return to combat conditions.[41] Under the Army's diagnostic criteria, "combat exhaustion" was a type of "transient personality reaction" defined as an "acute psychiatric casualt[y] of combat."[42] Investigators in the war zone undertook an intense study of the psychological and physiological effects of combat, and combat tours were shortened from the duration of the entire war (as had been the case in World War II) to a fixed term of nine months.[43] As a result of these measures, the incident rate of casualties attributed to psychological trauma dropped to 37 per 1000.[44]

Although PTSD entered the popular lexicon in connection with the postwar experiences of Vietnam veterans, the wartime incident rates of psychological casualties during the Vietnam conflict were actually lower than prior conflicts involving U.S. soldiers.[45] One author places the incident rate at 12 per 1000, a significant reduction from both the Korean conflict and World War II.[46] Soldiers reportedly benefited from fixed duty tours of one year, frequent rest and relaxation opportunities, and "the application of modern military psychiatry" in the theater of war.[47] Some commentators argue, however, that despite these advances, soldiers serving in Vietnam faced aggravating stressors distinct from those faced by earlier veterans.

Vietnam-era soldiers on average were 19.2 years old, compared to 26 years old in World War II.[48] Soldiers traveling to and from Vietnam traveled individually rather than as a unit, often arriving and departing on commercial aircraft.[49] Some even returned home on the same day they departed the battlefield.[50] Further, the war's shifting political and military objectives led to uncertainty and disillusionment among soldiers,[51] feelings exacerbated by a U.S. populace that was ambivalent at best and hostile at worst to the entire war effort.[52] With the benefit of historical hindsight, such aggravating factors caution against drawing a firm correlation between the incident rates of wartime psychological casualties and postwar episodes of combat-related trauma—a lesson to be remembered when calculating the potential psychological impact of the Iraq and Afghanistan wars on today's returning soldiers.[53]

Postcombat Behavior and PTSD

For purposes of this chapter, the critical question is whether and to what extent combat-related trauma suffered by wartime veterans lingers once they returned home from combat and reintegrated into society. Both anecdotal accounts and historical data are revealing. Jason Roberts, a Union soldier who had been a prisoner in Southern prisons during the Civil War, returned home to his wife and children on a stretcher exhibiting "peculiar actions," "curious" talk, and threatening behaviors.[54] "I kept him a little afraid of me, by threatening him with punishment," his wife said. "He got so that he did not mind me, & I saw that he watched me very closely. He had a wild angry look in his eyes and I got afraid of him at last." She eventually applied to have him committed for "chronic mania."[55] In England, using language not altogether dissimilar from that used to describe today's veterans, an article in the *London*

Times from March 1, 1920 documented the haunting postwar experience of World War I veterans when they returned home:

> Of the many problems calling for solutions, one of the most urgent is that of the man disabled in the war or suffering from shell-shock or neurasthenia. There exists a great army of men suffering from varying degrees of mental instability, and in the ordinary labour market, and particularly in the employment bureaux, such men are at a serious disadvantage. Employers have come to look askance at them.[56]

Aside from these brief anecdotes, historical data support the conclusion that veterans of prior wars also suffered from both acute and delayed onset of PTSD.[57] In the United States in 1921, the number of U.S. veterans receiving care for psychiatric disorders was 7499.[58] By 1931, the number had increased to 11,342.[59] Similarly, from 1923 to 1932, benefits paid to World War I veterans for psychiatric disorders jumped from $23,256 to $67,916.[60] Veterans of World War II exhibited similar postwar responses to combat stress. A cohort of veterans followed by researches for 20 years displayed "persistent symptoms of tension, irritability, depression, diffuse anxiety symptoms, headaches, insomnia, and nightmares."[61] Labeling the condition "veteran's chronic stress syndrome," researchers concluded: "These particular veterans cannot blot out their painful memories."[62] Significantly, one researcher observed in 1945 that "[the] majority of psychiatric admissions among returnees are not men who have returned with war neuroses, but those who develop signs of illness after completing a full term of duty."[63]

Like veterans before them, veterans of the Vietnam conflict also suffered from the trauma of war after returning home. Estimates in the 1980s placed the number of Vietnam veterans with PTSD between 500,000 to 1,500,000.[64] Those with significant combat experience had incident rates of suicide, substance abuse, marriage problems, and unemployment higher than those of the general population.[65] Because psychiatrists and psychologists viewed Vietnam veterans' combat and reintegration experiences as unique, however, they adopted new terminology to describe returning veterans' symptomatology—"Vietnam Syndrome," "Post-Vietnam Syndrome (PVS)," "Vietnam-Veteran Syndrome," "Re-Entry Syndrome," or "Post-Viet Nam Psychiatric Syndrome (PVNPS)" were all employed in the literature of the day.[66]

Too often these labels were reinforced by negative media images of angry, distrustful veterans returning home to an unwelcoming public, scenes far different than the idealized cheery parades and welcoming banners heralding the return of veterans of earlier conflicts. While some commentators have recently disputed the uniqueness of the Vietnam combat experience, arguing that veterans of earlier conflicts similarly suffered from dislocation, unemployment, family disintegration, and recurring trauma after returning from war,[67] the portrayal of troubled Vietnam veterans during the 1970s generated the sympathy needed in both political and medical circles for the advancement of combat trauma as a subject of serious psychological study and treatment.

Accordingly, in 1980, the American Psychological Association (APA) included PTSD in the third edition of the *Diagnostic and Statistical Manual of Mental Disorders* (*DSM-III*), the major diagnostic manual used by clinicians in treating mental disorders.[68] Earlier editions of the *DSM* had categorized combat trauma as "gross stress reaction" or "adjustment reactions of adult life," diagnoses which failed to articulate a description of trauma-induced symptoms sufficient to either diagnose or treat veterans.[69] In *DSM-III*, PTSD was characterized by the development of specific symptoms—including diminished responsiveness, hyperalertness, exaggerated startle response, insomnia, recurrent nightmares, aggressive behavior, depression, and anxiety—exhibited after a "psychologically traumatic event that is generally outside the range of usual human experience."[70] Both acute and delayed PTSD were recognized, and combat veterans were specifically referenced in the diagnostic description.[71] The fourth edition of the *Diagnostic and Statistical Manual of Mental Disorders* (*DSM-IV*) modified the diagnostic criteria, but remained focused on symptoms resulting from traumatic events, including "military combat."[72]

COMBAT TRAUMA AND THE PROBLEM OF CRIMINAL RESPONSIBILITY

In an April 2008 study titled "Invisible Wounds of War," the RAND Corporation approximated that 300,000, or nearly 20%, of the 1.64 million veterans who have served in Iraq and Afghanistan since 2001 suffer from PTSD.[73] These figures generally accord with a 2004 study which found that 15.6–17.1% of veterans of Iraq met the screening criteria for major depression, generalized anxiety, or PTSD.[74] Incident rates of PTSD were directly tied to the number of combat experiences, from a rate of 9.3% for soldiers involved in one or two firefights to

19.3% for those involved in five or more firefights.[75] More recently, the VA disclosed that 44% of Iraq and Afghanistan war veterans seeking treatment at VA medical facilities had been diagnosed with mental health disorders, with 23% diagnosed with possible PTSD.[76] In 2009, the National Center for PTSD published a bibliography of studies in which it found an overall PTSD rate of 10–18% for combat troops serving in Iraq and Afghanistan.[77]

PTSD and Criminal Behavior

The relevance of PTSD rates for justice system stakeholders lies in their correlation to risk factors which, themselves, are routinely linked to incidents of criminal activity. Surveys from the 1980s suggested a measurable link between PTSD and criminal behavior in Vietnam-era veterans,[78] with one study finding a heightened disposition toward violent crimes in incarcerated Vietnam veterans compared to incarcerated nonveterans[79] and another finding a relationship between PTSD and "self-reported aggression, hostility, and anger[.]"[80] Researchers elsewhere estimated that 25% of veterans who experienced heavy combat had been charged with committing a criminal offense since returning home.[81] Perhaps the most comprehensive assessment comes from the National Vietnam Veterans Readjustment Study, which determined the rate of violent acts in Vietnam veterans with PTSD to be nearly four times that of veterans without PTSD.[82] Study results further showed nearly half (45.7%) of veterans suffering from PTSD had been arrested or imprisoned, compared to only 11.6% of veterans without PTSD.[83]

Not surprisingly, emerging studies of Iraq and Afghanistan veterans show similar trends. A longitudinal study of Iraq and Afghanistan veterans six months after deployment revealed that "27 to 35 percent reported symptoms placing them at mental health risk, including symptoms of PTSD, depression, alcohol misuse, and suicidal ideation, as well as self-reported aggression."[84] Other reports have suggested an increase in drug abuse by Iraq and Afghanistan veterans,[85] and noted that veterans between the ages of 20–24 years are reportedly four times more likely to commit suicide than their nonveteran counterparts.[86]

Although environmental variables between Vietnam veterans and Iraq and Afghanistan veterans prevent direct comparison, current data indicate that Iraq and Afghanistan veterans who display PTSD hyperarousal symptomatology have greater difficulty—like their Vietnam veteran counterparts—in controlling aggressive impulses or urges, managing anger, and controlling violence.[87] These risk factors do not yet appear to have led to an increase in the percentage of veterans among prison populations, although the lack of recent data hinders firm conclusion. A 2004 study, the most recent available, found that 10% of state prisoners were veterans, a decline from 12% in 1997 and 20% in 1986.[88] During that same time period, veterans as a percentage of the U.S. population dropped to 11% in 2004 from 16% in 1985, suggesting that the downward trend of veterans in prison populations mirrors that of the decline of veterans among the populace generally.[89]

Of course, long before either the Vietnam conflict or the wars in Iraq and Afghanistan, writers, policy makers, and researches recognized the potential connection between combat and postwar criminal behavior. Sir Thomas More, writing in *Utopia* in 1516, referred to individuals who, in war, "had so inured themselves to corrupt and wicked manners [ ] that they had taken a delight and pleasure in robbing and stealing[.]"[90] In Machiavelli's *Art of War*, published in 1521, the character Fabrizio similarly contends, "War makes thieves, and peace hangs them."[91] Winston Churchill, in the aftermath of World War I, declared at a London dinner in 1919:

> People talk about the world on the morrow of the Great War as if somehow or other we had all been transported into a higher form. We have been transported into a sphere which is definitely lower from almost every point of view than that which we had attained in the days before Armageddon. Never was there a time when people were more disposed to turn to courses of violence, to show scant respect for law and country and tradition and procedure than the present.[92]

Edith Abbott, an early 20th century American economist and social worker, noted reports of "crime epidemics" in France after the Revolution of 1848, in France and Germany after the Franco-Prussian War (1870–1871), and in England after the Second Boer War (1899–1902).[93] In a detailed study of post-Civil War data, Abbott found "[a] marked increase occurred ... in the number of commitments of men to prison during the years following the war."[94] One prison warden of the time concluded that 90% of his new prisoners "had been more or less incapacitated and demoralized by an apprenticeship to the trade of war."[95] Following World War I, both France and the United States feared an increase in crime as battle-hardened veterans returned to the home front, with one French criminologist commenting that "[p]ersonal morality ... has deteriorated during the years of war with the breaking-up of homes and the perpetual vision of death, and has brought about a state of moral vertigo[.]"[96] After the conclusion of World War II, researchers in New York City found a substantial increase in violent personal crime, though they disputed whether it was attributable to the effect of combat on returning veterans, or simply the great volume of returning veterans themselves.[97] It should be noted that these historical studies rarely distinguish between the psychological and behavioral aspects of war, generally ascribing increased criminal activity to the "lost morality" of soldiers brutalized by war. Nevertheless, they provide an insightful connection between war and crime, and support the conclusion that present-day discussions about veterans and criminal behavior are trodding well-worn ground.

PTSD as a Defense Before 1980

While it may be well-settled that PTSD increases the risk factors for certain types of criminal behavior, the extent to which PTSD either excuses or mitigates associated criminal conduct as a matter of law remains a subject of lively concern. One of the earliest cases on point, *People v. Gilberg* (1925), addressed whether a World War I veteran accused of child molestation sufficiently raised insanity as a defense by introducing evidence of "shell shock" incurred during the war.[98] Testifying on the defendant's behalf, experts explained "with minute detail the symptoms of 'shell-shock' and epilepsy and the effect of each upon the nervous organism."[99] The Supreme Court of California, in language reflective of the prevailing view of the time, commented:

> [The soldier] received no battlefield wounds, but claims to have suffered an injury by falling into a "funk-hole." It appears that he spent considerable time during his enlistment, both overseas and in this country, as a patient in hospitals, under treatment for "shell-shock." "Shell-shock" is not a distinct type of nervous disorder, but a condition produced upon certain organisms by sudden fear or by highly exciting causes. It is a form of neurosis. It is not settled, general insanity, but, according to the testimony of the expert offered by the defense, a functional nervous disease, and not due to organic changes.[100]

Perhaps because of the nature of the alleged crime, or perhaps because the defendant's in-court antics made his condition appear contrived, the Court upheld the trial court's determination not to submit the matter of insanity to the jury.[101]

In *People v. Danielly* (1949), a World War II veteran attempted to introduce evidence that his conviction for murder should be reduced to manslaughter because he had no recollection of the incident due to his combat-related "nervous" disability.[102] The trial court denied introduction of the evidence and the defendant was convicted of first degree murder. Although the Supreme Court of California upheld the trial court's ruling, it noted that the defendant had been in the Navy 11 years, was wounded on August 18, 1944 "by the explosion of an enemy anti-personnel bomb," and was diagnosed and ultimately discharged from the military for "psychoneurosis neurasthenia."[103] Among other things, the defendant's symptoms included nervousness, tremors, sweating, irritability, insomnia, "easy startle," "battle dreams," and anxiousness.[104] While not rendering the defendant legally insane, the Court found that such symptoms nevertheless warranted sympathy: "[T]hat he is a victim of war in the sense that his original emotional stability and related ability to cope with the vicissitudes and demands of living in normal society have been to some extent impaired seems . . . reasonably certain."[105] At the conclusion of its ruling, the Court specifically commented on the governor's ability to commute sentences for such compassionate purposes.[106]

Finally, in the 1973 case of *Kemp v. State*, a Vietnam veteran pled not guilty by reason of insanity when he shot his wife in bed while dreaming "that he was in Viet Nam and being attacked by the Vietcong."[107] The defendant, who had witnessed multiple companions killed by a land mine in Vietnam, developed "battle fatigue" and "battle neurosis" during his combat tour. He began to drink heavily, experienced amnesia, and had recurring nightmares about the Vietcong. After being discharged from the military, he drifted in and out of VA hospitals and took to sleeping with a weapon beneath his pillow. Five days after being released from outpatient care, he turned up armed and intoxicated at a VA hospital with no recollection of recent events. Later that day, police discovered his wife's body in the couple's bed, the bullets in her body matching the gun the defendant carried into the VA. At trial, six psychiatrists testified. The defendant's psychiatrist and two court-appointed psychiatrists testified the defendant was legally insane. Two state psychiatrists testified they could not give an opinion. One additional state psychiatrist testified the defendant might be legally insane. Despite their testimony, the jury found the defendant mentally competent and he was convicted of murder. The Supreme Court of Wisconsin disagreed, however, stating, "We believe the weight of the testimony is such that justice has probably miscarried and that it is possible a new trial will result in a contrary finding."[108] Accordingly, the Court ordered a new trial on the issue of the defendant's sanity.[109]

As these cases anecdotally suggest, veterans who relied on combat trauma to prove insanity met with mixed results prior to the recognition of PTSD as a formal diagnostic category in *DSM-III*. Partly this may be a function of the skepticism with which combat trauma was generally viewed by the public prior to 1980. A more significant reason, however, seems to lie in the fact that clinicians had few diagnostic tools with which to diagnose chronic, delayed onset of combat-related trauma. "Gross Stress Reaction," the diagnostic category in *DSM-I* recognizing combat stress, was "seen as a situational disorder that would abate with reduction in exposure to the stressor."[110] The more generalized category of "transient situational disturbances" contained in *DSM-II* offered even less assistance.[111] Without adequate diagnostic tools, veterans facing criminal charges—and psychiatrists testifying on their behalf—ha understandable difficulty in establishing the foundational requirement for any insanity defense: the presence of a "mental disease."[112]

With the exception of four states without an insanity defense, states generally employ one of four tests in determining a defendant's insanity, all of which require an initial showing of a "mental disease."[113] Most states have adopted a strain of the *M'Naghten* rule, which articulates two alternative prongs for establishing insanity:[114]

> [T]o establish a defence on the ground of insanity, it must be clearly proved that, at the time of the committing of the act, the party accused was laboring under such a defect of reason, from disease of the mind, as not to know the nature and quality of the act he was doing; or, if he did know it, that he did not know he was doing what was wrong.[115]

The U.S. Supreme Court has described these two prongs in terms of a defendant's cognitive capacity (the ability to know the nature and quality of the act) and moral capacity (the ability to know that an act is wrong).[116] Although most states follow the *M'Naghten* rule, other states have recognized that some defendants' mental disorders may prevent them from controlling their actions even if they are aware their actions are wrong. Accordingly, these states utilize an alternative test—often called the Irresistible Impulse Test—based on a defendant's volitional incapacity.[117] Some of these states also follow the Model Penal Code, which combines elements of the Irresistible Impulse Test and the *M'Naghten* rule to obviate criminal responsibility when a defendant, as a result of mental illness, "lacks substantial capacity to appreciate the criminality . . . of his conduct or to confirm his conduct to the requirements of [the] law."[118] In addition to these tests, the state of New Hampshire employs a final variant called the Product-Of-Mental-Illness Test, which "simply asks whether a person's action was a product of a mental disease or defect."[119]

PTSD as a Defense After 1980

After PTSD was added to *DSM-III*, veterans and legal practitioners had substantially more success in raising PTSD as an affirmative or mitigating defense in state and federal courts.[120] Literature from the mid-1980s discussed the application of PTSD in defenses of insanity, diminished capacity, automatism (involuntary action), and self-defense.[121] One commentator identified PTSD's successful use in the early to mid-1980s in cases of "murder, attempted murder, kidnapping, and drug smuggling."[122] When offered in mitigation, PTSD similarly proved helpful "for crimes such as drug dealing, manslaughter, assault with intent to commit murder, and even tax fraud."[123] By 1985, the introduction of PTSD evidence at trial was credited with helping some 250 Vietnam veterans obtain sentence reductions, treatment opportunities, or outright acquittals at trial.[124]

One representative case is *State v. Heads*, in which a Louisiana jury found the defendant not guilty of murder by reason of insanity due to his PTSD.[125] Charles Heads had served as a Marine in Vietnam, performing 38 reconnaissance missions deep into enemy territory. On his first patrol, he witnessed his platoon commander killed by a land mine. Nine months later, with seven conformed "kills" himself, Heads was shot twice in the stomach and evacuated from the jungle by helicopter.[126] Seven years after returning home and marrying, Heads drove to his brother-in-law's home late one night in search of his wife. He rang the bell and shouted, but no one answered. Walking away, something "hit" Heads and he immediately returned to the house, crashing through the door with a gun in his hand. After firing multiple shots, he returned to his car for a rifle, continued firing, and eventually killed his brother-in-law, who also was holding a gun.[127] When the police arrived moments later, Heads surrendered quietly.[128]

Heads was tried by a Louisiana jury twice. The first trial, in 1977, led to a conviction for first-degree murder. That case was overturned on appeal when the appellate court determined the jury had been improperly instructed.[129] The second trial, in 1981, led to an acquittal by reason of insanity after numerous lay and expert witnesses recreated the horrors of Vietnam and the reality of PTSD for jurors. According to Heads' attorney, the difference in the two trials resulted from the addition of PTSD to *DSM-III* in 1980:

> I represented Heads the first time when they found him guilty. I was unable to prove that he was suffering from insanity; psychiatrists never found any evidence of any recognized mental disorder. In 1980, after the American Psychiatric Association recognized PTSD, I knew that's what it was—and I had what I needed.

Relying on the diagnostic criteria of PTSD in *DSM-III*, Heads' attorney successfully argued the relevance of Heads' military service, combat trauma, and troubled childhood in establishing the presence of a "mental disease." The jury then applied a modified version of the *M'Naghten* rule and, in acquitting Heads, apparently believed his PTSD had caused him to enter a dissociative state in which he could not distinguish right and wrong.[130]

In arguing the range of criminal offenses PTSD arguably could induce, legal practitioners and clinicians of the early 1980s were assisted by a key study presented by John P. Wilson, PhD, and Sheldon D. Zigelbaum, MD, in 1983. Over a period of two years, Wilson and Zigelbaum assessed the relationship between PTSD and criminal behavior in 114 combat veterans.[131] Study results revealed three distinct ways in which PTSD could motivate criminal behavior.

First, a veteran could enter a *dissociative state* in which he "is likely to function predominately in the survivor mode by behaving as he did in combat in Vietnam."[132] Dissociative states are most commonly linked to violent criminal behavior.[133] Second, a veteran could display a *sensation seeking syndrome*, characterized by attempts to seek out the same level of excitement, exhilaration, and stimulation as that experienced in combat.[134] Sensation seeking syndrome often manifests itself in risk-filled activities, such as motorcycle riding, sky diving, and gambling.[135] Third, a veteran could experience *depression-suicide syndrome*, which is accompanied by feelings of hopelessness, painful imagery, survivor guilt, and psychic numbing.[136] In an effort to end psychic pain, veterans with depression-suicide syndrome sometimes act out violently or recklessly knowing they will be caught or killed as a result of their actions.[137] Though based on limited data obtained nearly 30 years ago, the Wilson and Zigelbaum study continues to influence discussions of PTSD and criminal responsibility by providing a useful framework in which to connect particular criminal behaviors with specific PTSD symptoms.[138]

PTSD in Today's Courtroom

By 1985, the success of PTSD as an affirmative defense had begun to wane, as "juries ... rejected an increasing percentage of stress-related defenses."[139] "It seems there was more receptivity five years ago," Dr. Wilson (of the Wilson and Zigelbaum study) said at the time. "My batting average [as an expert witness] was once about .900 but now it's dropped."[140] Commentators ascribed the decline to shifting public attitudes over Vietnam,[141] overuse of the defense by defense counsel,[142] continued public resentment of the acquittal of John Hinkley, Jr., who had been acquitted on grounds of insanity in the attempted assassination of President Ronald Reagan in 1981,[143] and the public's fear of potentially false PTSD claims.[144]

More recently, however, PTSD as both an affirmative and mitigating defense has re-emerged, largely as a result of a growing national consciousness of the problems faced by veterans returning from the wars in Iraq and Afghanistan.[145] In one of the first successful PTSD cases involving a veteran of the war in Iraq, for example, an Oregon jury in 2009 found a veteran accused of murder "guilty but insane" due to the combat trauma he suffered as a result of his deployment.[146] At trial, the prosecutor argued the 26-year old former Army National Guard soldier had "hunted down and killed" the victim, a man who allegedly raped the defendant's fiancée.[147] In response, the defense attorney put on evidence that the defendant had returned from Iraq a changed man, living in the woods for days at a time patrolling with an assault rifle and unable to stay employed due to his explosive anger. Doctors at the VA had first rejected the defendant's claim of PTSD, then later awarded him a disability rating of 70% and then 100%. At the time of the shooting, the defendant told his attorney, it was like he was back in Kirkuk, "watching murderous events unfold around him. He saw somebody shooting [the victim], emptying all 10 rounds from the clip. [The victim's] 14-year-old nephew was shouting from the front porch, and [the defendant] saw him as an Iraqi woman screaming."[148] Believing the defendant needed treatment—not prison—the jury found him "guilty but insane" under Oregon law, and the defendant eventually was sentenced and moved from county jail to an Oregon state hospital.[149]

Of course, not all cases are as successful,[150] and questions have been raised about the fairness of allowing veterans to sidestep criminal responsibility by placing blame on their combat trauma.[151] The Oregon decision does suggest, however, that judges and juries remain sympathetic to receiving and considering evidence of defendants' combat trauma in determining the scope of criminal responsibility.[152]

A 2009 Supreme Court case, *Porter v. McCollum*, underscores this point.[153] In *Porter*, the Supreme Court addressed whether the defendant's Sixth Amendment right to counsel had been violated when his attorney failed to uncover or introduce at sentencing evidence of his significant combat experience.[154] In 1986, George Porter, a Korean war veteran, shot and killed his former girlfriend and her boyfriend. With standby counsel, he represented himself through most of the prosecution's case, then decided to plead guilty with representation by counsel. The defense attorney put on one sentencing witness. Other than a passing reference, the attorney made no mention of Porter's mental health. After being convicted and sentenced to death, Porter filed a petition for postconviction relief in 1995 and argued his defense counsel had been deficient in introducing mitigating evidence.

At a subsequent two-day hearing, Porter presented extensive evidence of his troubled childhood, history of substance abuse, and, in the Supreme Court's words, "his heroic military service and the trauma he suffered because of it."[155] Evidence from Porter and his former commander established that Porter's unit had been involved in two ferocious battles in Korea. In the first, Porter was shot as his unit protected the withdrawing Eighth Army from the advancing Chinese at Kunuri. In the second, less than three months later, at Chip-yong-ni, Porter's company was ordered to charge a hill under heavy fire. Porter again was wounded, and his unit sustained casualties of more than 50%.[156] The battles were "very trying, horrifying experiences," Porter's commander testified.[157] Porter's unit received the Presidential Unit Citation for their heroism at Chip-yong-ni, and Porter personally received two Purple Hearts and the Combat Infantryman Badge.[158] In addition to this evidence, Porter also introduced the testimony of a neuropsychologist who "concluded that Porter suffered from brain damage that could manifest in impulsive, violent behavior."[159] The neuropsychologist further testified that "Porter was substantially impaired in his ability to conform his conduct to the law and suffered from an extreme mental or emotional disturbance," both of which warranted mitigation under Florida law.[160]

In holding that Porter's Sixth Amendment rights had been violated, the Supreme Court strongly chided the defense attorney for failing "to uncover and present any evidence of Porter's mental health or mental impairment, his family background, or his military service,"[161] finding that such evidence could have been offered as both statutory and nonstatutory mitigation.[162] The Court then remanded the case for rehearing on sentence.[163]

Two key points readily emerge from the Court's opinion in *Porter v. McCollum*. First, *Porter* reminds both defense counsel and courts of the necessity of introducing and considering evidence of military service—especially when it involves combat—as a mitigating factor in criminal trials. Aside from its success as an affirmative defense, PTSD remains critically relevant in mitigation.[164] Second, far from being averse to PTSD-related evidence, the Court favorably embraced both lay and expert testimony regarding Porter's combat trauma, a point underscored by the language of the decision itself. In an opinion notable for its marked sympathy, the Court began the opinion with these words:

> Petitioner George Porter is a veteran who was both wounded and decorated for his active participation in two major engagements during the Korean war; his combat service unfortunately left him a traumatized, changed man. His commanding officer's moving description of those two battles was only a fraction of the mitigating evidence that his counsel failed to discover or present during the penalty phase of his trial in 1988.[165]

In its conclusion, the Court adopted a similarly moving tone in explaining the leniency traditionally shown veterans:

> Our Nation has a long tradition of according leniency to veterans in recognition of their service, especially for those who fought on the front lines as Porter did. Moreover, the relevance of Porter's extensive combat experience is not only that he served honorably under extreme hardship and gruesome conditions, but also that the jury might find mitigating the intense stress and mental and emotional toll that combat took on Porter.[166]

It is this historic leniency, coupled with the data linking combat trauma to criminal behavior, which serves as the historical underpinnings to the veterans court movement today.

THE TREND TOWARD VETERANS' COURTS

In January 2008, Judge Robert T. Russell presided over the first session of the Buffalo Veterans Treatment Court, the first court of its kind in the country "that specialized and adapted to meet the specific needs of veterans."[167] The idea for the veterans court grew out of Judge Russell's experience as a sitting judge in the Buffalo, New York city court, where he observed that a rising number of defendants on his docket were military veterans.[168] Having seen that veterans in both the Buffalo Drug Treatment Court and the Buffalo Mental Health Court responded more favorably to other veterans, Judge Russell developed a court model designed to pair veteran-defendants with veteran-mentors and directly link defendants with service providers who understood veterans' unique challenges and needs.[169] As Judge Russell explained, the Veterans' Treatment Court adopted a comprehensive approach to treatment:

> The mission driving the Veterans Treatment Court is to successfully habilitate veterans by diverting them from the traditional criminal justice system and providing them with the tools they need in order to lead a productive and law-abiding lifestyle. In hopes of achieving this goal, the program provides veterans suffering from substance abuse issues, alcoholism, mental health issues, and emotional disabilities with treatment, academic and vocational training, job skills, and placement services. The program provides further ancillary services to meet the distinctive needs of each individual participant, such as housing, transportation, medical, dental, and other supportive services.[170]

Implicit in the Veterans Treatment Court's initial methodology was an understanding that the risk factors for criminal behavior exhibited by some veterans—including alcohol and substance use, homelessness, broken relationships, unemployment, and mental health—would, if left unaddressed, likely result in future involvement with the criminal justice system.[171]

The Buffalo Veterans' Treatment Court: A Model of Therapeutic Justice

From an operational perspective, the Buffalo Veterans' Treatment Court diverts veterans with substance dependency or mental disorders to its docket by employing a court-initiated screening process.[172]

Participation is voluntary, and typical offenders are facing either felony or misdemeanor charges for nonviolent crimes.[173] Under the direction of the judge, veterans participating in the program receive a tailored package of cooperative assistance from community partners, including "the VA Health Care Network, the Veterans Benefits Administration, the Western New York Veterans Project, the Veterans' Treatment Court teams, volunteer mentors, and a coalition of community health care providers."[174] A VA employee attends every session of court, with a secure laptop allowing immediate access to veterans' VA records.[175] Veterans not already receiving services from the VA may register in court.[176] One-on-one mentoring by a veteran mentor is key. Some forty veterans of the Korean war, the Vietnam war, Operation Desert Shield, Operation Enduring Freedom, and Operation Iraqi Freedom volunteer as mentors, listening, coaching, and helping defendants set and reach goals.[177] The environment is therapeutic, but accountability is required. Veterans in the program must "attend regular status hearings, participate in the development of their treatment plans, and engage in community groups."[178] After completion of the program, which generally lasts at least one year,[179] "not only are veterans sober and stable, many also have their charges reduced or dismissed, or receive a commitment of non-incarceration."[180]

Methodologically, the Buffalo Veterans' Treatment Court has adopted a modified version of the 10 key components the Department of Justice described in its publication, *Defining Drug Courts: The Key Components.*[181] Now a model for other veterans' courts, these components serve as guideposts in developing comprehensive treatment plans for veterans throughout the country:

1. Key Component One: Veterans' Treatment Court integrates alcohol, drug treatment, and mental health services with justice system case processing.
2. Key Component Two: Using a nonadversarial approach, prosecution and defense counsel promote public safety while protecting participants' due process rights.
3. Key Component Three: Eligible participants are identified early and promptly placed in the Veterans' Treatment Court program.
4. Key Component Four: The Veterans' Treatment Court provides access to a continuum of alcohol, drug, mental health, and other related treatment and rehabilitation services.

5. Key Component Five: Abstinence is monitored by frequent alcohol and other drug testing.
6. Key Component Six: A coordinated strategy governs Veterans' Treatment Court responses to participants' compliance.
7. Key Component Seven: Ongoing judicial interaction with each veteran is essential.
8. Key Component Eight: Monitoring and evaluation measures the achievement of program goals and gauges effectiveness.
9. Key Component Nine: Continuing interdisciplinary education promotes effective Veterans' Treatment Court planning, implementation, and operation.
10. Key Component Ten: Forging partnerships among the Veterans' Treatment Court, the VA, public agencies, and community-based organizations generates local support and enhances the Veterans Treatment Court's effectiveness.[182]

While data on the Buffalo Treatment Court's success are necessarily limited, initial results are promising. Judge Russell reported in 2009 that only 2 of more than 100 veterans who had participated in the program had been returned to regular criminal court.[183] Of the 30 veterans who had graduated as of May 2010, none had been re-arrested.[184] Graduates from the program were free from substance abuse, had obtained adequate housing, and were either employed or were pursuing educational training.[185]

Veterans' Courts Across the Country

Seeing the Buffalo Veterans' Treatment Court's initial success, approximately 21 states have established more than 40 veterans' courts across the country, with courts currently operating or under development in Alabama, Alaska, Arizona, Arkansas, California, Colorado, Delaware, Florida, Georgia, Illinois, Michigan, Minnesota, Missouri, Nevada, New York, Ohio, Oklahoma, Pennsylvania, Texas, Washington, and Wisconsin.[186] The vast majority of these follow the Buffalo Veterans' Treatment Court treatment methodology by using the tenets of drug courts to build comprehensive, community-based treatment plans. Some differences, however, exist. For example, some veterans' courts operate as preconviction diversion programs, while others only accept veterans who already have pled guilty.[187] Most hear only nonviolent criminal cases,[188] though a few hear low-level violent criminal cases as well.[189] The veterans' court in Tarrant County, Texas limits program participants to veterans with brain trauma, mental illness, or a mental disorder such as PTSD.[190] The Buffalo Veterans Treatment Court, by contrast, accepts veterans with either substance dependency or mental illness.[191] In a third iteration, the veterans' court in Orange County, California accepts only combat veterans eligible for probation.[192]

Despite these differences, the goals of veterans' courts to date have been similar—to provide at-risk veterans, especially those with PTSD, with an opportunity to receive individualized help and treatment instead of incarceration. Two examples suffice.[193] In Harris County, Texas, one of the first veterans' court participants was a veteran who served a combat tour in Iraq and, after returning, was diagnosed with PTSD.[194] He was "arrested for evading arrest after a small auto accident when he panicked after seeing the police lights."[195] Because his PTSD was a contributing factor to his offense, he was accepted into the veterans' court program with the possibility of having his indictment dismissed and his arrest record expunged upon successful completion of the program.[196] In Rochester, New York, a former Marine who fought in Iraq returned home and was arrested for drug use and writing forged checks.[197] Struggling with combat trauma, he had self-medicated with Oxycontin, which in turn led to drug dependency and financial turmoil. By electing to have his case heard in veterans' court, he agreed to plead guilty and sign a contract with the judge to stay out of trouble for one year.[198] "This isn't a get-out-of-jail-free card," the veterans' court judge said when speaking about the court's program. "It's a 'Who are you? What are you doing? What can we do to provide you with the type of treatment to make you a citizen again?'"[199]

Community, State, and Federal Action

Paralleling developments at the local level, policy makers at the community, state and federal levels have taken proactive steps toward encouraging the establishment of veterans' treatment courts. The National Association for Drug Court Professionals has created Justice for Vets, a clearinghouse for information related to veterans' treatment courts, and launched a cooperative training program between the National Drug Court Institute (NDCI), the Bureau of Justice Assistance (BJA), the VA, the GAINS Center, the Battered Women's Justice Project, and numerous existing veterans' courts to assist additional locales in establishing their own veterans treatment court programs.[200] The VA has placed Veterans Justice Outreach officers in each of its regional medical facilities to work with courts in providing frontline mental health and substance services to veteran-defendants in the criminal justice system.[201] Embracing a community-based approach, the American Bar Association House of Delegates adopted a policy in February 2010 supporting veterans' courts and setting forth key principles for their establishment (Table 12.1).[202] Central among the outcomes proposed by the ABA are decreased recidivism, addiction recovery, veteran self-sufficiency, judiciary cost savings, and connection to local and federal service providers.[203]

In addition to these actions, both state and federal legislatures have considered or enacted legislation relating to veterans' courts. At the state level, five states—California, Colorado, Illinois, Nevada, and Texas—have passed legislation establishing veterans' courts or requiring existing courts to considering military-connected factors, such as PTSD, in adjudicating criminal cases.[204] In California, for example, legislation enacted in 2006 (modifying earlier legislation applying to Vietnam veterans) authorizes criminal courts to place veteran-defendants facing prison terms into treatment programs if the veteran suffers from "post-traumatic stress disorder, substance abuse, or psychological problems as a result of [military] service" and "alleges that he or she committed the offense as a result of post-traumatic stress disorder, substance abuse, or psychological problems stemming from service in a combat theater in the United States military [.]"[205] Legislation passed in Texas in 2009 authorizes local establishment of veterans' courts and dismissal of criminal charges following completion of a treatment program of at least six months.[206] Focusing on rehabilitation and community coordination, the jurisdiction of such courts is tailored to veterans accused charged with either a misdemeanor or felony who (1) suffer "from brain injury, mental illness, or mental disorder, including post-traumatic stress disorder," (2) that "resulted from the defendant's military service in combat," and (3) "materially affected the defendant's criminal conduct at issue in the case."[207]

At the national level, legislators in both the U.S. House of Representations and the Senate have introduced legislation to support the creation of additional veterans' courts throughout the country.[208] Entitled the Services, Education, and Rehabilitation for Veterans (SERV) Act, the proposed legislation authorizes grants to states, state courts, and local courts "for the purpose of developing, implementing, or enhancing veterans' treatment courts or expanding operational drug courts to serve veterans."[209]

Predicting Outcomes for Veterans' Treatment Courts

While the lack of available data prevents present analysis of veterans' court outcomes, two analogical measures give hope for success. First, veterans convicted of criminal activity appear generally to have lower recidivism rates than nonveterans convicted of criminal activity.[210] A 1993 study reviewing recidivism rates for veterans who were released from two New York correctional facilities after participating in an on-site veterans treatment program found that "[v]eterans who participated in one of the programs for a minimum of 6 months had a significantly lower rate of return to custody than veterans with less than 6 months program experience and those veterans with no program experience."[211] The same study found that "veterans . . . return to the [correctional] system at less than 80 percent of the rate at which similarly situated non-veterans return."[212] In 2000, a report released by the Bureau of Justice Statistics from the U.S. Department comparing criminal history rates of incarcerated veterans to incarcerated nonveterans concluded that "[v]eterans in State prison were less likely than nonveterans to be recidivists."[213] A 2007 follow-up report by the Bureau of Justice Statistics similarly concluded "[v]eterans in State prison had shorter criminal histories than their nonveteran counterparts,"[214] indicating that convicted veterans are less likely than nonveterans to reoffend following release. Other studies also have shown that veterans—especially those who complete treatment programs—have lower recidivism rates than nonveterans.[215] Taken together, these studies suggest that veterans participating in veterans' court treatment programs, who are paired with a veteran-mentor and connected with specialized service providers, are less likely to engage in future criminal behavior than those convicted by traditional courts.

Data from drug courts provide a second positive predictor of veterans' court outcomes. The initiative to create drug courts, which were the first specialized problem-solving courts in the country, began in 1989 when the first drug court opened in Miami, Florida.[216] Momentum built rapidly, and, by 1995, the number of drug courts had climbed to 75, joined by a variety of other specialized problem-solving courts: a women's drug court in Michigan; a community court in New York; a DWI court in New Mexico; a juvenile drug court in California; and a family drug court in Nevada.[217] By 2007, some 2147 drug courts were in existence, as well as 1057 other problem-solving courts.[218] Both independent and state researchers have consistently concluded that drug courts reduce future criminal activity for participants and deliver measurable savings for states. A study in California reported rearrest rates of 41% for drug offenders who did not participate in drug court and 29% for offenders who did participate in drug court.[219] A similar study in Massachusetts reported that drug court participants "were 13% less likely to be re-arrested, 34% less likely to be re-convicted, and 24% less likely to be re-incarcerated" than those on probation for similar offenses.[220] In four different "meta-analysis" studies, independent researchers have found "that drug courts significantly reduce crime rates an average of approximately 7 to 14 percentage points."[221] Further, researchers have found that while drug courts have significant start-up costs, they are more cost-effective in the longrun. An analysis of drug courts in Washington State found an average cost of $4333 per client, but an average savings per client of $4705 for taxpayers and $4395 for potential future victims.[222] A study in California found an average cost of $3000 per client, with an average savings of $11,000 per client.[223] Nationally, drug courts are estimated to save taxpayers $90 million annually.[224] Other studies reveal similar savings.[225]

Given that drug courts utilize the same tenet methodologies as those now employed by veterans' courts, drug court outcomes provide a useful comparator in estimating veterans' courts' recidivism rates and community savings. Additionally, several commentators have postulated that savings generated by veterans' courts should outpace those of drug courts because the VA offers at federal expense many of the support services participants in other problem-solving courts can obtain only at state or community expense.[226]

Advocates and Critics

Proponents of veterans' courts primarily base their support of specialized problem-solving courts for veterans on one of three grounds. First, veterans are "a niche population with unique needs."[227] Service members share experiences which are not common among members of the general public, including the trauma of combat, the strain of deployment, and the discipline inherent in military service. These experiences, proponents argue, can only be leveraged when the justice system both acknowledges and builds upon them.[228] Second, veterans' courts equip judges with rehabilitative tools beyond those available in a traditional criminal justice setting, where probation or incarceration is too often the only alternatives following conviction.[229] By including community partners in the process, veterans' courts connect troubled veterans to service providers offering a range of veterans benefits, such as the VA,[230] which veterans otherwise may not access.[231] Third, veterans hold a unique position in society because of the patriotic service they have rendered. As a result, they deserve both assistance and leniency whenever possible.[232] This mirrors the "grateful nation" language of earlier eras, most recently echoed by the Supreme Court in *Porter v. McCollum* when it stated, "Our Nation has a long tradition of according leniency to veterans in recognition of their service, especially for those who fought on the front lines as Porter did."[233] Veterans' courts, advocates argue, are the best and most appropriate manifestation of that leniency.

Although muted, some critics have expressed concern that veterans' courts unfairly benefit veterans by singling them out as a discrete population.[234] Unlike drug or DWI courts, critics might argue, participation in veterans court is not based on commission of a particular offense, but on membership in a particular group. Should states also create courts for individuals of other like-minded interest groups, such as those sharing similarities in income, religion, or life experience? The ACLU of Nevada made an argument similar to this when it challenged legislation in Nevada creating a court specifically for veterans. According to one ACLU of Nevada representative, the proposed legislation would have provided "an automatic free-pass based on military status to certain criminal-defense rights that others don't have."[235] A representative of ACLU of Colorado agreed, arguing "that the legal category of 'veteran' is both too broad and too narrow, sweeping in both Vietnam and World War II veterans who have very different experiences, but excluding non-veterans who also suffer from PTSD and aren't eligible for any special courts."[236] The national arm of the ACLU avoided weighing in on the issue, but a spokesman for the ACLU in Illinois stated the ACLU had no concern with veterans' courts that model drug treatment courts. The objections in Nevada, the spokesman said, were that the legislation "automatically" transferred veterans into a special court and "provided some options for lower-level sentences."[237]

Another objection centers on the perception that veterans' courts allow veteran-defendants to avoid criminal responsibility by blaming their actions on their PTSD. TESSA, an advocacy group for domestic violence victims, voiced concern on precisely these grounds when a Colorado veterans' court included on its docket low-level domestic violence cases. "We know that veterans who serve in combat have some unique, serious mental health issues as a result of that trauma," the group's Executive Director said, but "using PTSD or traumatic brain injury as the reason for violence is wrong[.]"[238] In objecting, TESSA's Executive Director noted that domestic violence victims routinely suffer from PTSD without resorting to violence.[239]

In the 2009 Oregon case discussed earlier, the victim's family objected to the trial's result on similar grounds as unfair. "We understand he has PTSD," the victim's brother told reporters, "But does that give him the right to just go murder somebody?"[240] At the heart of the family's complaint is a concern that criminal justice system lacks fairness when the perpetrator's rehabilitative interests are placed above the victim's retributive interests. Aside from the relative merits of these arguments, which have been discussed in broader contexts elsewhere,[241] the point they impress on those involved in developing veterans' courts is that the interests of *all* justice system stakeholders require consideration in establishing a sustainable treatment program.

CONCLUSION

Drawing on the history of combat-related trauma and its evolving reception in both the medical and legal communities, several lessons relevant to the establishment of veterans' courts present themselves. First, combat-related trauma is neither new nor unique. Three hundred years of military history in the United States provides more than sufficient evidence to conclude that a significant percentage of veterans from the Revolutionary War to the Iraq war (a) have suffered from combat-related trauma, and (b) had difficulty with social reintegration once they returned from combat. In light of this history, medical and social service providers should be proactively engaged in preparing for and treating returning combat veterans whose mental wounds, though invisible, exact an individual and social price no less than real than the physical wounds of war.

Second, combat-related trauma increases the risk that veterans will engage in criminal behavior. As the Wilson and Zigelbaum study suggests, veterans suffering from PTSD may respond by engaging in behaviors that, if left unattended, sometimes lead to criminal activity, including anger, violence, alcoholism, drug dependency, thrill-seeking, and despondency. Knowing this, justice system stakeholders should design criminal court procedures that emphasize treatment and rehabilitation over punishment whenever possible—a course that would result in fiscal benefits by reducing incarceration costs and, more importantly, social benefits by returning to society those members who arguably are among its most valuable and productive.

Third, judicial leniency toward veterans is part of the United States' historical tradition. Though perhaps not always shown, courts have long displayed sympathy for veterans whose military heroism on behalf of their country results in personal sacrifice and suffering, especially when that suffering later contributes to criminal misdeeds. Recognizing the liminal effects of combat in military veterans is thus a judicially appropriate response when the misconduct at issue arises from combat-related trauma.

Fourth, treatment methodologies employed by most problem-solving courts are well-suited to the needs of veterans facing prosecution in veterans' courts. Most operating veterans' courts adjudge misdemeanor and felony offenses committed by veterans with either substance abuse or mental illness concerns, both of which have been treated with marked success by drug and mental health courts. The ten key components of drug courts emphasize a voluntary, community-based approach to treatment. Coupled with involvement by a caring veteran-mentor and the VA, the success of veterans' courts should parallel—if not exceed—that of other problem-solving courts.

Fifth, veterans' courts that hear violent offenses should seek to ameliorate victim concerns while advancing treatment opportunities for veterans suffering from combat-related trauma. As a matter of law, combat trauma may provide an affirmative or mitigating defense to criminal responsibility, a matter of concern to critics who view it as an escape hatch for veterans. In veterans' courts, therefore, where courtroom adversity is sidestepped in favor of a collaborative, therapeutic approach to rehabilitation, victims' rights should be reconciled with veterans' interests to the fullest extent possible. Veterans' courts rely on community involvement and support. Harmonizing the retributive interests of victims with the rehabilitative interests of veterans provides a pathway for public acceptance of veterans' courts' existence and outcomes.

Writing in 1918, Edith Abbott summarized the debt due service members returning from war. "[T]he country is agreed," she wrote, "that no effort shall be spared to make the transition from war to peace as little onerous as possible to the great numbers of young men

TABLE 12.1 Key Principles to Veterans' Courts Policy 105A

American Bar Association, House of Delegates, February 8–9, 2010

The American Bar Association House of Delegates adopted a policy in February 2010 supporting veterans' courts and setting forth key principles for their establishment.[a] The principles identified by the ABA list specific outcomes for measuring veterans' courts' success, including decreased recidivism, addiction recovery, veteran self-sufficiency, judiciary cost savings, and connection to local and federal service providers.[a]

(1) Participation is voluntary and the constitutional rights of participants are retained.

(2) Veterans' Treatment Courts or the resources devoted to veterans within existing civil and criminal court models will utilize the participation of a caseworker and legal representative with coordination from federal Veterans Affairs employees, veteran service agencies, community-based service providers, and local agencies to assess the needs of and provide veterans with appropriate housing, treatment, services, job training, and benefits.

(3) Veterans' Treatment Courts or the resources devoted to veterans within existing civil and criminal court models include mentoring sessions with other veterans.

(4) In the criminal court context, participants in the program have all qualifying charges reduced or dismissed, or traditional sanctions waived, including where appropriate and feasible, more serious charges, commensurate with completion of appropriate treatment and services. Where charges are dismissed, public access to the record is limited, where appropriate and feasible as provided by state or local law, including through expungement.

(5) The Veterans' Treatment Courts shall address those criminal matters that involve serious violent felonies only at the discretion of local courts.

(6) The success of Veterans' Treatment Courts or additional resources devoted to veterans within existing civil and criminal court models is measured through the following outcomes:

(a) Prevention and reduction of homelessness among veterans.

(b) Reduction of recidivism.

(c) Recovery achieved through compliance with the individual treatment plan of the veteran.

(d) Improved communication and reunification with family members, when appropriate.

(e) Successful elimination of legal barriers to self-sufficiency.

(f) Reentry to the workforce, enhanced job opportunities, and reintegration with the community.

(g) Economic savings to the courts, criminal justice and public health systems, and the community.

(h) Connection to VA benefits, long-term supportive housing, and other benefits for participants whose service-related disabilities are so severe as to prevent their return to the workforce.[a]

[a]ABA Policy, *supra* note 204.

from whom we are already asking such heavy sacrifices."[242] Continuing, she stated:

> Great pity, kindness, toleration, and infinite patience will be needed on all sides when the men go back from the excitement of war to beat their bayonets into ploughshares, and adequate plans for reconstruction should be got under way if the new peace is to be worthy of those who have sacrificed their youth to secure it.[243]

In many ways, the language Abbott uses echoes from a bygone era. The lessons she urges, however, do not. Within the context of the criminal justice system, the establishment of veterans' courts is, perhaps, the best means yet of helping those who sacrificed so much "beat their bayonets into ploughshares"—a necessary repayment from the society that handed veterans their bayonets in the first place.

NOTES

1. Dan Herbeck, *Arrest Raises Questions on Care at VA; Inadequate Counseling Blamed for Assaults*, Buff. News, Feb. 21, 2010, at B1, available at http://bit.ly/bwEmgz.
2. *Id.*
3. Dan Herbeck, *Veteran to Undergo Psychiatric Evaluation; Judge Won't Rule Until After Treatment*, Buff. News, Mar. 12, 2010, at B1, available at http://bit.ly/dtaztg.
4. *Id.*
5. Dan Herbeck, *Veteran Held in Assault at VA Wins Approval to Rejoin Family*, Buff. News, Apr. 18, 2010, at C8, available at http://bit.ly/cSJ1B2.
6. *Id.*
7. *Id.*
8. Dan Herbeck, *Veteran Gets 2nd Chance from a Court with a Heart*, Buff. News, Sept. 14, 2010, at B1, available at http://bit.ly/dve3vq.
9. *Id.*
10. *Id.*
11. *Porter v. McCollum*, 558 U.S. ___, 130 S. Ct. 447 (2009) (per curiam).
12. *See generally* Daryl S. Paulson & Stanley Krippner, Haunted by Combat: Understanding PTSD in War Veterans Including Women, Reservists, and Those Coming Back from Iraq 8 (2007).
13. Note, *Post-Traumatic Stress Disorder—Opening Pandora's Box?*, 17 New Eng. L. Rev. 91, 92 n. 6 (1982) [hereinafter *Pandora's Box*] (quoting R. Lattimore, The Odyssey of Homer ¶ 230, at 204 (1965). For a comparison of the psychological wounds inflicted on soldiers of the Trojan wars and Vietnam war, see generally Jonathan Shay, Achilles in Vietnam: Combat Trauma and the Undoing of Character (1994).

14. WILLIAM SHAKESPEARE, THE FIRST PART OF KING HENRY THE FOURTH act 2 sc. 3. *See also* SHAY, *supra* note 15, at 165–166 (reviewing the text of Shakespeare's *Henry IV* in light of PTSD symptomatology).

15. Philip A. Mackowiak & Sonja V. Batten, *Post-Traumatic Stress Reactions before the Advent of Post-Traumatic Stress Disorder*, MIL. MED., Dec. 2008, at 1158.

16. *Id.* (quoting Benjamin Rush, *Results of Observations*, 7 LONDON MED. J. 77, 99 (1786)).

17. *See* Louis F. Bishop, Jr., *Soldier's Heart*, AM. J. NURSING, Apr. 1942, at 377–380 (describing "soldier's heart" as a cardiac neurosis that "is more than fear—it is an emotional state linked with fear"); Joel D. Howell, *"Soldier's Heart": The Redefinition of Heart Disease and Specialty Formation in Early Twentieth-Century Great Britain*, MED. HIST., Supp. 5, 1985, available at http://bit.ly/9twLJC; PAULSON & KRIPPNER, *supra* note 14, at 9; *Pandora's Box*, *supra* note 15, at 92–93. For in-depth treatment of combat trauma and the Civil War, see ERIC T. DEAN, JR., SHOOK OVER HELL: POST-TRAUMATIC STRESS, VIETNAM, AND THE CIVIL WAR (1997).

18. Michael J. Davidson, *Post-Traumatic Stress Disorder: A Controversial Defense for Veterans of a Controversial War*, 29 WM. & MARY L. REV. 415, 418 n. 21 (1988) (citing P. BOURNE, MEN STRESS AND VIETNAM 9–10 (1970)).

19. *Id.*

20. C.B. SCRIGNAR, POST-TRAUMATIC STRESS DISORDER: DIAGNOSIS, TREATMENT, AND LEGAL ISSUES 2 (1984). *See also* John Talbott, *Combat Trauma in the Civil War*, HIST. TODAY, Mar. 1996, at 41 (providing numerous anecdotal accounts of combat trauma among Civil War soldiers).

21. SCRIGNAR, *supra* note 22, at 2.

22. PAULSON & KRIPPNER, *supra* note 14, at 9

23. *See* SCRIGNAR, *supra* note 22, at 2; Bishop, *supra* note 19, at 377.

24. *See* SCRIGNAR, *supra* note 22, at 2–3; Bishop, *supra* note 19, at 377; Howell, *supra* note 19, at 43.

25. Bishop, *supra* note 19, at 377.

26. Perhaps the most thorough treatment of "shell shock" and psychiatry during World War I is BEN SHEPHARD, A WAR OF NERVES (2000).

27. *See* Howell, *supra* note 19, at 43; *Pandora's Box*, *supra* note 15, at 93 n. 11.

28. *See id.*; DEAN, *supra* note 19, at 30. *See also Sorenson v. State*, 188 N.W. 622, 624 (Wis. 1922) (doctor testified "he has found as a result of shell shock and other nervous and mental disturbances originating in battle, actual changes in the central nervous system produced by continuous proximity to shock and concussion caused by heavy artillery, in some cases actually causing more or less permanent derangement of the central nervous system").

29. *See Pandora's Box*, *supra* note 15, at 94. *See also* SHEPHARD, *supra* note 28, at 31 (observing by 1916 clinicians had concluded "shell shock" may be caused by "an emotional disturbance or mental strain"); Harold Merskey and August Piper, *Posttraumatic Stress Disorder is Overloaded*, CAN. J. OF PSYCHIATRY, Aug. 2008, at 499 (discussing the evolution of combat trauma

diagnosis from shell shock to combat neuroses to PTSD); C. Peter Erlinder, *Paying the Price for Vietnam: Post-Traumatic Stress Disorder and Criminal Behavior*, 25 B.C. L. Rev. 305, 313–314 (1984).

30. Howell, *supra* note 19, at 43.
31. *See id.*
32. *Id. See also* Dean, *supra* note 19, at 31 ("Attitudes toward the psychiatric casualties of the war varied widely over time; initially, many disoriented men at the front were treated as deserters and shot[.]"); Talbott, *supra* note 22, at 41 ("[M]en whom medical officers might have diagnosed for combat trauma in 1916, 1944, or 1968 were hauled before courts martial in 1864, and some of them probably wound up at the end of a noose or in front of a firing squad.").
33. Dean, *supra* note 19, at 30–31. Similar efforts to screen out "feeble-minded" and "neurotic" enlistees had been made toward the latter part of World War I. *See* Shephard, *supra* note 28, at 126.
34. Dean, *supra* note 19, at 35.
35. *Id. See also Pandora's Box, supra* note 15, at 95.
36. Dean, *supra* note 19, at 35.
37. *See id.*; Erlinder, *supra* note 31, at 314.
38. The "forward psychiatry" treatment methodologies employed on large scale by the U.S. Army in World War II, which brought psychiatrists to the front to treat soldiers immediately rather than return them rear asylums, had been pioneered in World War I by Dr. Tom Salmon. *See* Shephard, *supra* note 28, at 125–132.
39. For a detailed review of the possible explanations for the increase in psychiatric casualties in World War II, see *Pandora's Box, supra* note 15, at 95 n. 25. Also, at least one expert has "concluded that over ninety percent of chronic war neuroses were both undiagnosed and untreated during World War I." *Id.* at 94.
40. *Id.* at 95 n. 25, 97 n. 30.
41. *Id.* at 97.
42. *Id.* at 95 n. 25 (quoting War Dep't Technical Medical Bulletin (TB MED) 203, issued Oct. 19, 1945).
43. *Id.* at 97–98.
44. *Pandora's Box, supra* note 15, at 97 n. 30.
45. *See id.* at 98.
46. *See id. See also* Dean, *supra* note 19, at 40
47. *See Pandora's Box, supra* note 15, at 98; Dean, *supra* note 19, at 40. As a result of these advances, a leading psychiatrist concluded at the time, "[T]here is reason to be optimistic that psychiatric casualties need never again become a major cause of attrition in the United States military in a combat zone." *Id.*
48. Davidson, *supra* note 20, at 416 n. 11.
49. *See id.*; Dean, *supra* note 19, at 41; Dennis McLellan, *PTSD-Shellshock Hit Vietnam Vets Hardest: 20 Years After the Fall*, L.A. Times, Apr. 27, 1995, at 4, available at http://lat.ms/aEs0YL.
50. *See Pandora's Box, supra* note 15, at 99.

51. *See* Davidson, *supra* note 20, at 417.

52. *See Pandora's Box, supra* note 15, at 99; DEAN, *supra* note 19, at 41.

53. *See Pandora's Box, supra* note 15, at 99; DEAN, *supra* note 19, at 41.

54. *Id*. at 84.

55. *Id*. at 85.

56. *Id*. at 39.

57. *Id*. at 70.

58. DEAN, *supra* note 19, at 39.

59. *Id*.

60. *Id*.

61. *Id*.

62. *Id*.

63. DEAN, *supra* note 19, at 39.

64. Erlinder, *supra* note 31, at 305.

65. *Id*. at 311.

66. DEAN, *supra* note 19, at 42.

67. For a comparison of the psychological casualties in Vietnam to those of the Civil War, see DEAN, *supra* note 19, at 181–209.

68. AM. PSYCHIATRIC ASS'N, DIAGNOSTIC AND STATISTICAL MANUAL OF MENTAL DISORDERS (3rd ed. 1980) [hereinafter DSM-III]. *See also* Thomas L. Hafermeister & Nicole A. Stockey, *Last Stand? The Criminal Responsibility of War Veterans Returning from Iraq and Afghanistan with Posttraumatic Stress Disorder*, 85 IND. L.J. 87, 94 (2010).

69. Davidson, *supra* note 20, at 419–420. *See also* Erlinder, *supra* note 31, at 315. One of the shortfalls of "gross stress reaction" was that it assumed combat trauma was situational and "would abate with a reduction in exposure to the stressor." *Id*. at 315.

70. DSM-III, *supra* note 70, at 236.

71. *Id*.

72. AM. PSYCHIATRIC ASS'N, DIAGNOSTIC AND STATISTICAL MANUAL OF MENTAL DISORDERS 463–464 (4th ed., 2000) [hereinafter DSM-IV-TR].

73. RAND CTR. FOR MILITARY HEALTH POLICY RESEARCH, INVISIBLE WOUNDS OF WAR: PSYCHOLOGICAL AND COGNITIVE INJURIES, THEIR CONSEQUENCES, AND SERVICES TO ASSIST RECOVERY iii (Terri Tanielian & Lisa H. Jaycox eds., 2008) [hereinafter Rand Report]. *See also* Anthony E. Giardino, *Combat Veterans, Mental Health Issues, and the Death Penalty*, 77 FORDHAM L. REV. 2955, 2958. For a discussion of the possible over-diagnosis of PTSD, see Merskey and Piper, supra note 31, at 499. *See also* Hafermeister & Stockey, *supra* note 70, at 90 n. 12 (same). This chapter does not discuss Traumatic Brain Injury (TBI), a physiological injury estimated to have occurred in 300,000 combat veterans returning from Iraq and Afghanistan. *See* Giardino at 2598. Veterans suffering from TBI who commit criminal acts, however, also require sympathetic consideration and a problem-solving approach to rehabilitation. Accordingly, arguments supporting specialized courts for veterans with PTSD may be extended to veterans with TBI.

74. Charles W. Hoge, et al., *Combat Duty in Iraq and Afghanistan, Mental Health Problems, and Barriers to Care*, 351 NEW ENG. J. MED. 1, 13 (2004).

75. *Id.* at 13.
76. William H. McMichael, V *A Diagnosing Higher Rates of PTSD*, Marine Corps Times, Jan. 18, 2009, available at http://bit.ly/cA8Qj5.
77. Brett T. Litz and William E. Schlenger, *PTSD in Service Members and New Veterans of the Iraq and Afghanistan Wars: A Bibliography and Critique*, PTSD Research Quarterly, Winter 2009, at 1–3. By contrast, historical studies on Vietnam veterans following conclusion of the conflict indicate PTSD rates of 30%. *See* Hafermeister & Stockey, *supra* note 70, at 100.
78. *See id.* at 101; Elizabeth J. Delgado, *Vietnam Stress Syndrome and the Criminal Defendant*, 19 Loy. L.A. L. Rev. 473, 478–482 (1985); John P. Wilson & Sheldon D. Zigelbaum, *The Vietnam Veteran on Trial: The Relation of Post-Traumatic Stress Disorder to Criminal Behavior*, 1 Behav. Sci. & L. 69 (1983). p. 80–82
79. Bruce Pentland & James Dwyer, *Incarcerated Viet Nam Veterans*, *in* The Trauma of War: Stress and Recovery in Viet Nam Veterans 406 (1985).
80. Lynne Peralme, Predictors of Post-Combat Violent Behavior in Vietnam Veterans 13 (1995) (unpublished Ph.D. Dissertation, The Florida State University College of Arts and Sciences).
81. Erlinder, *supra* note 31, at 306 n. 5.
82. Peralme, *supra* note 82, at 14. *See also* Ann R. Auberry, Comment, *PTSD: Effective Representation of a Vietnam Veteran in the Criminal Justice System*, 68 Mar. L. Rev. 647, 650 (1985) (25% of Vietnam veterans involved in heavy combat had been charged with a crime, a rate higher than that of veterans not in heavy combat or nonveterans).
83. Peralme, *supra* note 82, at 14.
84. Debra A. Pinals, *Veterans and the Justice System: The Next Forensic Frontier*, J. Am. Acad. Psychiatry and L. (June 2010) at 164.
85. *See Serious Psychological Distress and Substance Use Disorder among Veteran*, The National Survey on Drug Use and Health Report, U.S. Dep't of Health & Human Services, Nov. 2007 [hereinafter NSDUH Report], available at http://bit.ly/c1uxq9 ("One quarter of veterans age 18 to 25 met the criteria for [substance use disorder] in the past year compared with 11.3 percent of veterans aged 26 to 54 and 4.4 percent of veterans aged 55 or older.").
86. Rick Little & Stacy Garrick Zimmerman, *Helping Veterans Overcome Homelessness*, 43 Clearinghouse Rev. 292, 295 (2009). *But see* Margaret E. Noonan & Christopher J. Mumola, *Veterans in State or Federal Prison, 2004*, Bureau of Justice Statistics, U.S. Dep't of Justice 7, May 2007 (finding no link between combat service and mental health problems among incarcerated veteran inmates), available at http://bit.ly/dxfBcc.
87. Eric B. Elbogen, et al., Correlates of anger and hostility in Iraq and Afghanistan war veterans, *Am. J. Psychiatry*, Sep. 2010, at 1051. *See also* Wilson & Zigelbaum, *supra* note 80, at 73–74; Melissa Pratt, *New Courts on the Block: Specialized Criminal Courts for Veterans in the United States*, 15 Appeal 39, 40 (2010); Deborah Sontag and Lizette Alvarez, *Across America, Deadly Echoes of Foreign Battles*, N.Y. Times, Jan. 13, 2008, available at http://nyti.ms/9Mc3zV. In January 2008, the *New York Times*

uncovered 121 media stories involving veterans of the Iraq and Afghanistan wars who had been accused of committing manslaughter or murder. *Id. See also* Pratt, at 40 (discussing the *New York Times* story). Many of the accused veterans reportedly suffered from combat trauma or substance dependency. *Id.*

88. Noonan & Mumola, *supra* note 88.

89. *Id.* at 2. In January 2000, the U.S. Department of Justice reported that "[m]ale military veterans are incarcerated in the nation's prisons and jails at less than half the rate of non-veterans[.]" Press Release, Bureau of Justice Statistics, U.S. Department of Justice (Jan. 18, 2000), available at http://bit.ly/aASjgn. Notably, the U.S. Department of Justice also reported that "[v]eterans were more likely to be in a state prison for a violent offense (55 percent) . . . than the non-veteran inmate population (46 percent . . .)." *Id.* Nonveterans had a higher incident rate than veterans for drug offenses (22% and 14%, respectively). *Id.* A study released in 2007 found similar results, though it also noted the incarceration rate was due to the difference in age distribution because prisoners who were veterans were older. Noonan & Mumola, *supra* note 88, at 1–2. *See also* Press Release, Bureau of Justice Statistics, U.S. Department of Justice (Apr. 29, 2007), available at http://bit.ly/acMCLf.

90. Abbot, *supra* note 2, at 46 (quoting THOMAS MORE, UTOPIA (1516)).

91. NICCOLO MACHIAVELLI, THE ART OF WAR 14 (Christopher Lynch trans., University of Chicago Press, 2003) (1520).

92. Abbot, *supra* note 2, at 212–213 (quoting MANCHESTER GUARDIAN, Nov. 28, 1919). Modern commentators parallel Churchill's remarks. Robert Jay Lifton, a Harvard researcher who has studied PTSD, recently observed: "When they've been in combat, you have to suspect immediately that combat has some effect, especially with people who haven't shown these [criminal] tendencies in the past." Sontag & Alvarez, *supra* note 89. Similarly, William Gentry, an Army reservist and prosecutor in California, remarked: "You are unleashing certain things in a human being we don't allow in civic society, and getting it all back in the box can be difficult for some people." *Id.*

93. Abbott, *supra* note 2, at 212–213.

94. *Id.* at 216.

95. *Id.* at 228.

96. Edith Abbot, *Crime and the War*, J. OF AM. INST. OF CRIM. L. & CRIMINOLOGY, May 1918, at 40 (summarizing the arguments of M. Roux, professor of criminal law at the University of Dijon). *See also* Milton H. Erickson, *Some Aspects of Abandonment, Feeble-Mindedness, and Crime*, AM. J. OF SOC., Mar. 1931 (finding a statistical correlation between military service and the commission of criminal offenses following World War I); SHAY, *supra* note 15, at 23–28 (discussing impact of war on soldiers' "Social and Moral Horizon").

97. Harry Willbach, *Recent Crimes and the Veterans*, J. CRIM. L. AND CRIMINOLOGY, Jan.–Feb. 1948, at 508.

98. *People v. Gilberg*, 240 P. 1000 (Cal. 1925). Prior to *People v. Gilberg*, several defendants elsewhere also had raised "shell shock" as part of an insanity defense, all without success. See *State v. Throndson*, 191 N.W. 628, 634 (N.D. 1922) (defendant argued mental incapacitation due to shell shock from World War I); *Sorenson v. State*, 188 N.W. 622, 624 (Wis. 1922) (same); *State v. Shobe*, 268 S.W. 81 (Mo. 1924) (same).

99. *Gilberg*, 240 P. at 1002.

100. *Id.*

101. *Id.*

102. *People v. Danielly*, 202 P.2d 18 (Cal. 1949).

103. *Id.* at 38–39.

104. *Id.* at 40.40.

105. *Id.* at 41.

106. *Id.*

107. *Kemp v. State*, 211 N.W. 2d 793 (Wis. 1973).

108. *Id.* at 797. See also Erlinder, *supra* note 31, at 308 n. 21(discussing *Kemp*).

109. *Kemp*, 211 N.W. 2d at 799.

110. Erlinder, *supra* note 31, at 315–316.

111. *Id.*

112. See Hafermeister & Stockey, *supra* note 70, at 113.

113. See *Clark v. Arizona*, 548 U.S. 735, 747 (2006); Hafermeister & Stockey, *supra* note 70, at 113.

114. See *Clark*, 548 U.S. at 747; Hafermeister & Stockey, *supra* note 70, at 109.

115. *Clark*, 548 U.S. at 747 (quoting M'Naghten's Case, 8 Eng. Rep. 718, 722 (H.L.) (1843)).

116. *Id.* See also Hafermeister & Stockey, *supra* note 70, at 109 n. 130.

117. See *Clark*, 548 U.S. at 750; Hafermeister & Stockey, *supra* note 70, at 109.

118. Hafermeister & Stockey, *supra* note 70, at 110 (quoting MODEL PENAL CODE § 4.01(1) (2001)). Interestingly, this was the test primarily used by federal courts until John Hinkley, Jr. was acquitted on grounds of insanity in the attempted assassination of President Ronald Reagan in 1981. Davidson, *supra* note 20, at 422 n. 53, 427. In the ensuing public firestorm, Congress passed the Insanity Defense Reform Act of 1984, 18 U.S.C. § 20 (Supp. II 1985), which eliminated the volitional component of the Model Penal Code test and returned the *M'Naghten* rule to federal court practice. *Id.* at 427.

119. *Clark v. Arizona*, 548 U.S. 735, 750 (2006).

120. See, e.g., Erin M. Gover, *Iraq as a Psychological Quagmire: The Implications of Using Post-Traumatic Stress Disorder as a Defense for Iraq War Veterans*, 28 PACE L. REV. 561, 562 (2008) ("PTSD has been used to prove existing criminal law defenses since 1978. Its use as a defense rose dramatically when the American Psychiatric Association officially recognized it as a mental disorder in 1980.") (citations omitted).

121. *Id.* (citation omitted). See also Hafermeister & Stockey, *supra* note 70, at 123; Adam Caine, *Fallen from Grace: Why Treatment Should Be Considered for Convicted Combat Veterans Suffering From Post Traumatic Stress Disorder,*

78 UMKC L. Rev. 215, 222–223 (2009) (discussing insanity, automatism, and mitigation).

122. Davidson, *supra* note 20, at 422–423 (citations omitted).

123. *Id.* at 423 (citations omitted). *See also* Comment, *PTSD: Effective Representation of a Vietnam Veteran in the Criminal Justice System*, 68 Marq. L. Rev. 647, 670 (generally discussing use of PTSD in mitigation).

124. *See* Christopher Hawthorne, *Bringing Baghdad Into the Courtroom*, 24 Crim. Just. 4, 7 (2009) (citing David Margolick, *New Vietnam Debate: Trauma as Legal Defense*, N.Y. Times, May 11, 1985, at A11); Davidson, *supra* note 20, at 422 n. 55.

125. *State v. Heads*, No. 106, 126 (1st Jud. Dist. Ct. Caddo Parrish, La. Oct. 10, 1981). For an account of the *Heads* case, see Erlinder, *supra* note 31, at 319–320; Myra McPherson, Long Time Passing: Vietnam and the Haunted Generation 219–224 (2002).

126. *See* McPherson, *supra* note 127, at 219.

127. *See* Erlinder, *supra* note 31, at 320.

128. *See* McPherson, *supra* note 127, at 219.

129. *See id.* at 219–220; Erlinder, *supra* note 31, at 320.

130. Erlinder, *supra* note 31, at 320–321.

131. Wilson & Zigelbaum, *supra* note 80, at 70.

132. *Id.* at 73.

133. *Id.*

134. *Id.* at 74.

135. *Id.*

136. Wilson & Zigelbaum, *supra* note 80, at 74–75.

137. *Id.*

138. *See, e.g.*, Peralme, *supra* note 82, at 11–12; Gover, *supra* note 122, at 567; Hafermeister & Stockey, *supra* note 70, at 101 n. 77.

139. David Margolick, *New Vietnam Debate: Trauma As Legal Defense*, N.Y. Times, May 11, 1985, at A1.

140. *Id.*

141. *See* Hawthorne, *supra* note 126, at 7–8.

142. *See* Margolick, *supra* note 141; Hafermeister & Stockey, *supra* note 70, at 119.

143. *See* Davidson, *supra* note 20, at 422 n. 53.

144. *See* Margolick, *supra* note 141; Hawthorne, *supra* note 126, at 7–8; Gover, *supra* note 122, at 582–583 (discussing *People v. Lockett*, 121 Misc. 2d 549 (N.Y. Crim. Term. 1983), in which a defendant who had never been in Vietnam misled both defense and state psychiatrists into diagnosing him with PTSD).

145. *See, e.g.*, Sontag & Alvarez, *supra* note 89; Hafermeister & Stockey, *supra* note 70.

146. For a discussion of the trial, see Melody Finnemore, *Firestorm on the Horizon*, 70 Or. St. B. Bull. 19 (2009); Kim Murphy, *Did the War Make Him Do It?*, L.A. Times, Nov. 28, 2009, available at http://lat.ms/ckTQua; Sarah Jane Rothenfluch, *Guilty But Insane Due to PTSD*

(Or. Public Broadcasting radio broadcast Dec. 11, 2009), transcript available at http://bit.ly/cUs3ri.
147. Murphy, *supra* note 148.
148. *Id.*
149. *See* Rothenfluch, *supra* note 148.
150. *See* Hawthorne, *supra* note 126, at 5–6 (comparing two recent cases involving traumatized veterans).
151. *See infra* text accompanying notes 240–243.
152. *See* Pratt, *supra* note 89, at 47 (discussing 2009 California case in which a court found a veteran accused of robbing a pharmacy not guilty by reason of insanity based on his PTSD).
153. *Porter v. McCollum*, 558 U.S. ___, 130 S. Ct. 447 (2009) (per curiam).
154. *Id.*
155. *Id.* at 449.
156. *Id.* at 449–450.
157. *Id.* at 450.
158. *Porter v. McCollum*, 558 U.S. ___, 130 S. Ct. 447, 450 (2009) (per curiam).
159. *Id.* at 451.
160. *Id.*
161. *Id.* at 453.
162. *Id.* at 454–455.
163. *Porter v. McCollum*, 558 U.S. ___, 130 S. Ct. 447, 456 (2009) (per curiam).
164. For a discussion of military service as a mitigating factor in caselaw, see Pratt, *supra* note 89, at 45–46 (discussing *United States v. Pipich*, 688 F. Supp. 191 (D. Md. 1988) (district court judge relied on exemplary military record to lower sentence under sentencing guidelines)). Note, however, that the Sentencing Commission has determined that "military, civic, charitable, or public service; employment-related contributions; and similar good works are not ordinarily relevant" in deciding whether a sentence should deviate from the guidelines. *Id.* (citing U.S. Sentencing Guidelines Manual § 5H1.11 (2007)).
165. *Porter v. McCollum*, 558 U.S. ___, 130 S. Ct. 447, 448 (2009) (per curiam).
166. *Id.* at 455.
167. Robert T. Russell, *Veterans Treatment Court: A Proactive Approach*, 35 New Eng. J. on Crim. and Civ. Confinement 357, 364 (2009). While the veterans court in Buffalo is often considered the "first" veterans treatment court, a less-well known veterans court had been established by two judges in Anchorage, Alaska four years earlier. *See* Michael Daly Hawkins, *Coming Home: Accommodating the Special Needs of Military Veterans to the Criminal Justice System*, 7 Ohio St. J. Crim. L. 563 (2009) (discussing creation of court for veterans in Alaska in 2004); Steven Berenson, *The Movement Toward Veterans' Courts*, 44 Clearinghouse Rev. 37, 39 (2010) ("The first small-scale effort at starting a veterans court took place in Anchorage, Alaska, in 2004, but most commentators locate the beginning of the current movement toward specialty courts for veterans in Buffalo, New York.").

168. Russell, *supra* note 169, at 363.
169. *Id*. at 364.
170. *Id*. at 364.
171. *See id*. at 357–363.
172. *Id*. at 367–368.
173. Russell, *supra* note 169, at 368.
174. *Id*. at 368–369.
175. Caine, *supra* note 123, at 233.
176. *Id*.
177. Russell, *supra* note 169, at 369–370. *See also* BUFFALO VETERANS COURT VETER-ANS MENTOR HANDBOOK § 2.1, available at http://bit.ly/duWdf9; Sergio R. Rodriguez, VA Secretary Eric K. Shinseki Visits the Buffalo Veterans Treatment Court, Erie County Veterans' Services: The Buffalo Veterans Treatment Court, http://bit.ly/dc2C8t (last visited Oct. 28, 2010).
178. Russell, *supra* note 169, at 369.
179. Caine, *supra* note 123, at 233.
180. Russell, *supra* note 169, at 369.
181. *Id*. at 364 (citing NAT'L ASS'N OF DRUG COURT PROF., U.S. DEP'T OF JUSTICE, DEFINING DRUG COURTS: THE KEY COMPONENTS (1997), available at http://bit.ly/drbEyz).
182. Russell, *supra* note 169, at 365–367.
183. Berenson, *supra* note 169, at 30 (citing Nicholas Riccardi, *These Courts Give Wayward Veterans a Chance: The First Veterans Court Opened Last Year in Buffalo, N.Y.: Its Success Stories Have Led to More Across the Country*, L.A. TIMES, Mar. 10, 1009, available at http://bit.ly/UiRJr).
184. Trauma Courts for Vets, The World (PRI radio broadcast May 10, 2010), transcript available at http://bit.ly/a5xCll.
185. Russell, *supra* note 169, at 370. *See also* Pratt, *supra* note 89, at 52–53 (discussing the successful experiences of two Buffalo Veterans' Treatment Court participants).
186. Nat'l Assoc. of Drug Court Prof., Justice for Vets: The Nat'l Clearinghouse for Veterans' Treatment Courts, http://bit.ly/bK67tT (last visited Oct. 28, 2010).
187. For example, the Veterans Court Diversion Program in Tarrant County, Texas, requires admission of guilt before entry to the program. Conditions for Veterans Court Diversion Program, Veterans Court Diversion Program, Tarrant County, Texas, http://bit.ly/9iMKrr (last visited Oct. 28, 2010).
188. *See, e.g.*, LA Opens New Criminal Court for Troubled Veterans, BBC News (Sept. 19, 2010), http://bbc.in/9Bl3l2 (last visited Oct. 28, 2010).
189. *See, e.g.*, Kevin Graman, *Special Courts Divert Wash. Veterans from Jail*, TRI-CITY HERALD, Sept. 19, 2010, available at http://bit.ly/aD4NAB (cases of domestic violence and fourth-degree assault heard by veterans court judge); Amy Gillentine, *4th Judicial District Creating Special Court for Veterans*, CO. SPRINGS BUS. J., Feb. 2, 2010, available at http://bit.ly/cLYdu1 (same); Lewis Griswold, *Valley Vets Get Court of Their*

Own: Tulare County Offers Victims of PTSD a Second Chance, FRESNO BEE, June 19, 2010, available at http://bit.ly/d0dKQI (same).

190. Veterans Court Diversion Program, Tarrant County, Texas, http://bit.ly/axkMDY (last visited Oct. 28, 2010).

191. *See* Russell, *supra* note 169, at 364.

192. *See* Pratt, *supra* note 89, at 54.

193. In addition to these examples, news outlets have reported many others. *See, e.g.,* John Schwartz, *Defendants Fresh from War Find Service Counts in Court,* N.Y. TIMES, Mar. 15, 2010, available at http://nyti.ms/9q9gpf; Jessica Mador, New Minn. Court Handles Vets Accused of Crimes, National Public Radio, May 12, 2010, http://n.pr/bWSkSG; Griswold, *supra* note 191.

194. Rodney Ellis, *Veterans Court Is a Dose of Good News,* HOUSTON CHRON., Dec. 20, 2009, available at http://bit.ly/9vqnbf.

195. *Id.*

196. *Id.*

197. Lindsay Goldwert, Tough-Love Judge a Veteran's Lifesaver, CBS News (Mar. 1, 2010), http://bit.ly/8ZjmtL.

198. *Id.*

199. *Id.*

200. *See* Nat'l Assoc. of Drug Court Prof., Justice for Vets: The Nat'l Clearinghouse for Veterans' Treatment Courts, http://bit.ly/bK67tT (last visited Oct. 28, 2010).

201. *See* Veterans Justice Outreach Initiative, U.S. Dep't of Veterans Affairs, http://bit.ly/beCyd0 (last visited Oct. 28, 2010).

202. Policy 105A, House of Delegates, American Bar Association, House of Delegates (February 8–9, 2010) [hereinafter ABA Policy], http://bit.ly/bygdsz. *See also* Rhonda McMillion, *Lingering Wounds: The ABA Enlists in Efforts to Help Homeless Veterans Deal with their Burdens,* A.B.A. J., Oct. 2010, at 66.

203. *Id.*

204. *See* Griswold, *supra* note 191; Marc A. Levin, *Policy Brief: Veterans' Court,* TX. PUB. POL. FOUND., Nov. 2009, available at http://bit.ly/b6jQTr; Pratt, *supra* note 89, at 50–51 (discussing California's statute requiring consideration of PTSD in mitigation).

205. CA. PENAL CODE §1170.9 (2010). *See also* Pratt, *supra* note 90, at 50 (discussing California legislation).

206. S.B. 1940, 81st Leg. (Tx. 2009) (enacted), available at http://bit.ly/beOR0R.

207. *Id.*

208. *See* Services, Education, and Rehabilitation for Veterans Act, H.R. 2138, 111th Cong. (2009), available at http://bit.ly/cXT1eW; Services, Education, and Rehabilitation for Veterans Act, S. 902, 111th Cong. (2009), available at http://bit.ly/chSGWZ. *See also* Pratt, *supra* note 89, at 50 (discussing congressional legislation).

209. H.R. 2138, 111th Cong. § 2(b)(2009), available at http://bit.ly/cXT1eW.

210. *See generally,* Pratt, *supra* note 89, at 40.

211. K. Canestrini, *Veterans' Program Follow-up July 1993*, N.Y. Dep't of Correctional Serv., available at http://bit.ly/cwKu1l.

212. Pratt, *supra* note 89, at 40 (quoting K. Canestrini, *Veterans' Program Follow-up July 1993*, N.Y. Dep't of Correctional Serv., available at http://bit.ly/cwKu1l).

213. Christopher J. Mumola, *Veterans in Prison or Jail, Jan. 2000*, Bureau of Justice Statistics, U.S. Dep't of Justice 7, Sept. 2000, available at http://bit.ly/8ZSEXL.

214. Noonan & Mumula, *supra* note 88, at 4.

215. *See, e.g.*, Pratt, *supra* note 89, at 41 (citing additional studies in Buffalo, New York and King County, Washington).

216. C. West Huddleston, et al., *Painting the Picture: A National Report Card on Drug Courts and Other Problem-Solving Court Programs in the United States*, National Drug Court Institute 1, May 2008, available at http://bit.ly/bNhOI9.

217. *Id.*

218. *Id.* at 1, 18.

219. *Id.* at 6 (citation omitted).

220. *Id.* (citation omitted).

221. Huddleston, *supra* note 218, at 6 (citations omitted).

222. *Id.*

223. *Id.*

224. Russell, *supra* note 169, at 371.

225. *See, e.g.*, Berenson, *supra* note 169, at 40 (noting financial savings of drug courts and citing Dwight Vick & Jennifer Lamb Keating, *Community-Based Drug Courts. Empirical Success: Will South Dakota Follow Suit?*, 52 S.D. L. Rev. 288, 304 (2007)).

226. *See, e.g.*, Graman, *supra* note 191 (discussing cost savings of veterans' courts).

227. Russell, *supra* note 169, at 363.

228. *See id.* at 363.

229. *See* Berenson, *supra* note 169, at 38.

230. *See* Russell, *supra* note 169, at 361; Pratt, *supra* note 89, at 51.

231. *See* Russell, *supra* note 169, at 361 (veterans reluctant to seek mental health assistance); *id.* at 363 (only 41% of soldiers involved in alcohol-related incidents referred to an alcohol program).

232. *See* Berenson, *supra* note 169, at 40 (arguing veterans deserve special treatment because they "were willing to sacrifice life and limb in service to their country").

233. *Porter v. McCollum*, 558 U.S. ___, 130 S. Ct. 447, 448 (2009) (per curiam). *See also* Pratt, *supra* note 89, at 45 (quoting *United States v. Pipich*, 688 F. Supp. 191 (D. Md. 1988) ("An exemplary military record, such as that possessed by the defendant, demonstrates that the person has displayed attributes of courage, loyalty, and personal sacrifice that others in society have not.")).

234. *See* Graman, *supra* note 191 (observing "[c]ritics of veterans' courts argue that the American justice system should single no one out for special treatment"); Hawkins, *supra* note 169, at 570–571 ("Of particular concern to civil libertarians is the disparity in treatment between non-violent drug offenders who are not veterans and those who are." (citation omitted)).
235. Dahlia Lithwick, *A Separate Peace: Why Veterans Deserve Special Courts,* Newsweek, Feb. 11, 2010, available at http://bit.ly/chHEMT.
236. *Id.*
237. Debra Cassens Weiss, ACLU Likes Veterans Court—If It Doesn't Include Special Sentencing Deals, A.B.A. J., Jul. 15, 2009, http://bit.ly/aCeb5v.
238. Amy Gillentine, *4th Judicial District Creating Special Court for Veterans,* Co. Springs. Bus. J., Feb. 2, 2010, available at http://bit.ly/cLYdu1.
239. *Id.*
240. Murphy, *supra* note 148.
241. *See, e.g., The Law of Mental Illness: Mental Health Courts and the Trend Toward a Rehabilitative Justice System,* 121 Harv. L. Rev. 1168, 1174–1175 (2008) (discussing swing of justice system pendulum between rehabilitative model of treatment and retributive model of punishment for criminal offenses).
242. Abbott, *supra* note 98, at 45.
243. *Id.*

13

THE FIRST RESPONDERS' BRIDGE TO PROTECTING VETERANS: A SOCIAL WORKER'S DESIGN ON STREET REACH

Elizabeth Rahilly, Kristen Tuttle, and David Gitelson

The greatest casualty is being forgotten.
THE WOUNDED WARRIORS PROJECT (www.woundedwarriorsproject.org)

Law enforcement, firefighters, emergency medical personnel, and other First Responders across the country are coming into contact with our returning servicemen and servicewomen. Unfortunately, many of the circumstances for this contact are not positive and actually involve any combination of reckless–aggressive driving, motor vehicle and motorcycle accidents, violence, emotional crisis, alcohol- and drug-related incidents, and in worst cases suicide (Brenda & Belcher, 2006; Friedman, 2006; Meichenbaum, 2009).

The VA Hudson Valley First Responder Initiative was created by two social workers employed by the Veterans Administration Hudson Valley Health Care System to provide useful and practical information to the local Law Enforcement and First Responder community[1] regarding the many issues that returning veterans from the Iraq and Afghanistan wars (Operation Iraqi Freedom [OIF] and Operation Enduring Freedom [OEF]) are facing. It was hoped this program would be helpful to the First Responder (FR) whose interaction with the returning service member might replicate some aspects of the wartime experience (sirens, loud noises, flashing lights, authority issues, and so on). The program was also designed to provide each First Responder with a tool they could use to easily inform returning service personnel and their families of the assistance available through the VA.

---

[1] Police Officers, Firefighters, Paramedics, Emergency Medical Technicians, Critical Incident Response Team members, Police and Emergency 911 Dispatchers.

ORIGINS OF THE INITIATIVE:
WHERE ARE THE UNREACHED?

An initial question, from which the idea for the program grew, was, "If there are veterans who served in Iraq and Afghanistan in the area, why aren't some coming to the VA to register for services? Do they know about the VA? Are we reaching out to them in the right ways?"

> The VA is a large complex bureaucracy with a wide variety of benefit programs and many entry points. It was very difficult for new veterans to navigate the system, despite VA benefits briefings. Compounding the problem was the fact that many of the troops serving in support of OEF/OIF are activated members of the National Guard and Reserves, who often are less knowledgeable about VA benefits and services than those on regular active duty. There had to be a better way.
>
> —*Manske, 2006*

This dilemma led the social workers to develop a program that would extend the arms of the VA to these unreached veterans. The social workers knew the VA had many resources and programs to offer this population, and were not satisfied with "waiting" for veterans to come to the VA to utilize them. According to Savitsky, Illingworth, and DuLaney (2009), veterans need to receive services from a multitude of outreach programs, town hall meetings and veterans' associations as well as partnerships that are adopted between nonprofit agencies, veteran service organizations, and other nongovernmental organizations in providing support to veterans and their families.

In addition to the research which influenced a desire to create this program, the social workers came from families with active members of the first responder community. One social worker's family is deeply embedded in the 911/Firefighter/EMS system: her mother is a county 911-dispatcher, her father a Fire Chief who has always been involved with the Fire Department; her brother is a paramedic and paid firefighter in the community; and her father and brother are also members of the county Critical Incident Response Team. Finally, her father is a Vietnam veteran. The issue of reaching unreached veterans was significant for her.

The second social worker's husband is a Gulf War veteran who was deployed during Operation Desert Storm & Desert Shield in the 1990's. He currently works in civilian law enforcement. Prior to that he worked as a paramedic and was a member of a volunteer fire company. This social worker herself had worked as an Emergency Medical Technician and has experience as a 911-dispatcher.

Separately, both social workers worked with returning veterans and had strong contacts in the First Responder community. While both social workers worked at the same VA facility with the same supervisor, one was hospital based, working in the OEF/OIF program, while the other worked in a community-based outpatient clinic.

Thus, the idea that they together develop a collaborative effort between the VA and the First Responder community emerged. What if they went out into the community to provide education and a tool to First Responders to link returning soldiers to the VA and which might also prove helpful to the First Responders in their interactions with returning soldiers.

Developing the Design

- Education is a fundamental element to the program design. First, the social workers planned to educate the First Responder community about what returning veterans might experience upon their return, and explain what the VA could do to help. They would travel to their police departments or firehouses, police academies or agencies, rather than have the First Responders come to the VA. This would make it more practical and appealing for the First Responders, and, as it was hoped, would reach more First Responders directly. To accomplish this, both social workers knew they would have to address several questions:
- Would the First Responder community be interested in participating in the initiative?
- How would the First Responders define their educational needs? What information would benefit them in their interventions with returning soldiers?
- Would it be possible to hold the presentations in the First Responders' settings?
- How could the design of the presentation represent a collaborative effort between the VA and the First Responder groups? (Brager & Holloway, 1992)

First, the social workers turned to their social network of First Responders and returning soldiers to explore what they believed the First Responder community needed to know. The ideas ranged from:

- What are veterans experiencing with the legal system?
- What interactions were they having with police?

- What do we need to know about the circumstances surrounding their auto accidents?
- What is the prevalence of domestic violence among this population and how is this related to PTSD and other combat-related issues?
- How do we address suicide attempts and volatile behaviors when responding to homes, job sites, or other public or private places where other individuals may be at risk?

While posttraumatic stress disorder (PTSD) and traumatic brain injury (TBI) were designated as signature wounds of OIF/OEF, First Responders are also witness to veterans' aggressive behaviors, public fighting, and reckless driving. These elements are closely connected to PTSD and TBI. Unfortunately, when veterans' issues with PTSD, along with other significant issues such as substance abuse, homelessness, and domestic violence are left untreated or unaddressed, contact with a First Responder is inevitable (Brenda & Belcher, 2006; Meichenbaum, 2009; National Center, 2004; Savitsky et al., 2009).

Also on the list of topics to cover, suicide was important. Suicide was a significant topic of discussion for veterans and their families, at the VA, and Urgent Rooms (Department of Veterans Affairs, 2009). Clearly, the First Responder community needs to know more about the signs and symptoms of suicide as many returning veterans are at risk. In fact, mental health issues are significant for returning combat veterans, especially since they

> ... can be just as damaging and life altering for our veterans as it can be for our troops ....
>
> —*Shea-Porter, 2009*

There is a great level of support for returning veterans within the First Responder community as they feel strongly about supporting and caring for those who have protected our country overseas. Many First Responders have served our county and feel a sense of responsibility to be helpful to returning soldiers. They often refer to the extended helping hand as, "Doing the right thing." Thus, the social workers believed First Responders' sense of responsibility, and comparable commitment to duty and honor, would be key elements that would result in their supporting the proposed initiative.

In addition to hearing from the First Responder community about rising concerns regarding returning soldiers, the social workers were hearing from family and spouses who "did not understand" their loved one who had returned home from combat. Family members noted the veterans were different and that "things were not the same as before."

To compound this, many veterans themselves were telling the social workers about their daily struggle to fit back into civilian and family life. They were finding it hard to manage their lives; they knew that they had changed and did not know why. Many of the soldiers did not have the ability to articulate their needs or describe what they were experiencing. This limited their ability to communicate, including in the presence of a police officer or other First Responders.

The social workers believed that with education, the First Responder community might feel better prepared to communicate with returning soldiers; understand the impact of PTSD, TBI, and suicidal and other cognitive distortions; and subsequently offer options and possible solutions—whether the engagement involved a medical emergency, a vehicular violation, or family issues.

PTSD, TBI, and cognitive/thought distortions are serious issues for the VA, helping professions, and the overall civilian community. For First Responders, dealing with PTSD and other behavioral maladies can prove challenging. Symptoms of PTSD and TBI can include *arousal symptoms* (Friedman, 2006; National Center, 2004; Savitsky et al., 2009), which include restlessness, hyper-alertness, inability to relax, jumpiness, and difficulties concentrating. *Intrusive symptoms* (Friedman, 2006; National Center, 2004; Savitsky et al., 2009) are the mental "replays" and dreams in which the veteran sees, hears, feels, smells, and tastes aspects of the event which appear real, vivid, and frightening.

The first snowfall can remind a returning soldier of a sand storm in Iraq or Afghanistan, making it difficult for them to drive. This, in turn, may cause the soldier to appear impaired, increasing the likelihood of a roadside investigation by highway patrol.

BUILDING A BRIDGE TO COMING HOME: *THE TRI-FOLD WALLET "STREET REACH"*

In order to reach the unreached and ensure that an increased number of returning soldiers registered and utilized the VA system, the social workers sought to bridge the VA with the First Responder community in the area they served. It was believed that through education, training, and resource information provided to the First Responders, returning soldiers might be more likely to register with the VA and utilize its services.

To accomplish this, the social workers designed a presentation which would benefit First Responders in their work. It included easily understandable information on PTSD, TBIs, and other mental health and social stressors confronting returning soldiers. They incorporated into their presentation a range of situations the First Responders might face with returning soldiers. These situations included reckless-aggressive driving, roadside investigations and motor vehicle/motor-cycle accidents, violence, emotional crisis, alcohol- and drug-related incidents, and attempted suicides.

Owing to time limitations for First Responders, presentations were designed for 15 minutes to 2 hours, depending on the FR requests. In addition, the social workers became certified as New York State Police Academy instructors in order to be credentialed to provide the training.

Reinforcing the training, the social workers developed a wallet-sized card (more commonly referred to as the Tri-fold) to be given to First Responders to distribute to returning soldiers with whom they interacted. The wallet card lists common symptoms of PTSD and TBI and provides vital contact information for the VA hospital and the National Suicide Prevention Lifeline 1-800-273-TALK. The wallet card is intended to be handed to returning soldiers during traffic stops and routine emergency or nonemergency calls. This would afford the First Responder an opportunity to provide important information to the soldiers they were meeting, including how to contact the VA. Finally, the wallet card was designed to be smaller than a driver's license so that it could be offered discretely and would be more likely to be carried by a First Responder.

After several iterations, the approved cover of the Tri-Fold stated "Coming home can be difficult, and we're waiting for you." The social workers felt this wording conveyed the VA's desire to help as well as its recognition of the struggles the soldiers might be confronting as they returned home.

Training

After approval to implement the program the social workers set training dates at three different sites within the first week. To accomplish this they relied on their family members who were First Responders, and their contacts within the FR community.

> At least if we needed to tweak things in the presentation we'd learn it in front of familiar faces.

The first presentations were the most important as they paved the way for other First Responder organizations to open the door to their agencies and departments. The social workers would have earned "street credibility" as family members who were First Responders were able to endorse their presentation. From the very beginning, word of the presentation spread. The social workers received telephone calls and emails asking them to present at many agencies, even beyond the County in which they were based.

The educational presentation and distribution of tri-fold wallet cards has resulted in a strong community and VA collaboration. During the trainings, First Responders asked numerous questions which included:

How long does PTSD last?

If untreated, symptoms can last forever . . . .

How do I know if someone's a returning soldier?

Ask them. From experience, returning service members don't always think of themselves as veterans. They may consider a veteran to be their father or grandfather or a soldier who has suffered a war injury . . . .

Could someone be diagnosed with PTSD 30 years later? I think I have it.

Yes. Someone could be diagnosed with PTSD years later, and the onset of PTSD does not always present itself immediately following a traumatic event. Someone may experience a delayed onset, or have symptoms for years before seeking treatment when it becomes too overwhelming . . . .

If a veteran is feeling or acting suicidal, should you ask them to talk about it? Or will that make it worse? If I ask if they feel like killing themselves will this plant the seed?

No. Just asking will not make them more likely to commit suicide. In fact, asking them may prompt them to ask for your help . . . .

If they want to go to the VA, can we just take them there?

Yes. If the veteran voluntarily asks to go to the VA, bring them. We have trained staff available 24 hours a day . . . .

I've had recent military service can I go to the VA?

Yes. Come in and talk to our eligibility department . . . . They will inform you of those services for which you may be eligible.

The ongoing discussions resulted in shared stories between the First Responders and the social workers. One campus security guard shared that a student at the college where he worked had recently committed suicide. He proceeded to say "maybe if I had known some of this information the outcome could have been different, maybe I could have recognized signs."

A police officer said "I wish I had this number (1-800-273-TALK) last night. There was a veteran in crisis and I would have had him call."

Unintended Outcomes

The feedback the social workers received from the First Responder community was overwhelmingly positive. As word of the program spread, they received calls from college security offices and mental health staff, VFW groups, and a president of an AARP chapter. Other organizations identified their roles with returning soldiers which ranged from assisting them to register in college, to roles as members of the AARP who wanted to be ready to help their grandchildren when they returned from Iraq and Afghanistan. Those groups whose members had also had war experience wanted to have information so that they were better prepared to guide the veterans they served.

The VA, a huge governmental health care system, was offering First Responders tools to support returning soldiers transition back home. Many of the First Responder community were veterans themselves— many of them understood the returning soldiers' struggles and were eager to help. The tri-fold provided them with that opportunity especially after they had received the education and information the presentation provided.

However, there were some unintended, yet positive outcomes. One was the requests for training beyond the First Responder community. Those requests were not intended, sought after, or expected. These contacts have come from academic institutions, the NYS Governor and Traffic Safety Council, AARP, Suicide Prevention Task Forces, Critical Incident Response Teams, libraries, and so on. The social workers also learned that it is not only the returning veterans, who may be given the information by a Police Officer or First Responder, who benefit from this program; it is also the veterans who are working in Law Enforcement and the First Responder Community who have themselves returned from Iraq and/or Afghanistan and other wartime eras, including Vietnam. In the beginning phases of implementation, it was not yet realized that this training would be speaking directly to First Responders who were veterans themselves.

One of the social workers was contacted by a recently returned soldier calling from his car. He informed her that a police officer, who had just stopped him for reckless driving, had given him "this card," the wallet card, and told him to "get some help." Soon after he came to the VA to register for care and meet with the social worker. He shared his embarrassment as he too was employed in law enforcement. He had returned from Iraq weeks earlier and was struggling with many of the common issues returning soldiers were facing. The wallet card was his bridge to VA care.

In another instance, campus security and faculty responded to a college student in emotional crisis. The previous week the safety and security staff had attended the First Responder Training. They remembered to ask the student if he had recent military service. The student indicated that he had served in Iraq and had recently returned. The student then described what the faculty remembered were possible symptoms of PTSD. One of the staff had a wallet card in his pocket and provided it to the student. Within hours that student was connected to and receiving VA care.

The social workers take many of their cues from the audience. If they are presenting to a campus security group, they focus on the class room and campus triggers for PTSD, and give examples based on anecdotes they've gathered at other college presentations. For police, the social workers tailor the presentations to situations that would commonly relate to their routine work, such as traffic stops, and emphasize returning soldiers' driving patterns as reported to them by returning soldiers with whom they work.

When discussing traffic stops, in particular, the social workers describe how flashing lights, sirens, being startled or difficulty hearing commands may trigger symptoms related to PTSD. They emphasize that in no way are they recommending that any of the agency or safety protocols be changed; they simply asked the First Responders to be aware that returning soldiers' behaviors may be related to PTSD, TBIs, or other wartime experiences. Finally, First Responders are shown slides of car stickers and emblems that are commonly displayed by returning soldiers, which can help in identifying them when they come into contact.

CONCLUSION: *STREET REACH IS OUTREACH*

Outreach initiatives are often one-dimensional in that the target population is not involved in defining a specific need or designing the program. An agency may design a program or outreach effort to promote its services, a date is agreed upon, a target population is invited to attend and attendees are free to roam the stationary tables and select material or information that may be helpful.

The First Responder bridge-to-VA-care initiative has been designed to be multidimensional. While the intended audience and recipients of the information are preidentified (returning soldiers), the information provided is tailored to each First Responder group and their specific work environment, thus increasing the possibility that more returning soldiers will be helped. In addition, the curriculum has been designed with direct input from First Responders and returning soldiers to ensure it addresses their concerns and the specific situations in which they interact.

Initially, 50% of the training presentation was designed to educate First Responders on the services provided by the VA. Ultimately, this was reduced to a smaller portion of the presentation as it became apparent that the target audience wanted to learn more about what soldiers are experiencing as they return home and how these experiences may affect their behaviors; how they, the First Responder, can be of better assistance; where they can bring a returning soldier voluntarily, if help is needed; and whom they can contact at the VA should the need arise.

Finally, a tool was designed (the tri-fold) to demonstrate the First Responder's and the VA's concern while providing important information to the returning soldier. Currently, there are approximately 55,000 tri-folds in emergency vehicles for First Responders. Each wallet card carries with it the opportunity for a returning soldier to be connected to the services and programs he or she is entitled to, and deserves. The program is currently viewed as an important component of the facility's services to returning soldiers and has received recognition from VA facilities around the country.

The focus of the initiative is to ensure that no returning soldier is ever overlooked when they return home. The commitment is to make the bridge-to-VA-care realistic and easier so that returning soldiers receive the support and services they have earned.

REFERENCES

Brager, G., & Holloway, S. (1992). Assessing prospects for organizational change: The uses of force field analysis. In D. Bargal & H. Schmid (Eds.), *Organizational change and development in human service organizations* (pp. 5–28). Hayworth Press.

Brenda, B., & Belcher, J. (2006). Alcohol and other drug problems among homeless veterans: A life course theory of forgiveness. *Alcoholism Treatment Quarterly, 24*(1/2), 147–170.

Department of Veterans Affairs. (2009, October). *Care management of Operation Enduring Freedom (OEF) and Operation Iraqi Freedom (OIF) veterans.* Washington, DC: Department of Veterans Affairs, Veterans Health Administration.

Friedman, M. J. (2006). Posttraumatic stress disorder among military returnees from Afghanistan and Iraq. *American Journal of Psychiatry, 163*(4), 586–594.

Manske, J. E. (2006). Social work in the Department of Veterans Affairs: Lessons learned. *Health and Social Work, 31*(3), 33.

Meichenbaum, D. (2009). Trauma and substance abuse guidelines for treating returning veterans. *Counselor: The Magazine for Addiction Professional, 10*(4), 10–15.

National Center for Post Traumatic Stress Disorder. (2004). *Iraq war clinician guide* (2nd ed., pp. 1–20). Washington, DC: Department of Veteran Affairs.

Savitsky, L., Illingworth, M., & DuLaney, M. (2009). Civilian social work: Serving the military and veteran populations. *Social Work, 54*(4), 15–16.

Shea-Porter, C. (2009). Posttraumatic stress disorder and government initiatives to relieve it. *Health and Social Work, 34*(3), 235–236.

14

THE 21ST-CENTURY VETERAN AND THE 19TH-CENTURY PENSION CODE: WHY THE VA CLAIMS PROCESS IS A STEAM ENGINE IN AN E-UNIVERSE

Thomas Reed

The VA claims process is complex, legalistic, and protracted. Clinical reports suggest that individuals with PTSD have particular difficulty managing the stress involved in submitting an application, undergoing a disability evaluation, and waiting for the uncertain outcome.

SAYER ET AL., 2005, p. 867

The VA system is not an automatic machine that requires the claimant to do nothing more than file a paper or turn a crank to get a favorable result. It is a quasi-judicial system for weighing evidence and allocating entitlements based on the law and the evidence. It is the administrative equivalent of a civil law suit against the United States for breach of contract. The VA investigates a claim, tries to amass evidence to prove the claim, then weighs the evidence discovered against the law. It is not easy to be the fact-gather and the judge in the same case.

Serious students of the Veterans Affairs Department agree that the VA compensation system has failed to accomplish its mission: prompt, fair adjudication of compensation and pension claims made by veterans or by their dependents.[1] The current system, originating with the Pension Act of 1862, is no longer functional. Decades of administrative debris preclude rapid, fair adjudication of a service member's disability claim.

On May 23, 2007, the House Veterans Affairs Committee convened an extraordinary roundtable discussion with veterans' advocacy groups and the United States Department of Veterans Affairs (VA). The discussion was provoked by the delays preventing returning disabled veterans of the Iraq and Afghanistan conflicts from receiving their VA benefits for uncontested service-connected disabilities.[2] The members of Congress who attended the roundtable focused on this narrow issue. The advocacy groups raised larger issues with respect to the fundamental fairness and efficiency of the VA's claims adjudication process. All the advocates and most of the members of Congress agreed that the Veterans Disability Compensation system was irretrievably broken and needed more than a band-aid applied by Congress to keep faith with U.S. veterans of every era.[3] The author was part of this round-table and submitted a position paper from which this article was derived. The author believes that the current VA claims adjudication process is an unjust system that harms veterans and dependents entitled to compensation by law by delaying the adjudication of claims for an unreasonable period of time after the claimant's original claim has been submitted.[4] The VA claims adjudication system is a antique paper-driven system that has changed little from its Civil War era beginnings. Congress so far has refused to modify the compensation system, even though it routinely asks veterans to put themselves in harm's way.

More importantly, a 1973 fire at the National Archives warehouse damaged or destroyed nearly all World War I Army records, most World War II records. Most Korean War Army and U.S. Air Force records for veterans, with last names from M to Z, were destroyed or damaged. Navy, Marine Corps, and Coast Guard records were not affected by the fire. The National Archives and Records Administration is the custodian of all military service records for all U.S. veterans. Records for Revolutionary War, Civil War, and Spanish American War veterans are kept in the National Archives in Washington. More recent records are stored in the National Archives warehouse complex in St Louis. However, several records for veterans are unavailable due to the fire of 1973.

THE CLAIMANTS AND THEIR CLAIMS

According to the Veterans Affairs Department, there are 23,976,991 men and women who are veterans. About 17.9 million living men and women were veterans in time of war as defined by title 38 U.S. Code.[5] More than 3.5 million veterans and dependents currently receive some form of VA compensation or pension benefits.

The class of people eligible for VA compensation or pension benefits consists of one living World War I veteran, several widows of

Spanish American War veterans, an unspecified number of children of Civil War veterans, and widows and dependent children of World War I veterans. Each member of this group is an important individual, but the group is too small to present any institutional problems. These people have long ago been awarded some form of compensation under Congress's pension acts, or under the original version of the Veterans Administration Act of 1930.[6]

More than 16 million men and women served in World War II.[7] About 2.8 million still survive, together with millions of dependent spouses and dependent children of World War II veterans.[8] The median age of this group is well past 80, and the ranks of these veterans are rapidly thinning. It is also an age when latent conditions become manifest that may be traceable to an in-service condition.[9]

The Korean Conflict cohort of veterans serving from 1950 to 1955, and dependents, exclusive of those who were also World War II veterans numbered about 6.8 million.[10] More than 3 million Korean War vets survive as well as many hundreds of thousands of dependent spouses and children of Korean War veterans.[11] The median age of this cohort is approximately 75 years.

More than 3,000,000 men and women served from 1945 to 1950 and from 1955 through 1963 during the first period of the Cold War. More than 2,500,000 survive today.[12] This cohort's military records were not destroyed in the 1973 fire. The average age of Cold War vets is around 65. Latent conditions arising from such activities as peacetime nuclear test participation, experimental use of certain kinds of medication, and similar incidents are becoming apparent among this cohort, as well as general worsening of such conditions as traumatic arthritis, high blood pressure, and heart disease. Few of these vets have dependent children, but most have dependent spouses.

More than 8 million men and women served during the Vietnam War from 1962 to 1975, whether or not they actually served stateside or abroad.[13] As of 2003, 7.9 million men and women who served from 1963 to 1975 survive.[14] The service records and medical records of this group, approximately 55 years of age, are intact and available for adjudication. This is the cohort that brought Agent Orange contamination to public attention,[15] and the group from which the mental condition known as posttraumatic stress disorder (PTSD) was originally brought into the annals of psychiatric medicine.[16] This group includes millions of dependent spouses and minor children.[17]

The all-volunteer, down-sized military force of the 1970s and 1980s contributed more than 3.5 million men and women who served from 1975 to 1991, a group that is represented by almost 3.5 million survivors,[18] and at least as many dependent spouses and children. This group has made the lowest percentage of claims.

The Gulf War of 1991 was the first of the "gray hair" actions in which a large portion of the military committed to active participation in combat and combat support was drawn from the Organized Reserves and National Guard. More than 4 million men and women served in this conflict.[19] More than 4 million survivors remain with at least as many dependent spouses and children.[20] It is the group that gave us "Gulf War Syndrome" a mysterious ailment like lupus that affected thousands of returning Gulf War veterans of all ages. The records of Gulf War era service are intact and available to the VA for adjudication. This group has made a significant number of VA claims since 1991, considering its relatively small size.[21]

As of September 30, 2006, the VA reported that more than 1.3 million men and women had served in the Global War against Terror (GWOT).[22] The Iraq and Afghanistan War veterans cohort includes older Reserve and National Guard members who served in the first Gulf War, and in the peacekeeping actions in Bosnia. It also consists of our nation's older adolescent and young adult men and women. The insidious nature of the insurgencies in both countries produced physical and mental disabilities unlike those seen in earlier cohorts. More noncombat soldiers, sailors, airmen, and marines were injured by improvised explosive devices (IEDs) and rocket-propelled grenades than by typical, or expected, combat-type shrapnel and gunshot wounds. This cohort has a high incidence of mild-to-extensive traumatic brain injury (TBI), as well as PTSD or other significant impairment.[23] In addition to the TBIs and the PTSD, this group is seeing a large need for vocational rehabilitation training due to the number of amputees returning home. Also, returnees have reentry issues and concerns such as financial damage done by loss of well-paying civilian wages or salaries, loss of opportunity to return to a preservice job, marital discord, and/or divorce from the stress of repeated deployments and the influence of combat-related stress on home life.[24]

Types of VA Claims and Elements of Proof

The Department of Veterans Affairs recognizes five types of claims against the United States for some form of disability benefits: (1) Compensation Claim; (2) Pension Claim; (3) DIC Claim; (4) Medical Malpractice Claim; (5) Vocational Rehabilitation Claim.

Compensation Claim

Congress mandates that the VA pay appropriate compensation to disabled veterans and their dependents for injuries or diseases that first occur, or are aggravated by military service. A service-member's enlistment contract implicitly includes this Congressional entitlement.[25]

VA compensation benefits are awarded when the claimant meets the statutory burden of proof set out in 38 U.S.C. § 5107. When the evidence for and against a claim are approximately equal, the claimant must prevail.[26] The VA standard for causality is similarly lenient: when a claimant submits competent medical evidence showing a nexus between the claimant's current condition and an in-service condition, the VA will accept service causality for the current condition. The claimant is not required to show that some service-related act or omission proximately caused the claimant's current injuries. The claim will be granted if the claimant's medical evidence shows that it is as likely as not that the claimant's current condition is related in some way to an in-service occurrence.[27] A service member is presumed sound on enlistment if no medical defects are noted in the preenlistment physical examination.[28] The burden of demonstrating any preexisting or later source of injury is on the VA. The VA must prove that the preponderance of the evidence is against the claim.[29] If the VA does not carry the burden of disproof by a preponderance, the claimant prevails.

A VA compensation claim requires proof of (a) satisfactory military service (honorable discharge or general under honorable conditions); (b) incurrence of an injury or disease in service; (c) present symptoms; and (d) medical expert opinion linking the in-service injury or disease to current symptoms.[30] Some claimants who are rated at least 60% disabled are eligible for 100% compensation based on Total Disability Individualized Unemployability using a standard similar to that employed by the Social Security Administration.[31] Claimants may also receive special monthly compensation for loss of use of a creative organ,[32] or under separate chapters of title 38 U.S. Code, for an automobile.[33] See also 38 C.F.R. § 3.808 (2008) for home renovations necessary to accommodate a veteran who has lost the use of lower or upper limbs, or in-home care or nursing home benefits for a claimant who has become totally incapacitated through a service-connected condition.[34]

Pension Claim

Pension is a special program for veterans in time of war who have been totally disabled by a nonservice connected disability.[35] A pension claim for a veteran who served in time of war requires proof of

(a) satisfactory military service during time of war,
(b) current disease or injury severe enough to
(c) preclude the veteran from holding substantial gainful employment.[36]

Pension benefits are need-based and at this writing are well below social security disability benefits for most individuals with a reasonable work history.[37] An eligible veteran receives a basic statutory maximum pension rate as an individual, plus additional pension payments for any dependent spouse, child, or parent. The VA takes into account household income that includes income from a spouse or children.[38] It does not take into account the income of an informal live-in boyfriend or girlfriend.[39] The VA calculates the pension payable to a disabled veteran by taking the maximum benefit payable under current pension law and subtracting from that maximum any countable income earned by the veteran or by family members. The amount remaining is divided by 12, yielding the monthly pension benefit payable. This system is called annualization of income.[40]

DIC Claim

Dependency and Indemnity Compensation (DIC) benefits are payable monthly to eligible survivors of dead veterans. A survivor's DIC claim requires proof of (a) satisfactory military service for a deceased veteran, (b) eligibility to receive DIC benefits (surviving spouse, minor child, helpless child over 18, or dependent parent)[41] (c) meet one of the three criteria for award of DIC benefits (i) death of service member from a service-connected disease or injury, (ii) death from any cause if the veteran was adjudicated 100% disabled for a period of more than ten years prior to death, or (iii) death from any cause if the veteran was adjudicated 100% disabled for a period of 5 years if the veteran did not survive for 10 years.[42] Surviving dependents of claimants receiving VA need-based pension may claim a similar award of DIC benefits at a lower rate based on some of the same criteria as a pension award and a DIC award for a service-connected veteran's dependents.[43]

Medical Malpractice Claim

A veteran or an eligible dependent may apply for compensation as if service-connected for medical malpractice committed by VA medical personnel.[44] The claimant must show that (a) the veteran was diagnosed or treated by VA medical personnel, (b) the diagnoses or treatment was negligent, and (c) the negligent diagnosis or treatment was the proximate cause of injury or death to the veteran.[45] A veteran who proves a malpractice claim will be treated as if he or she had a service-connected disease or injury and will be compensated accordingly.[46] DIC claims can be based on proof of medical malpractice that took the life of a veteran.[47]

Vocational Rehabilitation Claim

Section 1151 also provides for compensation payable as if service connected for a veteran who is injured or ill while enrolled in a VA vocational rehabilitation program. To prevail on a claim arising under 38 U.S. C. § 1151 for injury or disease arising from a vocational rehabilitation program, the veteran must show that (a) the veteran was certified and enrolled in a vocational rehabilitation program, (b) the veteran incurred an injury or disease during participation in the program that disabled the veteran.[48]

According to the Fiscal Year 2008 Veterans Benefits Report, 2.9 million veterans (about 12% of all living veterans) are receiving VA disability compensation. Of this group, 262,682 veterans (8.9%) are deemed 100% disabled. This figure does not include 244,186 veterans (8.4%) receiving Total Disability Individualized Unemployability benefits. In addition, 315,763 veterans are receiving VA pension benefits. In all, 320,966 spouses of dead veterans are receiving DIC benefits; 11,726 dependent children, and 5127 dependent parents are also receiving benefits. In the fiscal year 2007, the VA paid out $34,778,486 to compensation and pension benefits recipients.[49]

THE CURRENT CLAIM PROCESS

There are a minimum of three steps and a maximum of seven steps in the current VA claims process. The following describes all seven steps.

Step One: Initial Filing of Claim at Regional Office

A claimant[50] must start the claim process by filing a written claim at one of 58 VA Regional Offices.[51] This requires completion of one of several standard forms, the most common being Form 21-256—the veteran's claim for compensation and pension.[52] Once the completed claim form is received, the VA is required to pull together a veteran's service records, service medical records, VA treatment records, and civilian treatment records. According to the latest VA Performance and Accountability Report, the VA needed an average of 183 days to process a compensation claim in the fiscal year 2007.[53] An average of 127 days were classified as "pending," a special VA category for claims that have been triaged, developed, and moved to the rating specialists.[54] The same report estimated that 132 days were required to process a DIC claim.[55]

Step Two: Assisting the Claimant to Develop the Claim

When a claimant files a substantially complete application for compensation, the Regional Office sends a letter to the claimant that contains the following elements:

(a) A statement of the evidence necessary to prove the claim,
(b) assignment of the burden of presenting evidence to the VA,
(c) and an assignment of the burden of presenting evidence to the claimant.[56]

The Regional Office is also required to locate and obtain veterans' military service records and military medical records, from the National Archives in St Louis, for those veterans who are discharged and no longer under any reserve obligation.[57] Since 1992, the armed services have sent all discharged veterans' health records to the VA, which stores them in a different warehouse in St Louis. The records for veterans who have outstanding reserve obligations are maintained by the reserve component of their armed service. Typically, the armed services retain records for recently discharged veterans for up to three years after all reserve obligation has ended.

The Regional Office also has the obligation to obtain medical records from the VA medical facilities that have treated the veteran. If the veteran has had a disability adjudication from Social Security Administration, Railroad Retirement Board, or the Office of Personnel Management, the Regional Office is required to request those records if disclosed to it by the veteran.[58] The veteran may also authorize the Regional Office to obtain private medical records by signing a simple consent to release records form. The Regional Office is then under a duty to request those records from private medical sources.[59]

Since November 2000, every veteran applying for benefits has the right to a compensation and pension physical examination at the nearest VA Medical Center by a specialist or specialists competent to express an opinion on the connection (or nexus) between a current condition and an in-service disease or injury.[60] The examining physician is supposed to have the veteran's claim file and to have reviewed all pertinent documents in that file before making the examination.[61]

Developing the claim by and with the veteran does not stop with the accumulation of records from NARA or the VA. It can often include submissions from the veteran from private physicians, or statements from service buddies to confirm a service incident, and even civilian employment records showing time off the job for an illness or injury. This step overlaps with adjudication, because the Regional Office will continue to accumulate evidence while adjudicating a claim.

Step Three: Adjudication

After filing, claims are developed by a team of VA personnel who combine records together from all sources for review by VA Raters.[62] When development is completed this team forwards the claim file to a third team of rating specialists trained by the VA to read medical records, service records, and interpret medical diagnoses and opinions.[63] The rating specialists confer and recommend a rating decision on service-connection and degree of disability or entitlement to benefits such as pension or DIC. The file then goes to a fourth team that actually makes the written Rating Decision and sends it to the claimant together with a cover letter.[64]

Step Four: Initiating an Appeal

A disappointed claimant who has received an adverse Rating Decision has one year to send a written Notice of Disagreement (NOD) to the Regional Office.[65] A legally effective NOD must be in writing, dated and signed by the claimant and refer to the Rating Decision by date. The NOD should also show that claimant wishes to continue the appeal.[66] If the claimant does not file an NOD within one year from the date of the adverse Rating Decision, the decision becomes final and nonappealable.[67]

The Regional Office is obliged to send a chronological summary of the steps taken to develop a claim to a claimant who has filed a notice of disagreement. This document is called the Statement of the Case (SOC) and may contain additional adjudication by the Regional Office.[68]

A dissatisfied claimant must submit a substantive appeal on VA Form 9[69] to the Regional Office within 60 days after the date of the SOC or within one year from the date of the adverse rating decision, whichever is longer. If the claimant does not meet this deadline, the decision will become final and nonappealable.[70] The Regional Offices offer a claimant an alternative to an appeal to the BVA after issuance of the SOC: an informal meeting with a senior rating specialist known as the Decision Review Officer (DRO). The conference may include sworn testimony from the claimant and other witnesses. The DRO conference leads to a reevaluation by the DRO who then issues a Supplemental Statement of the Case (SSOC).[71]

Meanwhile, the RO can continue to accept evidence to develop the claim until the claimant's file is physically delivered to the Board of Veterans Appeals (BVA). The RO may even reverse itself and readjudicate a claim that was denied and grant benefits. Once the claim file leaves the RO to be delivered to the BVA, the RO can do nothing with respect to the claim until it is remanded to the RO for further action.[72]

Step Five: Board of Veterans Appeals

The BVA consists of 60 authorized veterans law judges appointed by the Secretary of Veterans Affairs.[73] The Chair of the Board is a Presidential appointee with no term limitation.[74] The governing statute for the BVA requires that an appeal be assigned to a single BVA Veterans Law Judge or to a panel of three judges for review.[75] The judges are divided into decision teams based on assignment to a number of geographically associated ROs from which cases arise. The decision teams do not provide support for one another when one team has a peak load.

When a claim file is transferred from the RO to the BVA, the BVA Director of Administrative Services dockets the appeal and assigns it to one of the decision teams, depending on geographic location. The case is then assigned to a single judge for hearing and review.

The claimant may choose to have an in-person Travel Board hearing at the Regional Office, a personal hearing in Washington, DC, at the BVA's headquarters, or she may waive an in-person hearing and proceed to adjudication.[76] Since 1998, a fourth choice has been available: a video-conference hearing on a remote connection from the Regional Office to the central office. This is considered to be a waiver of an in-person hearing by the VA.[77] The BVA schedules hearings within six months to a year from the date the claim file is received. The new video-conference hearings are usually the fastest track to a hearing.

A personal hearing before a single Veterans Law Judge is such that the Veterans Law judge informally introduces herself to the claimant and to the claimant's representative, if any. She explains the purpose for the hearing and asks who will be giving testimony under oath. When this introduction is completed, the Veterans Law Judge opens the formal hearing, swears all witnesses and then asks the claimant or the claimant's representative to make an opening statement.[78]

The claimant then gives a narrative statement or responds to questions put to the claimant by the claimant's representative, followed by questions from the bench. The claimant or claimant's representative may then make a brief closing statement and the hearing is closed. The Veterans Law Judge does not issue a decision from the bench. Instead, the judge waits for the transcription clerk to complete the transcript. The Board has its own in-house staff attorneys who are assigned as staff attorneys to the Decision Teams. The case is assigned to a staff attorney for review, who prepares a bench memo to the judge outlining the case and the merits of the claimant's appeal. The presumption is that the Regional Office correctly decided the case, placing the burden of persuasion on the claimant to demonstrate a mistake in the Regional Office's procedure or substantive fact finding and application of the law to the facts.[79]

The Judge refreshes his/her recollection of the case by reviewing the file and transcript and the bench memo. Then he/she reaches a decision and writes a formal Board decision disposing of the case. The Board review of a Regional Office decision usually takes about a year to complete. The Judge's choices are limited: he/she can remand the case to the Regional Office with instructions to the Regional Office to develop the claim further, he/she can affirm the Regional Office, and in rare cases, he/she can decide to service-connect the claimant, remanding the claim to the Regional Office to determine the degree of disability resulting from service-connection.[80]

BVA decisions were not reviewable in court under the Federal Administrative Procedures Act (5 U.S.C. § 701 et seq.),[81] or by any other statute until 1988. Congress passed the Veterans Judicial Review Act signed into law by President Reagan. An Article I Congressionally established court was set up to review BVA decisions under a series of legal constraints discussed below.[82]

Step Six: Appeal From the Board to the Court of Appeals for Veterans Claims

Since 1988, an unhappy claimant who received a negative decision or outcome from the Claims process is able to appeal to the U.S. Court of Appeals for Veterans Claims (CAVC, formerly known as the "U.S.

Court of Veterans Appeals"), the Article I court responsible for over-sight of BVA decisions. The Court consists of three to seven judges appointed by the President with the advice and consent of the Senate for a 15-year term.[83] The court's jurisdiction is limited to review of errors of law and to overturning a clearly erroneous finding of fact. It has no authority to make any findings of fact itself.[84]

A dissatisfied claimant starts an appeal by filing a Notice of Appeal (NOA) with the Clerk of Court. The NOA must be in writing, dated and signed by the claimant. It must reference the date of the BVA decision it is appealing. Although the Rules of Court provide a form to use for an NOA, any written document that meets these requirements will suffice.[85] The claimant has 120 days from the date stamped on the first page of the BVA decision to appeal to the Court from an adverse BVA decision. The claimant may also move the Chair of the BVA for reconsideration of the BVA decision during the same 120-day period.[86] The 120-day period will be tolled by a motion to reconsider until the Chair rules on the motion.[87] If denied, the claimant has 120 days from date of denial to file an NOA.[88] More than half of all appeals are filed by individual veterans or dependants without assistance from a lawyer.[89]

When a claimant is represented by an attorney, the claimant's attorney must file the NOA accompanied by a copy of the retainer agreement between attorney and client, and an appearance notice sent to the VA's Office of General Counsel, Appellate Litigation Group 027 (027 Group). A claimant filing on his own is also supposed to send a copy of the NOA to the 027 Group, but failure to do so will not result in dismissal of the appeal.[90]

Step Seven: Appellate Process Before the Court of Appeals for Veterans Claims

The Secretary must send a designation of the record to the appellant within 60 days from the date the claimant files the NOA.[91] The claimant has 30 days to agree or to disagree with the Secretary's designation of record.[92] The claimant can propose adding other documents contained in the claim file to the record, a proposal which the Secretary may agree to or oppose. In any case, once a record has been settled on, the record is recopied with Bates numbers overprinted on the individual pages and resent to the claimant as the Record before the Agency for the appeal.

According to Court rule, the appellant must file his/her principal brief within 60 days from the date of the filing of the record with the court.[93] Assuming that the appellant does not ask for an extension, and files on or before the 60th day, the Secretary has 60 days from the date of filing of the appellant's brief to submit his/her brief.[94] Once the Secretary's brief has been filed, the appellant has 14 days to file a short 10-page reply.[95]

The case is then submitted to the Court. The Clerk's staff assigns the case to a single judge for review. The single judge may choose to decide the case alone if it involves well-settled principles of law. If the case presents novel questions of law, the single judge may submit the case to a panel of three judges for review and decision. Since the Court rarely grants oral argument to the litigants, the Court panels meet and decide the cases without formal oral argument. The three judges vote on the case, and one judge is assigned to write the opinion. The written opinion is then circulated to the panel for comments and revisions. If and when the opinion is deemed acceptable, it is published and the Court issues its order affirming the Board, reversing the Board or most often, reversing the Board and remanding the case to the Board with instructions.[96]

This process takes more than a year from start to finish. According to the Court's own annual report for 2007, the average time from filing to disposition was 416 days, up from 2006 by 65 days.[97]

The party who loses before the CAVC may appeal that decision or move for a rehearing or rehearing before the full court. A motion for rehearing or rehearing before the full court must be filed within 21 days of the date of the order or decision.[98] When the time for filing a motion for rehearing has passed, the CAVC issues its judgment, and several days later its mandate.

An appeal to the U.S. Court of Appeals for the Federal Circuit must be filed within 60 days of the date of mandate.[99] Although a number of cases are appealed to the Federal Circuit each year, this article is not concerned with delay or efficiency before that Court or the U.S. Supreme Court.

A SYSTEMATIC VIEW OF THE VA CLAIMS PROCESS

The objective of the VA claims process is to move a claim from point of origin to destination in the most efficient manner. Unfortunately, the VA system suffers from a number of built-in procedural "choke points" that clog the system and impede progress. Unlike a traditional highway system, the VA system does not have one universally agreed-on destination. Although the VA claim system is "supposed to be a nonadversarial, ex parte, paternalistic system, that is uniquely pro-claimant,"[100] there are conflicting goals buried within the system itself that seem antiquated during a time when medical and compensation claims and case files are electronic and move quickly through the internet-based media.

To achieve this, there are three goals for the claims process. These goals are to (1) reduce fraud against the U.S. Treasury; (2) compensate veterans; and (3) promoting efficiency through the claims process.[101]

Guarding the Federal Treasury From Fraud

The VA requires sufficient documentary and testimonial evidence to show that it is as likely as not that the veteran has a payable claim. That is why witnesses before the Board and at DRO Conferences are sworn to tell the truth. That is why a claim not supported by documentary entry of an in-service injury or disease, with certain exceptions for chronic diseases, must be corroborated by sworn or unsworn statements from service members who recalled the event.

The burden of proof is on the veteran to establish the five elements of a claim. A VA claimant can succeed if the claimant establishes that it is as likely as not that the elements of a claim are proved.[102] This is less burdensome than showing the elements of the claim are proved by a preponderance of the evidence, as in civil litigation.

Some researchers have called for a self-reporting system similar to that of the IRS. The claimant should be allowed to make a claim that will be deemed valid and benefits will be paid to the claimant, subject to a later audit to determine fraud or legal baselessness.[103] The problem with this proposal is that it will hinder the prevention of fraudulent or frivolous claims at the expense of speeding up the process.[104]

The VA receives many frivolous claims and some fraudulent claims that have no legal merit.[105] A self-reporting system would not discourage frivolous claims. It would require the United States to pay frivolous claims until such time as a retrospectant audit of the claim is undertaken that demonstrates the legal baselessness of the claim. At this writing, it is impossible to determine the risk of paying on fraudulent or frivolous claims filed under a self-reporting system. Since the risk cannot be estimated empirically, one may be very wary of the proposed self-reporting compensation system.

Compensating a Veteran for Service-Connected Disorders and Awarding DIC or Pension Benefits

The second goal of the VA system is to award benefits to those men and women entitled to compensation or pension based on the law and the facts applied to the case. Critics of the VA system often ignore or forget that most claims are adjudicated at the Regional Office level without any appeal.[106] Less than one out of six Regional Office decisions are appealed to the Board. The VA Inspector General gathered up all the annual reports to Congress and other data submitted prior to 1997 and summarized it in its annual report to the Undersecretary for Benefits. According to this report, the average processing time for an initial disability compensation claim was around five months. Claims for additional diagnoses and increases wait an average of four months for adjudication. If a veteran took an appeal to the Board of Veterans Appeals, the average processing time for the claim on appeal was 36 months.[107] Later data show that the processing time for initial claims, claims for increases, and claims appealed to the Board of Veterans Appeals is much greater than was the case in 1997. In the fiscal year 2008, the average time for adjudication of an initial claim was 179 days.[108] There remains an irreducible 10–18% of all claims filed that are not settled to the satisfaction of all parties at the Regional Office. These are the hard cases, usually involving latent conditions, lost or destroyed records, and other complications. Some of the claimants are not eligible for compensation under current law. The claimant cannot prove one of the four elements for service-connection or DIC benefits. Others require difficult searches for evidence that may include declassification of reports. Other claims have frankly been fouled up by the claimant, a lay person who does not understand the law. These are the kinds of cases that the Widener Veterans Law Clinic encounters.

Claim Processing Efficiency

The present system is built upon the Pension Act of 1863 as remodeled by the Veterans Administration Act of 1930 and later amendments to Title 38 U.S. Code. The assignment of burden of proof to the claimant is part of that inefficiency. The development of a claim that requires accumulation of military, VA, and other federal and private records before anyone reviews the claim for decision is also part of that inefficiency. The requirement of a notification letter to the claimant allocating the burden of production of evidence to the claimant and to the VA before a decision is made is part of that inefficiency.[109] The requirement that a physician review all medical records to make a determination whether or not the veteran has the disorder claimed in the claim and determining the degree of impairment also impedes efficiency.

On the other hand, a system that rewarded perfectly healthy veterans with compensation based on self-serving declarations on a claim form without verifying the conditions asserted as service connected would be unjust and indefensible. The proposal to make the VA compensation system a "self-reporting" system like the annual income tax return has some appeal in respect to efficiency goals.[110] It does not meet the criteria for protecting the Treasury, since a fraudulent claim would be automatically payable until the VA conducts an audit at random and discovers the fraudulent payments. Recovering funds paid out on a fraudulent claim will prove as difficult as collecting a delinquent student loan. First, debts owed the U.S. Department of Veterans Affairs for claims improperly paid would have to be made nondischargeable in bankruptcy. Payments from other government agencies such as Social Security Administration benefits would have to be made subject to an off-set against a VA claim fraudulently paid out. Third, a system of objection to termination of payments with notice, hearing, and right of appeal would have to be built into Title 38 U.S. Code, and the Veterans Affairs Department would be required to make regulations for terminating such payments and appealing termination. Termination of public benefits is subject to Fifth Amendment Due Process protection as determined 37 years ago by *Goldberg v. Kelly,* [111] which was reaffirmed in *Matthews v. Eldridge.*[112] Any efficiency gained in the initial award of benefits under this proposal would be temporary, followed by a long-drawn out adjudication process when fraud or mistake is involved in the initial award of benefits.[113]

The front-end improvements that the automatic payment approach supports are counterbalanced by rear-end costs for audits, overpayment assessments, and a right to a hearing before the assessment is imposed. The proposed automatic system is not a good solution to the VA's problems.

A Systems Evaluation of the Process

VA claimants do not understand why it takes so long for their claims to be adjudicated favorably. Many veterans fail to understand the need to prove a claim. They are insulted when the VA denies their claim for want of proof of one of the elements of the claim. Veterans believe the

VA should take their word on faith and if not, the VA is accusing the veteran of dishonesty. Veterans who have service-incurred injuries or diseases that are disabling have an entitlement to benefits, that is, the right to establish the grounds for compensation or other benefits from the evidence. If the veteran cannot prove a claim, the entitlement ceases.

A Systems Evaluation: Eliminating the Choke Points

The system described above has some readily identifiable waste motion and four "choke points" that are the product of the difficulty involved in proving a claim. First, there is the *Development Phase* (*Acquiring Federal Records for Review*). During this phase, the Regional Office is under a regulatory duty to obtain records from sister federal agencies pertaining to a veteran's case.[114] The Regional Office must depend on the goodwill of sister federal agencies for the documents necessary to establish a compensation or DIC claim. The veteran's military service records are held by the National Archives in St. Louis, MO, as custodian for the military services of retired service records. The Social Security Administration, Office of Personnel Management and Railroad Retirement Board also hold important medical records affecting many veterans' claims. These agencies often do not reply to requests for copies of records pertaining to a veteran, even though the records are intact and stored in an archive under agency control.

The VA usually sends two requests for copies of records and gives up when the sister agency fails to send requested records.[115] This often works an injustice on veterans who proved disability retirement cases or Social Security disability entitlement for the same condition they now seek VA compensation for. The National Archives will respond to requests for records. It usually takes the overburdened archivists in St Louis six months or more to locate the records requested, copy the records, and send the copies to the regional office.

The development of a VA claim may be frustrated by the actions of employees of sister federal agencies who do not see copying records for the VA as part of their job description. Title 38's sections on duty to assist should be matched by complementary statutes that require the Social Security Administration, the Railroad Retirement Board, and other federal agencies to assist the VA in developing claims by prompt copying and submission of records requested by the VA.

The second phase is identified as the Adjudication Phase (*Waiting for Godot*), in which the VA's internal regulations provide for a rating board in each of the 58 regional offices in order to adjudicate claims. The rating board consists of at least three specialists. Rating individual claims has been delegated to a single specialist in most regional offices. When a claim is received it is reviewed by the triage team. It sends the remaining claims to the development team that obtains the claimant's service medical records and other supporting data. That team in turn sends the developed claim to the Rating Board that makes the rating decision. The rating decision is then written up by a fourth team. This four team system was devised by the VA to make the claim adjudication process more efficient. Discretionary review at the request of the claimant by a Decision Review Officer is like a check on false-negative decisions of the individual rater.[116]

The one-year limitation within which to file a Notice of Disagreement is from the Pension Act of 1873 and was ratified in 1962 by an amendment to Title 38. As such, this limitation is what informs the third phase in the Appeal (*The NOD, Statement of the Case & Substantive Appeal*). During this phase, Title 38 U.S. Code section 7105[117] requires that the regional office issue a rating decision, wait for an NOD to be filed within one year, then print and send a Statement of the Case to the claimant that must be perfected by a substantive appeal within 60 days from the date of the Statement of the Case, or one year from the date of the original Rating Decision. This section was added in 1962.[118] The 1962 amendments were adopted to afford a claimant who disagreed with a rating decision a due process notice of the process by which the decision was made.

Prior to 1962, a negative Rating Decision was little more than a conclusion that the claimant receive nothing.[119] In 2008, however, it is an anachronism that could be improved by shortening the one-year period for filing an NOD to a shorter period,* *from date of adverse Rating Decision. In fact, the present two-step process outlined in 38 U.S.C. § 7105 could be collapsed into a single step, as this very cumbersome two-step process is a built-in delay factor in claims adjudication. It would not prejudice claimants or the VA to add to the Rating Decision a summary of the steps taken to prove the claim that normally appears in the Statement of the Case. The claimant would then be obliged to file a Notice of Appeal either by mail, in person or online using the VA's current online filing capability. The VA has permitted original claims to be filed online for several years.*[120]

An online Notice of Appeal could be filed as readily and transmitted to the regional office. The Rating Decision could carry the

---

*Say 60–90 days.

same information now included in the Statement of the Case and one Notice of Appeal could replace the NOD and Form 9.

The final phase is the Deadlines. Even if these choke points were eliminated, the VA claims adjudication process would not move much more rapidly than it does today. Since title 38 U.S. Code has set no deadlines for the RO to act on a claim, and the claimant has no recourse when the RO fails to act on a pending claim for years. If the RO was compelled to grant or deny a claim within six months of date of receipt, the claims process would be sped up. An escape valve for delay due to good cause would be required in such a time limit.

The BVA also has no deadline for issuing decisions, and a claimant who takes an appeal to the BVA has no way to compel the BVA's Veterans Law Judge to act on a pending appeal. Congress provided no deadlines for BVA decision-making. Claimants may pursue a writ petition before the CAVC under the All-Writs Act when the BVA or the RO sit on a remanded claim for a period of more than two years without taking action.[121] A claimant may force a sluggish RO or BVA to act on a claim, but the usual result is a denial of the claim.[122]

Congress needs to redesign the VA compensation and pension process such that the VA has to adhere to deadlines established by a specific Act of Congress when adjudicating claims. Congress also needs to redesign the VA's development and adjudication process. Under the current system the VA is a paper tiger that cannot compel a sister agency to release vital information necessary to prove a claim. Under the current system, VA physicians who give compensation and pension examinations are not available for a Decision Review Conference or for a BVA hearing, nor can these individuals be deposed for purposes of furnishing accurate testimony at an upcoming hearing. Neither the claimant nor the VA has the right of compulsory process. As a result, claims development suffers from a lack of critical evidence necessary to prove the claim, evidence that is under the control of and in the hands of the United States.

CONCLUSION

Adopting the procedural reforms suggested in this article will not cure all the problems associated with the VA claims process. One should not expect a miracle. Eliminating obvious choke points in the claims process will not increase delay in deciding claims. Making the VA adhere to a system of time limits for decision and granting claimants compulsory process and deposition rights before the BVA will help to make the claims process function efficiently and fairly.

NOTES

1. See, for example, Government Accountability Office Report GAO-08-473T, *Veterans' Disability Benefits: Claims Processing Challenges Persist, while VA Continues to Take Steps to Address Them* (2008); Linda A. Bilmes, *Soldiers Returning from Iraq and Afghanistan: The Long-term Costs of Providing Veterans Medical Care and Disability Benefits* (2007); Veterans Disability Benefits Comm'n, *Honoring the Call to Duty: Veterans' Disability Benefits in the 21st Century* (Prerelease version, Oct. 2007).
2. See Press Release House Veterans Affairs Committee May 23, 2007 downloaded from http://veterans.house.giv/news/PRArticle.aspx?NewsID= 97 downloaded Aug. 12, 2008. See also House Committee on Veterans Affairs Oversight Plan for 110th Congress referencing review of VA compensation system, downloaded from http://veterans.house.gov/about/plan110.shtml. on Aug. 12, 2008.
3. See the remarks of Prof. Linda Bilmes, John F. Kennedy School of Government from her testimony given originally on March 13, 2007, and repeated at the round table, downloaded from http://www.ksg.harvard.edu/ksgnews/OntheHill/2007/Bilmes_031307.html on May 23, 2007.
4. See description of Veterans Affairs Veterans Benefits Administration at www:va.gov.
5. Dept. of Veterans Affairs Office of the Actuary, Policy Planning & Preparadeness, *Table 2L Veterans by State, Period, Age Group Gender 2000–2003* http://www1.va.gov/vetdata/page.cfm?pg=2 downloaded May 18, 2007 (hereafter "Table 2L").
6. U.S. Dept. of Veterans Affairs, Fact Sheet America's Wars, Nov. 2006, downloaded from http://www1.va.gov./opafact/amwas.asp. May 19, 2007 (hereafter "VA Fact Sheet 2006"). VA Adjudications Procedures Manual M21-1 § 1.07 (2008) (hereafter "M21-1").
7. Table 2L. According to *VA Fact Sheet 2006* 16,112,556 men and women served in World War II. 291,557 men and women died in battle, 113,842 died from noncombat causes. In all, 671,846 men and women were wounded but survived. Totally, 10.4 million men and women served in the U.S. Army (including the USAAF) during 1941–1945. The Army suffered 936,000 battle casualties and 83,400 nonbattle casualties, including 236,000 dead.
8. According to the *VA Fact Sheet 2006* 232,745 surviving spouses and 15,636 dependent children, and 227 dependent parents of World War II veterans were receiving VA compensation in Sept. 2006.
9. The National Archives and Records Administration is the custodian of all military service records for all U.S. veterans. Records for Revolutionary

War, Civil War, and Spanish American War veterans are kept in the National Archives in Washington. More recent records are stored in the National Archives warehouse complex in St Louis. The 1973 fire at the National Archives warehouse damaged or destroyed nearly all World War I Army records, most World War II records, and Korean War Army records, as well as the last half of U.S. Air Force service records for the Korean period. Navy, Marine Corps, and Coast Guard records were not affected by the fire.

10. *VA Fact Sheet 2006.* 5,720,000 men and women served between 1950 and 1955. Totally, 33,741 died in battle, 103,284 were wounded. *VA Fact Sheet 2006. Id.* The actual number for 2003 was 3,151,481. 2,821,966 men and women served in World War II only; 99,227 who served in the Korean Conflict and Vietnam as well as World War II, and 229,496 who served in the Korean Conflict and World War II.

11. *VA Fact Sheet 2006.* The VA's 2003 estimate was 3,086,149 living veterans of the Korean War. This includes 229,496 men and women who also served in World War II and 220,717 men and women who served in Vietnam. In all, 3243 children, 419 parents, and 61,423 surviving spouses of Korean War veterans were receiving compensation in Sept. 2006.

12. *Id.* The actual number is 2,538,348 who served from 1953 to 1963, and 155,594 who serve from 1945 to 1950 before the start of the Korean War.

13. *Id.* The official reported number was 8,744,000.

14. *Table 2L.* This group consists of 7,286,528 who served during the Vietnam era, 220,717 who also served in the Korean War, and 99,277 who served in World War II and Korea.

15. For a detailed history of Agent Orange litigation up to 1987 see In re Agent Orange Product Liability Litigation, 821 F.2d 139 (2nd Cir. 1987). For an explanation of Boyle's law that protected government contractors from liability to injured service members, see Anthony DiSarro, *Boyle's Law and Agent Orange Litigation,* 238 N.Y. Law J. No. 111 June 10, 2008.

16. See, for example, description of Post Traumatic Stress Disorder on MedicineNet http://www.medicinenet.com/posttraumatic_stress_disorder/article.htm downloaded Aug. 12, 2008.

17. *VA Fact Sheet 2006.* The VA is paying compensation to 9819 children, 3614 parents, and 151,507 surviving spouses of Vietnam era veterans.

18. *Id.* This group has 3,447,955 surviving members.

19. *Id.* The official number was 2,322,000. Overall, 694,500 men and women were deployed to the Persian Gulf, 147 died in battle and 467 were wounded.

20. *Id.* 4,646,527 men and women were in this group as of 2003. In total, 4,297,284 served only during the 1990–1991 conflict; the remainder included 342,899 who had service in the Vietnam era, 5552 who also served in the Korean War, and 792 who were World War II veterans.

21. See, for example, *Frontline, Last Battle of the Gulf War* http://www.pbs.org/wgbh/pages/frontline/shows/syndrome/published Jan. 1998; see also *Merck Manual, Gulf War Syndrome* http://www.merck.com/mmhe/sec25/ch306/ch306c.html downloaded Oct. 25, 2008.

22. *VA Fact Sheet 2006.* In all, 1,384,968 men and women have served since September 11, 2001. Overall, 165,000 have been deployed to Afghanistan or Iraq. Totally, 2333 died in battle, and 21,649 wounded survived. The VA's estimate of living veterans is 588,923.

23. See, for example, Michael Phillips, Sharing war stories to ward off trauma, *Wall Street Journal,* Apr. 12, 2003, downloaded from http://www. tgorski.com/Terrorism/ptsd_operation_iraqi_freedom_030412.htm Oct. 25, 2008.

24. See, for example, MSG Colleen McGee, Reservists *Deal with Homecoming Stress,* Air Force Reservist Nov. 29, 2006 downloaded http://www.afrc. af.mil/news/story.asp?id=123033219 Nov. 2, 2008; Mental illnesses appear common among veterans returning from Iraq and Afghanistan *ScienceDaily* (Mar. 13, 2007) downloaded http://www.sciencedaily.com/ releases/2007/03/070313114409.htm 2 Nov. 2008.

25. 38 U.S.C. § 1110 (2008) (veterans in time of war), 38 U.S.C. § 1113 (2008) (veterans not in time of war).

26. 38 U.S.C. § 5107 (2008).

27. This standard is usually referred to as the "reasonable doubt" standard and is explained by 38 C.F.R. § 3.102 (2008). See also the discussion of the burden or proof in *Ortiz v. Principi,* 274 F.3d 1361, 1364–1366 (Fed. Cir. 2001) and *Gilbert v. Derwinski,* 1 Vet. App. 49, 54–55 (1990).

28. 38 U.S.C. § 1111 (2008).

29. See *Gilbert v. Derwinski,* 1 Vet. App. 49, 54 (1990).

30. This requirement is a judge-made rule construing provisions of Title 38 U.S.C. §§ 1110 (award of compensation in time of war), 1112 (award of compensation not in time of war) and 7261 (clearly erroneous rule). See, for example, *Cotant v. Principi,* 17 Vet. App. 116, 132–133 (2003); *Hickson v. West,* 12 Vet. App. 247, 252 (1999); *Hicks v. West,* 12 Vet. App. 86, 89 (1998); Barton F. Stichman and Ronald B. Abrams, eds., *Veterans Benefits Manual* § 3.1.5 (2007) (hereafter "Veterans Benefits Manual").

31. See 38 C.F.R. § 4.16 (2008). The VA requires a special claim form, Form VA 21–8940.

32. See 38 U.S.C. § 1114 (k) (2008).

33. 38 U.S.C. §§ 3901–02 (2008).

34. See 38 U.S.C. §§ 2101(a) and 2102(a) (2008). Congress added this benefit for service members on active duty in 2006. See Pub. L. No. 109–233, 120 Stat. 397 (June 15, 2006).

35. 38 U.S.C. § 1521 (2008).

36. The Department of Veterans Affairs requires a veteran to prove several elements to be eligible for pension set out in 38 U.S.C. § 1521(j) and in 38 C.F.R.§ 3.3:

    1. Satisfactory military service under "other than dishonorable conditions" (see 38 U.S.C. § 101(2); 38 C.F.R. § 3.12(a) (2008) for determination of character of discharge).

2. Proof that the veteran served at least 24 months' active duty or the full period for which the veteran was called to active duty, whichever is least. This period of active service must include one of the following criteria as well:

   (a) at least 90 days' service during one or more periods of war as defined by 38 U.S.C. § 1101;

   (b) 90 or more consecutive days, one of which is during a period of war; or

   (c) one or more days of wartime service that was terminated by a discharge for service-connected disability;

3. Veterans whose first enlistment was earlier than September 8, 1980, do not have to meet this standard limited income and net worth that does not provide adequate maintenance (the "need test") asset out in 38 U.S.C. § 1522.

37. The current pension benefit payable to a veteran is determined by a complex formula that ensures the disabled warrior does not receive anything like enough to live on from the Veterans Affairs Department (describe formula with reference to Vets Benefits Manual).

38. 38 C.F.R. § 3.23(d)(4) (2008).

39. The pension system shares this peculiar quirk with AFDC and other programs using countable income from both spouses to off-set benefits, but not income from a "companion."

40. The steps involved in annualization of income are theoretically simple, but can be very difficult in the case of an individual veteran with a very diffuse income history. First, the VA establishes the maximum pension benefit payable to the veteran depending in number of dependents, living situation (i.e., housebound or not housebound) and need for special assistance. This is called the maximum annual pension rate (MAPR). In step two, the VA deducts from the MAPR all the countable income available from all other sources (i.e., Social Security, retirement, spousal earnings, etc. (IVAP). The amount derived from this subtraction exercise is then divided by 12 to give the monthly pension rate for the veteran, exclusive from the MAPR. That amount is divided by 12 to calculate the monthly pension payment rate payable to the veteran. Note that both entitlement and income for dependents are involved in this calculation. A veteran with a dependent spouse has a MAPR of the base rate plus $3256 for the spouse. If the spouse has earnings, the earnings are included in the IVAP and deducted from the MAPR. The result may be that the spouse's income outweighs the stipend payable for a dependent spouse.

41. See, for example, *Valiao v. Principi*, 17 Vet. App. 229 (2003); 38 U.S.C. § 101(14) (2008); 38 C.F.R. § 3.5(a) (2008). Benefits under 38 U.S.C. § 1151 may also be paid when treatment results in a foreseeable bad result that was not disclosed to the veteran prior to securing the veteran's agreement to the treatment procedures. This is known as "lack of informed consent."

42. 38 U.S.C. § 1318 (2008).
43. See *Veterans Benefits Manual* §§ 7.7.5.1 through 7.7.5.3 (2008).
44. 38 U.S.C. § 1151 (2008).
45. *Stoner v. Brown*, 5 Vet. App. 488 (1993). See also 38 U.S.C. § 1151 (2008); 38 C.F.R. § 3.358 (2008).
46. 38 U.S.C. § 1151 (2008); 38 C.F.R. § 3.358 (2008).
47. 38 U.S.C. § 1151(a) (2008).
48. *Cottle v. Brown*, 14 Vet. App. 329 (2001).
49. See Veterans Benefits Report Fiscal 2008 at http://www1.va.gov/vetdata/docs/4X6_summer08_sharepoint.pdf for the information on benefits and types of claims. See also geographic distribution of VA Expenditures for Fiscal Year 2007 at http://www.vba.va.gov/reports/abr/2006_abr.pdf.
50. Defined as "any individual applying for, or submitting a claim for, any benefits under the laws administered by the Secretary." 38 U.S.C. 5100 (2008).
51. 38 U.S.C. § 5101(a) (2008) provides that a claim "must be filed in order for benefits to be paid or furnished to any individual under the laws administered by the Secretary."
52. See, for example, *Mitscher v. West*, 13 Vet. App. 123, 127 (1999); 38 C.F.R. § 3.155(a) (2008).
53. *Performance and Accountability Report Fiscal 2007* at 8 (Performance Scorecard) (hereafter "PAR"). See also Key Measures at 144.
54. PAR Table I at 221.
55. PAR Scorecard at 8.
56. 38 U.S.C. § 5103A (2008).
57. 38 C.F.R.§ 3.159(c)(3) (2008).
58. 38 U.S.C. § 5103(c) (2008); 38 C.F.R. § 3.159(c)(2) (2008).
59. 38 U.S.C. § 5103(c) (2008); 38 C.F.R. § 3.159(c)(1) (2008).
60. 38 U.S.C. § 5103A(d) (2008).
61. 38 C.F.R. § 3.159(c)(4) (2008).
62. *Veterans Benefits Manual* §12.6.6.1 and 2 (2008).
63. *Id*.
64. *Veterans Benefits Manual* § 12.6.2.2.1 through 6.5 (2008).
65. 38 U.S.C. § 7105(b)(1) (2008); 38 C.F.R. § 20.201 (2008).
66. 38 U.S.C. § 7105(b)(1) (2008).
67. 38 U.S.C. § 7105(c) (2008).
68. 38 U.S.C. § 7105(d) (2008).
69. 38 U.S.C. § 7105(a) (2008); see also 38 C.F.R. § 20.202 (2008).
70. 38 U.S.C. § 7105(d)(3) (2008); 38 C.F.R. § 20.202 (Rule 202); 20.302(b)(1) (2008).
71. See 38 C.F.R. § 3.2600 (2008).
72. See 38 U.S.C. § 7104.
73. *Annual Report of the Chair of the Board of Veterans Appeals 2008* at 3 (here after "2008 BVA Report").
74. 38 U.S.C. § 7101A(a)(1) (2008).
75. 38 U.S.C. § 7102 (2008).

76. 38 U.S.C. § 7107(d) (2008); *Veterans Benefits Manual* § 13.1.2, 13.3 (2008).
77. 38 U.S.C. § 7107(e)(1) (2008); *Veterans Benefits Manual* § 13.7 (2008).
78. For a description of the hearing see *Veterans Benefits Manual* § 13.3.3 (2008). In fiscal year 2008, the 60 Veterans Law Judges held 10,652 personal hearings, an average of 178 hearings per judge. *2008 BVA Report* at 3.
79. *Veterans Benefits Manual* § 13.9.1 (2008).
80. *Id.*
81. P.L. 71–536 ch. 863, § 1, 46 Stat. 1016 (1930); Economy Act, Ch. 214, § 401–08, 47 Stat. 382 (1932); *Johnson v. Robison*, 415 U.S. 361, 94 S.Ct. 1160 (1974) (narrow exception for constitutional issues found by court).
82. P.L. 100–687, 102 Stat. 4105 (1988) codified under title 38 U.S.C. § 7251–99 (2008).
83. 38 U.S.C. § 7253 (a) (2008).
84. 38 U.S.C. § 7252 (2008).
85. 38 U.S.C. § 7266 (2008). See also U.S. Ct. App. Vet. Cl. R. 3 and Form 1.
86. 38 U.S.C. § 7266(a) (2008).
87. A judge-made rule construing "final decision of the Board of Veterans Appeals" in 38 U.S.C. § 7266(a) to mean that a timely filing of a motion to reconsider within 120 days of date of original decision keeps the Board decision from becoming final until the Chair rules on the motion. *Rosler v. Derwinski*, 1 Vet. App. 241 (1991). See also 38 C.F.R. § 20.1000 to 1003 (2008) (Procedure on Motion to Reconsider).
88. Rosler, 1 Vet. App. 249.
89. *U.S. Ct. of Appeals for Veterans Claims Annual Report for 2006*. The percent varied from 73% pro se in 1997 to a low of 58% in 2002 and 2005.
90. U.S. Ct. App. Vet. Cl. R. 3(c).
91. U.S. Ct. App.Vet. Cl. R. 10(a).
92. U.S. Ct. App. Vet. Cl. R. 10(b).
93. U.S. Ct. App. Vet. Cl. R. 31(a).
94. *Id.*
95. *Id.*
96. *Veterans Benefits Manual* § 15.4.4 (2008).
97. *Annual Report of the United States Court of Appeals for Veterans Claims* (2007) downloaded from http://www.vetapp.uscourts.gov/annual_report/8 Aug. 2008.
98. U.S. Ct. App. Vet. Cl. R. 35(d).
99. 38 U.S.C. § 7292 (2008).
100. *Collaro v. West*, 136 F.3d 1304, 1309 (Fed. Cir. 1998).
101. For example, in 2005, the VA Inspector General reported to the Secretary that some veterans had obtained PTSD benefits by fraud on the VA. The Secretary ordered a review of 72,000 claim files for veterans receiving benefits for PTSD to check out whether the documentation supporting PTSD was full and complete. Thanks to pressure from the veterans service organizations, the Secretary called off the review in November 2005. *Veterans Benefits Manual* § 3.6.2 (2008) (Advocacy Tip).
102. *Gilbert v. Derwinski*, 1 Vet. App. 49, 54 (1990); 38 U.S.C. § 5107(b) (2008).

103. Dr. Linda Bilmes of the John F. Kennedy School of Government is the principal advocate for this system. She describes the self-reporting claims process in detail in her position paper before the House Veterans Affairs Committee. See Linda A. Bilmes, *Soldiers Returning from Iraq and Afghanistan: The Long-term Costs of Providing Veterans Medical Care and Disability Benefits* (2007) a report issued by the John F. Kennedy School of Government.

104. This fear is aroused by recommendations such as those put forth by the Dole–Shalala Commission. (See Serve, Support Simplify: the Report of the President's Commission on Care for American's returning Wounded Warriors, Recommendation 2 at 6–7 at (2007)) and Dr. Linda Bilmes, who proposes a self-reporting compensation system similar to the self-reporting system for individual income tax assessment. See Linda Bilmes, *Soldies Returning from Iraq and Afghanistan: The Long-term Costs of Providing Veterans Medical Care and Disability Benefits* (2006) and Linda Bilmes, *Testimony before the House Committee on Veterans Affairs*, Mar. 13, 2007 downloaded from Bilmes website, Kennedy School of Government, Harvard University.

105. The VA publishes no statistics on the number of fraudulent or frivolous claims filed each year.

106. See Statement of Daniel L. Cooper Undersecretary for Benefits Department of Veterans Affairs Before the House Appropriations Subcommittee on Military Construction, Veterans Affairs, and Related Agencies, March 13, 2007 downloaded from http://www.va.gov/OCA/testimony/hac/smqlva/07031320.asp 1 Nov. 2008.

107. Report of the Inspector General of the Department of Veterans Affairs to the Undersecretary for Benefits at 1 (1997).

108. Dept. of Veterans Affairs, Performance and Accountability Report FY 2008 at 118 (2008) (hereafter "PAR2008"). The average time was 183 days in 2007. See also Veterans Disability Benefits Comm'n, Honoring the Call to Duty: Veterans Disability Benefits in the 21st Century, at 306 Figure 9.01 (2007) The VA does not report the characteristics such as standard deviation and outcomes of adjudication that would allow an analyst to make some judgments about the claim process at the Regional Office Level.

109. See 8 U.S.C. § 5103(a) (2008).

110. Dr. Bilmes proposed a "self-reporting" system in some respects similar to the Income Tax return system. The veteran files a single document stating that the veteran is disabled and lists the diagnoses for the disabling conditions. Compensation would be automatically paid to the veteran at the maximum rate available for the listed conditions. The VA could challenge an "automatic rating" and require the veteran to prove the claim at that time. See n. 135 supra.

111. 397 U.S. 254,262–63 (1970) (held: welfare benefits are "property rights" that could not be terminated without a meaningful prior hearing.

112. 424 U.S. 319,333–34 (1976).

113. For a good description of this process see Karen M. Streisfeld, *Note: The Denial of Due Process: The Unrecognized Right to an Attorney for Jeopardy Assessed Taxpayers*, 75 Cornell L. Rev. 1426 (1990). See also Leslie Book, *The Collection Due Process Rights: A Misstep or a Step in the Right Direction?* 41 Hous. L. Rev. 1145 (2004) (describing post 2002 reforms in tax collection process raising due process concerns).
114. M21-1 Part II ¶ 1.02 (e) (2008).
115. See M 21-1 Part II ¶' 1.02 (e)(3) and (5).
116. See 38 C.F.R. § 3.2600 (2008) for the rules pertaining to Decision Review Officer review of adjudicated claims.
117. 38 U.S.C. § 7105 (2008).
118. Sept. 19, 1962, P. L. 87–666, § 1, 76 Stat. 553.
119. See, for example, the 1945 Rating Decision in the case of Peter J. Mozzo (now deceased) in the author's possession.
120. The VONAP program for electronic application is described on the VA website at http://vabenefits.vba.va.gov/vonapp/main.asp.
121. See *Erspamer v. Derwinski*, 1 Vet. App. 3, 9 (1990). The Court established a two pronged test for obtaining a writ to compel adjudication of a long-delayed claim: (1) whether his entitlement to the writ is clear and indisputable, and (2) whether he lacks an alternative means to obtain the relief sought. See also *Herrman v. Brown*, 8 Vet. App. 60, 62 (1995); *Veterans Benefits Manual* § 15.2.7 n. 178.
122. *Veterans Benefits Manual* § 15.2.7.

REFERENCE

Sayer, N. A., Spoont, M., & Nelson, D. B. (2005). Post-traumatic stress disorder claims from the viewpoint of veterans service officers. *Military Medicine, 170*(10), 867.

Epilogue

Meeting the Need and Respecting the Voice: Our Final Words

Diann Cameron Kelly, David Gitelson,
Sydney Howe-Barksdale, and William Valente

I just want to be normal.

A Young Male Veteran of OIF to His Social
Worker Two Years Posttransition

When we embarked on this journey to bring the issues of veterans to the public, we wanted it to be a labor of service and honor to our veterans. The contributors enthusiastically provided their research and observations to this endeavor, and the reviewers (scholars whose research is committed to the well-being of veterans) gave everything they could to ensure this work met expectations to affect the well-being of veterans. But it was ourselves who were greatly affected.

Through the course of our editorial journey, we understood even more the depths of the sacrifices made by veterans and their families. However, there is so much more that we began to learn—especially that the toll of war is everlasting on the veterans, their spouses, their children, and their communities. When veterans are removed from our communities, we lose social capital and cultural capital. You cannot quantify this in dollars and cents. Institutional memory revolving around their civilian jobs is also lost. But, what is lost even more is social connectedness.

It is hard to call a man or woman our national pride or joy and ignore that when they return to us as civilians—the "man" or "woman" they knew or thought they knew cognitively and spiritually changed on the battlefield and another individual emerged from transition. They now speak a language that is indiscernible to the average citizen. They walk the perpetual path of loss and suffering, which is incomprehensible to the average citizen and entertainment industry that seeks to exploit their services. These individuals have memories locked away and stored on some dark side of the moon that, as Edgar Allen Poe says, are never shown to anyone.

More than 40 years ago, men and women returned from Vietnam and our response was limited because we did not know or understand the gravity of their needs. Now, we know too much. Knowing what we know about the needs of returning servicemen and servicewomen and how these needs differ between the active and reserve components, no veteran should be lost to us. What do we mean by lost?

We should know before a veteran returns home whether there is a propensity for addiction and/or suicide. We should know before a veteran returns home whether their family life is stable and secure to ensure against homelessness, divorce, or loss of child custody. We should know before a veteran returns home whether their community can support them in their old job or they need retraining to ensure gainful employment with significant earnings potential. We should know before a veteran returns home whether they are self-destructive or socially impaired, thereby placing themselves and others at risk. No veteran should return home after liberating a foreign people only to lose their own freedom.

There needs to be a national "welcome wagon" for our veterans that identifies and intervenes as they physically transition home from the combat zone to their distant home community. Our version of a welcome wagon would include (1) comprehensive assessment and contact with their state-side service manager before they leave the combat theater; and (2) a partnership (programmatic and fiscal through RFPs) between Department of Defense/Department of Veterans Affairs (DOD/VA) and nonprofits and community associations to provide modest-to-extensive intervention services to veterans. Such an initiative would constitute a bridge that facilitates reintegration and ensures stability of the veteran and his or her family, and use VA and non-VA professionals to accomplish these and other tasks.

Sadly, even if the DOD/VA were able to provide a more comprehensive assessment before leaving the combat zone and if the veteran received a state-side service manager who communicated with them and facilitated services and registration with the VA, it would not be enough. Professionals at the VA and those working in private industry with the VA say that more physicians, psychiatrists, nurses, social workers, and other helping professionals are needed as the requirement is too great for an already overwhelmed system.

Further, these same individuals would tell you that more women's clinics are needed to accommodate the multitude of needs of female veterans including residential programs that address military sexual trauma (MST), sexual abuse that may have existed prior to their deployment, as well as a substance abuse treatment program that is gender-focused. In addition, creative treatment is essential as there are a rising number of dual-diagnosis programs where veterans exhibit both substance abuse and mental health issues. Combine the dual diagnosis with the presence of a traumatic brain injury, and you have a serious treatment problem that requires creative treatment plans. In addition, veterans require advocates that can fight on their behalf to ensure treatment services are not discontinued.

We must remember that not all veterans want or need treatment. There are many resilient warriors who are able to meet their own needs. However, the civilian community must be vigilant to make certain that veterans are respected, valued, and their needs addressed.

It is said that we hide what we do not understand. I ask that we open the curtains, dispense with the delicate pleasantries, and serve the men and women who have served us so well with honor.

Diann Cameron Kelly

***

Approaching 40 years working for the Veterans Administration Health Care System I have had the privilege of working with veterans living with spinal cord injuries, dealing with mental health issues, or facing the aging process. These experiences have taught me much about courage and resilience. The opportunity to be involved in this project, to explore the experiences of our returning soldiers, continues this journey.

My hope is that those who read this book will better understand the impact that war has had on many of our servicemen and servicewomen, the courage and strength that they exhibit, and the important need to address the physical, mental, and social stressors they deal with upon their return.

David Gitelson

***

What I have learned from this project is that stronger families lead to healthier veterans. When our troops return from combat to their previous lives, there are many adjustments that they face in order to

thrive in civilian society. What most alarmed me is the affects of deployment on the women veterans as well as minority veterans. They are
more likely to leave families with minimal resources, and return
home at risk of a myriad of socio-economic challenges beyond finding
jobs in an already constricted economic climate.

From a legal perspective, knowing that veterans are more likely to
face divorce, loss of child custody, along with extensive homelessness,
and/or joblessness is also equally alarming. Posttraumatic stress disorder (PTSD) affects so many aspects of family life from increased difficulty in communicating with each other to being involved in the
community. Criminal activity is not expected. Unfortunately, when
combined with social disconnectedness and isolation from society,
increased substance abuse, and the inability to distinguish a decorated
veteran from our stereotype and stigma of "vagrants," we are more
likely to absorb these individuals into our criminal justice system.

The most minimal treatment for veterans and their families is a far
better option than the isolation they may experience while trying self-
manage their needs or fend for themselves without supportive services
and outreach. We know that many families often deny or ignore the
escalating socio-emotional and behavioral health needs because they
are not as visible, mirroring society's lack of acknowledgement of the
veterans' concerns. Thus, by hiding our shame, our veterans unfortunately come face-to-face with domestic violence shelters, prisons, or
something even more deadly.

I implore us to institute as many meaningful interventions as possible to strengthen and sustain the family unit as a cohesive supportive
bond for the veteran during his or her reintegration. When the family
is stronger, more aware of the veterans' needs, the veteran is more
likely to be engaged, socially connected and contributing to society,
and experiencing a life postcombat that is honorable, stable, and secure.

Sydney Howe-Barksdale

***

When individuals serve the country, they make a contract to offer their
bodies, minds, and lives. When society accepts this contract with the
individual, society should also make a pledge to do its utmost to
ensure that the veteran is given back his or her body, mind, and life
to the greatest degree possible after service. This is not only the honorable thing to do, it is the most practical thing to do. It is healthier for
society, less expensive, and more humane to offer support before

PTSD turns into domestic violence, before readjustment turns into chronic unemployment, and before desperation turns into suicide.

In working on this book, I have been reminded that it is not an abstract army that is fighting wars in Iraq and Afghanistan but individuals. The force and strength of the U.S. military is made up of people, a next door neighbor, a mother picking up her kids from school, a man on an unemployment line, a person dealing with PTSD who is losing contact with friends and family and does not know why. As with all social issues, veteran affairs play out in the individual, in the struggles and successes of daily life. It is in these struggles and successes that helping professionals can step in, offer a hand, and provide the services that are necessary for well-being to be established and maintained in the lives of veterans and the lives of all they encounter.

William Valente

INDEX

Note: n = Footnote